Hans Hörmann

Psycholinguistics

An Introduction to Research and Theory

Translated from the German Edition by
H. H. Stern

With 69 Figures

Springer-Verlag Berlin · Heidelberg · New York 1971

Dr. Hans Hörmann, o. Prof. der Psychologie an der Ruhr-Universität Bochum, Direktor des Psychologischen Instituts der Universität, 4630 Bochum-Querenburg

Dr. H. H. Stern, Director of the Modern Language Center, Ontario Institute for Studies in Education, 252 Bloor Street West, Toronto 5, Ontario, Canada

This English Edition is a revised version of the German Edition "Psychologie der Sprache" (Revised printing 1970)

ISBN 3-540-04879-0 Springer-Verlag Berlin-Heidelberg-New York
ISBN 0-387-04879-0 Springer-Verlag New York-Heidelberg-Berlin

ISBN 3-540-05159-7 Springer-Verlag Berlin-Heidelberg-New York
ISBN 0-387-05159-7 Springer-Verlag New York-Heidelberg-Berlin

We want to establish an order in our knowledge of the use of language: an order with a particular end in view; one out of many possible orders; not *the* order.

WITTGENSTEIN, Philosophical Investigation, § 132

Preface[1]

A German work on the psychology of language which has become a classic, KARL BÜHLER'S *Sprachtheorie (Theory of Language)*, appeared over thirty years ago (1934). The political events of the time have robbed this work of the rightful and immediate influence that it should have exercized; for psychology in Germany had once again turned away from its empirical foundations, which had nurtured, in a most productive way, the earlier work from FECHNER and WUNDT down to Gestalt psychology. The only exception to the stagnation which had set in was the monumental work of KAINZ which began to appear in 1940 and which by now has reached Part I of Volume 5. This work constitutes the end of the Bühler era of psycholinguistics.

In contrast to the situation in Germany, psycholinguistics in the Western world and, by the way, also in the East has in recent years advanced in a most remarkable way. This development is not to be viewed as an achievement of orthodox behaviorism; rather it is the achievement of a psychological science, which has struggled through behaviorism, and, having recognized the strengths as well as the weaknesses of this school of thought, has acquired new foundations and a renewed impetus, and has gained a research methodology.

The object of this book is to present, and place into a context, the methods and findings of the new era of psycholinguistics and, thus, to outline one of several possible approaches to the study of the psychological laws of verbal processes.

Anyone faced with the task of presenting a particular branch of present-day psychology has a difficult decision to make because of the vast and overwhelming growth in the sheer mass of available research: which theoretical position is one to adopt so as to order and punctuate the information? In psycholinguistics, as in other branches of psychology, the multiplicity of methods, the diverse antecedents of the research workers and the different orientation and objectives of the various approaches make it impossible to adopt a single and consistent point of view.

---

[1] *Translator's note.* This is a shortened and adapted version of the Preface to the original edition.

I have attempted to make a virtue out of this necessity. In this book the reader will be obliged to change his standpoint again and again; he will be asked to view the subject from different angles and, at the same time, to take note of these changes. I am attempting to familiarize the reader with the field of psycholinguistics by making him aware of the fact that research results are dependent upon particular viewpoints, that each viewpoint is based upon certain assumptions, and that each has its own limitations. If this book succeeds in its purpose, these maneuvers, the obstacles in the way, the bridging operations needed, the sight of the barren stretches as well as of exciting perspectives should fit together to form a cognitive map of psycholinguistics. But even if it is possible to open up the territory to the reader, he will soon discover that, in this map, the unknown and explored areas are very unevenly distributed.

It is impossible to consider the *psychology* of language without taking into account certain *philosophical* points of view. Yet, to do so is extremely difficult. Without a philosophical orientation one cannot appreciate the limitations imposed by historical origins, nor can one understand the full implications of the given point of view. But these philosophical aspects cannot be presented in advance, as a separate introduction, because they form part of the psychological arguments which, at the same time, presuppose some familiarity with philosophy.

I have chosen the questionable expedient of interposing a sketch of the philosophical background at a point where an understanding of the development of psycholinguistics without such knowledge seemed impossible, namely in the discussion of NOBLE'S work.

Similar problems arose in the presentation of the concept of meaning. The psychological implications and aspects of this basically philosophical notion appeared in so many different places in the entire field of psycholinguistics that it was impossible to bring them together into a single chapter. The reader will meet this concept again and again in a variety of contexts.

From what has been said it will be seen that the different chapters of this book have not been written as separate entities and they should not be read as such. It might almost have been better to abandon altogether the division into chapters.

Certain limitations should be noted. This book does not offer a clear separation of sociolinguistics from psycholinguistics. It might well be argued that studies with a predominantly sociolinguistic orientation should have been taken into account and should have been looked at from a psycholinguistic viewpoint. The same criticism can be made with regard to the treatment of studies in the area of content analysis.

The book can further be criticized for paying insufficient attention to psychopathology. In recent years, observations on speech deficit have made increasingly significant contributions to psycholinguistics. In my view, the greatest advances in psycholinguistics may, in fact, be expected in this area.

In a work on psycholinguistics one necessarily operates not only with concepts of psychology but also with those derived from linguistics. It should be noted that the latter are introduced and defined here only to the extent that was regarded necessary for a predominantly *psychological* discussion. Linguists may well regard this treatment as grossly oversimplified.

In conclusion, it is worth mentioning that this book originated in a series of lectures given in the academic year 1964-1965. The particular interest these lectures aroused among students is acknowledged with gratitude.

Berlin, 1967 H. Hörmann

Translator's Foreword

During the last fifteen years psycholinguistics has advanced rapidly in the English-speaking world. But curiously, in spite of intense research activity and theoretical debate, very little has been written to help the serious reader and the student with little or no previous knowledge of psycholinguistics to become acquainted with this expanding field of study. The great classic to this day has remained GEORGE MILLER'S *Language and Communication*, a work which initiated the development of psycholinguistics nearly twenty years ago.

The obvious lack of a more modern introduction has been met by several books of 'readings' and collections of papers, e.g., SAPORTA (1961), FODOR and KATZ (1964), LENNEBERG (1964), ROSENBERG (1965), LYONS and WALES (1966), DE CECCO (1967), JAKOBOVITS and MIRON (1967), OLDFIELD and MARSHALL (1968), ROSENBERG and KOPLIN (1968). Excellent though these collections are, they do not replace a systematic exposition of the field as a whole, and they are no substitute for an introduction to the more specialized articles and researches such as may usually be found in books of readings or in the scholarly journals.

Professor HANS HÖRMANN, who until 1969 was Professor of Psychology in the Free University of Berlin and is now Professor of Psychology and Director of the Psychological Institute at the University of the Ruhr at Bochum, in the Federal Republic of Germany, has produced the kind of introduction to psycholinguistics which is so badly needed today, particularly in the English-speaking world. Work in psycholinguistics has progressed at such a pace that most scholars in English-speaking countries have simply not taken the time to survey and review the development, current state, and achievements of psycholinguistics. The result is that the uninitiated reader is faced too early and in too haphazard a fashion with particular problems and controversies. He is led to taking sides and following fashions before he has even had a chance to find out the background of existing studies, and before he has had time to understand and appreciate what links present-day theoretical issues and research interests with the work on language in the recent past of merely a decade or so ago.

One does not have far to seek for the causes of this unsatisfactory state of affairs. In the early fifties the young discipline of psycholinguistics established a theoretical framework within which to undertake empirical research. Two major and now classical studies (OSGOOD and SEBEOK, 1954, and SKINNER, 1957) provided this framework. But the work was hardly underway when the whole theoretical structure was badly shaken by CHOMSKY'S review of SKINNER'S *Verbal Behavior* (1959). The inadequacy of a behavioristic approach to language was exposed. Scholars, such as GEORGE MILLER, whose earlier work had been entirely within the behavioristic and probabilistic framework, revised their theoretical positions and research interests (e.g., MILLER, GALANTER and PRIBRAM, 1960). Yet others continued to work and to produce valuable studies on the foundations established in the 1950's. The result is that present-day scholars and students in psycholinguistics find it very difficult to see the field as a whole and in perspective, to value adequately the work that has already been done, and to pursue different lines of arguments on some of the great classical questions of psycholinguistics, such as the problem of meaning, the relationship between thought and language, or the acquisition of language in early childhood.

Professor HÖRMANN, who has undertaken the formidable task of writing a new introduction to psycholinguistics, has obviously not composed this work with the needs of English-speaking readers in mind. But, by a strange coincidence, the German audience addressed by this book in the original as well as the English-speaking readers of this translation may find that the book provides what is, at present, needed by both audiences, i.e., *an introductory, detailed review and discussion of psycholinguistic thought and research.*

If one attempts briefly to understand what this book sets out to achieve for its German readers, he will be able to see, at the same time, what it can offer to an English-speaking audience.

In German psychology of the twentieth century, behaviorism and neo-behaviorism have never had the hold that they have had for many years in North America and in the English-speaking world generally. Although an empirical approach to psychology largely originated in Germany, psychology there has maintained a much more strongly philosophical orientation than in English-speaking countries. Hence, one of Dr. HÖRMANN'S major objectives has been to make German readers, who are basically skeptical towards behaviorism, aware of the existence of ingenious and thought-provoking empirical studies in the behaviorist tradition.

In the English-speaking world, the onslaught by CHOMSKY and his school on the behavioristic approach to language and verbal behavior, necessary though it was, has today produced a strongly antibehavioristic mood of thought, not only in psycholinguistics but in psychology and linguistics generally. The present book can help to redress the balance and give the reader a renewed appreciation of the behavioristic approach to the study of language. Meanwhile, the author discusses fully and constructively the weaknesses of the behaviorist position. What emerges is a much more differentiated picture than is currently available elsewhere.

At the same time, this book is, as one would expect, in the best German scholarly tradition: it views the psychological study of language in its philosophical context. This approach has been somewhat neglected in the English literature except for some recent studies, e.g., by FODOR and KATZ (1964) and CHOMSKY (1966, 1968), which have opened the way. A text which places psycholinguistics in a philosophical framework will be valuable also for English-speaking readers today. For example, in the heat of recent debates one was led to believe that a philosophical approach to language must necessarily stand in contrast to behaviorism. Dr. HÖR-MANN, however, shows that behaviorism itself and its various offshoots imply philosophical positions worthy of consideration.

One regrettable effect of the development of psycholinguistics as a subdiscipline of psychology has been that the psychology of language has become diverted from the main stream of psychological inquiry. Some psychologists have even questioned the significance of psycholinguistic research to psychological theory. By looking at language from the point of view of a psychologist, this book attempts to relate findings on verbal behavior and language to general psychology, e.g., to work on thinking, perception and personality. This is timely in the context of current discussions on language in relation to psychology.

For German readers, this book is further meant to provide an introduction to work which, for the most part, has been published in English. The wide-ranging understanding of the psycholinguistic literature written in English and the author's truly staggering command of it constitute one of the great merits of this work. But English-speaking scholarship has itself tended to remain insular in its own way. While it is no doubt good for Germans to get to know North American and British work, it is equally rewarding for English-speaking readers to be introduced to the work of European scholars and to understand the presentation of psycholinguistics with a European orientation.

Lastly, although an important function of this book has been to describe theoretical issues to the reader and to explain research methods and results without necessarily taking sides on a particular question, one would seriously underrate this work if he regarded it purely as a research review. The attentive reader will discover that the author's own points of view emerge in the course of the study. The positions he adopts on several issues are of greatest interest to students of psychology and linguistics. They deserve, in fact, the attention of all scholars concerned with questions of language and should contribute to a better understanding of language, speech, and the concept of meaning.

There is a necessary time lag between the first appearance of a work such as this in the original (1967) and its translation. Even though, then, the state of knowledge represented here reflects the mid-sixties rather than the very latest developments, this is no serious disadvantage. Having gained the necessary perspective with the help of this book, the reader should be able to approach with increased understanding and interest the more recent studies, as well as the papers, in the books of readings on psycholinguistics which would form an excellent companion or follow-up to this scholarly introduction.

The translation was carried out in the Modern Language Center of The Ontario Institute for Studies in Education, Toronto, Canada. As translator, I wish to thank, first, the Institute for generously putting facilities at my disposal in order to make this translation possible, and, second, the members of the Modern Language Center team for their ever ready assistance. I am especially grateful to my Research Assistant, Miss K. McTavish, for her skilled, perceptive, and painstaking help in seeing this fascinating, but arduous task of translation through to its completion. I also wish to express my gratitude to the author, Dr. Hörmann, who has read the translation with greatest care and, thanks to his superb knowledge of English, has been able to provide numerous corrections. In addition, he has updated the text by a few additions and modifications wherever it was felt that recent developments made such updating imperative. This English translation, therefore, constitutes at the same time a revision of the original German publication.

Toronto, Summer 1970

H. H. Stern

Table of Contents

Chapter 1

Introduction: Organism, Language and World

Characterization of the field in which language becomes
possible and necessary — Organism and environment —
Language as stimulus — Language as response — Speaker
and listener — Language as a system of signs — Development from a historical to a structural orientation in linguistics — SAUSSURE's distinction between *langue* and *parole* —
CARROLL's definition of language — Linguistics and psycholinguistics.

The possession of language distinguishes man from animal. Our whole
capacity of being truly human is implicit in language. Truth is only
possible in language or, at least, by means of language. Even a lie presupposes language.

Language, it has been said, is "man's greatest invention" (THORN-
DIKE, 1943, p. 60). As we think about this statement, a number of questions arise which serve as our first landmarks at the beginning of our
inquiry. Was the inventor of language already human before his invention? What kind of situation made such an invention possible and
necessary? Can it be studied phylogenetically by comparing man and
animal in relation to language? Or ontogenetically by tracing the
development of language from prelinguistic infancy to early childhood?

The feature of language is so specifically human that it would b
hopeless to think that we might be able to trace and observe the gradu
evolution of this feature itself. Phylogenetic comparisons can, at b
give us hints from what points of view to study the complex speech
of man. Needless to say this limitation is not a comment upo
relevance of a biological perspective. LENNEBERG (1964 b) has estab
the notion that a definite constellation of biological peculiarities a
for the presence of language in man and only in man: linguistic
correlates highly with a large number of special morpholo
functional developments; the onset and the course of linguist
ment in the child are an extraordinarily regular process; ev

serious handicaps, such as blindness or deafness, language is still possible; no non-human species can acquire language, in the sense in which it is here understood; there are linguistic universals (see, p. 321 f.), i.e., universal principles found in natural languages, which cannot be explained in terms of historical causation. According to LENNEBERG, the capacity to acquire and employ a human language does not depend upon the intelligence of the organism or the size of its brain, but upon the fact that it is a human organism.

Moreover, a biological or genetic viewpoint will be useful to us in a different sense. We will attempt to explain the function of language by observing the genesis and process of the individual speech act. "Speech, in its true essence, is constantly and at any moment ephemeral. It is itself not a product (*ergon*) but an activity (*energeia*). Its true definition must therefore be a genetic one. Language is the ever recurring activity of the mind endeavoring to make the articulated sound express thought. Taking it quite literally and strictly, this is the definition of each act of speech; but in a more real and fundamental sense, only the totality of these speech acts can, as it were, be understood as language" (HUMBOLDT, translated from the 1949 edition, p. 44).

It is at this point that HUMBOLDT, the linguistic scholar and philosopher, has raised the question of the fundamental nature of language. For a psycholinguistic study this orientation is hardly appropriate because psychology does not ask questions about the *nature* of the object it studies, e.g., the nature of the psyche; but, presupposing its existence, it asks how the psychic event happens. The question of the nature of language is beyond the domain of an empirical psychology. Yet, if the philosopher recognizes the nature of language as an *energeia*, an activity or a process, this approach offers a basis which is entirely acceptable to the psychologist because in other branches of psychology as well, e.g., in the psychology of learning or of motivation, psychological insight is increased if we treat the object of scientific inquiry as a process. Such a dynamic viewpoint gives a clear and broad perspective, especially for a study of language, but in principle also for psychology as a whole. It is our intention to adopt this point of view, although with some caution, so as to be able to analyse the factors which determine speech events and language. We will discover what the nature of these factors is if, before examining language itself, we begin our inquiry at an earlier stage, so to speak, or at a more fundamental level.

The event which we call 'organism' can be described in terms of two groups of factors: broadly speaking, and without being unduly inhibited by theological or philosophical considerations, there is what, on the one hand, might be called *spontaneity* or the life force which, from inside the organism, strives towards fulfilment, BERGSON'S *élan vital*. On the

other hand this spontaneity is surrounded by the *life space* within which the vital process takes place. Determinants of the 'life space' shape the spontaneous strivings of the organism's capacities and potentialities into its unique, precise and recognizable biography. The spirituality of the highest form of life, man, manifesting itself through the will, adds a further dimension of freedom to this interplay of spontaneity and life space.

In psychology, ALLESCH adheres most clearly to such a dynamic-biological basic viewpoint, which is characterized by the assumption that spontaneity and life space are in harmony with each other. For a particular kind of spontaneity, a characteristic life space is, as it were, 'predetermined'; e.g., the bird's instinctive nesting behavior is designed for an environment which provides twigs.

The relationship between spontaneity and life space can be more or less intimate, more or less variable. Varying degrees of closeness of fit characterize different organisms. Some organisms fit so precisely and neatly into their vital space that even a slight variation in the environment is sufficient to exceed the tolerance level of the organism which then succumbs. Interesting instances of this interplay are certain cases of symbiosis and similar forms of interaction: thus, future generations of the yucca plant are endangered by anyone who disturbs the yucca moth.

The relationship between life force and life space can attain greater degrees of freedom in other species. Here a variation in one group of factors is not always nor inevitably accompanied by definite variations in the other. In these organisms the framework within which the events of life take place is much less fixed, and the life of the organism is no longer dependent upon a definite realization within a narrowly defined life space.

We come to a similar point of view if we compare—as UEXKÜLL (1928) has done—environment in lower organisms and in man. In the animal, spontaneity and milieu are almost like a closed world which is nearly perfectly divided into the two hemispheres of action (*Wirkwelt*) and perception (*Merkwelt*). UEXKÜLL says about the animal: "The stimuli of the environment surround the animal like the walls of a self-made dwelling cutting off the entire world outside it" (translated from CASSIRER, 1932).

Life in such an enclosed space is unlike human life because it can never transcend its own field of action and look at it from outside (CASSIRER, 1932). To make this possible the close fit must be relaxed; this tight world must somehow come apart so that finally consciousness, representation, language and knowledge can develop. Such a loosening has already begun at the lower levels of phylogenesis, and we must be able to recognize such early beginnings if we want to come to grips with the psychological dynamics of speech events. This does not mean to say that language has gradually evolved from non-linguistic preformations. What it does mean is that the concepts with which we operate in explaining the linguistic event have something in common with those factors which —at a pre-linguistic stage—determine the relationship between spontaneity and environment.

At this point it may be appropriate to interrupt the argument briefly in order to consider an obvious objection. It may be argued that such biological and teleological interpretations are inappropriate in general psychology, hence equally so in psycholinguistics. Concepts such as BERGSON's *élan vital* are in bad odor in an empirical science—and psychology is an empirical science.

Such doubts are justified and they would become critical if the attempt was made to establish a non-empirical psychology of language exclusively on the basis of teleological speculations. The value of this way of looking at language lies purely in the leads it gives us to a point of entry and the orientation it offers in the choice of researches.

In general, this book represents the view that it is helpful in psycholinguistics to be able to vary procedures and approaches. To uphold a method which has proved fruitful at one point, knowing that few new insights can be gained, would be less desirable than a certain flexibility in method. Such flexibility must, however, fulfil one condition, namely, that we are always aware of the change of method and its implications. Only such a procedure would offer the prospect of steering us safely between the simplification of a pure stimulus-response model and the premature systematization of linguistic philosophy. We want to avoid the "mystification of age-old anthropomorphisms" and study psycholinguistics in a way which does full justice to the epistemological criteria of psychology as well as to the object of enquiry itself, viz, language, ranging from "the physics of air vibrations to the philosophy of the objective mind."

After this digression let us return to our principal argument. The loosening of the tight interlocking fit between spontaneity and life space creates the precondition for the emergence of speech. The disturbance in the adjustment gives rise to a new group of devices whose function is to compensate for the discrepancies and the imbalances. Such devices which control the adaptation to the environment are unnecessary as long as the organism—assuming a borderline case—fits so perfectly into its environment that, for example, periodic changes in the environment are taken care of by simultaneous changes in the plan and structure of the organism. In this case the organism would not require, for instance, sense receptors to be informed about the momentary state of the environment.

However, if spontaneity and life space are no longer perfectly attuned, and if they no longer obey the same rules and rhythms, and if, in consequence, discrepancies and tensions occur, a controlling device is needed to bridge the two worlds which have moved apart. This bridging operation makes behavior possible and indeed necessary.

Perception, for example, may be looked upon as such a controlling device; for perception is not primarily the cause or initiator of behavior. Behavior, after all, occurs continuously from the moment the organism begins to live. Perception steers behavior and is one of its co-determinants. A school of psychology which views behavior and especially perception as a sequence of stimuli (S) and responses (R) can, indeed, explain a great deal but it remains incomplete. We shall later examine more closely the potentialities of an S-R analysis in the field of psycholinguistics.

Behavior, then, is viewed here as the process in which the interaction of life space and spontaneity becomes manifest. Perception is, in a peculiar way, both a part and a determinant of this process. If we adopt this point of view, language may be considered to be similar. It originates, too, in the indeterminate sphere between the spontaneous impulses of the individual and his life space. In the last resort, language is, as ARISTOTLE already said, an *organon* or tool which comes into use between the self and its surrounding world as a means of coming to terms with its environment. But whereas perception links the self and objective reality, speech links man with other kinds of realities: he is surrounded by the social world of his speech community. Verbal thinking relates him to the world of the mind; and in the 'intercourse of mind with itself' (PLATO) man creates the world of his own self. If, in this preliminary and sweeping way, we ascribe to language a function which, in principle, is analogous to perception, it is tempting to test this analogy a little further and to examine the applicability to language of the notions of stimulus and response.

Speech as stimulus: verbal signals can guide and determine behavior. But speech can also be perceived. The nature and conditions of such speech perception will therefore have to be investigated.

Speech as response: we note that many chains of events end in a verbal utterance, just as other chains of events end in motor behavior. The question is what are the antecedents to the verbal response.

Within the framework of an S-R analysis, we must not simply look upon language as stimulus and response but also as an intervening variable, using this term in its widest sense. In other words, language intervenes in the bond between stimulus and response. If a particular R and no other follows a specific S, this may well be the result of the kind of linguistic categories which are at our disposal in dealing with a particular S. Or looking at it differently, an empirically discovered relationship between a given R and an S can sometimes only be explained if we assume linguistic links as mediating elements. The mechanism of an action can often only make sense if it is assumed that a verbal component, without necessarily appearing overtly, modifies the S-R sequence in a qualitative way. For instance, purposeful human acts which extend over a period of time, almost inevitably involve intermediate purposes expressed in verbal forms which are like bridge supports carrying the event from the original stimulus to the final response. The concept of *mediation* which should be mentioned here is one that must engage our attention to a considerable extent at a later stage.

These initial reflections on an S-R analysis of language already indicate that the explanation of language demands, under certain conditions, that we have to operate with variables which have no equivalent in externally observable behavior. The question of how necessary and yet how risky it is to go beyond observable behavior has been an important aspect in the discussion on behaviorism in general and has affected the psychology of language.

One important distinguishing feature of *speech as stimulus* is: it is, at least in principle, a stimulus directed towards us with intent by other members of our species. With this observation, we touch a problem which we will take up again later. In the psychology of perception, once we are beyond the purely physical description, we face this question: is the 'real' stimulus the light-waves, or is it a discharge in the receptor; is it the glass of water before us, or is it the object of our thirst? Similarly, in psycholinguistics, the air vibrations which we can regard as stimuli do not so much exercise their effect because of the energy they hold (a bang could have as much) but they act as stimuli because they convey meaning. It is as if the physical stimulus, at the same time, was a stimulus carrier of a totally different order. Studies in the psychology of language can often assume that *stimulus equals meaning*; but, for instance, in speech perception we must note the characteristic interplay of physical and semantic aspects of stimulation.

Similar distinguishing characteristics can be noted in looking upon *language as response*. The speech event produced by an individual A is hardly ever the last link in a stimulus-response chain; it is generally a directed response transmitted from A to B. The linguistic response is produced by A with the intention of making B react. In other words, a verbal response can only be regarded as the last link in a chain of events if the unit of observation is the individual. But the social nature of language demands the embedding of the speech event into a social field which comprises a speaker and a hearer. The dynamic structure of this field arises from the fact "that the essentials of language reside in purpose. Looked at teleologically, language is particularly powerful as a means of communication." (RÉVÉSZ, 1946, p. 109). FREYTAG-LOERINGHOFF has described communication as the ontological locus of language. If we want to understand language, he argues, we must enquire into the nature of interpersonal communication (1962, p. 240).

The social field in which speaker and hearer represent the two poles is characterized by certain lines of force. Speech as an event occurring in this field manifests the influence of these lines of force in various ways. While we initially discussed in very general terms the dynamics of the processes occurring between organism and environment, we shall now, in a parallel manner, but closer to language, discuss the social field as a language-forming structure. In doing so, we will not treat language as a unitary substance (see CASSIRER, 1944, pp. 129f.) but will attempt to analyse it from ever-changing perspectives in such a way that the totality of the various components will reveal the functional unity of language.

One line of force which marks this field is relatively simple: it is the social contact between the 'I' and 'thou' in its quite primitive form. Speech as *contact-sound* is, according to RÉVÉSZ, the first and lowest stage of linguistic evolution. The contact-sound repeats, as it were, the most reassuring of messages which says: 'Here too is someone' and thus maintains a social hond.

We operate with RÉVÉSZ' concepts, not because we believe language has developed according to the sequences which RÉVÉSZ proposed, but because these notions —outside their evolutionary context—are convenient in making apparent the forces at work to which a language, even at its most advanced level, is subjected.

This first and most simple line of force in the social field appears in many different manifestations. It occurs, in the animal kingdom, well below the mammals, e.g., in the cry of wild geese on the wing. It ranges from the phatic communion—as MALINOWSKI (see OGDEN and RICHARDS, 1923) has called the vocal utterances which serve to establish social relations— to the highly stylized forms of social conversation, where talk occurs, because it would be rude to be silent. HAYAKAWA calls the prevention of silence an important function of speech (1949, p. 72).

Close to the line of force represented by the undirected primitive contact-call, the social field in which speech events occur carries another similar line of force. To make it evident, we adopt HAYAKAWA'S presentation. According to HAYAKAWA, a community or a social group is a network of 'mutual agreements'. Being in vocal contact with one another is not insignificant; it has affective meaning. The *emotional charge* of the sound turns a mere sound into a call which moves the listener to establish or demonstrate the 'mutual agreements' which, according to HAYAKAWA, are the framework of society.

At this point another feature comes into evidence which will be important for our later discussion. Speech is more than an exchange of information; for example, a question can be more than, or different from, a request for factual knowledge. It may well be an attempt to seek confirmation, to be assured of the mutual agreement and thus to orient oneself with regard to one's own place in a social situation. Like HAYA-KAWA, GLINZ writes in an essay devoted to this function of language: "The effect of talk among two or more persons is that it interposes between them values which are already held in common or have yet to be accepted. In this way, it is not only that objects or phenomena find their place and are related to people but lines of thought are drawn between persons like streamers stretched from one to another" (1959, p. 104).

The manifestations of this line of force range from the *hailing-call* (*Zuruf*), which RÉVÉSZ considers to be the second stage of language above the contact-sound, to the post-symbolic use of words which are no longer intended to transmit information but 'merely' serve the ritualized communion of social contact. Between these extremes is the area of social manipulation through language.

It was stated earlier that the field of force in which speech events occur has two poles, speaker and listener, transmitter and receiver. The 'existential situation' of the speech event lies in the imbalance between the two poles. This discrepancy or gradient produces the tensions which we are investigating.

There is either an imbalance of information or an imbalance of intention. The imbalance of information—or to put it more precisely: of informed-ness—cause the person who has less information to be on the look-out for information-bearing signals or to question the other person who has more and who makes this more available in some form of presentation. The imbalance of intention impels the one to send out signals or commands and the other to act upon these signals or commands.

It is because of this dynamic imbalance that language functions as a tool — in this case in the social field, in other cases, to be explained later, in the area of thought or philosophic orientation.

Language is a tool for the speaker, because with its help he can obtain from someone else what he himself lacks, or he can get someone else to do what he himself is unable or unwilling to do. But language is also a means to give help *to* the other fellow. Information or signals which are useful to the receiver may be transmitted to him. In the *demand-call* (*Anruf*)—the third stage of the evolutionary scale of RÉVÉSZ—the imperatives in both directions are combined; the demand-call 'come here' is meant to get the listener moving: it may be for *my* benefit because *I* want something from him — or for *his* benefit, because I want to guide him round a treacherous stretch of the road.

The inequality between listener and speaker is not the only dynamic factor of the linguistic field. The speaker is engaged in purposive behavior, and so is the listener. The goal towards which the speaker strives was treated above in terms of social psychology. We referred to the social field of force in which verbal behavior occurs. But the social domain is only one of the domains with which we are linked by language. We must also study the role of verbal processes in behavior sequences which are not directed towards social objects, but towards such activities as eating, drinking, having a nap or repairing a lighter.

With this observation we reach a point which has bearing on the social function of language but which at the same time transcends it: language is essentially a system of signs. Signs, meaning, signification—these are concepts which in every treatment of psycholinguistics play a decisive role. But, fundamentally, they are not so much psychological as philosophical concepts.

It follows that it will not be possible to allocate them a definite place in a system, to treat them, and then to move on, relieved of this somewhat awkward baggage. Instead we will find that these notions crop up again and again, and only after numerous encounters can we hope to get the psychological aspects of these concepts into some perspective.

Language, we said, is essentially a system of signs. Language presupposes signs, but signs are possible even before any language. A Pavlovian dog, conditioned to the sound of a bell, accepts this sound as a sign or signal that food is on its way, and he reacts to this sign. The rat, which in a Lashley 'jump' box faces one card with stripes and another with squares, treats the sight of the striped card as a sign for food behind it and acts accordingly. The animal in a Tolman maze learns to react to signs, to expect signs and to be guided by signs. The sign directs to something that is not the sign itself. The sign is generally a biologically irrelevant object (e.g., striped cards are totally irrelevant to rats not trained in a Lashley 'jump' box) which gains biological value only through learning and experience and thus becomes relevant for the behavior of the animal.

We discussed earlier in detail the phylogenetically increasing separation of organism and environment necessitating simultaneously the creation of control mechanisms by means of which mutual adjustment becomes possible. The most important part in this control mechanism is played by the sign. Nowhere is this so clearly expressed as in the work of Russian psychologists. LEONTIEV writes, for example: "The fundamental fact is that initially the direct, unmediated connections of organisms with the external medium at a certain stage in evolution formed the basis for the development of connections which were indirect and mediated. Animals acquired the capacity to react in the same way to agents which *of themselves* had no biological significance for them ... This type of agent ... became a signal stimulus" (1961, p. 228). This *first signal-system*, which already exists in the animal world, leads, in man, to a second one, based on language (PAVLOV, 1960, 1963). In this *second signal-system* the immediate sense impressions are transformed. "The second signal-system must not be treated as a kind of abstraction. It is rather the neuro-dynamic system of conditioned associations, which, in turn, are indirect and generalized signals of reality. Human concepts result from the generalization of conditioned associations in the first signal-system. This process of generalization occurs on the basis of the verbal repertoire" (ALBRECHT, 1959, p. 129).

The possibility of generalization is one of the most important functions of language. But it must be remembered that even below language, within the first signal-system, a form of generalization is already possible, i.e., *stimulus generalization*. A dog conditioned to a tone of 1,000 cps. reacts also to a similar tone of 800 cps. But the generalizations in the first signal-system run along physically or biologically given dimensions (in our example, the dimension of pitch measured in cps.). In the linguistic medium generalization is not predetermined in extent or direction and, as a result, is open to ideational or sociological influences.

Signs, then, occur wherever purposive behavior occurs. The act of substitution, distinct from direct action, or the sign which stands for something else originates at a prelinguistic stage; but the sign comes truly into its own only in language, for only in language does it become a sign which can be used at will. "Between the clearest animal call of love or warning or anger, and a man's least trivial *word* there lies a whole day of *Creation*—or in modern phrase, a whole chapter of evolution" (LANGER, 1963, p. 103). For the whole further mode of procedure in psycholinguistics it is important to recognize these two sides: the parallels and analogies between animal and human behavior, and the distinctively new in human language. Language opens up the dimension of the intellect and, at the same time, is an expression of this dimension, a duality already thoroughly explored by HUMBOLDT. By making available the not-here and the not-now, language enables us to step out of the firm stimulus-response chain. An event may be 'wished', an action 'planned', an experience 'remembered' and 'told'. Whereas the speechless animal remains almost completely in the prison of action and reaction and only makes, as it were, preliminary moves towards breaking out with the help of its primitive use of signals, language makes possible explicit representation, and thus the possibility is given of drawing on knowledge at will.

serious handicaps, such as blindness or deafness, language is still possible; no non-human species can acquire language, in the sense in which it is here understood; there are linguistic universals (see, p. 321 f.), i.e., universal principles found in natural languages, which cannot be explained in terms of historical causation. According to LENNEBERG, the capacity to acquire and employ a human language does not depend upon the intelligence of the organism or the size of its brain, but upon the fact that it is a human organism.

Moreover, a biological or genetic viewpoint will be useful to us in a different sense. We will attempt to explain the function of language by observing the genesis and process of the individual speech act. "Speech, in its true essence, is constantly and at any moment ephemeral. It is itself not a product (*ergon*) but an activity (*energeia*). Its true definition must therefore be a genetic one. Language is the ever recurring activity of the mind endeavoring to make the articulated sound express thought. Taking it quite literally and strictly, this is the definition of each act of speech; but in a more real and fundamental sense, only the totality of these speech acts can, as it were, be understood as language" (HUMBOLDT, translated from the 1949 edition, p. 44).

It is at this point that HUMBOLDT, the linguistic scholar and philosopher, has raised the question of the fundamental nature of language. For a psycholinguistic study this orientation is hardly appropriate because psychology does not ask questions about the *nature* of the object it studies, e.g., the nature of the psyche; but, presupposing its existence, it asks how the psychic event happens. The question of the nature of language is beyond the domain of an empirical psychology. Yet, if the philosopher recognizes the nature of language as an *energeia*, an activity or a process, this approach offers a basis which is entirely acceptable to the psychologist because in other branches of psychology as well, e.g., in the psychology of learning or of motivation, psychological insight is increased if we treat the object of scientific inquiry as a process. Such a dynamic viewpoint gives a clear and broad perspective, especially for a study of language, but in principle also for psychology as a whole. It is our intention to adopt this point of view, although with some caution, so as to be able to analyse the factors which determine speech events and language. We will discover what the nature of these factors is if, before examining language itself, we begin our inquiry at an earlier stage, so to speak, or at a more fundamental level.

The event which we call 'organism' can be described in terms of two groups of factors: broadly speaking, and without being unduly inhibited by theological or philosophical considerations, there is what, on the one hand, might be called *spontaneity* or the life force which, from inside the organism, strives towards fulfilment, BERGSON'S *élan vital*. On the

Chapter 1

Introduction: Organism, Language and World

Characterization of the field in which language becomes possible and necessary — Organism and environment — Language as stimulus — Language as response — Speaker and listener — Language as a system of signs — Development from a historical to a structural orientation in linguistics — SAUSSURE'S distinction between *langue* and *parole* — CARROLL'S definition of language — Linguistics and psycholinguistics.

The possession of language distinguishes man from animal. Our whole capacity of being truly human is implicit in language. Truth is only possible in language or, at least, by means of language. Even a lie presupposes language.

Language, it has been said, is "man's greatest invention" (THORN-DIKE, 1943, p. 60). As we think about this statement, a number of questions arise which serve as our first landmarks at the beginning of our inquiry. Was the inventor of language already human before his invention? What kind of situation made such an invention possible and necessary? Can it be studied phylogenetically by comparing man and animal in relation to language? Or ontogenetically by tracing the development of language from prelinguistic infancy to early childhood?

The feature of language is so specifically human that it would be hopeless to think that we might be able to trace and observe the gradual evolution of this feature itself. Phylogenetic comparisons can, at best, give us hints from what points of view to study the complex speech act of man. Needless to say this limitation is not a comment upon the relevance of a biological perspective. LENNEBERG (1964 b) has established the notion that a definite constellation of biological peculiarities accounts for the presence of language in man and only in man: linguistic behavior correlates highly with a large number of special morphological and functional developments; the onset and the course of linguistic development in the child are an extraordinarily regular process; even in case of

Trial and error as a principle of language acquisition — MOWRER'S autism-theory — 'Mama' — Language as part of the total dynamics of the child — Language as a link between practical events — The interaction of language and total situation — Language and thought in the work of VIGOTSKY — The role of consciousness — Meaning as awareness of constancy — Classification processes in language acquisition — The word as a 'lure to cognition' — Genesis of predication — The acquisition of linguistic rules — The role of imitation.

Semantic implications of grammatical word classes — The object-forming function of language — Formation of categories through language — Language as a teacher of discrimination and non-discrimination — Kinship terms as an illustration — Status and solidarity of address — WHORF and the thesis of linguistic relativity — LENNEBERG'S methodological argument — Color coding and its problems — GLANZER'S verbal-loop hypothesis — Towards linguistic universals — General Semantics.

The making of generalizations creates order which transcends the sequence of concrete events, gives each single event a place in a hierarchy and treats it as 'a case of ...' or 'an instance of ...', an instance of bread, kindness, schizophrenia, etc. This higher-order something is no longer concretely accessible; it is a fact of language, which we create, or of which we can take possession because it is already available to us through culture and society. Language enables us to extract from the fleeting mass of phenomena the common elements or qualities essential for our experience, and to give them permanence. The Greek word *logos* expresses this function of language. STENZEL (1934) speaks of the primal phenomenon of the "crystallization, from the buzzing confusion, of an object by means of the word. The word is so powerful that without it the object would not exist for the mind, but once the mind has a word it seems to be able to do what it likes with it. Mental activity, which reaches awareness only through language, helps to define more clearly the essential qualities of an object in all its manifestations and makes it possible to ask questions about the essence of the object, and thus the mind itself shapes it in the way it will appear to consciousness ...". "As a result (the word) now becomes an inherent part of the object and expresses it, and must henceforth be used to refer to it" (p.38). "The transformation of experience into concepts ... is the motive of language" (LANGER, 1963, p. 126). The close connection between language and thought is the consequence of all this. Certainly language and thought cannot be treated as identical, but language is "thought made directly real" (K. MARX).

The abstraction of essentials, conveyed by language, makes it possible to accumulate experience in form of knowledge and thus—in the long run—to establish a culture. Human cunning and human rationality are based on the capacity to operate with signs.

In language biological, psychological and socio-historical determinants converge. Language is a product of the social field; consciousness in the individual is largely verbal in character: the consequence of these two facts is that man is basically a *zoon politikon*.

Thus language presents itself to us as the characteristically human instrument. With a minimum of energy this instrument reaches beyond the arm's length of the language user; it surrounds the speaker and in its applications is not confined to straight-line communication, nor is it —like vision—restricted to use in daylight. Community and consciousness, rationality and knowledge are in their human form only possible with the aid of language. Its influence—as HUMBOLDT says—extends over everything man thinks or feels, decides and achieves. "It transforms the world into a possession of the mind" (HUMBOLDT, 1905 b edition, p. 420).

This transformation of the world into a possession of the mind — in Humboldt's view, the primary achievement of language — is of interest to many sciences. Hardly anywhere else can one see so clearly as here that the sciences differ from each other not so much in the object of inquiry, as in their approach, the unit of analysis and the methodology they employ. Linguistic events engage the attention of such diverse disciplines as phonology and historical linguistics, acoustics and psycholinguistics. We shall understand better the procedures, viewpoints, possibilities and limitations of the psychology of language or psycholinguistics if we give some thought to the relationship of the other disciplines to language, the common object of study.

The science of language or linguistics was, right into the nineteenth century, a discipline with a historical orientation. Linguistic science meant historical linguistics. Or, more precisely, it consisted of the telling of individual 'histories' (LOHMANN, 1962), for example, the evolution of a given word or of a grammatical category. The model on which the development of language was conceived was — under Darwinian influences — that of a developing organism (BOPP, SCHLEICHER), whose growth and changes were to be studied biographically. The *Neogrammarians (Junggrammatiker)*, who also had historical leanings, were in agreement with the psychologist WUNDT in that the historical changes ought to be explained psychologically. PAUL called psychology "the most eminent foundation for all human sciences conceived in a higher sense" (1909, p. 6). But this psychologizing in historical linguistics confined itself to the construction of motives for particular historical processes after the event, based on psychological insight. For WUNDT language belonged to the psychology of nations *(Völkerpsychologie)* which he conceived in ideographic terms; it was not — as in the modern conception — part of general psychology which has a nomothetic orientation and is fundamentally a-historical (cf. SOMMERFELT, 1962a.)

This kind of linguistic science was therefore close to comparative grammar and to philology with its texts and consequently also to classical education, as MARTINET (1962) has rightly pointed out. Language, for nineteenth-century linguistics, was a product of the human mind which was final and static, but had a history, just as a landscape was the static product of a geological evolution which could be laboriously reconstructed.

A second characteristic of the conception of language which was current at the time was the view represented, for example, by BECKER (1841), that the whole of grammar could be derived from formal logic. The logical order of the world is "explicitly used as the theoretically demonstrable measuring rod for linguistic order" (APEL, 1962, p. 205), a conception which goes back to OCKHAM: language as a system of signs, fitted as an afterthought upon a 'given' primary, prelinguistic world, and presenting an undistorted picture of this world. This fundamental conception—as we shall see later—is of decisive importance for all sciences which study the problem of *meaning*. The name of WITTGENSTEIN characterizes the extreme opposite to this viewpoint.

The rejection of these two features of nineteenth-century linguistics (i.e., historicism, and the identification of laws of language with laws of nature) and the consequent emancipation of modern linguistics go back to HUMBOLDT. After HUMBOLDT language was viewed not as an invention of the human mind, or *ergon*, but as *energeia*. As a result, its psychological interest became something quite different from that in Paul's work: an activity can only be understood psychologically if agent and objective are included in the analysis.

In contrast to KANT, HUMBOLDT had also recognized the determining role of language in the way humans construct a world-view: language does not so much reflect a world which exists apart from it; language moulds a world. "Language is the thought-shaping organ. The subjective activity of thinking gives form to an object" (1949 edition, pp. 53 and 55). This aspect will be treated in greater detail at a later stage. We now turn to a line of thought in the development of modern linguistics which has quite recently become important for the psychology of language.

The suggestion to view language not so much as *ergon* but as *energeia* gave the impetus to a far-reaching change in many of the sciences interested in language as a whole. This change, without which psycholinguistics in the modern sense would not have become possible, was furthered by DURKHEIM and completed by SAUSSURE. DURKHEIM intimated that language should be regarded as a social phenomenon; he was interested in how social facts, scattered throughout a society, have an existence of their own, independent of individual manifestations, and, because of this non-individualized existence, exercise *une contrainte extérieure*, i.e., external constraints, upon the individual. The further development of Humboldtian thought in the work of SAPIR and WHORF will later show that language imposes not only external but also internal constraints. To consider speech as a social event, as a process comprising speaker and listener in a social field, is axiomatic for any modern form of linguistics which has not a purely historical orientation.

The confrontation, already indicated in Durkheim's work, of supra-individual facts on the one hand and of individual manifestations on the other was given a precise form—probably independently of DURKHEIM—by the Swiss linguist SAUSSURE (1916, posthumously): *langage* is divided into *langue*, the system of language existing in the abstract, and *parole*, the individual speech acts. The form in which *langue* exists is, according to SAUSSURE, that of a totality of impressions, deposited in the brain of each member of a speech community, rather like a dictionary of which many identical copies have been distributed. In other words, *langue* is present in every individual, but it has no individuality.

Parole is, at every moment, in a process of creation under the determining and prescribing influence of *langue*. For psycholinguistics the genesis of *parole* is the central issue; SAUSSURE had practically no interest in it.

The distinction between *langue* and *parole* recurs in similar forms repeatedly. In the analysis offered by information theory 'code' equals *langue*, whereas 'message' corresponds to *parole*. HERDAN (1956) who understands *langue* as the engrams of language plus the statistical probability of the appearance of these engrams, views *langue* as statistical population, while *parole* assumes the character of a sample of this population. MALMBERG (1953), however, raises the objection to this viewpoint that it does not adequately describe the relationship between *langue* and *parole*: *langue* provides rules for what is possible or impossible in *parole*; and this regulating function, as we shall see, cannot be fully grasped in terms of probability. Also worth mentioning is Jakobson's conception of *langue* as a totality of pre-arranged and available possibilities. The totality of possibilities—it will be shown—plays an important part in information theory. BUBER (1951) distinguishes three modes of language: available repertoire *(präsenter Bestand)*, potential repertoire *(potentialer Bestand)* and actual event *(aktuelles Begebnis)*. But he points out emphatically that the repertoire *(Bestand)* cannot be regarded as something that can be found outside the human being.

Both *langue* and *parole* are characterized by form rather than substance. The linguistic reality lies in their function and in the dynamic relationships among the units into which language can be divided.

SAUSSURE traces these dynamic relations in two different directions, diachronically and synchronically. The diachronic approach is approximately in line with that which is customary in a historically oriented science of language, whereas synchrony represents a "transverse cut through diachrony" (MERLEAU-PONTY, 1952, p. 95). As for the time dimensions with which SAUSSURE tacitly operates, diachrony predominates in the scientific exploration of *langue*, synchrony in the treatment of *parole*. We shall later become acquainted with sequential psycholinguistics which lies between diachrony and synchrony.

Synchronic linguistics describes *états de langue*, snapshots of temporal cross-sections, or whatever lies "along the axis of simultaneity."

Next, we have to ask ourselves *what* it is that can be arranged diachronically in a sequence, or side by side synchronically. Here we face the problem of the search for units of linguistic analysis. "Language then has the strange, striking characteristic of not having entities that are perceptible at the outset and yet of not permitting us to doubt that they exist and that their functioning constitutes it" (SAUSSURE, 1959 edition, p. 107). This unit is the *sign*. Sign is defined in a twofold way: firstly as a combination of content *(signifié)* with a sound pattern *(signifiant)*, and secondly as something that is different from another thing, i.e., another sign. The proposition that "dans la *langue* il n'y a que des différences, sans termes positifs", means that the linguistic form as such has no meaning or content (LOHMANN, 1962). The entire mechanism of language is built upon differences and similarities. "In language, as in any semiological system, whatever distinguishes one sign from the others constitutes it" (SAUSSURE, 1959, p. 121). Synchronic linguistics—as far as *langue* is concerned—deals with a system of linguistic signs which is valid for all members of a speech community. In this system every sign is demarcated from signs in its vicinity; each part of the system supports all the rest.

This brief historical sketch of developments in linguistics in more recent times, incomplete though it is, is adequate for the purpose of further discussion here.

We now take up the fact which SAUSSURE had emphasized, viz, that language can be looked upon as a system transcending the individual or as a structure characterized by formal relations. This system or structure has a direct effect on individual acts of speech in as much as it commands how things may be said.

This approach, which is formal rather than substantial, goes well with nomothetic procedures which are as customary in modern linguistics as they are in modern psychology. CARROLL has significantly called linguistics the *science* of language.

If we take the two key concepts which we evolved earlier—*language as a tool* and *language as a social phenomenon* and add to that *language as structure* we are now ready for a first definition of language which originates from CARROLL (1955, p. 10) and reads as follows: "A language is a structured system of arbitrary vocal sounds and sequences of sounds which is used, or can be used, in interpersonal communication by an aggregation of human beings, and which rather exhaustively catalogs the things, events, and processes in the human environment."

The determination of purpose, contained in this statement, makes Carroll's definition particularly good as a point of departure for a *psychological* study of language, because—as we have repeatedly emphasized—in psychology purposive activity in social beings plays a decisive role.

With the help of a diagram, (Fig. 1, based on OSGOOD and SEBEOK, 1954) we shall now describe that event which psycholinguistics attempts

Fig. 1

to elucidate. We start from the fact that language occurs in a social field, determined by the two poles, speaker and listener (or source and receiver). The information links the two. The information or message is that part of the speaker's *output* which, simultaneously, forms the listener's *input*. Under output we understand here what the speaker produces and under input what the listener receives. The activity of the speaker which constructs and edits the message and sends it on its way is called *encoding*; the activity of the listener which, in turn, makes sense out of sound waves is called *decoding*.

The concepts 'encoding' and 'decoding' suggest translating into and from a code. *Code* represents the systematic aspect which has proved so important in the analysis of the linguistic event. Linguistic communication is always communication by means of a system; this is what distinguishes it from primitive communication, e.g., by means of contact-sound.

With the help of the above diagram we can now demarcate psycholinguistics from linguistics proper. Linguistics deals with the structure of messages. The linguist describes the message—*en route*, so to speak—as an objective configuration, whose rules of organization have to be discovered. Linguistics "confines itself to the analysis of the characteristics of signal system or 'codes', as it may be derived from the structure of messages" (LOUNSBURY, 1956, p. 158). Naturally the analysis of the language system of a speech community is only possible through the study of particular instances, i.e., concrete speech events; but the object of the linguistic effort is the presentation of the system which underlies all the particular manifestations. In the terminology of BÜHLER or KAINZ we might say: the linguist studies *Sprachgebilde* (linguistic forms).

It will be clear that we confine the use of the term linguistics to formal or structural linguistics. In this respect we are in agreement with most linguists (e.g., GREENBERG) and nearly all psycholinguists (e.g., CARROLL). Such an emphasis on form or structure is consonant with a scientific approach. Following GLINZ (1964) we might comprehensively apply to structural plus semantic linguistics—the work of WEISGERBER and TRIER comes to mind—the wider expression of 'the study of language'.

The object of psycholinguistics is not to describe language scientifically, but to describe the processes of language use. Psycholinguistics is concerned with the relation between messages and the individual transmitting or receiving these messages. In other words, if linguistics deals with language as an objective, structured system, psycholinguistics is concerned with language as a process[1].

Going back to the model in Fig. 1 we might say following OSGOOD: "Psycholinguistics deals ... with the processes of encoding and decoding

---

[1] The corresponding terms, employed by BÜHLER, are 'linguistic form' *(Sprachgebilde)* and 'linguistic event' *(Sprachereignis)* or 'speech event' *(Sprechereignis)*.

as they relate states of messages to states of communicators" (Osgood and Sebeok, 1954, p. 4).

Encoding and decoding are transitions from one behavior modality to another. In encoding, the perceptions, thoughts and feelings of the speaker are translated into a behavior modality, i.e., verbal behavior. This sequence can be made explicit in the following diagram (following Carroll and others).

Intentive	Encoding		Decoding	Interpretive
behavior ⟶	behavior ⟶	Message ⟶	behavior ⟶	behavior
of speaker	of speaker		of hearer	of hearer

Fig. 2

The markedly behavioristic flavor of this conception is evident. What the speaker has to encode, and what happens when the listener decodes is, of course, behavior, and certainly nothing so 'mentalistic' as imaging or knowing. Carroll (1955, p. 89) points out emphatically that the intentive behavior of the speaker consists of events which have the characteristics of responses. In our view, it is questionable whether the concept of response in this interpretation is not over-stretched in a way which, although permissible, is unfruitful. Verbal behavior is not only anchored in stimuli on the one side and responses on the other but is also subjected to the determining influence of the over-riding system, the *langue* of Saussure.

But even if we do not entirely accept the implications of this terminology, the sequence in the model is useful as a base from which to move in two directions.

First, encoding and decoding can be treated as series of decisions. Decisions occur between discrete choices. This leads us to the problem of what to consider as the unit of linguistic analysis and further to interpretations in terms of information theory.

Secondly, the model shows that the linguistic process involves a kind of translation in two places. The sound cluster is produced by the speaker in lieu of something else and is understood by the listener as standing for something else; in other words, the sound complex functions as a sign; it has meaning.

In the following pages we shall take up again (and indeed not the only time in this book) the character and function of signs, while the ideas which lead from this model to information theory will be discussed in a later chapter.

Chapter 2

Sign, Expression and Symbol

BÜHLER'S *organon* model of the sign — Expression and
language — Animal language and evolution of language —
LANGER'S treatment of the tendency to symbolize — Meaning
as representation — Behavioristic and neobehavioristic
approaches to psycholinguistics.

BÜHLER in his work *Sprachtheorie* (1934), a monumental investigation
on the concept of the sign, set out from the *stat aliquid pro aliquo*
of Scholasticism. This 'standing for something else' can occur in different
modes, which are not distinguished so much by substance as by function.
BÜHLER conceives these modes of sign-quality in terms of an 'organon
model' of language (or more precisely of the sign), in keeping with the
Platonic statement that language is a tool or *organum* so that "one person
can talk to another about things." One person (A) — to another (B) —
about things: these are the three elements which are related to each other
in this model.

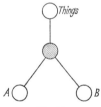

Fig. 3

BÜHLER gives the following example: A hears the patter of rain and
says to B, 'It's raining.' B on hearing these words looks towards the
window. To represent these events with greater accuracy the first
drawing can be developed as follows:

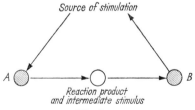

Fig. 4

Let us note in parenthesis: even in the interpretations of a scholar such as BÜHLER, who can hardly be suspected of behavioristic inclinations, the analysis of sign function leads to a presentation in terms of stimulus and response. "Reaction product and intermediate stimulus" are central to what modern mediating-response theories are about (see chapter 10).

At the next stage BÜHLER makes use of a more powerful magnification which permits him to identify differences in the various relations. In the center we find again the concrete event or phenomenon (ph):

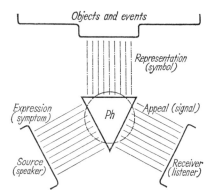

Fig. 5. BÜHLER's *organon* model (adapted from BÜHLER, 1934, p. 28)

Three features of this phenomenon turn it in a threefold way into a sign. BÜHLER represents these three features as a triangle. Corresponding to its three sides are the three modes of sign-quality. The phenomenon is a *symbol* in relation to objects and events; it is a *symptom* because of its dependence on the speaker whose inner state it expresses, and it is a *signal* because of its appeal to the receiver whose behavior it guides.

Representation, expression and appeal — these are, according to BÜHLER, the three characteristic functions of language (or of signs, as we would more cautiously be inclined to say).

Suppose we want to understand two people talking to each other in a foreign language, we can undertake the analysis under the three aspects; the phenomena, i.e., the sound patterns, may be related to:

(1) the events in the real world ('Whenever it rains, he utters this sound');

(2) the state of the speaker ('Whenever he trembles, he utters this sound');

(3) the effect on the hearer ('Whenever he hears this sound, he comes').

In the first case the sound pattern is viewed for its representational function, i.e., it functions as a symbol; in the second case it is taken as an expression or symptom, and in the third case as a signal which directs an appeal to the receiver.

2*

By treating a sign as an expression or symptom, we infer something: because we know of, or assume, a connection, we conclude that the appearance of the phenomenon implies the occurrence of what is connected with it, although it cannot be directly observed. Thus, if we observe marked variations in voice intensity we conclude that the speaker is excited. This is, according to BÜHLER, the inference *quoad existentiam*. It is quite different in the case of the representational function of the sign. Here the perceived phenomenon does not act as an indicator by its appearance, *quoad existentiam* with which it is linked through *connexio rerum*; it stands *quoad essentiam* for something outside itself (BÜHLER, 1932, p. 102f.). A high color on the cheeks is connected with a fever *(connexio rerum)*, but the fever does not draw the curve on the temperature chart; the chart represents certain abstract moments of the course of the fever. In this form of representational relatedness, there is no *connexio rerum*, but an *ordo rerum*, produced by the ordering activity of the mind.

If we consider the cogency of the relationship between the sign and the object signified we find, in BÜHLER'S model, only two possibilities: either the relationship is natural (derived from a *connexio rerum*), or it is conventional (i.e., arbitrarily established).

A more detailed scale of necessity in the relation between sign and what it designates has been established by PEIRCE (1932): he distinguishes *icon* (the sign has similarity to what is signified), *index* (the sign is causally connected with the thing signified) and *symbol* (the sign is connected with what it designates according to a conventional rule). The varying degrees of necessity in the connection between sign and denotatum will be discussed once more in greater detail in connection with the claim of an 'inner relationship' between sign and the thing signified: in onomatopoeia, in WERNER'S theory of linguistic physiognomy and in sound symbolism, also in connection with the reverse of this theory, the *General Semantics* of KORZYBSKI and HAYAKAWA.

SAUSSURE stresses the arbitrariness of the connection between the sign and what it signifies. *Signe* is the unit which is produced by the association of *signifié* and *signifiant*. *Signifié* is not the object itself but the concept, *signifiant* not the sound, but the psychological trace of the sound. *Signifié* and *signifiant* are, therefore, abstractions which in the system are placed into the area of *langue* (cf. MALMBERG, 1963). A consequence of this shift of *signe* into the 'objective' sphere of *langue* is that it unwittingly confirms the Saussurian view of the meaning of a word as something definite. The inevitable relativity of meaning produced by the situation is a feature still to be discussed in greater detail. The point here is that we now meet for the first time the difference of opinion as to what the object really is in the dual relationship between sign and signified object.

A particularly noteworthy further development of the Bühler theory of signs is the treatment by JASSEM (1961) who in his discussion of the sign distinguishes three levels of analysis, derived from concepts of information theory: (a) 'signal', (b) 'sign' (in a narrow sense) and (c) 'symbol'. To these levels correspond certain linguistic units, which will be introduced below (p. 42).

In BÜHLER'S model (see Fig. 5 above) the three modes of sign quality are represented by a triangle. This triangle is somewhat smaller in places than the circle which represents the concrete phenomenon. If a concrete object or process (e.g., a sound pattern) functions as a sign, the sign function is exercised by certain features—and only those (1932, p. 110). In traffic signals only the color functions as a sign, not their size or degree of brightness. This is what BÜHLER calls 'abstractive relevance' (abstraktive Relevanz). This principle, according to which only part of a sound cluster has sign function, whereas all the rest is irrelevant, is important for the discussion of linguistic units (see chapter 4).

The triangle which represents the three modes of sign quality (Fig. 5 above) in certain places extends beyond the circle of concrete phenomena. According to BÜHLER this is meant to indicate that the acoustic data are supplemented by others which cannot be immediately perceived by the senses, but derive, for example, from memory, motivation and so on. This filling-out process by the organism occurs according to principles which in modern psychology are studied under the heading of social perception.

A certain deficiency in BÜHLER'S model—which results from the philosophical climate of his time— is that the world of objects and events is treated as completely detached from language. This is the Aristotelian notion that language depicts the world. There is no place in this model for the object-creating function of language which was stressed by HUMBOLDT and later by CASSIRER, SAPIR, WHORF and others. This essential addition has been made by linguistic research with a behavioristic orientation and also by linguistic analysis in philosophy (see chapter 15).

Moreover, BÜHLER'S 'organon theory' overlooks another problem: does the sign have its function (or functions) so to speak 'intrinsically', or is it only the intention of the sign-user which 'tunes' the sign into a certain direction?[1] This question is not discussed by BÜHLER, because he is more concerned with the isolated sign than with the complete speech event.

The sign is undoubtedly the nucleus of language, but language is more than mere sign. The blurring of these distinctions has caused an old controversy: to what extent can expression—mime, facial expression,

---

[1] On the signifying intention see HUSSERL (1929) and MERLEAU-PONTY (1952); in the psychology of language ACH (1932) has treated this aspect. MORRIS' theory —to be described in chapter 8—leads to advances on this point.

gesture and certain phenomena of the autonomic nervous system—be considered to be a language or to belong to language? One can speak of 'the language of the human face' or of a 'telling' blush.

Such views can be accommodated in the model under discussion; in BÜHLER's conception the sign is a symptom whenever it can be understood as an expression of the inner state of the speaker. The symptom relationship between sign and what is signified is in this case, as we have seen, a natural one because of the *connexio rerum*. But MALMBERG rightly notes in this connection that a symptom does not have to be natural. Even such apparently 'primitive' utterances as cries of pain have a different form in different languages; i.e., they are, to a certain extent at least, co-determined by conventions. Where the sign functions as a symbol (i.e., for reference), the arbitrary conventional association is dominant, but even in these cases, as we shall see in the discussion on sound symbolism, there are, so to speak, 'natural' preferences. In the signal and the symbol functions, then, the border-line between conventional and natural causation is either vague or non-existent. If the poet says that the heart is worn like a posy of violets—is this using language for representation or as expression?

And again: is the presence of the expressive function alone sufficient to speak of 'language'? This question may seem to lead to a purely terminological dispute about the definition of language; but it is this kind of questioning which has for centuries given the impetus to thought about the origin and evolution of speech.

The expressive movements and sounds in animals manifest themselves for emotional reasons or in connection with instinctive actions. Can animals speak? HERDER (1772) has answered this question succinctly by saying that the sounds of emotion can only become language if an intellect is added which can cause the sound to be uttered intentionally.

Consequently, the similarity of animal and human language is external; it refers purely to the appearance of sound, but not "to the specifically linguistic sound which emanates from the urge to speak and which is determined by an inner faculty of language" (RÉVÉSZ, 1946, p. 37). The total character and intention of the uttered sounds indicate that animal language is not language in the real sense. In these observations RÉVÉSZ shows that he is still entirely in the tradition of the psychology of consciousness. "If the tendency or intention of entering into contact with others is added to the expressive movement, the latter ceases to be purely expressive movement and becomes either a signalling sign or a linguistic symbol" (p. 39). RÉVÉSZ, therefore, assumes that expression and what is expressed are co-existent poles in a psychic unity. It follows that expression, produced with intent or employed for whatever purpose, e.g., to make contact, is no longer simply expression. If, on the other hand, expression—or, more precisely, expressive behavior—is in principle regarded as separable from an inner state, as was discussed above, there is no clear distinction between expression on the one hand and symbol and sign on the other. According to our present state of knowledge on the role of tradition in expression, of the directive function of expressive movements and the role of learning in understanding of expression (cf. KIRCHHOFF, 1965, on this point), it is certain that expression can, to a certain extent, be used purposefully. We must therefore assume a broad field of transition between symptom, signal and symbol; one might place in this area, for example, threatening gestures of animals or the display behavior of geese. These result in communication and, yet, we do not have to presuppose communicative intent in the source.

RÉVÉSZ would be prepared to ascribe a language to certain animal species, if they disposed of a well-ordered system of signs, or—to use the terms of our earlier discussions—of a structured *langue* or *code*. In this case animals would have to have "e.g., not one warning call but several, one for the approach of a human, another for a member of his family coming into view *(sic)*, another again for a hostile animal" (p. 47). RÉVÉSZ no doubt believed that it would not be possible to find animal utterances which satisfied these criteria. He was mistaken. It is known—thanks to observations by HEINROTH and LORENZ—that various species of birds make just these distinctions in their warning sounds. For instance, one may find in one and the same species different warning sounds for flying enemies and for enemies on the ground.

The point of view, which has thus been introduced into the discussion, of a systematic differentiation of messages has never been more clearly demonstrated than in the fascinating researches of FRISCH on the language of bees. One can hardly think about the psychology of language without taking note of the results of these investigations. They are therefore briefly described here.

In 1919 FRISCH observed a bee which, having just returned from a feeding place to the hive, danced around and caused excitement among the worker-bees. After a three-year period of intensive research he believed he had come to understand the language of bees. Twenty years later, FRISCH himself remarked that he had overlooked the most important factor and that the language of bees was exceedingly complex (1962a).

When a honey bee returns from a forage and performs a dance, the other worker-bees experience the characteristic smell of the feeding place because of the scent which adheres to the returning scout. FRISCH held at first that it would be impossible for the bee to provide, in addition, an exact description of the location. But when the foragers fly off they search at the right distance as well as in the right direction. Has the language of bees a word for distance? A bee coming from a nearby feeding place performs a round-dance; if it returns from a more distant place it executes a tail-wagging-dance. But the indication of distance is even more differentiated. The message transmitted through the wagging-

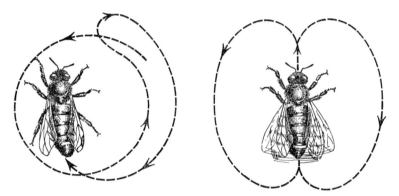

Fig. 6. Dance patterns of the bee: round-dance (left) and wagging-dance (right) (from FRISCH, 1962a, p. 126)

dance contains more information than merely 'more than 50 meters'. If the goal is at a distance of 100 meters the bee repeats the straight run of the dance pattern approximately 9 or 10 times in 15 seconds. At greater distances the speed of the dance declines in a regular manner; a definite tempo corresponds to each distance.

This is the internationally accepted form of communication among bees; various strains of the species *apis mellifera* can communicate with one another; but there are 'dialects': Austrian and Italian bees can co-operate harmoniously: the Austrian dance stimulates the Italian bee; but the indication of a distance of 100 meters is misinterpreted as 80 meters, whereas 100 meters danced in the Italian dialect is interpreted by the Austrian bee as 120 meters (FRISCH, 1962b).

The direction of the target is indicated by the direction of the straight line in the wagging-dance pattern, with the position of the sun as a point of reference. In the darkened beehive this angle on the sun is represented by a corresponding angle on the direction of gravity. The differences in the dialects described above stand in contrast to a phylogenetically earlier and simpler form of communication: Indian dwarf bees, a more primitive ancestor of the *apis mellifera*, are not capable of this trans-position from light to gravity. A less developed language corresponds to a more primitive social organization. Even lower in the phylogenetic scale are the stingless *meliponini*; in this strain the information about the target is not transmitted to the foragers in the hive, but traces of scent and pilot bees act as guides (LINDAUER, 1961).

It had been thought for a long time that the capacity of the communicative system in the honey bee is restricted to transmission of information on quality and position of feeding places. LINDAUER (1955 and later) was able to demonstrate that swarming bees can signal the position of a good place for a dwelling with a similar code.

The communicative system of the honey bee is also important for linguistics from another point of view. A number of different sense modalities are brought into use to transmit information: the kind of food found by the scout is indicated by a minute particle of the substance itself or by the scent of the substance, and the distance of the feeding place is communicated by the dance. Investigations by ESCH (1961) suggest that sound utterances of bees equally contain information on quality and distance.

Different strands of development lead from the communicative achievements of honey bees to phylogenetically higher species. These strands seem to disappear in one place, re-appear in a changed form elsewhere and finally lead to strange and puzzling forms of 'linguistic' behavior such as those which are found in dolphins and chimpanzees in the wild (GOODALL, 1963). It will be seen that the various strands or components are sometimes cumulative, sometimes disappear and re-appear in a new place and develop afresh. The study of communication in the animal world can present informative analogies for the study of human speech, as, for instance, CARMICHAEL (1964) has brilliantly demonstrated.

BÜHLER has regarded the signals used in a colony of bees as steering devices which represent a prehuman analogue to language. GREENBERG (1961), who 'as a human' insisted on giving the bees not just 'a technical knockout', has claimed that genuine (i.e., human) language must be capable of being used metalinguistically: one must be able to speak in language about language, e.g., to exchange opinions on the meaning of an utterance. But it is not certain whether even this criterion enables us to keep apart animal and human language; rhesus monkeys exchange metalinguistic information in order to distinguish between play and reality (SEBEOK, 1963).

The question 'Can animals speak?' turns out to be a terminological one; it can in fact only be answered by a definition of what one is prepared to recognize as language. But the lengthy discussion on this question has not been useless; it has taught linguistic science and psycholinguistics to take note of certain aspects and to make distinctions which, in quite a general way, —also outside this particular problem area—have proved to be important and fruitful.

The inability to find a genuine answer to the question 'Can animals speak?' also has consequences for the study of the origin of speech. What we are inclined to accept as the origin of speech will depend upon what we accept as 'real language'. But here again we will find what we have just noted: the discussion on the origin of language, without reaching a satisfying conclusion, yields a number of viewpoints which, in a general way, ease operations in the area of psycholinguistics. This is why it is justifiable to take up this problem in the following remarks.

In our inquiries on the behavior of bees the communicative aspect of language was prominent. But it is by no means certain whether from an evolutionary point of view communication is the earliest strand in the tissue of language.

Theories on the origin of speech which have appeared again and again over the centuries have often given greater prominence to other aspects.

THORNDIKE (1943) has summarized these theories under three most memorable headings: ding-dong theories, bow-wow theories and pooh-pooh theories. A ding-dong theory assumes that certain attributes of objects, which cannot be explained further, motivate man to utter certain sounds. As the sounds are associated with the sight of a given object, they designate the object. The bow-wow theory represents the view that man mimics the noises produced by animals, things or events, and this habit leads him to invent significant sounds for other animals, things or events. The pooh-pooh theory starts from the unlearned or 'instinctive' sounds of expression and assumes that it leads to a conventionalized vocabulary of pain, surprise, fear and so on. STEVENSON (1944) sees such a connecting link between sighing, moaning and laughing on the one hand and exclamations on the other.

In more recent times, SUZANNE LANGER (1963) has approached this problem in a way which is particularly interesting for a *psychology* of language and we shall therefore briefly describe it. She starts out from a view expressed by SAPIR who has declared that the attempts to unravel the origin of language are hardly more than exercises in speculative imagination. As for the reason for this failure, SAPIR argues as follows: "The primary function of language is generally said to be communication ... The autistic speech of children seems to show that the purely communicative aspect of language has been exaggerated. It is best to admit that language is primarily a vocal actualization of the tendency to see reality symbolically, that it is precisely this quality which renders it a fit instrument for communication and that it is in the actual give and take of social intercourse that it has been complicated and refined into the form in which it is known today" (SAPIR, 1933, p. 159). This "tendency to see reality symbolically" is for LANGER the nucleus from which language has originated. It follows that the search for the roots of language should not be directed so much towards preformations of communication as towards earlier forms of symbolic behavior.

What should we imagine these early forms of *symbols* to have been like? To begin with, there was probably no more than a vague feeling that an object, a certain pattern or a sound is not insignificant, but that it has some meaning. LANGER documents with a series of examples that in certain anthropoid apes there are indications of an aesthetic sense or of superstitious fear directed towards objects which in themselves were trivial. Often such an object is treated literally as a fetish. Such behavior is evidence for the tendency to see more in an object than what is immediately and objectively given: the emotional tendency is a rudimentary form of symbolic behavior.

A genuine symbol evolves from these earlier forms through a process of dissociation and objectivization. The process originates most clearly "where some object, sound, or act is provided which has no *practical* meaning, yet tends to elicit an emotional response and thus hold one's undivided attention" (LANGER, 1963, pp. 116—117)[1]. This emotional tendency to *see* symbolically can be aroused in apes and in man by objects and gestures, but only in man can this tendency be elicited by *sounds*.

The earliest symbolic value of words originates in a vague emotional arrest at the use of words; it is therefore connotative in character. Only a later stage frees the symbol "from its original instinctive utterance and marks its deliberate *use*, outside of the total situation that gave it birth" (LANGER, 1963, p. 133). Thus, connotation becomes denotation, the factual relationship of the sign to the object signified is established, and this, as LANGER says, is the essence of language.

LANGER traces here the same line of development as CASSIRER[2] who sees it as a transition from emotional to propositional language or, in other words, to the power of conceptual use of language. The symbolic transformation makes possible the great discovery that in principle everything has a name.

Basically, then, these considerations lead us to a final criterion: whether something is or is not a symbol depends on the subjective manner of possessing it, or, in other words, on the awareness of having full control over it and of being able to use it at will. If, thus, we accord a decisive role to the subjective factor in symbol formation we touch upon problems and difficulties which reach beyond the question of the origin of speech. The presence of a genuine symbol and consequently of meaning is in this way made accessible only to an act of introspection but not to objective observation or to scientific treatment.

Sign, symbol and meaning are, as we have seen, concepts which always imply a relation between at least two poles: sign and what it

---

[1] The view that the symbol does not arise from practical aspects of behavior but from emotional projections directed towards behavior elements of no functional significance is a theory which stands in extreme contrast to a conception which will be discussed in detail at a later stage (see p. 210).

[2] See particularly the 4th edition of *Philosophie der symbolischen Formen (The Philosophy of Symbolic Forms)*.

signifies; symptom and inner state; symbol and object. We have already pointed out the uncertainty of the nature of the object which corresponds to the sign. BÜHLER does not hesitate to speak without any reservations about "objects and events", i.e., objects of the real world which can be perceived without language and apart from it. But who has ever come across an *animal* as such? In SAUSSURE the object, which he calls *signifié*, is not the object itself, but the concept, something rather like an idea or an ideal image of the object. This view has led psycholinguistics again and again to the conception of the object as an *image*. The meaning of a word such as 'Eiffel Tower', then, consists in the image of the edifice that the word evokes in the hearer. But what image corresponds to the word 'animal'? Has it fur, feathers or scales; and has it fins, feet or wings? And what does the image of 'justice' look like?

The impossibility of giving an answer to such questions together with the fact that many humans understand messages they hear without having any definite images[1] have brought about that in the psychology of language the notion of image has been treated with increasing scepticism.

These difficulties which have appeared on the frontiers between psychology of language and philosophy are the ones which, in general psychology, have led to the development of *behaviorism*. Behaviorism has set for itself the goal of employing only operations and concepts which can be communicated and tested without any trace of subjectivity. Yet, communicability and testability are valid as the decisive criteria not only for behaviorism but for every exact science.

This perfectly understandable desire has, as is of course known, led behaviorism to overshoot any reasonable target. Its refusal to consider anything that is not externally visible or any event that is only accessible to introspection has led many investigators into the most peculiar contortions around and away from the really interesting problems.

Even more dangerous than this restriction in the choice of objects and methods of investigation which is found in orthodox behaviorism is the tendency which goes with it to overextend the use of concepts (e.g., the concept of conditioning) which have proved useful in the analysis of certain modes of behavior without realizing that in the study of a new mode of behavior they are used far less rigorously. One bathes, as it were, in the reflected glory of scientific rigor acquired elsewhere.

These difficulties have had two consequences. Firstly, in the analysis of meaning, they have led to rather complicated models. In order to understand these models, we must familiarize ourselves with certain findings in the psychology of learning and language: the problem of meaning will, as was already pointed out, be encountered again and again.

---

[1] The studies on the psychology of thought of the Würzburg School come to mind in this connection.

A second consequence of these difficulties of behavioristic orthodoxy in psycholinguistics has been that it has led to a more tolerant and less purist form of behaviorism. We call neobehaviorists those psychologists who no longer anxiously avoid such notions as idea, thought or image but who, nevertheless, endeavor to use such notions only if some objectively available indices give them the right to do so.

In psycholinguistics this neobehavioristic position is particularly well represented by CARROLL who writes: "I take the initial position that subjective events can be regarded as behavioral, that they play an important role in many behavior sequences, and that appeal to them in a psychological context bears no necessary trace of philosophical dualism. I further take the position that there are publicly observable indices of subjective events (not the least of which is verbal behavior) and that subjective events may be assumed to follow much the same laws as those events observable as neurological, motor, and glandular responses... Psychologists constantly behave on the assumption that subjective events occur; they are willing to talk about 'thought', 'images', 'dreams', and 'percepts', though they prefer to speak of these things as events and processes rather than states ... The problem of subjective behavior becomes critical only when one speaks of consciousness, for there is a danger that one may lapse into philosophical dualism again by stating that something happens in consciousness which independently guides or directs overt behavior. We can regard the problem of consciousness as a spurious one, however, for if we think of subjective behavior as a series of responses, the notion of consciousness need not enter our discussions" (1955, p. 72).

'Behavior', in this interpretation, is acceptable without question; subjective, covert behavior, if necessary, as well; but consciousness as a state — no.

In our view, however, the achievement and significance of language is to be found just in this area. Language makes it possible to transcend the behavioral level which is bound by the time dimension. Through language we can bring past events to consciousness in memory (and have them precisely only there). Language makes it possible to make verbal plans of future activities, to have the chain of future acts reeled up and simultaneously present in thought; and to release it from this timeless form of existence—like Athene from the head of Zeus—into the time dimension of actual behavior.

Chapter 3

Linguistic Units

Description of the speech event — Phonetics — Articulatory, acoustic and auditory approaches — The morpheme — MARTINET'S dual scheme of analysis — The phoneme — Distinctive feature analysis — Grammar as combinatorics of language — CHOMSKY'S generative grammar.

In the preceding chapters the attempt was made to fit together largely philosophical and epistemological ideas in order to lay a general foundation for psycholinguistics. This attempt cannot be said to have been successful; we have not discovered a readily available philosophical basis for empirical enquiries in psycholinguistics. However, these chapters can give us points of view, hints and warnings which we would be well advised to bear in mind in our forthcoming discussions. We will find that, from time to time, the empirical inquiries will yield new glimpses of the epistemological questions which we have already considered.

Let us start once more from the model of the speech event we had outlined in chapter 1.

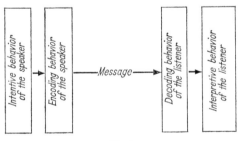

Fig. 7

Encoding and decoding are processes of translation — from and into language. The translator must choose among the possibilities which the lexicon and the grammar put at his disposal. Language, understood in this way, demands a series of decisions or choices; it is not an undivided total stream, but a sequence of different, separable events. We can study these events in the speaker, in the message, or in the listener. The separable events are connected with each other like members of a family because they form part of a *structured* sequence, but in spite of that, this 'family', the language, is composed of units which are individual and distinguishable. SAUSSURE who describes language not as substance but as form implies that the reality of language lies in the function of linguistic units and in their mutual relationship.

Our object now is to get to know these units. Why, it may be asked, should a *psychology* of language concern itself with the units of *linguistics* ? In psychology, generally the experimenter or investigator decides what he wants to treat as the units of inquiry[1]. In the psychology of language, however, the psychologist cannot define what the unit should be; he must know what the language user, the listener or speaker, treats as a unit. Language, or, more precisely, the use of language, is not a field which can be divided into units for the purpose of scientific analysis; the object of investigation is already structured. To find out what the structure is like, is the task of linguistic science; to find out how the structure functions and how it is acquired, is the task of psycholinguistics.

For this reason psychology of language —more than any other branch of psychology— is dependent upon co-operation with its non-psychological sister discipline. In the following pages we will attempt to describe the units of investigation which linguistics has developed, without studying in detail how psycholinguistics strives to investigate the functioning and acquisition of these units.

To begin with, the description of a speech event can be undertaken from two points of view: (a) *articulation*, i.e., the production of sound sequences; and (b) *acoustics*, i.e., the physical characteristics of the sound sequences, thus produced. It is not uncommon to find a good deal of switching from articulatory to acoustic description, as the need arises.

A corresponding description of the listening event can equally be undertaken from two points of view: (a) the physical characteristics of the sound sequence which acts as a stimulus, in other words from an *acoustic* point of view, and (b) what is heard by the receiver, the *auditory description*.

The total event comprising speaker and hearer can therefore be divided into three different phases and be described in three different terminologies: *articulatory*, *acoustic* and *auditory*.

Speech sounds are made by modifications of the air-stream which is produced by exhalation. (We are not, at this point, taking note of exceptions.) The two cavities which participate in the modification of

---

[1] An illustration from personality research will make this clear: one may, for example, regard a movement, an act, a need, a motivational pattern or a stage of life as a unit.

the air-stream, the chest and the pharyngeal-oral cavity, are separated
by the larynx which contains mobile folds of tissue, ligaments and
muscles, the *vocal cords*.

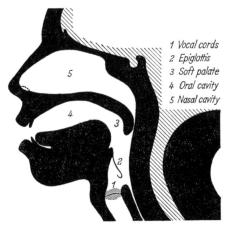

1 Vocal cords
2 Epiglottis
3 Soft palate
4 Oral cavity
5 Nasal cavity

Fig. 8. Schematic diagram of the organs of speech (from STEINBUCH, 1965, p. 90)

Attempts —partly with the help of primitive resonators— to understand the physical nature of speech sounds and the physical consequences
of the processes of articulation have a long history. The acoustic analysis
of speech sounds undertaken in the framework of phonetics recognizes
three dimensions: intensity, frequency and duration. Through sound
spectrography acoustic patterns can be converted into visual ones and
thus be made more amenable to investigation.

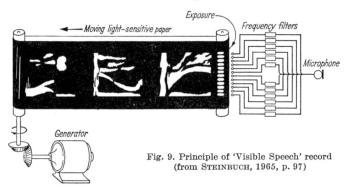

Fig. 9. Principle of 'Visible Speech' record
(from STEINBUCH, 1965, p. 97)

Thanks to the spectrograph the energy of continuous speech is distributed,
by means of filters, over 10 to 20 frequency-bands. The moving, light-
sensitive paper is blackened according to the relative intensity of the
energy at different bands.

An even more ingenious instrument, called a pattern playback, can reconvert graphic patterns into sound. It is possible, first, to darken the paper in order to indicate certain intensities and distributions, and in this way emphasize some frequencies and omit others, and then to hear what the sound, constructed by this procedure, is like. The analysis of a sound pattern can thus be tested by a subsequent synthesis for accuracy and exhaustiveness.

The following sketch indicates certain results of phonetics which have important implications for psycholinguistics.

The cavities through which the air-stream passes act as filters, filtering out some frequencies, and as resonators, reinforcing others. The principle involved is well-known: if we blow over the opening of a bottle, the size and shape of the cavity determine the frequency of the sound produced in this way. This principle is at the basis of vowel sounds. If we examine a spectrogram for the frequencies which are produced, for example, by the vowel sound [i], the pattern will normally reveal two peaks. In other words, two frequencies have more energy than others. These are the so-called *formants*. A formant is a concentration of energy in a relatively narrow frequency-band.

That vowels are characterized by such formants has been made known above all through the research of CARL STUMPF (1926) whose work —without any electronic devices— has led to astonishingly exact results even by present-day standards.

However, position and number of formants are not the only constituents of a given vowel. The formants of the vowel [a] spoken by a man are different from those spoken by a woman; and yet both can be clearly recognized as [a]. Nor is the relative position of the formants the only decisive factor; it may well be that learning and experience play a part.

The mark of a consonant is a sudden change in the even pattern of the formants. While in vowels the time dimension plays no important part, it is decisive for consonants. The change in the structure of the formants can be caused by a sudden complete stoppage or by transition to an irregular, non-periodic noise spectrum. The open vocal tract is closed once or several times and thus variation and repetition, having the effect of a disturbance, are brought into the even course of sound production. We do not have to go into detail here on further differences caused by stops, fricatives, and so on.

So far we have described the sounds of speech in acoustic or physical terms. If such a description is greatly refined, it will be found that no speaker can twice produce the same sound, nor can different speakers produce two sounds which are the same. Since, strictly speaking, there are no events which can be repeated, this account of a physical

event could not be lawfully related to other processes, e.g., the comprehension of spoken utterances. In order to establish regularities, the
separate events must be classified, as we have already done by speaking
of 'vowels' and 'consonants'.

The same conclusion is reached, i.e., a categorizing process must be
assumed, if we leave the articulatory-acoustic interpretation of speech
production and move on to the acoustic-auditive description of speech
perception.

An experiment of the Haskins Laboratories is perhaps a suitable link
between the production phase and studies on speech perception (cf.
LIBERMAN, 1957, and LIBERMAN et al., 1963).

Seven different vowels, each consisting of two formants, were recorded
on magnetic tape. Each of these vowels was preceded by a burst of noise
lasting 1.5 cs. The frequency span of this explosion remained 600 cps;
but the absolute height of the explosion was varied. Different [a] sounds
and different [i] sounds were produced, etc.; among them, for example,
an [a] preceded by a noise lasting 1.5 cs between 400 and 1,000 cps, or
an [a] preceded by a noise between 600 and 1,200 cps, or an [i] preceded
by a noise between 400 and 1,000 cps.

What does a subject hear who listens to these sound sequences?
If the noise explosion lies at a level above 3,000 cps. it is generally heard
as [t]; if it is below 3,000 cps it is heard as [k], as long as it occurs above
the second formant of the vowel; otherwise it is heard as [p]. This means
different explosions are heard as identical consonants, provided they
occur above 3,000 cps; on the other hand, identical explosions are
perceived as different consonants depending on the relationship to the
subsequent vowel.

This experiment has three interesting implications for us:
(1) What we perceive as vowels and consonants are not invariant sounds
or noises, but classes or categories of different noises. The differences
between classes determine our perceptions; differences between noises
within the same class are overheard or disregarded. The course of a speech
event —and, as we shall see later, both in its articulatory and its perceptive phase— has a built-in device which takes note of certain distinctions
and orients itself in accordance with them, but it ignores other distinctions and declares them as non-existent. We are reminded of SAUS-
SURE'S 'differences and identities' which are decisive for language (see
p. 15 above). By introducing the concept of classification, i.e., both noting
and ignoring differences, we have of necessity come to include a psychological point of view.
(2) In physical terms a sound is always fully defined by the characteristics of the sound wave. But what sort of consonant this sound is

perceived as, is psychologically determined by the subsequent vowel, or by the sequence within which the sound is embedded. In chapter 5 we shall return to this sequential feature.

(3) The three aspects which we have so far distinguished in a speech event —the articulatory, acoustic and auditory aspect—are not completely compatible. This means that, for instance, not all articulatory movements of the speech organs have an acoustic effect, and it further implies that a particular acoustic process does not always result in the same auditory experience. To put it differently: the articulatory space has different dimensions from the acoustic one, and the acoustic space, in turn, has different dimensions from the auditory space. There is a higher degree of agreement between the articulatory and the auditory dimensions than between the acoustic and the auditory ones: this peculiar state of affairs will occupy us again at a later stage when we discuss LIBERMAN'S theory (see pp. 62 ff.).

We now return to the question we discussed before our digression on the Haskins experiment. The search for linguistically and psycholinguistically relevant units, which we began in the field of phonetics with the help of the Saussurian 'clues' of likenesses and differences, has yielded the following results: differences that the speaker produces are not necessarily perceived as differences; identical utterances do not always exercise identical effects. The attempt of phonetics to determine the sounds of speech as events in their own right has shown that psychological factors must inevitably be taken into account. But this is not surprising; the speech sounds produced by the human voice are not random vocalizations, they are *linguistic* sounds; i.e., they have sign quality or meaning. A sign which, according to SAUSSURE, belongs to a system of signs is characterized by its difference from other signs. Since the approach via physical absolutes as distinguishing marks has not led very far, the search for linguistically relevant units must make use of differences and identities of *meaning* as the instrument of analysis.

A similar position is reached from the point of view of communication theory: "To be a practicable medium for the transmission of information, a language must be susceptible of description by a finite number of distinguishable, mutually exclusive sounds. That is, the language must be representable in terms of basic linguistic units which have the property that if one replaces another in an utterance, the meaning is changed" (FLANAGAN, 1965, p. 14).

In order to discover linguistic units, or to recognize distinct boundaries between them an analysis of the choice processes which occur during the speech act must be made. The speaker and the hearer must make a series of decisions. For each unit a choice has to be made or, conversely, what is selected at each single choice point constitutes a unit.

3*

In the sentence, 'The beer is good', a choice has been made before 'good'. During speaking (encoding) or listening (decoding) the decision might have been 'bitter', or 'stale' or 'pale'. Another decision has to be made before 'is': 'tastes' or 'was' might well have been chosen. And instead of 'beer' the decision might have been to say 'house' or 'child'.

The units which thus occur are, following MARTINET (1960), called 'units of the first articulation' or *monemes*; another common designation is also *morpheme*. It should be added that these units are not identical with words: the sentence, 'He feels unwell', has five morphemes: 'he', 'feel', 's', 'un', 'well'.

Each of the units of the first level of articulation displays meaning and phonic shape. Some thousands of such units in every new combination serve to communicate whatever we want to say. "What characterizes linguistic communication and opposes it to prelinguistic groans is precisely this analysis into a number of units which, because of their vocal nature, are to be presented successively in a linear fashion. These are the units which many contemporary linguists call 'morphemes'" (MARTINET, 1962, p. 22).

If a morpheme is analyzed further, its meaning is lost. The meaning of 'toe' is not a combination of the meanings of /t/ and /o/. The only analysis that is still possible is that of the phonic shape. It follows that the morpheme is the smallest meaningful unit. It is a segment of an utterance which recurs in different utterances with more or less the same meaning. The word 'older' consists of two morphemes, because the suffix '-er' has independent meaning. It is the comparative. The same sound '-er' in the word 'hunter' represents a different morpheme; it is an operator appended to a verb (from BERKO and BROWN, 1960).

While here the same sound (or as we shall call it below: the same 'phoneme') is recognized as two morphemes according to the environment in which it occurs, the morpheme can be said to form a class or category. In English, for example, we find the morpheme /s/ with the meaning of plural. This constitutes a class, composed of various *allomorphs*, with the same meaning: 'cats' with voiceless /s/, 'boys' with voiced /z/ 'roses' with /iz/. Which of these allomorphs is selected, is determined by what precedes and is not open to the free choice of the speaker; hence these three forms are not three different units, but only one. Sometimes the allomorphs of a morpheme are totally different in sound. 'Am, is, are' are allomorphs of the morpheme 'be'; which of these is used in a given utterance is not determined by the speaker but by the context; for example, the allomorph 'am' occurs only together with 'I'.

The morpheme as the 'smallest semantic vehicle' (JAKOBSON and HALLE, 1956, p. 3) is not the lowest level of decision-making. The morpheme 'toe', phonemically /to/, can be further analyzed into units, which —although they no longer *contain* meaning— still *convey* meaning. If instead of /o:/ we choose /i:/, we signal a different meaning: 'tea'.

This 'articulation at the second level' (MARTINET) into units of sound, the *phonemes*, again makes it possible to use decision-making as a criterion: for each unit a particular choice must be made; what is selected through one such act of decision, constitutes a unit.

The first articulation may be found in nearly all symbol systems, whereas the possibility of the lower-level articulation is the mark only of human language (MALMBERG, 1963). It is therefore possible to construct signs and messages of infinite length from a small number of units which themselves are not signs.

This dual articulation is so fundamental to language that MARTINET has placed it in the center of his definition of language. "A language is a medium of communication according to which human experience is analyzed, differently in each community, into units (monemes) with a semantic content and a phonic shape. This phonic shape, in its turn, is articulated in distinctive and successive units (phonemes) whose number in a given language is fixed and whose nature and mutual relations also vary from language to language" (1962, p. 26).

The great merit of this dual articulation is the economy which is thus attained. With the help of some 12 to 65 phonemes on the second level and some thousands of morphemes on the first it is possible to say everything that ever has been or ever will be spoken. The number of phonemes and the length of morphemes stand in a relationship to each other which can easily be established on the grounds of information-theory. If a language had only a small number of phonemes, the morphemes must correspondingly be longer (i.e., consist of more phonemes) in order to be mutually exclusive. If it had a large number of phonemes, the phonemes would be less easy to differentiate (CARROLL, 1964a).

In *phonetics* we have become acquainted with a discipline which investigates the physical characteristics of human speech sounds in their own right (BÜHLER).

Phonology is concerned with those aspects of speech-sounds which are relevant for the purpose of sign-functioning. The development of phonology has been decisively influenced by the Russian prince TRUBETZKOY (1929) and the so-called Prague Circle, a group with which, incidentally, KARL BÜHLER was closely associated. Phonology classifies the sounds of a language according to the smallest units which account for differences between various utterances in this language.

With the concept of the phoneme we have moved once more into the neighborhood of BÜHLER's arguments on the nature and function of the sign. The example with which BÜHLER in his *Sprachtheorie* introduces the phoneme makes this clear:

Suppose two persons agree to communicate by means of flag signals. In the code they arrange, the size and shape of the flags are irrelevant, only the shade of the color matters. Three grades of color saturation are agreed upon as relevant for meaning. Firstly, the shades of the black-white range with the least degree of saturation have meaning A; secondly, an intermediate degree of saturation is said to always have meaning B, but whether the color is sky-blue, pink or brown does not matter. Thirdly, the most saturated colors always have meaning C. Whether in a particular case a rich red, blue, green, or yellow appears makes no difference.

Supposing one of the partners wishes to send message C, the weather, his mood or his supply of flags may dictate whether he chooses dark-red, dark-yellow, dark green, or dark-blue. Thus, weather, mood or supply influence the particular choice, and yet are irrelevant for the sign function of the flags.

Let us now move from this hypothetical example to a concrete illustration. A West-Caucasian language has vowel sounds not unlike those of German. Among them, for example, are the sounds /u/, /y/ and /i/. But whereas in German it is possible to distinguish two words through the contrast of /u/ and /i/, e.g., 'Tusche' (Indian ink) vs. 'Tische' (tables), this is not possible in the West-Caucasian language, because in this language /u/, /y/ and /i/ have no distinguishing or diacritical significance. In German /u/ and /i/ function as two different phonemes, in the West-Caucasian language they belong to the same phoneme.

It follows that phonology recognizes in the phoneme those aspects of speech sounds which —in the original sense of the term— are significant, i.e., sign-forming, or distinctive within a code. Besides these significant differences there are many insignificant ones. In English the /l/ in 'light' and 'feel' are differently produced; nevertheless the difference in meaning of the two words does not depend upon this difference in articulation. In Russian, however, these two forms of the same sound must be clearly distinguished, or else misunderstandings might arise. In English these sounds are different *allophones* of the same phoneme; in Russian they are two different phonemes.

In English it does not matter whether /t/ is aspirated or not. In the words 'top' and 'stop' the difference in the /t/ is not used as a distinguishing mark. Whereas in English the aspirated and non-aspirated /t/ are allophones of the same phoneme, in Chinese and several other languages they are two different phonemes.

The notion that a phoneme can be considered as a class or category of allophones, and a morpheme as a class of allomorphs, links up with two interesting lines of thought. One of these takes us back to Saussurian 'differences and likenesses': the production and perception of sounds is channelled through a sorting device which disregards irrelevant differences and classifies sounds according to criteria which matter in the particular language. These criteria must therefore be *acquired*.

The other classification of morphemes and phonemes can be related to the *constancy phenomenon* well known in general psychology. The form constancy of a table as rectangular, however distorted it may appear on the retina, is clearly analogous. Whatever /l/ sounds like, provided it is clearly differentiated from, say, /m/ and /k/, we disregard any distortion.

BÜHLER'S introductory example of flag signals starts from the assumption that the partners have made an agreement. We must now consider the situation of an anthropologist who visits an unknown tribe and wants to find out what variations are meaningful. In this situation, which is often referred to in the American literature, it is customary to operate with the notion of the 'native speaker'. A speaker for whom the language in question is the first language is asked to repeat the relevant utterances. Or the anthropologist copies him and finds out what copy is acceptable as repetition and what therefore would be tolerated as allophonic variation or, alternatively, what would constitute a change in meaning. An English native speaker would tolerate if 'right' were pronounced 'roight' but he would reject it if it was pronounced 'rot'.

At first sight this procedure appears simple and unambiguous, but it conceals a psychological problem: much depends on the motivations of the native speaker. If he thinks he is being tested for his auditory discrimination, he will declare 'right' and 'roight' as different.

A more difficult problem can be illustrated by the following example from German. Suppose an anthropologist in an investigation on the German language wants to compare 'Donnerwetter' (thunderstorm) without aspirated initial /d/ with 'Donnerwetter!', with aspirated initial /dh/, uttered as an emotive expression ('Heavens', 'Good gracious') in order to find out whether unaspirated and aspirated /d/ in word-initial position are distinct phonemes or allophones. He will therefore ask his informant whether there is a difference in meaning. The answer to this question will depend upon how widely the concept of 'meaning' is interpreted. This issue takes us back to an earlier point in our argument: we are reminded of BÜHLER'S distinction between symbol, symptom and signal or of the division into denotative and connotative meaning, and of the discussion on the distinction between language and expression.

Another aspect, illustrated by the last example, is that a phoneme is not only what we globally refer to as a vowel or consonant, but it may also be the intensity, pitch or duration of a sound. Thus in Italian *fatto* must be distinguished from *fa:tto*.

By introducing the phoneme as a functional unit phonology has effectively reduced the multiplicity inherent in the acoustic events. Yet, the complicated interplay of contrasts and identities which is at the basis of this element leads to the further question of whether the distinction between two phonemes can be made more tangible. The minimal difference is a so-called *distinctive feature*. This term originated in the studies of the Prague Circle, in particular in the work of ROMAN JAKOBSON who now lives in USA. According to this view, a phoneme is characterized as

a bundle of distinctive features. One phoneme is separated from another
by at least one such feature. In this conception the distinctive features
can be regarded as the atoms of linguistic structure (MALMBERG, 1963).
The addition, exchange or subtraction of a single distinctive feature is in
effect a qualitative jump at the phonemic level: it converts one phoneme
into another.

The heuristic value of this further division into distinctive features is
the following: a feature which distinguishes one pair of phonemes is likely
to differentiate also another pair. Thus /t/ and /d/ are distinguished by
the feature voiced/unvoiced; but the same feature distinguishes also /p/
and /b/.

By comparing in a given language each phoneme with every other
phoneme it is possible to work out which bundle of distinctive features
forms (or better: defines) the phoneme in question. Table 1 describes
such a grouping for English.

To sum up, the phoneme consists of a *complex* or bundle of features,
whereas the morpheme consists of a sequence of phonemes (LÜDTKE,
1961).

The hierarchial structure of distinctive features as far as the syllable
is described by JAKOBSON and HALLE in the following terms: "The
distinctive features are aligned into simultaneous bundles called phonemes;
phonemes are concatenated into sequences; the elementary pattern
underlying any grouping of phonemes is the syllable ... The pivotal
principle of syllable structure is the contrast of successive features within
the syllable. One part of the syllable stands out from the others. It is
mainly the contrast vowel *vs.* consonant which is used to render one part
of the syllable more prominent" (1956, p. 20).

In recent years JAKOBSON'S line of approach has been further
developed in an interesting way. If we look at the table of distinctive
features it will be seen that each of these qualities is two-valued:
voiced/unvoiced, nasal/oral, etc.

It follows that the composition of a phoneme can be represented as a
series of two-valued judgments. But this observation leads to the analogy
of the computer which also works with binary operations. JAKOBSON
regards the principle of the binary opposition as a fundamental characteristic of his system. According to this theory, the perception of a phoneme
can be regarded as a sequence of yes-no decisions on each distinctive
feature of the bundle of features which make up a particular phoneme.
The English phoneme /p/ could be described by the following properties:
consonantal+, plosive+, voiced—, grave+, nasal—.

This approach lends itself particularly well to an analysis in terms of
information theory. MILLER (1956, p. 83f.) has related the number of
distinctive features to the channel capacity of the human; that is, the

Table 1. Jakobson-Fant-Halle's *analytic transcription of the phonemes of English (Received Pronunciation).* "*The phonemes may be broken down into the inherent distinctive features which are the ultimate signals*" (*Preliminaries*) (from MALMBERG, 1967, p. 118).

	o	ɑ	e	u	ə	i	l	ŋ	ʃ	ĵ	k	ʒ	ĝ	g	m	f	p	v	b	n	s	θ	t	z	ð	d	h	#
1. Vocalic/Non-vocalic	+	+	+	+	+	+	+	−	−	−	−	−	−	−	−	−	−	−	−	−	−	−	−	−	−	−	−	−
2. Consonantal/Non-consonantal	−	−	−	−	−	−	+	+	+	+	+	+	+	+	+	+	+	+	+	+	+	+	+	+	+	+	−	−
3. Compact-Diffuse	+	+	+	−	−	−	+	+	+	+	+	+	+	+	−	−	−	−	−	−	−	−	−	−	−	−	−	−
4. Grave/Acute	+	+	−	+	+	−								+	+	+	+	+	+									
5. Flat/Plain	+	−		+	−																							
6. Nasal/Oral								+							+					+								
7. Tense/Lax									+	−	+	−	+	−		+	+	−			+	+	+	−	−	−	+	
8. Continuant/Interrupted									+	−	−	+	−	−		+	−	+	−		+	+	−	+	+	−	+	
9. Strident/Mellow									+	+	−			−		+	−	+			+	−	+	+	−			

basic limitation of the capacity to cope in a given period with more than a restricted number of stimuli. An increase in the number of distinctive features would inevitably lead to a slowing down of speech. The number of distinctive features which differentiate neighboring consonants is regarded by SAPORTA as a compromise between the speaker's striving towards simplicity of articulation (he does not want to change the position of his vocal apparatus too frequently) and the demands of the hearer for the largest possible number of differences in order to be able to choose with greatest ease.

MEYER-EPPLER (see MALMBERG, 1963, p. 126, footnote) has questioned that this development of the theory of distinctive features can be sustained. "The fact that a phoneme can be analyzed into binary components does not permit the conclusion that the distinction between the phonemes as sound-signals rests on binary judgments. It is perfectly imaginable that ternary judgments or judgments of an even higher order play a part." FRY has pointed out that it is a weakness of the binary theory that it never states quite clearly on which side of the borderline between psychology and physics it operates. Against this viewpoint it must be noted that both physics and psychology of speech can surely make progress only if they are prepared to allow such overlapping between the two disciplines. As long as the investigator knows and bears in mind the adjustments needed by 'trespassing' in this way this objection of FRY'S carries little weight.

JASSEM (1961) has in an interesting manner related distinctive feature, phoneme and morpheme to different levels which must be distinguished in the analysis of the sign. The distinctive feature corresponds to the first level ('signal'), the phoneme to the second ('sign') and the morpheme to the third ('symbol').

From the morpheme, the unit of MARTINET'S first level, we have moved to the next smaller unit, the phonemes, and finally to the distinctive features. If we now return to the first level, it is also possible to turn in the opposite direction, towards larger units. We first come across the *syllable* which stands in a peculiar relationship to the morpheme. Both generally consist of several phonemes, but the syllable is not clearly related to meaning. In the syllable the possible sequences of phonemes are restricted by rules (LÜDTKE, 1961). The word 'tigers' consists of two syllables 'ti-gers' which separately contain no distinct meaning. But the same word also consists of two morphemes: tiger + s both of which, by definition, have meaning (e.g., 's' means plural). From the point of view of psycholinguistics the division into morphemes is more important than the division into syllables.

We therefore now turn to those structures which regulate the order of appearance of morphemes. In a given language how can morphemes be put together into meaningful utterances ?

The answer to this question is the object of *grammar*; that is, the combinatorics of language. Within grammar the distinction is made between morphology and syntax.

Morphology is concerned with combinations below the level of word, while syntax deals with those above it. Morphology and syntax are closely connected with each other, because the syntactic structure of a sentence influences the morphological structure of the words in the sentence.

We thus come to the peculiar problem of the role of the unit *word* in linguistics. The non-linguist is inclined to regard the word as the most obviously defined linguistic unit because there is the evident discreteness manifested in the written form. Here it should be pointed out that in all linguistic and psycholinguistic studies it is taken for granted that there is not necessarily a consistent relationship between speech and written language. In contrast to the layman, the linguist, who is equally interested in languages, written, for example, in syllabaries and ideographic scripts, has great difficulties in finding a definition of the word which is equally applicable to all languages.

The first attempt which is nearest to the popular view is to define the word semantically or by its content, i.e., to identify the word with the concept which it designates. This leads quickly into those difficulties which can best be characterized by a remark made by SAPIR, according to which there is a word in Nootka which must be translated: "I have been accustomed to eat twenty round objects (for example, apples) while engaged in (doing so and so)" (quoted from CARROLL, 1955, p. 40). It would hardly be possible to treat this meaning as a unit.

It is therefore better to attempt once again a formal definition. A common one is BLOOMFIELD's: "A word is a minimum free form." This means that what can stand on its own is a 'free form'. For example, 'child' is a free form. Although '-ish' is meaningful —it indicates 'relating to', 'befitting'— it cannot be used independently; it is a bound form: 'childish' is therefore a word, because it cannot be divided any more into parts *each* of which is both meaningful and independent. Although this definition has wide application it, too, runs into difficulties. For example, 'je' ('I' in French) would not be a word according to BLOOMFIELD, because it is not a free form. It is always used with a verb. If 'I' is to be used independently, 'moi' is employed.

Another quite serviceable definition is the formal one offered by LÜDTKE (1961), according to which a word is that smallest unit which is at once a complex of syllables and of morphemes. 'Tiger' is a word because the division into morphemes (one morpheme) co-incides with the division into syllables (two syllables).

The principles of classifications in morphology are also formal. Whatever has the same distributional value within an utterance is placed in the same class. Identity or difference of distributional value is established by tests of substitution and interchange.

The *sentence* forms the largest unit. The structural rules of a language
are effective within the sentence. The choice of the constituent of one
sentence influences at the most only indirectly the construction of the
following sentence. For example, a personal pronoun may refer to a
previously mentioned person. According to BLOOMFIELD, a sentence is
"a construction within an utterance which is no longer dependent upon
a larger construction" (1926). The sentence is the playing field in which
the game follows the rules of grammar.

We now approach the question, 'What is grammar?' with the help of
the following argument. A sentence is more than the sum of the meanings
of the individual words. Grammatical structures, in which the words are
placed in the sentence, signal structural meanings (FRIES, 1952, p. 56).
The sentence, 'The man gave the boy some money', tells us that the man
carried out the action, not the boy, and that only one man and one boy
took part in the action, that what happened was not only planned or just
happening but that the action had already been completed. The information is represented as a fact, and not as a question or demand.

FRIES recognizes, besides this structural meaning, a sociocultural meaning which
consists of the stimulus value of the sentence for the behavior of the hearer. The
above sentence varies in sociocultural meaning if it is part of a police-report or
functions as a stage instruction in a play.

From a different point of view the following aspects in the sentence may be
distinguished: conceptual content and *set* towards this content. Set is reflected in
the well-known 'moods', indicative, interrogative, imperative, and so forth; it can
be signaled through a particular word (e.g., 'or'), a structure or intonation, etc.
According to BRINKMANN the noun as subject in a progressive sentence ('Vorgangs-
satz') determines the place towards which attention is turned in anticipation.
Several directions might be taken from this position. The one chosen is determined
by the verb as predicate (1952, p. 14). Besides this type of sentence BRINKMANN
distinguishes action sentence ('Handlungssatz'), attitude sentence ('stellung-
nehmender Satz') and sentence of identity ('Identitätssatz').

The grammar to which the arguments of FRIES and BRINKMANN lead
is a theory of linguistic combinatorics. In its usual form it describes each
single sentence by identifying and labelling the linguistic units in the
sentence and the relationship between them. It is, in other words, a
taxonomy which provides criteria to determine and describe the linguistic
units (cf. N. F. JOHNSON, 1965).

The importance of such a grammar has always been recognized by
linguists. GLINZ, for example, writes:

"Language is ... mental organization within a community. It is based on the
fact that mental concepts and attitudes to experience are defined by being linked
with characteristic sound patterns. But this mental organization, however pervasive
its effect, is in general not consciously experienced by the language user. Grammar,
since its beginnings in ancient Greek times, sets itself a threefold task. It makes the
user conscious of this common mental organization; it elaborates its structural laws

and fundamental units, and it elucidates its overall organization down to the *minutiae* of each determining quantum, if one may use this analogy from physics" (GLINZ, 1965, p. 47). WEISGERBER expresses these ideas in a similar vein: "The task of grammar as one of the most ancient studies of humanity borders almost on the impossible: it attempts to create an awareness of a mental condition of human existence. Not only is the range of this condition beyond our grasp but its inner workings are also impenetrable" (1962a, I, p. 403).

Clearly, these conceptualizations, which use the word 'mental' four times in eight lines, hardly offer an approach which is appropriate for the psychology of language. Psycholinguistics must begin by formulating the relevant problem and then see whether a congenial grammar can be found.

The psycholinguist asks the following question: what knowledge and skill must a human being possess so as to produce sentences which are felt by a *native speaker* to be grammatical and acceptable? It is certain that this knowledge cannot consist of a stored description of all possible sentences. If it were, the production would admittedly be a 'simple' process of selection, but the store would be overloaded and several decades would be needed to fill it, even if it were assumed that each sentence, heard only once, would be stored. Therefore it is not language items in the form of ready-made sentences which are learned and stored, but rules for the formation of grammatical sentences. It is only in this way that a speaker is capable of producing new sentences which he has never heard before[1].

The psycholinguist, interested in discovering how the processes which lead to the production of sentences work and how they are acquired, expects from the linguist, therefore, not so much a grammar which consists of a static description of grammatical sentences, but a grammar which formulates a system of rules according to which the formation of grammatical sentences can be described.

Such a grammar, in a form which is useful for psycholinguistics, is CHOMSKY'S *generative grammar* which leans much more towards the natural sciences in its orientation than towards the humanities.

CHOMSKY (e.g., 1961, 1965) sets out from two essential distinctions. The first is that between 'competence' and 'performance'. The linguistic theory is based on the assumption of an ideal speaker or listener who is not hindered by any limitations or deficiencies (e.g., of a psychological nature) in his perfect functioning as a language user. What this ideal speaker or hearer knows about his language, i.e., what he must know in order to produce well-formed sentences is what CHOMSKY calls 'competence'. In contrast to it 'performance' is the term used for those

---

[1] BROWN has described the fact that there are responses in human behavior which are novel and yet fitting as one of the most important aspects which psychology can learn from linguistics (1958a).

utterances of the real speaker or listener with his weaknesses and limitations when he actually speaks (or listens) in a concrete situation.

CHOMSKY himself points out that this dichotomy is related to the Saussurian distinction between *langue* and *parole*.

A generative grammar describes the regularities of the ideal processes of production which constitute competence. The study of performance is perhaps less the task of linguistics than of psycholinguistics, but according to CHOMSKY an understanding of competence must be the basis for this study.

A second distinction which is presupposed by CHOMSKY is that between data and facts. The linguist's data consist of observations on forms and uses of utterances. The facts of linguistic structure which he hopes to discover go beyond these observations; *in toto* they constitute the grammar. "A grammar of a particular language is, in effect, an hypothesis about the principles of sentence formation in this language. It represents a factual claim concerning the rules that underlie the data that have been collected. We judge the truth or falsity of this hypothesis by considering how well the grammar succeeds in organizing the data, how satisfying an explanation it provides for a wealth of empirical observations, how far-reaching are its generalizations, how successfully it accommodates new data" (p. 219).

It follows that a grammar is what is called a theory in the sciences; it is *the theory of a language*.

The fundamental principle on which a generative grammar is based is the following:

A sentence S is divided into its *immediate constituents* (IC). As an illustration let us take the sentence, 'The dog bites the child'. This sentence is divided into a noun phrase NP ('the dog') and a verb phrase VP ('bites the child'). The units on this level can be divided again into their constituents or replaced by units on the next lower level: the noun phrase can be divided into 'the' (D = determiner, e.g., article, etc.) and 'dog' (N = noun); the verb phrase is divided into 'bites' (V = verb) and 'the child' (NP = noun phrase). This second noun phrase is again analyzed into D + N or 'the' + 'child'. In the terminal string of the analysis each constituent represents only one class of morphemes, in which are enumerated whatever items can be the constituent concerned without modifying the grammatical structure:

    D → the, a, an, our ...

    N → fire, chain, car, child, wool, dog ...

    V → plays, bites, likes, dislikes, sees ...

The phrase-structure grammar which has been described here consists of a sequence of substitution or rewrite rules:

$$S \rightarrow NP + VP$$
$$NP \rightarrow D + N$$
$$VP \rightarrow V + NP$$
$$\cdots\cdots\cdots$$
$$D \rightarrow \text{the, a, our } \ldots$$
$$\cdots\cdots\cdots$$

Such a phrase-structure grammar, if it wants to do justice to the reality of language, must, however, be so complex that it becomes improbable as the exclusive model of the *psychological* events in the speaker. CHOMSKY, therefore, introduces the following modification: he distinguishes the phrase-structure component from a transformational component. Transformation rules are applied to what constitutes the output of the phrase-structure component. This output of an application of phrase-structure rules is the so-called 'kernel string'. By applying a minimum of transformation rules the kernel string becomes a 'kernel sentence', i.e., a simple declarative active sentence. More complex sentences result from the application of further optional transformation rules to kernel strings produced by phrase-structure rules. Such a transformation would be, for example, the passive transformation; e.g., 'I hit him' is transformed into 'He is hit by me'. The *negative* would be another transformation.

In this way the generative grammar becomes a very economical system (and thereby a psychologically more probable model). Once the negative transformation has been learned it is possible to change the sense of *every* sentence. It is not necessary to learn separately the positive and negative form of each sentence, as the model of descriptive grammar would demand. One does not even always have to learn one positive and one negative phrase-structure sequence for each kind of sentence, as a pure phrase-structure grammar would require.

BROWN has pointed out that there is an analogy to the above mentioned transformation of a sentence in the so-called conditioned reaction investigated by LASHLEY. A rat can learn to select from the two signals ⬛△⬛ ⬛▽⬛ the triangle which stands on its base. It can also be trained to accept the reversal of this meaning if the triangles appear against a striped background ⬛△⬛ ⬛▽⬛. The stripes transform the total meaning and therefore function in an analogous manner to the above mentioned negative.

A key concept in transformational grammar is that of grammaticality: the sentences to be produced are those and only those which in the estimation of a native speaker are grammatical. CHOMSKY has demonstrated how grammaticality is to be understood by an example which has become famous. If we compare the following two sentences:

(a) Colorless green ideas sleep furiously
(b) Furiously sleep ideas green colorless

it will quickly be seen that sentence (a) has a higher degree of grammaticality than (b). But this example also serves to show that grammaticality must not be equated with making sense. Sentences (a) and (b) are both nonsense. The understanding of grammatical relations does not depend upon a prior independent understanding of the constituents of the sentence. Grammar is—to a large extent at least—independent of meaning.

Admittedly, the line of demarcation between semantics, as the study of conceptual meaning, and grammar is hard to draw. BÜHLER has pointed out that in German compound nouns it is meaning which determines how the vaguely indicated syntactical relationship between the parts of the compound is to be understood. As an illustration he points out the change in syntactical function of the morpheme 'back' (German for 'bake') in such compounds as 'Back-ofen' (an oven for baking), 'Back-stein' (brick: a stone which has been fired or baked), 'Back-huhn' (a roasting chicken: a chicken which can be roasted), 'Back-pulver' (baking powder: powder with which one can bake). Thirty years later PUTNAM wrote: "The reason that we would add a category to our grammar is mainly that it enables us to note a larger number of regularities. If these regularities concern only a very restricted class of sentences, we prefer not to call them grammatical regularities; but if they apply to a large number of sentences or to the use of important classes of morphemes, e.g. pronouns or articles, it is traditionally more acceptable to call them grammar rules. From this point of view it is more a matter of usefulness and convenience and certainly not a genuinely theoretical question where to draw the dividing line between grammar and semantics" (PUTNAM, 1965, p. 1120).

"A generative grammar is a system of explicit rules that assign to each sequence of phones, ... a structural description that contains all information about how this sequence of phones is represented on each of the several linguistic levels — in particular, information as to whether this sequence of phones is a properly formed or *grammatical* sentence and if not, in what respect it deviates from well-formedness" (CHOMSKY, 1961, p. 220).

"Anyone who writes a grammar of a natural language, classifies therefore certain sentences as non-deviant and others, tacitly, as deviant" (PUTNAM, 1965, p. 1111). These remarks show that it is not possible in linguistic theory to work without an ideal as a standard. Generative grammar is the program which forms a standard for a speaker if he wants to produce sentences which are experienced by members of the language community as grammatical. A generative grammar is therefore different from a functional model of language which describes what the language user actually does. The integration of these linguistic and psychological considerations forms one of the most interesting topics of modern psycholinguistics which will be taken up again in detail in chapter 13.

Chapter 4

Language and Communication

The concept of information — Sender, channel of communication, receiver — 'Bit' as unit of information — Continuous
variation and discrete events — Capacity of communication
— Classifying processes in speech perception — LIBERMAN'S
motor theory of speech perception — Disturbance of speech
perception through masking noise — Competition of speech
events — The concept of channel capacity.

In chapters 2 and 3 we considered three characteristic features of
modern psycholinguistics: (a) the importance of the sign concept, (b) the
necessity to transcend overt behavior, and (c) the rise of structural modes
of operation in linguistics. These three characteristics converge towards
a concept which, since 1948, has rapidly spread more and more widely,
namely, the concept of *information*.

In order to see the place of this concept in psycholinguistics in the
right perspective, let us briefly remind ourselves of the argument which
was presented in the Introduction. We noted an area of indeterminacy
between the spontaneity of the organism and its vital space. The imbalance between the two poles 'self' and 'world' appeared to us as the
generator which keeps the business of life going. As human life is characterized by the existential fact that *world*, to a large extent, is represented
by other persons, this imbalance between them generates language. There
is first of all an imbalance of intent, and secondly an imbalance of information. A knows more than B; A can transmit to B what B lacks.

The concept of information has the function of describing exactly
what it is that must be transmitted so as to remove uncertainty. "The
idea of transmission of information is based upon the polarity between
transmitter and receiver" (SCHMETTERER, 1960, p. 156).

An act of communication, e.g., a telegram, a letter or a speech, *is*
information or *contains* information. It is the 'or' in the preceding sentence, as WEIZSÄCKER (1959) has shown, that is a particularly good starting
point for an introduction to a discussion of the concept of information.
The following remarks present the main lines of WEIZSÄCKER'S argument.

4   Hörmann, Psycholinguistics

Is the telegram information or does it *contain* information ? Do we mean by information the printer's ink on the telegram form, i.e., something objectively given, or is it the content of consciousness which develops as the telegram is being read, i.e., something subjectively experienced ? It is in fact neither. The printer's ink did not come through the cable. What the sender wrote is not the same stuff the receiver of the message holds in his hand. And it may also be assumed that the content of the mind of the sender is different from that of the receiver. Neither printer's ink nor mental content have been transmitted. "Information is not a particular act of consciousness, but something that the act of consciousness 'knows', something that is held in common by the two persons, however different their minds may be. We are getting accustomed to looking upon information as a third thing, different from mind and matter. This discovery is an old truth in a new guise. It is the Platonic *eidos*, the Aristotelian form, dressed up in such a way that even man in the twentieth century can get a glimmer of it" (pp. 44f.).

The notion of information belongs, therefore, to the area of abstraction in which the concepts of language or of grammar are located — an area, as we shall see in chapter 11, which SKINNER regards as enemy territory.

Information is structure. Carrier of this structure may be printer's ink, sound waves or electric impulses. The telegram, sent by cable, and the telegram, read over the telephone by the operator, contain the same information.

With this proposition the concept of information is already narrowed down. Supposing I live in Toronto and receive a long-distance call from New York and hear that it is cold there, then information in the sense in which it interests us here is contained in this message. But what I hear contains yet another kind of information. The voice tells me something about the speaker: it is the voice of a woman who must have lived in New York for a long time; she also sounds rather bored. The sound spectrum, the speed of utterance, and characteristic pauses, etc. may lead me to the conviction that the speaker is my aunt Mathilda.

It is interesting to note what we did when we ignored the content of the message ('It is cold') and used the message to find out about the speaker. We have treated the message as 'symptom' in BÜHLER'S sense, or we have looked at what MEYER-EPPLER has called the *ecto-semantic sphere* and what MOLES has described as the *information esthétique*.

In the following remarks information is to be understood purely as semantic information (MOLES, 1963). It is that which is held in common by two persons if one person tells the other something that the other person did not know before. In this sense a communicative act contains information if and only if, by means of this act, uncertainty is removed or reduced in the receiver. Thus if I come into the house shivering and I am told, 'It is cold outside', I have received no information, because I, as the receiver of this message, was not in a state of uncertainty with regard to its content.

It should be added that the uncertainty of the receiver must be matched by the unambiguity of the message. WEIZSÄCKER has elucidated this point with the following illustration: "The sentence of HERACLITUS 'The father of all things is war' can be a profound truth, only because it contains no information, and it can contain no information because the words 'father' and 'war' in it are not unambiguous. If they referred to what they normally mean, the statement would indeed be nonsense. It cannot even be said that they have simply been redefined, so that they could be considered as speculative concepts in the philosophy of HERACLITUS. It should rather be assumed that it is in the nature of genuine speculative concepts not to be unambiguous" (p. 48).

Information, then, in the sense in which the term is used here presupposes a state of uncertainty in the hearer and unambiguity of the message. If we toss a coin, it is uncertain whether it will come down 'heads' or 'tails'. If someone looks and then says 'heads', the hearer receives information, for the unambiguous message has removed uncertainty. The amount of information, the information content of the message, equals the amount of uncertainty that has been reduced through the transmission of information.

The same facts will now be considered from a slightly different point of view. SHANNON, the initiator of information theory, characteristically served as a mathematician to the Bell Company, the large telephone and telegraph concern. His basic problem was to produce, at the output end of an information-transmission system, a message which at the input end had been selected for transmission. (It will shortly be seen that the formulation 'selected for transmission' is of some importance.) The meaning of the transmitted message is of no concern to the communications engineer — another statement which is important for our discussion. The information content of a message must not be confused with the meaning of this message. Once a tossed coin has come down it has a definite content of information, i.e., one bit, regardless of whether the result of the toss might mean a man's death or paying for a round of drinks.

SHANNON attempted to find an exact quantitative term for what is transmitted in a given communications system so as to be able to make an exact statement about the efficiency of the system. The communications engineer wishes to understand the utility of a transmission system. The model of such a communications system may be represented as follows:

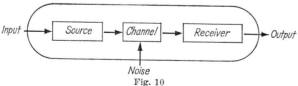

Fig. 10

This is basically the same diagram which has been made use of elsewhere in this book. What happens in the Shannon model between the microphone of the transmitter and the loudspeaker of the receiver corresponds to the events occurring between speaker and hearer. In precise terms, therefore, what we are concerned with is not so much a theory of information as a theory of information *transmission*.

The basic model assumes that at the input end *one* message, out of several possible messages, is selected for transmission. If a coin is tossed two messages are possible: heads or tails. Before the message reaches the output end of the channel, the receiver is in a state of uncertainty as to which of the two messages will reach him.

This has very important consequences: the receiver must know in advance which messages are possible. In other words, the receiver must have at his disposal the same repertoire of possible messages as the transmitter who selects from it the message to be sent.

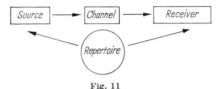

Fig. 11

It may happen, however, that transmitter and receiver do not draw on identical repertoires, because the events which have led to the development of the repertoires are different in the biographies of sender and receiver. This situation can be represented by the diagram in Fig. 12.

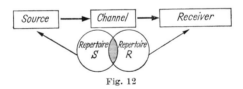

Fig. 12

In this case a communication is only possible to the extent to which the two repertoires overlap ◖ (based on MOLES, 1963).

Let us briefly digress once more to relate this to the organon model of BÜHLER (see pp. 18ff.). At first sight one would tend to assume that information is what is called the representational function in this model. But are 'symbols' transmitted in a communication system? What is transmitted are 'signals', i. e., instructions for action by the receiver, selection orders or commands according to which a receiver is to choose from his repertoire.

Yet, the conclusion that information theory is concerned with the signal function of the linguistic sign would not be quite accurate. The behavior of the receiver which is guided by *signals* consists in the selection of *symbols*. In other words the sharp division that BÜHLER makes between signal and symbol function (or between expression and representation) cannot be maintained here.

This fact has implications for psycholinguistics as well as for information theory. Information is certainly not identical with language. It presupposes language. Or to put it more precisely in the terms in which WEIZSÄCKER has expressed it: "Anyone who talks about language must not forget that language can be used for information, and anyone who talks about information must never forget that language as information is only possible against the background of knowledge that language cannot be transformed into unambiguous information" (1959, pp. 52f.).

We return once more to our basic model. The information about the face of the coin, i.e., which of the two possibilities has occurred, reduces to nil the uncertainty in the receiver. If two coins are tossed in succession four messages are possible: both heads; first heads, then tails; first tails, then heads; both tails. The uncertainty is greater than in the first example, so that the message when received, because it removes a higher degree of uncertainty, possesses a higher information value.

If the information value equals the uncertainty which is removed by the message, we go on to ask what determines the amount of uncertainty. The answer is: it is determined by the number of possible events. When a coin is tossed two events are possible; when a die is cast, there are six. The message concerning a coin contains less information than a message concerning a die.

Although these reflections may seem simple, they have far-reaching consequences. From them we can infer that, in the analysis of linguistic events, we must take into account not only what happens at the stimulus and response end, but also what does *not* happen but might have happened. The amount of information depends on the relationship between the actual event and all other possible events. The question therefore arises whether perhaps the number of possible events might be used as a measuring unit of information. Accordingly, tossing a coin where two events are possible would yield two units of information. Two coins would produce four units. If three coins are tossed there are eight units. The number of units rises steeply. It would be more convenient to operate with a unit of measurement which increases at a uniform rate; in this case this is the logarithm.

The measuring unit for information is called 'bit', an abbreviation for binary digit. It is the power to which two must be raised in order to obtain the number of possibilities. The information on the fall of the tossed coin removes the uncertainty with regard to which of two possible events has occurred. The message contains one bit of information; for $2^1 = 2$.

Another example may further illustrate the use of bit as an information measure. There is a well-known party-game in which the players agree upon an object which 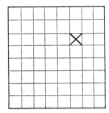 has to be discovered by a player who has, meanwhile, been sent out of the room. On his return this player is only allowed to ask questions in such a way that they can be answered by yes or no. To illustrate this, let us assume that, instead of a concrete object one of the 64 squares of a chessboard has been selected. The questioner is supposed to find out which square has been chosen, and the object of the game is to do so in the most economical way, in other words, with the smallest number of questions[1].

How many questions are needed to reduce the questioner's uncertainty to nil? The answer is precisely six.

1. Is it a square in the upper half? (Yes)

2. Is it a square in the left half of the remainder? (No)

3. Is it a square in the lower half of the sixteen remaining? (Yes)

4. Is it a square in the right half of the eight remaining? (No)

5. Is it one of the two right ones of the four remaining? (Yes)

6. Is it the lower one of these two? (No)

Six yes-or-no decisions are needed to specify 64 equally probable possibilities. Six bits of information are required to reduce the uncertainty contained in this system to nil, for $64 = 2^6$.

In general terms: if the number of equally probable possibilities of a system is called m and the amount of required information H bits, then $m = 2^H$. Or expressed in another way, the number of bits equals the logarithm of the number of possibilities to the base of 2.

Logarithmus dualis (logarithm to the base of two) means that in contrast to the usual logarithms it is not the figure 10 but 2 which is used as a base. This is an arbitrary decision; it is also possible to work in information theory with a decimal system. But the binary system has a number of advantages: apart from the one already mentioned that, with the doubling of the possibilities, uncertainty increases by one bit, one should mention above all the advantage in terms of communication engineering. The binary system which knows only yes or no or only the figures 0 and 1, is most convenient for communication engineering: if the current is *on*, this can represent 1, and if it is *off*, 0. The human nervous system seems to operate in a similar way: firing or no firing.

So far we have talked about systems in which each possibility is equally probable. In the tossing of an unbent coin heads or tails have equal probability p, viz, 1 divided by the number of possibilities m: in this case $\frac{1}{2} = 0.5$. In the chess-board example each square had equal probability of having been selected, viz, $\frac{1}{64}$. To express it in more general

---

[1] It should be remembered that what interested SHANNON was precisely a measure of the economic capacity of a communication system.

terms, the probability p of the appearance of a particular possibility is 1, divided by the number of possibilities m, or

$$p = \frac{1}{m} .$$

Therefore

$$m = \frac{1}{p} .$$

The content of information H had earlier been defined as $H = \log_2 m$, which can be rewritten as

$$H = \log_2 \frac{1}{p} .$$

This is now to be generalized to such cases where the various possibilities have different probabilities of appearance.

Since previously all possibilities were regarded as equally probable, we were able to summarize them in a single measure H. If now all possibilities are no longer equally probable, each requires its own measure of information: h_i is the information which results from the appearance of the possibility i. This is represented by $h_i = \log_2 \frac{1}{p_i}$.

One example: a bent coin is tossed, which in 90 percent of tosses shows heads, and in 10 percent tails. The probability that it is heads is therefore $p_{Hd} = 0.9$; the probability that tails is uppermost is $p_T = 0.1$. Accordingly, the information which is contained in the message 'heads' would be

$$h_{Hd} = \log_2 \frac{1}{0.9} = \log_2 1.11 = 0.15 \text{ bits.}$$

The information that is contained in 'tails' is

$$h_T = \log_2 \frac{1}{0.1} = \log_2 10 = 3.22 \text{ bits.}$$

These two messages, therefore, do not contain an equal amount of information. This is quite easy to understand: in the bent coin we expect *a priori* 'heads' in 90 percent of the throws, the message that it is 'heads' is therefore not surprising; it removes little uncertainty. However, if it is 'tails' we are very surprised.

We next inquire after the average information in a long series of tosses with the bent coin. Each message 'heads' will contribute 0.15 bits to this average, whereas each message 'tails' will contribute 3.22 bits. Now 'heads' is likely to appear very much more frequently than 'tails', because the probability of 'heads' is .9, the probability of 'tails' only .1. This fact must be taken into account in working out the average: 'heads' must contribute nine times as much as 'tails'.

$$(0.90 \times 0.15) + (0.10 \times 3.22) = 0.47 \text{ bits}$$

This average value is again designated as H.

If this average value of 0.47 is compared with the information value of straight coins (1.0 bit) it will be seen that the tosses with a bent coin on the average yield less information than those with a straight coin. The results of tosses of a bent coin are less uncertain.

At this point we can find an interesting link between information theory and thermodynamics, especially with regard to the concept of 'entropy'. A system has maximal entropy when all its possible states are equally probable. In this situation uncertainty is at its maximum. In a system with less than maximal entropy some states are more probable than others and therefore their occurrence has lower information value.

What was calculated as average value here was based on the formula:

$$H = p_1 h_1 + p_2 h_2 + \ldots + p_x h_x$$

H is therefore the sum of all products: p multiplied by h;

$$H = \overset{i}{\Sigma} \, p_i h_i,$$

where i designates each possibility.

Earlier h was equated with $\log_2 \frac{1}{p}$. In the above summation formula $\log_2 \frac{1}{p}$ can take the place of h. This yields the following:

$$H = \overset{i}{\Sigma} \, p_i \log_2 \frac{1}{p_i} \, .$$

In order to avoid fractions one can write:

$$H = - \overset{i}{\Sigma} \, p_i \log_2 p_i.$$

This is the well-known Shannon-Wiener measure of information.

The above presentation of the mathematical side of information theory (which leans heavily on the excellent introduction by ATTNEAVE, 1959) is sufficient for our purpose.

As a first step from pure information theory towards its application to psycholinguistics let us now resume the arguments first developed in chapter 3 where it was shown that our mechanism of perception classifies acoustic sounds as phonemes.

Information theory is applicable to discrete events. The die must fall on one of its six sides; in a wire the current is either on or off; there are no gradual transitions. Language, looked at from a linguistic or psycholinguistic angle, consists of such discrete events. A sound either is or is not in a certain class of phonemes. A graphic symbol is to be pronounced as a voiced or unvoiced sound. Viewed in this way the operations of information theory may be applied to language.

However, these facts look quite different from the point of view of the acoustician. If linguistic utterances are recorded, for instance, by means of an oscillograph or a spectrograph, no clear differentiations can be made between voiced and unvoiced or between 'a' and 'non-a'. The acoustician describes the speech sound through a series of measurements, and these measurements are not discrete choices of an 'either-or' character, but are variations on a continuous scale.

This difference between acoustic and linguistic descriptions of speech events had already become clear through the earlier discussion of the concept of the *phoneme*. For the acoustician there are indefinite numbers of intermediate stages and transitions between /bid/ and /bed/; for the linguist and psycholinguist there is only a single clear-cut change.

The input in form of sound waves, the physical event, no doubt has the character of a continuous variable. Even if, as in HOCKETT'S model below, we confine ourselves to the dimension voiced/unvoiced this variable may appear in the spectrogram of the acoustician as varieties of values. On the other hand all possible values are not likely to occur with equal frequency, but the frequency distribution will probably look as follows:

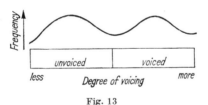

Fig. 13

In the perceptual system of the receiver this input is 'quantized', i.e., the continuous input is analyzed into discrete events.

HOCKETT (1961) attempts to make this explicit by means of a model: imagine two photo-electric cells side by side. The degree of voicing of the acoustic event is to be represented by a moving light dot. If the degree of voicing is high —in acoustics such gradations do indeed occur— the light dot moves to the right; if it is low it moves to the left. The frequency curve of the accompanying model has two peaks, because the light beam occurs more frequently at these sections of the horizontal axis than at others. If the light beam is *anywhere* within the area of one cell, it will trigger off a signal 'voiced'. If it is anywhere in the area of the other cell it will signal 'unvoiced'. Thus the continuous variable of the acoustician is transformed into the discrete events of the linguist because he must assume the dichotomy.

The same process occurs in reverse order when we speak: the articulation process transforms the discrete sequence of inner events into the continuous variables of the acoustic phenomenon[1].

HOCKETT summarizes these arguments as follows: The seemingly incompatible observations of the acoustician and the linguist can be explained by the fact that the two disciplines study the process at different points: the acoustician studies it in the channel of information-transmission while the linguist or psycholinguist studies it in the speaker or hearer.

This process of transformation was described in such detail because psycholinguistics operates both with acoustic concepts, which describe continuous variables, as well as with linguistic ones, which describe discrete events. The processes of encoding and decoding are transformations from one to the other. The information the speaker transmits to the hearer is the command to adopt a certain state of mind or to switch his system into a particular state, e.g., either [i] or [e].

The next question is: how *complicated* can the command or message which is transmitted through the communication channel linking speaker and hearer be per time unit? The complexity of the message to be transmitted per unit of time depends upon the distinctions which the mechanism of perception is capable of handling in processing the sound signals which carry the message. That is to say the answer to the above question is a task for psychophysics.

This can be made clear by an analogy from the field of vision. How much information can be transmitted through flag signals? Different flags could, among other distinctions, be varied according to size. This means that as many distinctions can be made as the visual apparatus can handle. The observer would not be able to distinguish two flags, one of which measured 1030 cm^2 while the other measured 1029 cm^2; hence difference in size cannot be used to transmit different messages with these two flags. Color and shape, besides size, could have been used as distinguishing features.

It is accepted that the sound event can be analyzed according to frequency, amplitude, phase and duration. Frequency is measured in cycles per second, abbreviated cps, i.e., the number of vibrations per second. The concert pitch has a frequency of 440 cps. Psychologically, the pitch of a heard sound corresponds to the physical 'frequency' variable.

Corresponding to amplitude is the loudness of a sound. It is generally measured as intensity or sound pressure. It is the relation of P_x, the pressure to be measured,

---

[1] In technology the principle of the digital-to-analogue converter offers a parallel.

to a standard intensity P_0. This standard pressure P_0 is conventionally fixed at 0.0002 dyne per one square centimeter. The unit of measurement, customarily employed in acoustics, db or decibel, is defined as 20 log P_x/P_0, i.e., the logarithm, multiplied by 20, of the relation between the pressure in question P_x and the standard pressure P_0. The low whisper of a person 5 feet away has approx. 20 db, the noise of a cinema audience about 45 db, the noise in a department store approx. 60 db, while a train passing through a subway station registers approx. 100 db.

The discriminatory capacity of the ear for frequency and amplitude (ignoring for the moment the other two dimensions) is not equally good over the whole range of these dimensions, as can be represented by the following diagram based on the work of STEVENS and DAVIS.

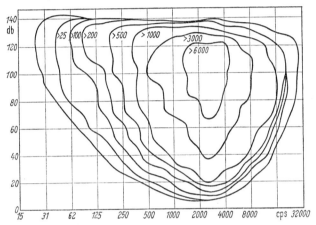

Fig. 11. The curves link points of equal discriminatory sensitivity. The peak of the 'mountain range' lies between 80 and 120 db and between 1,500 and 3,000 cps. Within these ranges the ear is capable of the most delicate discriminations, and therefore these are the most frequent (based on ROSENBLITH, from MOLES and VALLANCIEN, 1963, p. 69)

Frequency is indicated in cps on the x-axis, amplitude on the y-axis in decibles. The curves link points of equal discriminatory power. It should be noted that the most sensitive area for the auditory organ lies between 1,500 and 3,000 cps and between 80 and 120 db. Therefore within this range the hearer can receive a maximum of information.

We will now attempt to answer the question asked previously: How complex a message can be sent per time unit over the communication channel and can be received by the hearer? The human ear can distinguish intensities between 0 and 125 db[1] and frequencies between 10 cps and 20,000 cps.

But how sensitive is the power of discrimination along these two dimensions? How close together may two stimuli be so that the human

---

[1] At about 125 db is the upper limit beyond which pain and possible lesions may occur.

ear still recognizes them as two, i.e., as differing from each other ? Can we distinguish a sound of 1,000 from one of 1,001 cps ? According to ROSEN-BLITH (1963), whose presentation we follow here, the threshold of discrimination for intensity amounts to approx. 0.50 db, for frequencies it amounts to approx. 20 cps. Thus a sound of an intensity of 20 db is perceived as louder than one of 19.5 db; a sound of 1,020 cps is perceived as higher than one of 1,000 cps. The dimension of intensity which extends from 0 to 125 db yields, therefore, 250 possible distinctions, the dimension of pitch approx. 1,000. Each of these 1,000 sounds varying in pitch could again be perceived in 250 degrees of intensity, so that our hearing should be able to distinguish approx. 250,000 different sounds—"chiffre fantastique comme nous le verrons" (ROSENBLITH, p. 70).

Human speech uses approx. 50 different sounds, i.e., the phonemes of each language. What explains this discrepancy, this inadequate use of the channel of communication ?

In order to answer this question we must once more examine the approach to the problem we have just outlined. It is true that the hearing —as psychophysical studies of thresholds have shown—can distinguish closely neighboring stimuli when they are presented closely together. But speech sounds are not normally offered so as to be distinguished from each other, but in such a way that they must be identified independently. The question is not: 'Are these sounds alike or different ?' but 'Which sound is this ?' Investigations by POLLACK (1952, 1953, 1954) illuminate particularly well this aspect of the capacity of hearing. Subjects were given pure tones with the instruction to identify them. It was found that subjects can admittedly distinguish or identify a 'high', 'medium' and a 'low' tone; they can even operate with a five-point scale (very high, high, medium, low, very low), but beyond more than five different degrees they had difficulties.

The object of this investigation is similar to what is often referred to as *perfect pitch*, but ROSENBLITH has rightly pointed out that perfect pitch is customarily tested with a piano which does not produce pure sounds. Musicians do not do better than others in the Pollack experiments, and even a preliminary practice phase has little effect on performance.

Along another dimension, e.g., intensity, the results are again similars. Subjects can distinguish absolutely between five and seven different intensities. POLLACK's results approach what MILLER (1956) has called "the magical number 7 ± 2" on the basis of his investigations on immediate recall. We classify items of the same kind into categories which range between five and nine. The stimuli may be as differentiated as we like. We put them into one of these categories and thus perceive them in a classified form. "Perception involves an act of categorization ... we stimulate an organism with a suitable input, and the organism reacts by sorting the input into a class of things or events" (BRUNER, 1957b, p. 123).

It is clear, then, that in the study of the capacity of speech perception we meet once more the same process of classification that we came across before.

In POLLACK'S investigations which have so far been mentioned subjects were asked to identify sounds for single dimensions, either frequency or intensity. If in each of these dimensions seven absolute judgments are possible (in contrast to the relative distinctions of 'more' or 'less' in the above mentioned threshold studies), in the combination of two dimensions we reach a figure of approximately 50 absolutely distinguishable sounds, whereas in the case of distinguishing thresholds a figure of 250,000 was calculated. However, POLLACK has shown experimentally that even this calculation does not do justice to reality. If sounds are to be identified for pitch and loudness simultaneously (e.g., 'This sound was medium-high and very loud') the subject is not capable of identifying 50 but only about 8 or 9. If we take more than two dimensions, it is true the number of identifiable sounds increases, but the rate of increase steadily declines.

In other words, one dimension can carry about seven distinctions or—to speak in terms of information theory—2 or 3 bits. If a stimulus is assessed simultaneously for six dimensions, each of the six dimensions has only 1.2 bits of information content, and altogether they have about 7 bits.

"What happens in speech perception is an identification which does not take place on the basis of a single dimension, it is an identification of several simultaneous aspects on the basis of several distinctive features" (ROSENBLITH, 1963, p. 73).

This leads us back once more to JAKOBSON'S theory, discussed in chapter 3, according to which a phoneme is a bundle of distinctive sound features, each of which is binary. According to ROSENBLITH'S and JAKOBSON'S views linguistic perception is roughly as follows: Each input signal is received with the binary question: vowel or non-vowel? voiced or unvoiced? etc. Choices are made upon as many alternatives as are needed for the recognition of the particular signal.

Speech perception, therefore, functions in a manner which exploits only a fraction of the possibilities offered by the communication channel[1].

One might feel tempted to ask a purely teleological question: what is achieved by this 'inadequate' exploitation of the channel capacity? The answer is: *certainty*, i.e., certainty of the effectiveness of communication. Speaking is facilitated because it is not necessary to 'hit' a definite

---

[1] It has already been mentioned that, in addition, a sound event may yield 'ecto-semantic' information, e.g., information about the age of the speaker or whether he has a cold. This, however, in no way affects the above arguments.

sound but only a class of sounds or a 'phoneme'. Likewise, comprehension is eased. The listener does not have to analyze a sound in minute detail, but only to the point that he can classify it without danger of confusion. Often a minor part of the qualities of a sound sequence is enough to classify this event and to recognize it, for example, as a case of /i/.

This classifying process must proceed with extraordinary rapidity. Approximately ten phonemes are uttered per second (FLANAGAN, 1965), i.e., on the phonemic level alone ten decisions have to be made every second. Can this mechanism which leads so rapidly to absolute judgments be further elucidated? Beginnings of such an explanation are to be found in the investigations by LIBERMAN and his associates, to be described in the following paragraphs.

It is possible with the help of a pattern playback (see chapter 3 above) to produce an acoustic event which is perceived by the listener as a definite phoneme, i.e., distinguished from other events. If this same acoustic event, the identical piece of magnetic tape, is cut out from the linguistic context and offered as part of a non-linguistic noise sequence, the listener can no longer distinguish it without difficulty from other events in this sequence. A given acoustic event or signal is perceived by the listener correctly as a particular phoneme only if the input mechanism is tuned for language. This tuning-in of the apparatus of perception is therefore needed from the start so as to turn an acoustic event into a speech event.

Further information on the way this process operates is provided by the investigations of LIBERMAN et al. (1963). Fourteen synthetic speech patterns were selected in such a way that small stepwise variations led from /b/ via /d/ to /g/. In the first part of the experiment these stimuli were presented to the subjects singly and in random order; subjects were asked to identify them as /b/ or /d/ or /g/. In this experiment again subjects were offered an acoustically almost continuous variation; but perception turned it into three sharply divided categories; within a category no gradual transitions were perceived. The alteration of the acoustic variable is perceived only at the boundary between two phonemes.

In the second part of the experiment the stimuli were presented paired, and the subjects were asked to state whether they noticed differences between the stimuli. This procedure showed that the power of discrimination is more acute in the vicinity of the phoneme boundaries than in the middle of a phoneme category.

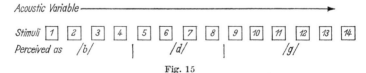

Fig. 15

The difference between stimuli 4 and 5 is noticed with greater frequency than the objectively equal difference between 2 and 3, or 5 and 6. Acoustically equal differences are perceived more easily near the boundaries of the phoneme than within the phoneme category, although the subject has a set for acoustic discrimination and not for linguistic distinction. This phenomenon was so marked that the author came to the conclusion that the hearer can only distinguish the sounds when he identifies them as different phonemes, or in other words, when he assigns them to different classes[1].

This experimental finding, it would seem, has important and far-reaching implications. First of all, it demonstrates that, even at this basic level, below the stage of meaning, perception of the world around us is dependent upon the language we have learned to speak. As HUMBOLDT said, it is only through language that world is recreated as mind.

This finding is, secondly, of interest from the point of view of *learning*. The phonemes are linguistic units which the hearer masters. Since there are no phonemes-in-general, but only phonemes of Arabic, English or German, etc., the phonemes, or more precisely, phonemic differentiations, are acquired. Hence there must also be an element of learning in the capacity to make differentiations at phoneme boundaries.

There are two possible explanations for this. It may be argued (a) that originally all acoustic stimuli of these speech events were equally as distinguishable as at a later stage are only the most clearly differentiated ones. Subjects have learned to neglect distinctions which are unimportant for communication: this is called *acquired similarity*.

Or, alternatively, (b) that acoustic stimuli were originally all equally difficult to distinguish. Man learns to discriminate more sharply where this is important for comprehension, namely at phoneme boundaries. This would be the case for *acquired distinctiveness*.

LIBERMAN is of the opinion that what is learned are the subtleties of discrimination at critical points; in other words, he argues for acquired distinctiveness.

It will be recalled that the mechanism of perception functions according to the principle of absolute judgments. The question now is: how is it that this mechanism can make clear discriminatory judgments at these points while elsewhere it can only make absolute judgments? According to LIBERMAN, this is made possible through a feedback mechanism from speech articulation to speech perception. The discriminatory power is acquired as a combination of heard sounds with the articulation necessary for the production of these sounds. Since in the hearer the incoming acoustic stimulus triggers off the tendency to produce this

---

[1] Incidentally, these results only apply to consonants, not to vowels.

sound himself and this tendency is perceived by the hearer as a preparatory set in the appropriate muscles, it is possible to make use of these proprioceptive stimuli as additional criteria of discrimination.

This argument has quite far-reaching consequences. It suggests that the process of perception is determined less by the physical nature of the linguistic stimulus, than, above all, by the articulatory processes which are needed to produce this linguistic stimulus and which the hearer imitates subvocally. Hitherto it was customary to symbolize the sequence of a speech event as in Fig. 16: the articulatory response R_A forms a stimulus S_P which has to be described in acoustic-physical terms and which in turn leads to the perceptive response R_{Per} in the hearer. A correction of this model as described in Fig. 17 is now indicated.

$$R_A \longrightarrow S_P \longrightarrow R_{Per}$$

Fig. 16   Fig. 17

The articulatory response R_A of the speaker forms a physical stimulus S_P which leads to a non-manifest articulatory response $R_{A'}$ in the listener. The listener, as it were, repeats in a sketchy way what the speaker must have done to produce the speech stimulus S_P. The articulatory innervations and movements, produced by the hearer ($R_{A'}$), are experienced by him proprioceptively as a definite stimulus pattern (S_{pro}). And it is only this stimulation, produced, so to speak, as an echo, which leads to perception R_{Per}.

This is the central proposition of LIBERMAN'S *motor theory of speech perception*[1] to which we had already drawn attention before (see p. 35). This theory stands so clearly in contrast to the usual and obvious view, according to which speech perception has more to do with the acoustic stimulus than with the necessary articulatory processes in the speaker, that a whole series of supporting experimental evidence is needed if this view is to carry conviction. The investigations will be briefly reported below with examples.

The first experiment shows that in certain cases a continuously varying perception corresponds to a discontinuous variation of the acoustic stimulus which in turn corresponds to a continuous variation of articulation; thus, in these cases audition parallels articulation. Fig. 18 shows the spectrograms of the consonant-vowel sequence [di/de/d...] and [gi/ge/...]. In the [d] series the direction and course of the transition of the second formant are different according to the variation in the subsequent

---

[1] On this point see also LANE (1965).

vowel, but all these transitions start out from identical frequency positions, i.e., 1,800 cps. Because of this acoustic invariance the same consonant is perceived before each vowel.

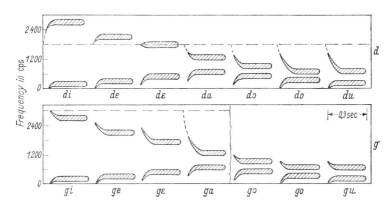

Fig. 18. Spectrograms of consonant-vowel sequences (based on LIBERMAN, from SAPORTA, 1961, p. 149)

It is quite different in the case of [g]. For the vowels [i] to [a] there is again an invariant point of departure leading to the transition round 3,000 cps. But the acoustic picture—and only the *acoustic* picture—completely changes for [ɔ], the vowel which is closest to [a]. Again one hears [g] before a subsequent vowel, and the speaker *produces* a [g] as before, but *acoustically* the [g] looks quite different. From the point of view of articulation and perception [gi/ge] to [gu] form a continuous series—only the properties of the acoustic stimulus mediating between articulation and perception display discontinuity at one point.

The result of an experiment by LANE (1962) can be regarded as a confirmation of the LIBERMAN theory. In this investigation it was shown that changes in the amplitude, duration or spectrum of a vowel appear larger to the speaker than to the listener. The speaker can perceive smaller differences than the hearer, although the latter receives the same acoustic stimulus. But the speaker has at his disposal, in addition, the feedback which results from the proprioceptive stimulation resulting from his own articulation.

In summary, it may be said that the LIBERMAN theory rests on three groups of findings: (a) acoustically *similar* stimuli, which were produced by *different* patterns of articulation, lead to *different* perceptions; (b) acoustically *different* stimuli, which were produced by *similar* patterns of articulation, lead to *similar* perceptions; (c) if both articulation and acoustic stimulation are continuously varied, changes in perception correlate most highly with those of articulation[1].

Let us now once more return to the starting point of this discussion. We questioned (p. 62) the nature of a mechanism which can make so many absolute judgments so rapidly and which can carry out so many classifications. The LIBERMAN motor theory of speech perception points out that speech sounds are perceived by being related to the speech movements necessary to produce these sounds. We can identify absolutely only a small number of sounds, but we can differentiate one or two hundred times as many. When a child learning to speak attempts to imitate a sound, his entire capacity for making differential judgments is at his disposal: for in this situation his task is to find out whether the heard sound produced by others and the sound produced by himself are alike or different. Even if [b] and [d] at first sound quite similar, the child, as he imitates, learns that [b] needs quite different muscular movements than [d]. These delicate differences derived from the feedback of muscle action serve at a later stage to differentiate even the less clear-cut distinctions between the acoustic signal for [b] and the acoustic signal for [d].

There is more of a one-to-one relationship between the articulation of a phoneme—or to put it more precisely—between the neural stimulus-configuration or the motor 'plan' for its production, on the one hand, and the perception of the phoneme on the other, than between the much more obviously relevant acoustic event and perception.

A further support for the LIBERMAN theory of perception is to be found in the phenomenon of delayed speech feedback. If the utterances of a speaker are fed back to him through headphones with a slight delay (of approx. 180 milliseconds) his articulation is markedly disturbed. The speech behavior which results can be described as artificial stammering[2].

The relationship between articulation and perception operates not only in the direction described by LIBERMAN, but also in the opposite way. Articulation not only influences perception, it, in turn, is also influenced by perception. This in itself is a convincing argument for the reality of such a relationship.

Researches with quite a different orientation, viz, deriving from learning theory, further suggest that hearing of a stimulus is followed immediately by a fractional imitative motor response. As we shall see in chapter 7, the psychology of association has —mainly for formal reasons— introduced the concept of *implicit response*: the perception of a speech stimulus always leads in the first instance to a 'subvocal mimicking' of the heard stimulus. What further responses follow, e.g., an expressed answer, is to be understood primarily in combination with this first implicit response.

---

[1] See in this connection the (otherwise very critical) article by LANE (1965).

[2] For a more detailed treatment see SCHUBENZ (1965).

However, the objections that have been raised against the LIBERMAN motor theory of speech perception should also be mentioned. JAKOBSON reports the experience that in certain Caucasian languages he could distinguish their numerous phonemes, without being able, in spite of all his efforts, to produce them himself. Parallel to that, he noted that he was able to read these languages but not to write them. Similar phenomena are of course generally observed in the learning of a foreign language: it is easier to understand than to speak and this has no doubt other causes besides the difference between an active and passive vocabulary. BAY regards the fact that the expressive aspect of language presents greater difficulties than the receptive one as an essential feature of language[1]. This is shown above all in the acquisition of speech in the child, where, for a time, the understanding of language is clearly in advance of its productive use. LENNEBERG (1962) describes a case in which learning to speak was impossible because of a pathological defect, and yet this did not affect the development of speech comprehension[2].

If we want to consider whether the learning processes through which articulation participates in speech perception, operate through a loss of unimportant distinctions or the emphasis of important ones (acquired similarity *versus* acquired distinctiveness), an observation of child psychology mentioned by LANGER, is important: "In a social environment, the vocalizing and articulating instinct of babyhood is fostered by response, and as the sounds become symbols their use becomes a dominant habit. Yet the passing of the *instinctive phase* is marked by the fact that a great many phonemes[3] which do not meet with response are completely lost.

Undoubtedly that is why children, who have not entirely lost the impulse to make random sounds which their mother tongue does not require, can so easily learn a foreign language and even master several at once ..." (1963, p. 122). Looked at in this perspective it appears likely that acquired similarity is more important than acquired distinctiveness, because the number of various sounds declines.

If this problem is to be viewed in somewhat more general terms, it is possible to cite a large number of Russian studies which show that there is a motor component which plays its part in processes of perception. Studies from SETCHENOV and PAVLOV onwards down to work by LEONTIEV and SMIRNOV[4] provide evidence, again and again and under the most varied circumstances, for the role of proprioceptive-motor processes in perception, cognition and retention of linguistic events.

---

[1] See BAY, 1964, p. 140, Discussion.

[2] The discussion of the LIBERMAN theory will be taken up once more in chapter 13.

[3] The justification to speak of 'phonemes' appears questionable at this pre-linguistic stage *(The Author)*.

[4] See, for example, SMIRNOV'S paper at the 16th International Psychological Congress 1960.

If we want to draw a general conclusion to the whole issue which has been discussed here under the heading of 'motor theory of speech perception', it is necessary to point out the fact that speech perception in comparison with the perception of all other stimuli occupies quite a special place. Only in the case of speech is the receiver himself able and willing to produce in such a large measure what is offered to him as a stimulus. Linguistic stimulation is a kind of stimulation which can always be produced by the receiver himself. The transformation of experience into conceptualization, which was discussed on p. 11, is made possible by the fact that the symbol as a store and generalizer is not just received passively by the hearer, but can at any moment be actively seized by him and conceptualized. In the last resort language is perhaps such a specifically human creation not because we can yield to it passively but because in order to grasp what we receive we must first of all make it actively our own.

Speech perception is geared more towards a high degree of security of communication than towards a maximum exploitation of channel capacity.

The certainty of communication reaches a high level if only a portion of the possible distinctions is sufficient to identify a speech event as belonging to the class of signal x. The certainty we thus attain will prove its worth particularly under conditions when the communication is far from the ideal we have so far assumed.

In the ideal channel of communication the input of the source reaches the receiver undiminished, undistorted and without the addition of a disturbing noise. In reality such an ideal channel hardly ever exists. Thus the air vibrations of speech on their way from the speaker to the hearer are deviated by obstacles and distorted, e.g., fewer high frequencies occur behind the speaker than in front of him; the intensity of the air vibrations declines with distance; the channel—because its width is restricted—transmits perhaps only a part of the signal; and—the most important source of disturbance—extraneous sound events and signals which do not originate in the speaker penetrate into the channel.

For the purpose of our discussion these disturbances may be divided into omissions, distortions and additions.

If most of the qualities which can be distinguished in an acoustic event are not exploited, it must be possible to deprive the event of a considerable part of these qualities without impairing the linguistic message and without disturbing the transmission of information.

Investigations in this problem area have been carried out, among others, by FRENCH and STEINBERG (1947). The spectra of the utterances coming from a speaker were artificially modified by inserting filters into the channels which allowed only high or only low frequencies to pass through.

If a high-pass filter is used, for example, a filter which allows all parts of a speech event above 1,000 cps to pass through, only 85 percent of syllables are intelligible. If only frequencies above 3,000 cps are allowed to pass, comprehensibility goes down to 30 percent. The effect of a low-pass filter, which only lets through frequencies below a certain level, is correspondingly similar; if, for example, all speech components above 300 or 400 cps are filtered out, it is almost impossible to understand anything.

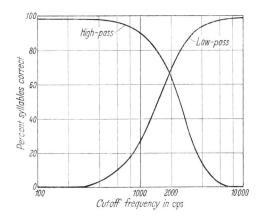

Fig. 19. Dependence of discrimination on the frequency range (based on FRENCH and STEINBERG, 1947, from MILLER, 1951a, p. 64)

The point of intersection of these curves at approx. 1,900 cps indicates that, if only the frequencies above this figure are used as signal carrier, approx. two thirds of the syllables are intelligible; the same result is obtained if only the frequencies below this figure reach the listener. In other words, it hardly matters *which* frequency bands are used as signal carrier: communication occurs as long as in the total spectrum there is a margin for variation, an area which allows for those distinctions which carry information.

As one would expect the exact position of these curves is a function of the sex of the speaker. CARTERETTE and MØLLER (1963) obtained similar results for different subjects, a different context, and in a different language — which suggests that fundamental characteristics of the mechanism of perception are involved.

In the experiments we have just discussed the frequency spectrum of the language was selectively filtered out. Other investigations have left intact the frequencies of the acoustic event but have selectively varied amplitudes.

In the simplest case the peaks of amplitudes are cut off; having done this we can transmit to the listener either these peaks or the remaining center portions of the wave. LICKLIDER was able to demonstrate that intelligibility of speech is hardly affected if the peaks are omitted, whereas in the case of the omission of the center portion of the wave and the exclusive use of the peaks intelligibility is nearly down to zero.

How can this result be explained? There must be signals which are characterized by the following qualities: they have very high intensities; yet they can be omitted without affecting intelligibility; at the same time they have not enough information content to transmit messages without a center portion. Such signals are the vowels. Clipping wave peaks

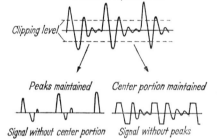

Fig. 20. Two kinds of distortion of the wave form produced by amplitude selection (based on MILLER, 1951a, p. 72)

affects the vowels, but the consonants hardly at all, since only vowels have such high intensities. The finding confirms that consonants carry more information than vowels because the number of consonants is greater. As was explained above the amount of information transmitted by a signal depends upon the number of possibilities from which the signal has been selected.

From quite a different point of view the example of Arabic can show that the loss of vowels affects the intelligibility of a language less than the loss of consonants: in Arabic script it is customary to write only consonants; for beginners in the language and also wherever it is regarded as important vowel signs are placed above or below the consonant.

So far we have discussed the effect of disturbances on communication when the signal on its way from the source has been mutilated in its acoustic band-width and, as a result, has probably been distorted. More important from a practical point of view are those cases in which something is added to the signal on its way. On the telephone one hears a speech event which is not only reduced in its frequency spectrum, but to which are added electrical disturbances and perhaps also a conversation on another line. The listener in this case receives a mixture of desired, genuine information and of misinformation from a source of disturbance.

The problem the listener faces is: how can the genuine information which comes from the speaker be picked out from the mixture?

There are two aspects to this problem: one mathematical which has been thoroughly investigated by SHANNON and which will not be treated here, and the other psychological in a narrower sense: how much is perception of speech sounds affected by competing acoustic events or *noise*? In this context noise is defined as all undesired information.

One of the concepts which is frequently used in this context is that of *masking*. In experiments on masking or covering up of the 'real' information it is customary to use a random mixture of all audible frequencies. In analogy to white sun light, which is a mixture of all visible wavelengths, this random swishing noise is called *white noise*.

If the disturbing effect of this white noise on speech perception is to be studied, a measure for the intensity of the noise is needed, because this intensity is the independent variable in the experiment to be described below. The measure is the decibel already defined on page 59 above.

By way of introduction to such experiments, it may be helpful to remind the reader of the fact that the sensitivity of the human ear is dependent upon the frequency of the sound to be perceived. As can be seen (Fig. 21), the threshold of detectability is lowest for sounds of 2,000 to 3,000 cps; here the sound needs the lowest intensity to be perceived.

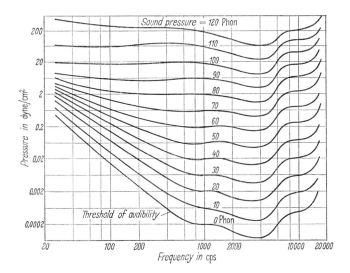

Fig. 21. Curves of identical loudness in binaural hearing as a function of frequency and sound pressure. Frequency is plotted along the abscissa and pressure along the ordinate, both on a logarithmic scale. At 1,000 cps the phone scale corresponds to the decibel scale (based on FLETCHER and MUNSON, from REIN and SCHNEIDER, 1964, p. 688)

If the audibility threshold is to be determined not only by transmitting the tone to be detected but also white noise, the following diagram results:

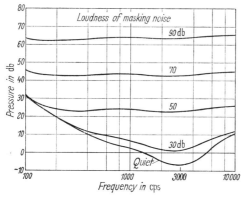

Fig. 22. Threshold for pure tones when masked by white noise: the parameter is the level of the masking noise (based on HAWKINS and STEVENS, 1950, from MILLER, 1951 a, p. 55)

Even noise of 30 db requires a rise in the threshold level for tones around 2,000 cps; in order to detect these tones their loudness must be increased beyond the point which would be necessary without white noise. If the white noise has an intensity of 50—60 db, all frequencies are affected.

In the following figure the same result is presented in a somewhat different form:

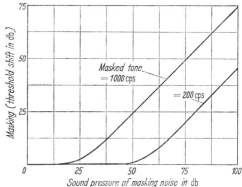

Fig. 23. Shift of the threshold of detectability for two tones when masked by white noise. The upper curve results from a masked tone of 1,000 cps, the lower one for one of 200 cps (based on MILLER, 1951a, p. 56)

The co-ordinates in this case are the intensity of the masking noise and the size of the threshold shift, resulting from the increase in noise. It will be seen that once the threshold shift has begun it rises in a linear fashion. If the noise level for a tone of 1,000 cps is raised by 10 db, the threshold for the perception of the tone also increases by 10 db. The so-called *signal-to-noise ratio* is constant in this instance; it is —25 db, i.e., the tone will no longer be heard if it is more than 25 db weaker than the noise.

For the sake of simplicity we have so far confined ourselves to the masking of pure tones; of greater interest is the question to what extent noise affects speech perception.

As Fig. 24 shows, the detection of speech occurs if the noise level is not higher than 17 db above speech. The *comprehension* of speech is dependent upon a number of other factors still to be discussed.

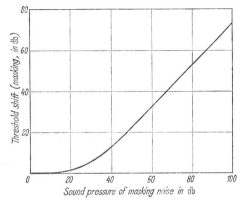

Fig. 24. Shift in the threshold of detectability for speech as a function of the intensity of white noise (based on HAWKINS and STEVENS, 1950, from MILLER, 1951a, p. 62)

The masking effect of the interfering noise depends not only on its intensity, but also on the spectrum. The more the spectrum of the interfering noise is similar to the spectrum of speech the more affected is the perception of speech.

To explain the masking of tones by noise MILLER now reasons as follows. Suppose that the signal to be detected has a component of 1,000 cps and that accurate discrimination of this component is decisive for the perception of the signal. If noise is present (assuming it is white noise) it will also have a component of 1,000 cps. As noise is produced randomly it is not possible to say whether the 1,000 cps component is in phase with the signal and added to it or if it is out of phase so that the 1,000 cps component of the signal and the noise cancel each other. The addition of noise to the 1,000 cps speech component would add a certain fuzzy effect, but an exact determination of this component is not possible. If the area of fuzziness is large, large changes of the corresponding signal component are needed, so as to perceive these changes as such and not as accidental fuzziness. In other words: the smaller the *signal-to-noise ratio* the fewer distinctions of the signal can be detected by the receiver, i.e., the fainter is the possibility for him to receive information.

Suppose now a language employs many delicate distinctions, these could perfectly well be detected over an undisturbed channel, i.e., in the quiet, and would permit a very high rate of information transmission per time unit. But under conditions of noise, communication operating with such delicate distinctions would soon break down.

While in the studies reported so far the influence of noise on speech *perception* has been investigated, DREHER and O'NEILL (1957) have studied the effect of noise on the *production* of speech. In their investigation the quality of production was measured in terms of comprehension by the listener. Fig. 25 explains the design of the experiment.

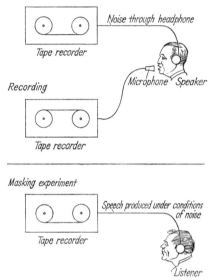

Fig. 25. Modified from DREHER and O'NEILL, 1957

The speaker speaks under conditions of noise. This produces the so-called lombard effect which consists above all in a heightening of the intensity. Speech produced in this way is recorded and then examined for its effect on the listener in a usual masking experiment, i.e., under addition of noise. The result is interesting in as much as the noise causes the speaker to produce a kind of utterance which is more intelligible under conditions of noise than an utterance produced without noise[1]. External deterioration is within certain limits automatically compensated for by improved speech output.

The effect of masking is, from a physiological point of view, a relatively peripheral event as it can already be detected in the reaction potential of the auditory nerve (ROSENZWEIG and ROSENBLITH, 1950). However, an experiment by HERNÁNDEZ-PEÓN et al. (1956), which is extremely interesting for the entire psychology of perception, makes it clear that

---

[1] In the other masking experiments it was only the listener who was under influence of noise not the speaker.

even this very peripheral event is under the influence of central factors: in the *nucleus cochlearis* of a cat the action potentials produced by the tick of a metronome can be registered. If a mouse in a glass is then shown to the cat, the potential produced by the tick disappears.

This means that through a shift of attention even peripheral physiological processes may be altered, and that such a shift is not confined to higher cortical centers. Peripheral perception, therefore, can be modified not only in the centripetal but also in the centrifugal direction. It is even more probable that such interaction between the incoming stimulus and the characteristics of the perceiving organism may be found in higher centers. These characteristics of the organism can be of various kinds: they can range from ephemeral states of shortest duration to the permanent 'knowing' of the frequency profile of linguistic elements.

While the study of masking by white noise gives information on quasi-physiological processes in the peripheral sectors of perception, the studies which use a second interfering event for masking instead of white noise probe the interaction of the stimulus on the one side and the characteristics of the organism at more central sectors of perception on the other. These last-named investigations have of course also a greater practical application; and for this reason we shall describe them in somewhat greater detail.

To what extent is the perception of a speech event disturbed by the simultaneous occurrence of a second speech event? BROADBENT whose research on this question has been of particular merit has carried out the following basic experiment. The subject receives a piece of squared paper. The squares are numbered and within each square are signs, e.g., a cross or a circle. The subject hears through headphones such questions as: 'Is there a cross in square two?' If the answer is yes, the subject has to record this on an answer sheet. A second voice comes in over the same headphones, asking similar questions. The result is that subjects have great difficulties when both voices ask these questions simultaneously.

One might be tempted to explain these difficulties in purely sensory terms: the two questions mask each other, are overlaid in the hearing and can therefore not be understood. That this view is not at all correct, and that therefore the masking is not a peripheral event is shown by the following variation of the experiment: one voice is called A and the other B and the subject is instructed to pay attention only to the questions asked by A. In this case the second voice (B) hardly interferes at all.

It is true that the subject must have the instruction to pay attention only to A *before* the input of questions. If he is asked afterwards to answer only the questions of A, the subject finds it just as difficult to do so as if he had the task of answering both A and B. The prior instruction 'Answer only A's questions' sets in motion a selection mechanism which annuls part of the incoming information, i.e., B's questions, and thus enables the subject to receive undisturbed the messages coming from A.

What can we learn about the selection mechanism ? To clarify this question let us again look at some further investigations by BROADBENT and his collaborators.

Two simultaneous messages may be understood if they contain little information. If the information content increases, a point is soon reached where comprehension can no longer keep up. It follows that the capacity for registering and handling messages is limited with regard to the *quantity* of information it can process. If the message contains little information and a second message with equally little information is added, the limit of this capacity is not yet reached. If the number of bits is raised at input (i.e., what the listener receives) the number of bits at output (i.e., what he records as having understood) is also increased. If one of the messages, however, already contains a great deal of information the rise in input is no longer followed by a corresponding rise in output. The channel capacity, i.e., the capacity of the receiver to handle information, is transcended.

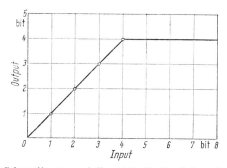

Fig. 26. Schematic representation of the limits of channel capacity

In the previously mentioned experiments, in which the listener simultaneously receives two messages only one of which, according to instructions, is relevant, it is all the easier to exclude or filter out the irrelevant one, the more clues are present for a distinction between the two messages. If one of the messages comes from the left and the other from the right, or if one is spoken by a man's voice and the other by a woman's, a separation is easily possible.

It was just pointed out that the irrelevant message would be 'filtered out', 'suppressed' or 'not registered'. This demands some further elucidations which will at the same time explain how the selection mechanism functions. If the 'irrelevant' speaker repeats the message of the 'relevant' speaker but with a delay of ten seconds, the subject is enabled to concentrate entirely on the relevant message without even noticing that the irrelevant voice after a delay of ten seconds repeats the message. However, if the delay of the second message is reduced to four seconds, the listener suddenly notices that the two messages are identical (CHERRY, 1957).

This has two implications: the relevant message must leave a kind of trace for about four seconds; and the irrelevant message, it appears, is not simply discarded; the apparatus of perception in a certain way takes cognizance of it. This suggests that the selection mechanism has a kind of store at its disposal. How this storing device works can be seen from certain experiments by BROADBENT. Messages are heard over separate loudspeakers each of which begins with a call signal: 'This is Fred speaking', 'This is Bill speaking'. The subject is instructed to pay attention only to what Fred says. Both signals are simultaneous. The responses of the subject show that both signals and both channels are received and then a decision is made which of the two voices should be listened to. The filtering-out process of the irrelevant one must be imagined roughly as follows: the receiver listens only to one channel but if he realizes that it is the irrelevant one, he can switch to the other channel and can find in it what has just recently occurred. It must be remembered that the event in channels one and two are objectively speaking strictly simultaneous. The events which lead to an acoustic input are definitely preserved for a brief span of time. If it is decided that the input is irrelevant, it is not passed for further processing and is quickly forgotten.

The effect of this store, which is set before the selection mechanism, can be demonstrated by the following experiment. The subject hears over the left headphone the figure 723 and simultaneously over the right one 954. Subsequently he is instructed to repeat all the numbers he has heard. He says '723954' or '954723', i.e., the response consists of *all* the information transmitted over one channel followed by all the information on the other channel. The subject cannot proceed in any other way; he is incapable of uttering the sequence which objectively occurred.

This experiment shows that in the course of the process of acoustic perception (and accordingly also in the process of speech perception) memory enters into the formation of units. The process of retention demands the formation of such units or chunks, as MILLER has proved. According to MILLER (1956), the number of such chunks may under certain circumstances be the decisive variable for retention, not the information content of what has been retained. (Compare on this point also EHRLICH, 1961). This relationship between perception (where the *information content* of the item matters) and retention (which is determined by the number of items) must also be considered in psycholinguistic research.

It had previously been observed that two simultaneously heard messages would only be understood if their information content was not too high. We can now add a further restriction: the information content must not exceed the channel capacity except for a short spell of time so that this excess can be stored until it is processed. Such storing is possible so long as the input in the seconds immediately following is not too high.

BROADBENT'S *filter theory* which is based on these and numerous other results need not be considered here in greater detail. The investigations we have described will be sufficient to show that the study of mechanisms in the psychology of language must go beyond psycholinguistics in a narrow sense and be related to insights gained from general psychology.

Chapter 5

The Probability Structure of Language

Speech perception and probability of occurrence — ZIPF'S curve and its interpretation — Thorndike-Lorge frequency count — Coding processes in speech perception — Language as a Markov process — Approximations to genuine language — Transitional probabilities as determinants of the perception and learning of verbal material.

The preceding chapter was concerned with the 'channel capacity' linking speaker and listener. It was found that this concept, among various ideas derived from information theory, has been fruitful. The information content of messages—as was discussed in detail in the last chapter—is closely related to the number of possible signals and the probability of the occurrence of a given signal. The present chapter is intended to explore what insights into the psychology of language can be gained by considering it from a probabilistic point of view.

As an introduction to the field as a whole a study by MILLER, HEISE and LICHTEN (1951) is particularly useful. In this inquiry the subjects were given the task of identifying words heard under conditions of noise.

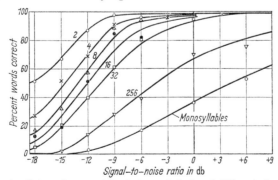

Fig. 27. Percentage of words correct for test vocabularies of different sizes; the bottom curve 'monosyllables' was obtained with a vocabulary of app. 1,000 monosyllabic words (based on MILLER, HEISE and LICHTEN, 1951, from MILLER, 1951a, p. 77)

In each case the size of the vocabulary from which the words were chosen
was exactly known. It comprised 2, 4, 8, etc. words respectively. For
example, when the vocabulary consisted of eight words, the subjects knew
that what they would hear through their headphones could only be one
of these eight words. The larger the vocabulary from which the test
words are selected the greater must be the intensity of speech with which
the words are uttered relative to the noise in order to ensure that an
equal percentage of words is understood correctly. The following figure
gives a second result of the same investigation. It appears that digits

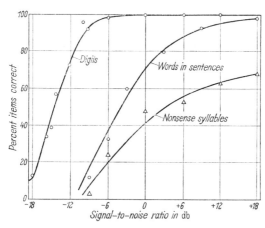

Fig. 28. Percentage of items
recognized correctly for different signal-to-noise ratios for
digits, words in sentences and
nonsense syllables (based on
MILLER, HEISE and LICHTEN,
1951, as reported by MILLER,
1951a, p. 75)

(0—9) are understood by far the best; next follow words in sentences,
whereas nonsense syllables even under a much more favorable signal-to-
noise ratio yield lower scores. The digits have, of course, the lowest
information content, because there are only ten possibilities. Words in
sentences contain very much more information, whereas the information
content of syllables is particularly high, because here almost anything is
possible.

The percentages of items recognized correctly in these three series
—digits, words in sentences and nonsense syllables—are different, but
the content of information, received at a given signal-to-noise ratio, is
fairly constant: in the case of the digits many items are understood but
they have little information content, while in the case of nonsense
syllables few have been correctly heard but they have a very high information content.

How can this result be explained? When the listener hears digits he
needs only few acoustic clues of the incoming message in order to decide
that it can only be 'five' if he hears /fai/. In the case of a meaningful
word the listener must of course receive more acoustic clues, but even if
a few are drowned by the noise, he can supplement these missing clues

by his previous knowledge of common sound combinations in his language. Isolated words at a given signal-to-noise ratio are less clearly understood than the same words at an equal noise level in sentences, for the sentence structure already gives a clue as to which word is possible in a given position.

POLLACK (1953a) attempted to find out the relative influence on the extent of information loss of two variables: the number of items in the message (i.e., the length of the message) and the number of possibilities per item. He transmitted to his subjects messages of a given number of items: each item in turn was one of a definite number of possibilities. The immediate result was that per message item the loss of information is greater the larger the number of items in the message and the larger the number of possibilities per item. If the length of the message (i.e, the number of items) is held constant, the percentage of information loss is independent of the number of possibilities per item. In other words, if the number of possibilities per item is great, some items will certainly not be received, but the items which have been registered yield a great deal of information because in every case they represent one of several possibilities. Fig. 29 represents a model of these relationships.

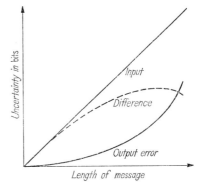

Fig. 29. Schematic presentation of information received. The information received is equal to the difference between information input and the information loss, i.e., output errors (adapted from POLLACK, 1953a, p. 430)

If the message is short, the information received by the listener is equal to the information transmitted by the source: there is no information loss. If the messages are a little longer the size of the error is small; but this means that the information content received rises. At a medium length of message the difference between input and output is roughly constant; a certain amount of information transmitted is always lost. If the message is very long the loss of information rises steeply, more steeply than can be compensated for by the increase in transmitted information.

It follows that for each number of possibilities per item there is a definite length of message which allows comprehension of a maximum of information. If a shorter message is transmitted, less information than would really be possible is sent; if longer messages are sent, the loss of information rises disproportionately. In other words, in these inquiries we again come across the notion of channel capacity which we discussed in the previous chapter.

From the point of view of information theory, understanding a message always involves more than is contained in the signal itself; it implies reference to the totality of possibilities which is available to the receiver and from which the signal in question has been selected. This totality of possibilities is by no means uniform, but has in each case a characteristic profile: some possibilities are more probable than others, and the variations in the degrees of probability influence the decoding process in the receiver. If the receiver knows that digits are contained in a message with a higher degree of probability than words, he will perceive 'si...' more likely as 'six' than as 'sits'. The listener—and in a similar way the speaker too—has not only learned the meanings of words and the grammatically correct use of the word, but apparently also the probabilities of occurrence of words (or of phonemes, letters or syllables, etc.); at any rate, the above mentioned experiments by MILLER, POLLACK and others demonstrate that such a knowledge of probabilities of occurrence is a co-determinant in the listener's act of perception.

In its simplest form this probability profile of a language is met as the average value of the occurrence of a certain unit—and unit may be taken to mean an element on a certain level, e.g., phoneme, letter, syllable, word, etc. Such average values can be calculated by counts of fairly large spoken verbal products, such as lectures, telephone conversations, etc., or of written verbal products, e.g., newspapers, letters or books.

Such frequency counts of linguistic units have been undertaken in Germany by KAEDING (1897) and MEIER (1964) and in America by THORNDIKE and LORGE (1944) and ZIPF (1949). It is largely thanks to ZIPF's long-standing efforts that the conviction has gradually spread that linguistic events can be investigated with the same objectivity as such 'natural' events as sun-spots or the social behavior of ants. As late as 1964, however, MEIER'S work contains a passionate plea for such investigations.

MEIER grouped into 14 levels the frequencies of the words in the texts he analyzed, which consisted of a total of ten million words. Table 2 illustrates the astonishing result which in all such investigations has been found again and again:

Table 2. *(Based on* MEIER, *1964, p. 53)*

Level	Number of word types at each level	Percent of word types	Number of word tokens representing these word types	Percent of all word tokens
Ia	30	0.01	3 468 082	31.79
Ib	70	0.03	1 670 379	15.31
Ic	107	0.04	791 693	7.25
II	305	0.12	925 035	8.48
III	510	0.20	695 265	6.37
IV	995	0.39	690 029	6.32
V	1 278	0.50	488 995	4.48
VI	1 396	0.54	341 669	3.13
VII	3 303	1.28	469 057	4.30
VIII	5 221	2.02	369 338	3.39
IX	12 391	4.80	386 882	3.55
X	15 477	6.00	209 515	1.92
XI	38 633	14.96⎫		
XII	178 457	69.12⎭	404 838	3.71
Total	258 173	100.00	10 910 777	100.00

The thirty most frequently occurring words in German constitute almost a third of all texts. One half of the texts consists of 200 of the most frequent words of the German language, or to express it in another way: not quite one percent of the different words makes up half the texts. Against this, the 15,477 word types on frequency level 10 (6 percent of all different words) constitute barely two percent of the texts. Which are the thirty most frequent words occurring in German? They are: die, der, und, in, zu, den, das, nicht, von, sie, ist, des, sich, mit, dem, daß, er, es, ein, ich, auf, so, eine, auch, als, am, nach, wie, im, für[1].

ZIPF goes one step further: he compares the frequencies of occurrence of different words by relating graphically the rank order of frequency with the frequency of occurrence of a particular word. ZIPF's famous law is represented in Fig. 30.

In order to understand this diagram correctly it is important to explain the co-ordinates: the rank sequence n of the words in terms of decreasing frequency is plotted on the abscissa: the most frequent, the second most frequent, the third most frequent word, etc. The ordinate records the actual frequencies P_n in a given text. Both scales are logarithmic. The resulting straight line indicates that the product $n P_n$ is constant.

---

[1] *Translator's note.* Approximate English equivalent of these are: the (and various other case forms), and, in, to, not, of, they/she, is, himself (and similar reflexive pronouns), with, that, he, it, a/an, I, on, so, also, as, at, towards/after, how, in, for.

Curve *A* resulted from a count of JAMES JOYCE'S *Ulysses,* curve *B* from a count of a large sample of American newspapers.

If we want to make a correct interpretation of these curves, which have been found again and again in the most varied samples, it must be made clear that the two variables, rank and frequency, are *not* independent. Since the rank position of a word depends on the frequency of its occurrence, the direction of the curve is, at least partially, simply the expression of the mathematical relationship between the two variables; i.e., the curve cannot be higher on the right than on the left

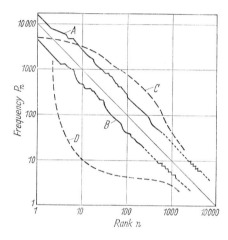

Fig. 30. Rank frequency of words.
A: JAMES JOYCE'S *Ulysses;*
B: American newspapers;
C and D: hypothetical curves (based on ZIPF, from CHERRY, 1963, p. 141)

because a word with a low frequency cannot occupy a higher rank position than a word with a higher frequency. But if all words were equally frequent the curve would be nearly horizontal; and if there were only some very frequent words and some very rare, it would be nearly vertical. Between these two extremes the shape of the line is, therefore, determined by the empirical facts. Our next question is how are we to interpret this strange finding ($n P_n$ = constant)? What conditions must be present to produce it?

According to ZIPF, human behavior in many spheres is founded on the *principle of least effort.* The organism strives to maintain as low an average level of exertion as possible. Not only does word frequency obey this principle, but it applies equally to the relative size of cities in a country or to the arrangement of tools at a work bench. According to ZIPF, language—from the speaker's point of view—would be at its simplest if the speaker had only to utter the same word again and again, or, in other words, if the language consisted only of a single word. From the listener's point of view, on the other hand, the language would be most rational and most convenient if every distinctive meaning had its own word. To put it differently, in language two tendencies confront each other: one to say things as economically as possible, and the other to be explicit. ZIPF names the first the tendency of unification and the second the tendency of diversification[1]. ZIPF'S law can therefore be viewed as the equilibrium between these two tendencies.

A flatter curve *(C)* would result if the speaker would use common words not quite so frequently, and rare words not quite so rarely, so that the tendency to diversify would predominate and therefore language would be used in a way which the hearer desires. Conversely, a steeper curve *(D)* would indicate the tendency of unification or a certain egocentricity in the speaker. The linguistic products of schizophrenics appear to be characterized by a greater steepness of these rank-frequency curves.

A clearer picture than that of the relative steepness of ZIPF'S curves is presented by individual preferences of frequency classes relative to a norm, on the basis of MEIER'S *spectrum* (Fig. 31). The 'language of

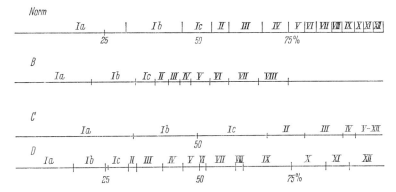

Fig. 31. Comparison between different frequency spectra (based on MEIER, 1964, pp. 54, 58, 66, and 112)

prescriptions' *(B)*, for example, is syntactically somewhat reduced; this is indicated by the decline in frequency of those very frequent words which in 'normal' texts predominate. Equally, in an investigation by KELCHNER (1929), a letter of a young female factory worker, analyzed under *C* in Fig. 31, confines itself to a very general vocabulary. MEIER describes texts of this type as *lexically-restricted*. MEIER'S use of this concept offers an example of a content analysis from a formal point of view.

MEIER demonstrates that lexically-restricted spectra emerge in moments of genuine stress. Such regression to the most usual words can no doubt be related to the well-known psychological observation that stress leads to increased rigidity of thought and to a reduction of creative ideas. Spectra with a wide lexical spread are found in descriptions, in

---

[1] JESPERSEN noted similar dynamics in language, particularly so in lexical choice: a maximum of effectiveness with a minimum of effort.

scholarly papers, in reports of lexically specialized character, such as on the sports page or the fashion page, or in ironical discourse. The analysis D in Fig. 31 represents a police warrant.

It should, however, be noted that the connection between frequency and the rank order of words, found by ZIPF, could also be interpreted quite differently. We follow GUIRAUD in this brief outline. The observation on which this interpretation is based is the empirically established correlation between frequency of occurrence and length of words.

We start out from a system consisting of four random elements a, b, c and the interval element z. If we now create sequences from these elements quite at random, e.g., azbazbbczcccaz..., it can be imagined that z always acts as a boundary between 'words' which in this illustration are a, ba, bbc, ccca. We are interested in the relationship between length of 'words' created in this manner and their frequency. It can easily be seen that shorter words will appear more frequently than longer ones; longer words are infrequent because it is unlikely that z would not appear in the sequences. It can in fact easily be proved mathematically that between a ranking of frequencies according to length and a ranking according to probability there appears the same perfect correlation which is expressed in ZIPF'S straight line. If we now equate phonemes with the chance elements in the above example, the following empirical data (Table 3) can be explained equally well on the basis of chance as on the basis of motivated tendencies in ZIPF'S manner; therefore it is unnecessary to appeal to a motivated choice if chance alone leads to same result, i.e., that shorter words are more likely to occur with greater frequency than longer ones.

Table 3. *Based on* GUIRAUD *(with modifications, from* MOLES *and* VALLANCIEN, *1963, p. 40)*

Mean rank	Mean length in phonemes	Frequency
100	3.50	500
500	4.37	150
1000	4.75	75
2000	5.75	33
3000	5.95	16
4000	6.00	12
5000	6.12	9
6000	6.30	5

If the view that the length of words used is determined by chance is unacceptable, one can still argue along the following lines. The logarithm of the probability of occurrence of a word expresses the content of information of that word. It follows that the number of phonemes in a word is proportional to the information content of that word. Words consisting of many phonemes are infrequent and therefore have more information content. If in a text frequent words were to be used even more frequently—and consequently rare words even more rarely—such a text would become shorter because frequent words are short ones. A shorter text requires less effort, but its total information content is lower. Vice versa, if infrequent long words are used, the total length of a text increases; admittedly, the information content rises too, but the effort increases at the same time. Thus, even from the point of view of information theory, ZIPF's formula describes an equilibrium, i.e., that state in which the transmission of messages displays an economic optimum.

MANDELBROT (1954) who is not concerned with the relationship between information content and word length starts out from the observation that the act of receiving a message involves a translation or decoding process: the word received must be stored in some way. Sheer economy certainly demands that frequently occurring words are transformed into abbreviated storing signals; it is only in this way that comprehension of a word sequence, of a sentence, and so forth can take place with least delay. According to MANDELBROT, the recognition of a message depends on the statistical characteristics of the memory which undertakes the decoding process. ZIPF's formula expresses the fact that the vocabulary with which the speaker and hearer operate consists of discrete individual signs which combine according to statistical laws.

Other lines of thought lead from ZIPF's results to certain other interesting problems. One of these is the determination of the *size of the vocabulary* of an individual. The spoken and written texts produced by a single person can be considered a sample of the total universe of words at the disposal of this person. HOWES (1964, p. 57) is of the opinion that, however large the sample, it can never exhaust the total vocabulary; if the size of the sample is further increased, new words—according to ZIPF's formula—will continue to appear. A numerical comparison of the vocabularies of different persons is therefore only of little value; what can be compared are the parameter values of their ZIPF functions.

We can relate an observation from psychopathology to this argument. GOLDSTEIN has observed that in many cases of aphasia the patient has special difficulties in finding abstract words and in carrying out abstract thought operations, whereas the use of concrete words is less affected. From this observation GOLDSTEIN has derived a well-known theory of aphasia, i.e., that aphasia is a pathological shift from abstract to concrete levels of behavior, or a loss of the capacity to abstract. Against this view HOWES argues that ZIPF's law applies even in extreme cases of aphasia; only the parameters are shifted. There is no genuine loss of vocabulary; in a sample of a given size the patient tends to use only fewer different words than a healthy person. If the size of the sample is sufficiently large, he can also use all the words that are at the disposal of a healthy individual. Since abstract words are normally already less frequent than concrete words, they are especially affected in aphasia through the shift of parameters; but those concrete words which are equally infrequent suffer the same deficit; i.e., aphasia is not concomitant with a loss of the capacity of abstraction[1].

The thoughts which relate ZIPF'S law to individual vocabularies tend to contribute more to a psychology of individual differences than to general psychology. Whereas ZIPF himself strives to discover average word frequencies in the language generally, vocabulary studies are intended to discover differences among members of different social, age, or intelligence groups. Such comparisons are more suitably made with the help of the so-called type-token ratio (TTR) than with the individual or group parameters of the ZIPF formula. The type-token ratio, which was introduced by W. JOHNSON following CARROLL (1938), is based on the relationship, already referred to earlier, between the number of different words in a text and the number of running words in that text. In type-token ratio studies the basic unit is the word, whereas ZIPF functions can be established with reference to all other possible units. In a text which comprises 65 words in which one word occurs four times, 5 words three times each, 9 words twice each, and 28 words once each, the type-token ratio would be 43 : 65 or 0.66.

There is a significant relationship between the TTR score of a text and the intelligence of its author, as indicated in Fig. 32.

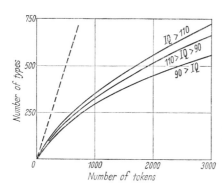

Fig. 32. The average number of different types is plotted against the total number of words used (tokens) by children of different intelligence levels (based on CHOTLOS, 1944, from MILLER, 1951a, p. 123)

A weakness of this ratio lies in the fact that it declines with the increasing length of a text, but this decline unfortunately happens in an irregular manner and therefore cannot be compensated for mathematically. On page one of a novel a writer need hardly repeat himself in the choice

---

[1] BROWN (1958a) offers an excellent discussion on the whole psycholinguistic problem involved in the concepts, 'concrete' and 'abstract'.

of words (the TTR would therefore be high) but after a few hundred pages he must necessarily re-employ words he has used before. By means of suitable sampling this defect can be obviated in the case of very long texts.

Whereas ZIPF as well as CARROLL and JOHNSON, the 'inventors' of the TTR, aimed at finding functional relationships within language, THORNDIKE aimed at straightforward description: together with his student LORGE he made the attempt to count which words in the English language occurred frequently and which occurred infrequently. The sample consisted of many millions of words in periodicals.

A similar count had already been made before the turn of the century by KAEDING who in 1897—98 produced, as a private publishing venture at Steglitz near Berlin, a frequency dictionary of the German language. This work served as a basis for MEIER's *Statistics of the German Language (Deutsche Sprachstatistik (1964))* already referred to, the imposing work of a lone scholar who had recognized earlier and more effectively than many linguistic scholars the necessity and value of statistics in linguistic inquiries. If in the following remarks the less complex THORNDIKE-LORGE studies are treated in greater detail, this is done only for one reason: THORNDIKE-LORGE has had considerable influence on psychological research, which can hardly be said of KAEDING and, not yet, of MEIER.

THORNDIKE was prompted to undertake his count by the necessity to grade quantitatively the difficulty of reading matter employed in schools. The less frequently the words in a text are used in everyday language, the more difficult is the text.

The Thorndike-Lorge count has become the basis for two trends of development, one of which is more practical and the other more theoretical in its orientation. The first is concerned with the systematic study of the *readability* or *intelligibility* of texts. The other trend has expressed itself in the use of frequency indices, worked out by THORNDIKE and LORGE, for the purpose of systematic variation of verbal materials in psychological experiments. Both trends will be briefly discussed in the following paragraphs.

Some documents are written in a way that makes them difficult to understand, whereas others manage to express complicated thoughts in easily intelligible language. For example, legal language is so unintelligible to the layman that a good portion of a lawyer's time is spent in explaining what it 'really' means. What causes this lack of intelligibility? What makes one novelist harder to read than another? Both after all write grammatically correct sentences[1].

If a series of texts is ranked for readability by different judges, it is found that easily readable texts consist of words which—according to the

---

[1] *Translator's note.* The author here contrasts two German novelists, MUSIL as a difficult writer and HEINRICH BÖLL as a more readable one.

THORNDIKE-LORGE lists—occur very frequently in the language. Texts which are difficult to follow contain many rare words. Short words make a text more readable than long ones. It should be remembered that, according to ZIPF, short words are more frequent than long ones. Short words at the same time are those without prefixes or suffixes. The use of short and frequent words without pre- or suffixes leads to a low TTR. In other words these different statistical indices correlate highly with one another.

Next to frequency of use of common words in a text, another factor influencing comprehension is of course sentence length. According to MEIER'S statistical analysis of the German language roughly half of all German sentences have in general a length of less than eighteen words. In scientific texts, however, sentences of this length constitute only about a third of all sentences; in sermons they constitute 60 percent.

In addition a number of other factors influence readability. One of the best and most commonly used formulae for quantifying readability is that developed by FLESCH (1946).

FLESCH has in fact developed two formulae, one for *reading ease* and the other for *human interest*. At least five passages from an article or thirty from a book are selected as random samples. Each sample consists of the first 100 words of a paragraph. The average number of syllables in the 100-word samples *(W)* is calculated; likewise the number of sentences, marked off by a period or semicolon, which are complete nearest to the 100-word mark in the sample. The number of words in these sentences divided by the number of sentences yields the average sentence length S. The formula for readability is:

$$\text{Reading ease} = 206.84 - 0.85\ W - 1.02\ S.$$

A score of 0 is practically unreadable, a score of 100 is 'readable' for any literate person.

For the *human interest* score the average number of personal words is calculated. Personal words are nouns with natural gender, pronouns referring to persons and words like 'people' or 'folks'. This gives the value w. The average number of personal sentences (i.e., direct speech, commands, requests, exclamations and grammatically incomplete sentences whose meaning can be inferred from the context) gives per 100 sentences the score s. The human-interest formula is as follows:

$$\text{Human interest} = 3.64\ w + 0.31\ s.$$

The exact measurement of readability in quantitative terms is no doubt of great practical significance—and not only in advertising. Of much greater scientific interest, however, is the use of THORNDIKE-LORGE frequency scores in experimental psychology. Many investigations make use of verbal material, e.g., studies of perception, learning, or memory. Previously almost the only variation in the verbal material had been the distinction between meaningful and nonsense materials. The inclusion of the frequency aspect has made it possible to relate the psychological events of perception, learning or memorizing to the frequency or probability structure of the verbal material. A wealth of new findings has resulted from this combination. Studies in this area are illustrations of synchronic psycholinguistics; they explore relationships between co-existing linguistic and nonlinguistic events.

This inclusion of aspects derived from statistical linguistics has been particularly fruitful in the study of the so-called *perceptual defense*. In the forties a number of investigators—McGinnies is a good representative of this group—had discovered that the tachistoscopic threshold of perception for taboo words lies higher than for non-taboo words. This means that words with a negative emotional connotation, when presented for brief moments, are perceived less easily than emotionally neutral words. The problem that this raises, i.e., that the observer must somehow 'see' that it is a taboo word before 'not seeing' it, this problem has stimulated intensive studies in this area which need not be discussed at this point. In the present context the objection advanced by Howes and Solomon (1951) is of interest: taboo words are infrequent words and some of them are unlikely to have been seen in writing. It might well be that it is not so much the negative emotional connotation but their infrequency which accounts for the higher recognition threshold. Howes and Solomon have confirmed this hypothesis by producing evidence of a clear connection between frequency of occurrence of a word in everyday language (Thorndike-Lorge values) and speed of perception. Infrequent words have a high recognition threshold even if they are not emotionally charged.

Starting from these investigations, it has been proved in a long series of studies that the frequency of previous occurrence of certain events influences the perception of these events. Everyday language can—following Thorndike-Lorge—be described as the supplier of such frequencies; but these frequencies can also be produced experimentally. The established connections are surprisingly strong: the coefficients of correlation between threshold of perception and the logarithm of frequency are throughout in the region of -0.7 to -0.8.

Not only perception but also learning and retention are determined by such statistical word frequencies. To cite only a simple example, Hall (1954) found a significant correlation between the frequency value of a word and the number of persons who retain this word in a memory experiment.

Let us now attempt to review the theoretical outcome of this series of studies which stretches from Miller-Heise-Lichten via Zipf to Thorndike-Lorge. During decoding the receiver goes through a sequence of discrete states. Which state comes next is partly determined by what is received as a signal, but partly also by what has the greatest probability for the receiver. The world with which we enter into contact is not amorphous; it has a probability profile. This enables us in perception to go beyond the information given. If we hear /si/ and expect figures, the next state that clicks is 'six'. This click occurs because this state has the greatest probability of occurrence on grounds of acquired verbal habits, of expectancy, and also on the basis of the stimulus that has occurred.

This feature of going beyond the information actually given is basic to all higher processes of perception and cognition. BRUNER (1957a) has written a well-known article on this subject whose main arguments will now be discussed.

A first form of this going beyond the available information consists in the process of assigning an object, as it presents itself, to a class of objects; i.e., the thing is understood as an exemplar of a certain class. We have already met this kind of process once, in our discussion of the discrimination of phonemes; it will be encountered again at a later stage in connection with certain psychological thougts expressed by BROWN. In principle, the mechanism involved in this process of classification is clear: the class is characterized by a number of qualities; if parts of the characteristics of a new object are identical with the defining characteristics of the class, this object is treated as an exemplar belonging to this class. Nevertheless the apparent ease of this ordering process has remained on a restricted and purely formal level. The inductive step from the individual thing to the class is often already taken when only few characteristics are available—e.g., in the case of verbal material when only fragments of the word are heard—so few that 'it is positively irresponsible' to make a decision on class membership ('That's six'). It is not the weight of the argument of actually noted characteristics of the object which acts as a driving force; the class is like a magnet that pulls the object towards it, and this 'magnetic force' is all the greater the more frequently the class has previously occurred. This can well be illustrated by the dynamics which exist between two neighboring phonemes: here it is not a process of gradual weighing of one quality against another, as if a gradual shift occurred from one phoneme class to another; on the contrary at the point of maximum uncertainty ('Is it still /g/ or already /d/ ?') we find a strange but most ingenious built-in 'tipping' device.

The same process, interpreted somewhat differently, is called *closure* by Gestalt psychology; what is needed to complete the configuration is added. HEBB'S explanation of closure in empiricist terms, different from 'Gestalt' psychology (the phase sequence, corresponding to the complete gestalt, can be set in motion by any part), could be most helpful in accounting for the processes we have just outlined.

Of a similar nature is the notion of *type* in the psychology of personality and in social psychology. Whether a particular person is to be classified as type x or type y can only be really decided after a considerable number of qualities of this person have already been found identical with the qualities characterizing this or that 'type'. Yet, classifying an individual under a type is mostly done whenever we do not know very much about him—it is a kind of biological economy. If we had to learn to react to each single object or to each particular event, our capacities would soon be overloaded. But if we succeed in assigning the particular object or the single event to a class of objects or events, the multiplicity in the world is thereby reduced.

It must be recognized how very much this tendency towards a biologically meaningful economy permeates all behavior and experience. It begins at the lowest, almost physiological level, with what in general psychology is known as constancy phenomena. A table is perceived as rectangular—regardless of the fact whether it is viewed from above or obliquely from the side. It is seen as rectangular, as one constant object; the various views are, as it were, separate examples of the single class which alone matters, the class 'this table'.

And at much higher levels we again meet this tendency towards a biologically meaningful economy in the area of social psychology as prejudice or stereotype. As soon as we identify someone as Chinese, Catholic, a Southerner or as a Communist, characteristic features for each class are immediately available. That this reduction of variety frequently does not have a desirable result, is perhaps caused by the fact that—to put it crudely—culture has complicated nature and thus it is no longer possible to rely on the energy-saving device of prejudice.

WILLIAM JAMES, as early as 1890, stressed the importance of this classification process when he said that cognitive life begins when it is possible to exclaim, 'Hollo! Thingumbob again.'

Placing an individual event into a class of events is one form of going beyond the information given. Another closely related form occurs when we complete missing elements on the basis of present data and the total array of various likely possibilities. In the word PXYCHXLINGUXSTICS the missing elements are supplemented without difficulty. What we meet as an 'event'—as we have already learned, for example, from the investigations by MILLER, HEISE and LICHTEN—does not only go with other actual events, but also with other unrealized possible events. Thus, in a concrete speech event, one part of a network of possibilities offered by the structure of the language is lifted into reality. Our perception and behavior are determined by this network as much as by the external stimulation that impinges upon us. The acquisition of this network of probabilities, the knowledge of the probable sequence of events A and B indicate that we have abstracted rules from the continuous sequence of real events—a fact to which HEIDER (1957) has drawn attention. These formal schemata lie on a higher plane of abstraction than the concrete events. Their acquisition is called *coding* by BRUNER. The acquisition of coding systems is probably the most important learning process in the construction of language and cognition.

Looked at from the point of view of language one of the most decisive problems of the psychology of learning is: how can anything be abstracted, learned and retained from a concrete event or from sequences of events which are in essence unrepeatable? Among the concepts developed by learning theory to come to grips with this problem are the notions of 'generalization' and 'transfer'; but, we must ask, are the mechanisms denoted by these terms powerful enough to account for these processes? Is successful transfer perhaps less a prerequisite than a consequence of the formation and use of a coding schema? More specifically in terms of language, verbal habits, on the one hand, are the foundations from which to go beyond the information given, but, on the other, the formation or learning of a verbal habit is already a going beyond the concreteness of individual events in the direction of an abstract, general rule. As ALLESCH put it, we grasp generalities *in* things and *by means of* things.

Thus, man faces a world which is not ruled by wild chance, but structured by probabilities. Man is not oriented towards expecting anything and everything that is possible; he anticipates certain possibilities more than others. It is in this area of probability that the regularities which psycholinguistics explores are found. These regularities become evident on the level of concrete reality, but the laws themselves are statements about probabilities. The rules describe the profile of possibilities, and concrete events follow its contour. One objective of a psychology of language is to gain access through concrete events to the probabilistic structure of linguistic processes. By allowing language to happen, man as a speaker or listener makes use of his freedom to link the randomness of reality with the laws of probability.

We must presuppose that man has an organ to be sensitive to this world of latent possibilities. Indeed, what we have described could be interpreted as another expression of the ingeniously designed interaction of organism and environment which has been mentioned repeatedly. What good would it be—to put it in starkly teleological terms—if the events of the world were ordered and lawful, but if the organism were incapable of deriving such order and lawfulness from these events and of taking them into account in his own behavior?

It should be added that we speak of 'organism' here quite deliberately and not, for example, of 'human intellect', because this 'coding' process or abstracting of rules from events does not occur only in humans, and in humans not only in conscious activity.

There is no more impressive illustration of this ingeniously designed relationship between world and organism than the subtle to and fro between the order which we derive from events and the order which we impose upon them. Are the classes into which we sort concrete events something we find *in* the world or something that we invent *for* the world ?

That the linguistic realm possesses a particularly distinct probabilistic structure may be due to the fact that it is built up of discrete elements. In the selection and combination of such elements statistical regularities can manifest themselves with particular clarity.

We meet the probabilistic structure of language in its simplest form in the average values of the appearance of certain items, which add up to millions of word sequences. These are the values which ZIPF and THORNDIKE have made use of in such a profitable way.

So far we have spoken globally of the probability with which a particular word x in the English language is likely to occur. In the following section we will, so to speak, interpose a kind of more powerful magnification; or, to put it differently, we will adopt a more dynamic point of view. We are now no longer concerned with the probability of the appearance of word x in general in a given language, but with the probability of the appearance of word x supposing it was immediately preceded by word w. Therefore, our task is now no longer to discover probabilistic rules of the language as a whole and to determine their consequences, but to understand the probabilistic rules of individual speech events: phoneme sequence, syllable, word, or sentence.

Consider a sequence of events, e.g. phonemes or letters, a, b, c, d, e, f. In the previous section the question was asked whether, and in what way, for example, the perception of the event d was dependent upon the probability of appearance of d in this language in general. Now we are asking: does the perception of the appearance of the event d depend on the fact that the listener has previously perceived a, b, c ? Would the same event d be perceived differently if, instead of a, b, c, the preceding events had been, for example, x, y, z ?

Whereas in the previous part the probability in general of the appearance of d in this language, regardless of context, was evinced, we are now concerned with probabilistic relationships within certain sequences and the consequences of such relationships, or to put it in more general terms, we are studying the effect of certain states or events upon later states or events in a sequence.

Such effects can be noted already in very simple events, which *prima facie* would appear to be determined entirely by their physical, i.e., acoustic, structure. In the description of vowels it was pointed out that a vowel is determined by the position of its formants; this is a fundamental principle of phonetics. An investigation by LADEFOGED and BROADBENT (1957), however, shows that this view is oversimplified. These two authors asked the following question: does the identification of a vowel depend upon the absolute values of its formants (this is the commonly accepted view), or does it depend on the relationship of these formant values to the values of other vowels which the hearer has already heard from the same speaker ?

The experiment was conducted in the following manner. The subject hears a synthesized, i.e., artificially produced, introductory statement: "Please say what this word is", followed by the test word: 'bit', 'bet', 'bat' or 'but'. The introductory statements are distinguished only by the formant structure of their vowels, i.e., one, for example, might sound a little 'darker' than another. The result is that, for example, the test word A is identified by 87 percent of the listeners as 'bit' if it is preceded by version one of the introductory statement, but the *same* test word A is identified as 'bet' by 90 percent of the listeners if it is preceded by version two of the introductory sentence.

It was said previously that a sequence of discrete states occurs at the source during encoding and in the receiver during decoding. We can now add to that in more general terms: each state of the sequence is linked to the one following by certain probabilities. If we know that state w has just occurred we cannot say with certainty which state will come next, but we have more information than if we did not know that w had just occurred. State y is now very likely to follow, x somewhat less likely, and z, a and f are quite improbable.

These indications of probability no longer refer to the occurrence of w or x in everyday speech in general—as in ZIPF'S or THORNDIKE'S work; they refer to the probability of x, if w has preceded.

By way of example let us take an utterance in English. Suppose we have started with the consonant b. It is highly probable that the next state in the sequence will be a vowel; it is in fact more probable that this vowel is going to be e rather than oo. It could also be an r or l whereas a second b, a t or an n would be extremely unlikely in English. These probabilities apply, although in the language as a whole in a Thorndike type of count, n is more frequent than r or l[1].

The problem to which we have turned our attention can now be formulated as follows: how do succeeding states of a linguistic sequence influence each other ? This question introduces us to one of the most interesting areas of the psychology of language, sequential psycholinguis-

---

[1] *Translator's note.* The author has illustrated the transitional probabilities in his work by reference to German sound sequences. The illustration in this case turns out to be equally applicable to German or English.

tics. This area, as OSGOOD has put it, is a meeting ground between information theorists, linguists and learning psychologists.

Sequential psycholinguistics stands, as it were, between the diachronic and synchronic approaches of SAUSSURE. Although it investigates sequences in time, these sequences are so short that sequential psycholinguistics is in effect very close to a synchronic approach.

In sequential psycholinguistics it is usual to operate on the assumption that linguistic events are structured as a Markov process.

A Markov process is a stochastic process, i.e., an event which proceeds according to laws of probability. The probability of the occurrence of a certain state in the future can be fully predicted from the present state. This prediction cannot be improved upon by additional information on the past of the system (based on KENDALL and BUCKLAND, 1960, p. 174). A Markov model is therefore a so-called finite-state model.

The conception of a linguistic event as a Markov process, which largely goes back to SHANNON, conceptualizes the present state in terms of its history and the future state in terms of its present. It raises questions about relations of probability which link a single event or state with a preceding event or state.

This model views the communication process above all from the point of view of the receiver. The hearer or receiver of a message has no means of knowing in advance what will come next except for what he can derive from the probability structure which links preceding and subsequent events.

This model is less suitable for the description of the encoding or transmitting aspect of the communication process. We shall see later that at this point in particular the incompleteness of this approach will become apparent.

Linguistic events consist of structured sequences. The units whose probabilistic relationships are examined in sequential psycholinguistics are always units of one definite order, thus always phonemes, or letters, or words. For the purpose of the analysis, whatever unit is chosen is adhered to. By contrast, in certain other linguistic analyses the investigator switches, for example, from words to sentences.

It was just noted that linguistic events consist of structured sequences. This can be expressed in another way by saying that linguistic events are redundant or contain redundancies. Redundancy is not a characteristic of a single event but of a sequence of events. If the degree of redundancy is zero all possible events have equal probability of occurrence. Suppose we write each letter of the alphabet on separate pieces of paper, put all the papers into a hat, then pick one at random and after copying the letter put it back, the sequence of letters we will thus make up will have zero redundancy, e.g., ZSBKBJPGXEVAOOWGAS. In such a sequence the knowledge of one letter has no predictive value for the next; a maximal degree of uncertainty remains. Each letter has the equal probability of occurrence of 1 over 26. In other words, each letter has an information content of approx. 4.5 bits ($26 = 2^{4.5}$).

But supposing now that individual letters or definite sequences of letters (or also of other units) appear more frequently than others the average information content in each unit decreases. The extreme case would be of 100 percent redundancy in which events succeed each other according to a fixed rule, so that if one event is known all subsequent ones can be predicted. A sequence AAAAA... is completely redundant, but so is the sequence XFKXFKXFKX...

Linguistic sequences have a redundancy degree from zero to 100 percent. The more redundant a language is the more individual events or single symbols are needed to transmit a message.

Taking a telegram as an example, let us analyze it at the word level (i.e., with the word as the unit of analysis). It reads: "I am arriving on Monday, the 4th of February, 1963, at 12 o'clock noon." This telegram contains redundancies. As soon as one has read 'I' the subsequent verb form must be 'am' with the verb 'arriving', and likewise 'am arriving' can only go with 'I'. The message that the 4th of February, 1963 is a Monday is also redundant, because a calendar can establish this. And if one assumes a 24-hour clock, the message that 12 o'clock is noon would be equally redundant.

An economical sender could shorten this message by cutting out redundancies. Redundancy is therefore the non-economical element in the transmission of information.

We came across a similar phenomenon previously when we noted that the information capacity of the human voice was only exploited to a small degree. Just as it would be possible in the case of vocalization to manage with a smaller number of intensities and frequencies, in the present case far fewer words, and far fewer symbols would be sufficient if all of them had the largest possible information content and if therefore all would be equally probable. In both instances, instead of extreme economy, preference is given to safety of communication. In a message which contains redundancies it does not matter if one or the other mistake occurs; it does not affect the sense or create a misunderstanding: I UM ARIVING ON MANDAY 44 EEBRUARY 1963 AT 112 O'CLOCK NOOM.

The mistakes caused by the operator or apparatus characteristically make the details of the message appear less probable than normal redundancy of language would customarily lead us to expect.

Up to this point we have confined ourselves to the purely formal properties of these so-called transitional probabilities and redundancies.

Transitional probabilities are of the 'if...then' variety: *if* event A precedes, *then* event X will follow with a probability of, say, 80 percent. In the following discussion we shall attempt to show with illustrations from empirical investigations how these concepts can be employed in the psychological analysis of the listening and speaking processes. To do so we must first, however, introduce the idea of approximation to natural language: zero-order approximation, first or second-order approximations, etc.

We mentioned earlier a sequence of letters in which the 26 letters of the alphabet have equal probability of appearance. Such a completely random

Table 4. *Mean frequency of occurrence of letters in a German text comprising one million lexical items (based on* ZEMANEK, *1959, with modifications taken from* STEINBUCH, *1965, p. 42)*

Letter	
Interval	151490
E	147004
N	88351
R	68577
I	63770
S	53881
T	47310
D	43854
H	43554
A	43309
U	31877
L	29312
C	26733
G	26672
M	21336
O	17717
B	15972
Z	14225
W	14201
F	13598
K	9558
V	7350
Ü	5799
P	4992
Ä	4907
Ö	2547
J	1645
Y	173
Q	142
X	129
Total	999985

sequence is a zero-order approximation to English. Following the principle of THORNDIKE-LORGE it can be stated how often each letter of the alphabet appears in a very long text in a language. A table (Table 4) with such values for German is presented on page 99 above.

If we put into a hat from which we want to draw random sequences of letters quantities of letters corresponding to the frequencies indicated in the table (and not as in a zero-order approximation all letters in equal quantities) a first-order approximation can be drawn. A German example is: NTDE SWNIKRUTARH ENIAS. An English example of a first-order approximation would be the following letter sequences: OCRO HLI RGWR NMIELWIS EU LL NBNESEBYA[1] etc.

With the next step we move from the discrete probabilities to the transitional probabilities which concern sequential psycholinguistics. We want to study the occurrence of two-letter sequences or digrams in English and German. A technique which is frequently employed in such studies is the following. A two-letter sequence is picked first, e.g., LE. Then the next occurrence in the text of E is looked for and the letter immediately following, for example, G. Subsequently we pick the next G in the text and the letter after it. The following item might, for example, be a space. A second-order approximation to German, produced in this way, looks as follows:

LEG OMSOFER ZE AN MEMENEIT SES KLACH

An example based on an English text would be:

ON IE ANTSOUTINYS ARE T INCTORE ST BE S DEAMY etc.

An illustration of German third-order approximation or trigram is:

NICH UND EIN WARTE TICHEN

English third-order approximations are:

IN NO IST LAT WHEY CRATICT FROURE BIRS GROCID etc.

What has been done so far on the level of the letter symbol can equally be done with the unit 'word'. The zero-order approximation consists of words picked at random from the dictionary. A first-order approximation contains words proportional to their general frequency as determined in the Thorndike-Lorge manner. Approximations of a higher order are commonly developed in the following way: the first person is given a word, e.g. 'come', with the request to add a word which might follow. A subject responds with the word 'with'. The next subject is given 'with' and might write 'sugar', the following subject adding to

---

[1] *Translator's note.* Besides the author's German examples, examples based on English and taken from SHANNON (1948) have been added.

'sugar', writes, for example, 'or'. This yields as a second-order approximation sequence: 'come with sugar or'[1].

This procedure which goes back to SHANNON uses verbal habits to arrive at statements on the structure of the language or to study the relationships between this structure and the psychological processes involved in speaking and hearing.

Approximations of the various orders at the word-unit level lead to the following English examples taken from SHANNON. First-order word approximations (chosen independently but with the appropriate frequencies): REPRESENTING AND SPEEDILY IS AN GOOD APT OR COME CAN DIFFERENT NATURAL HERE HE THE A IN etc.

Second-order word approximations: THE HEAD AND IN FRONTAL ATTACK ON AN ENGLISH WRITER THAT THE CHARACTER OF THIS POINT IS THEREFORE ANOTHER METHOD etc.[2].

As the order of approximation rises the influence of preceding elements on a subsequent item steadily increases. At a fourth-order approximation at word level, each individual word is determined by three preceding words. The context—this is in the nature of redundancy—produces certain constraints, but not an absolute compulsion, as to what may or may not occur in this context.

This series of approximations to genuine language is regarded by MILLER as a continuum starting with 'nonsense' at one pole and moving more and more towards meaningful utterances at the opposite pole. In other words, MILLER regards the difference between meaningless and meaningful utterances not as strict alternatives but as a finely graded dimension.

If it is heuristically profitable to equate the series of approximations with the dimension sense/nonsense, it should be possible to come to grips with a problem which has for a long time troubled the psychology of

---

[1] *Translator's note.* The author's German example starting from 'komme' has led to the sequence: 'komme ich bin doch ...'

[2] The following German examples are taken from an investigation by HERRMANN.

Zero-order:	Beweis Ausraufung stabil Linde Stiel gemäß der ...
	(Proof tearing-out stable lime-tree stem according the ...)
First-order:	Aus wurde Kino von über wir Thema noch Korn Grund ...
	(Out became cinema of over we topic still corn bottom ...)
Third-order:	Arbeit gedeiht im Januar schneit es oft lieber geschwätzig als Putzfrau fegen ...
	(Work thrives in January it snows often rather loquacious as cleaner sweep ...)
Sixth-order:	Mainz fand vorige Woche der Kongreß statt und endete mit Applaus aller ...
	(Mainz took place last week the congress and ended with applause of all ...)

learning, as well as psycholinguistics, viz, the problem why meaningful material should be learned and retained more easily than nonsense material. What was and was not meaningful, could hitherto only be determined subjectively; some critics consider the writings of EZRA POUND as less meaningful than the works of GOETHE. If MILLER's view is confirmed, the series of approximations to genuine language offers a possibility of determining operationally the dimension of meaningfulness.

Using words as units, MILLER and SELFRIDGE (1950) constructed approximations of different order. These were arranged in lists of varying length (10, 20, 30 and 50 words) so that there were: one set of four lists of different lengths of zero-order approximation, another set of four lists of varying lengths of first-order approximation, and so forth. Each list was recorded on magnetic wire, and subjects were asked to listen to these recordings. Each subject's task was to write down immediately what he had retained. The score was the percentage of words remembered correctly.

In Fig. 33 the co-ordinates are order of approximation and percentage of correctly remembered words. The parameter is the length of the list. The same results are represented in Fig. 34 with the order of approximation as the parameter and the length of the lists plotted along the abscissa.

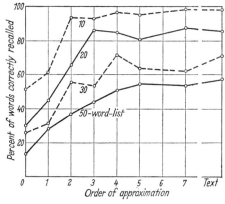

Fig. 33. Word-lists of varying length were presented (10, 20, 30 or 50 words). The figure shows the percentage of words recalled correctly as a function of the order of approximation to English (from MILLER and SELFRIDGE, 1950, p. 181).

As one would expect, the evidence shows, first of all, that the percentage of correctly remembered words declines, as the length of the list increases. Secondly, the evidence shows—and this is what interests us here—that the percentage of correctly remembered words increases with the rising order of approximation.

What stands out is that there is no variation in retention from about the fifth order of approximation, not even with 'genuine' text. Strictly speaking, all degrees of approximation are nonsense, but memory, it appears, does not function according to the dichotomy of philosophers; a passage of fifth or sixth order of approximation is retained as well as genuine text. Thus, the psychologically relevant distinction is not the sharp division between sense and nonsense, but the distinction between material in which earlier learning can become effective and material in

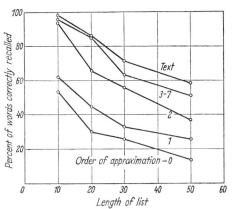

Fig. 34. Data as in Fig. 33. Percentage of words recalled correctly presented as a function of the length of the word-lists for different orders of approximation (0, 1, 2, 3 − 7) and authentic text.

which earlier learning has less influence. What has been learned earlier is the structured nature of language. As language is acquired, such learning includes the transitional probabilities which lead from one event to the next. The experiment by MILLER and SELFRIDGE is designed to make the effect visible upon retention of these acquired transitional probabilities. If in the past it used to be said that meaningful material is easier to retain because it is meaningful, we can now be more precise by saying: meaningful material is easier to retain because it contains, to a higher degree than nonsense material does, the transitional probabilities of everyday language.

The notion of transitional probabilities serves to conceptualize the sequential probability structure of the speech event. Investigations based on this concept study the relationship between the probability structure of language on one side and cognition, learning and retention of verbal material on the other.

The investigation by MILLER and SELFRIDGE was an attempt to study the effect of a certain form of redundancy. In MILLER'S experiments redundancy is a higher degree of approximation to English structure, or greater contextual determination or lowered content of information per unit. Such redundancy normally eases or improves the performance. MILLER made subjects learn redundant and less redundant letter sequences, ADELSON, MUCKLER and WILLIAMS (1955) letters in redundant and less redundant lists, RUBENSTEIN and ABORN (1954) an artificial language of varying degrees of redundancy: in every case learning improves with redundancy. However, this proposition is only applicable as long as the learning achievement is measured by the quantity of learned material. But as redundancy lowers the information content per unit, redundancy does not, or at least does not inevitably, increase the learning performance in terms of information theory.

The influence of order of approximation upon learning and retention of the material can of course be interpreted as positive transfer of verbal habits acquired through the use of everyday language. Whatever is in keeping with such habits does not have to be learned afresh again.

An effect of redundancy on the perception of speech was seen in a different context in the investigation by MILLER, HEISE and LICHTEN: under conditions of noise isolated words are not recognized as well as words in sentences. Speed of reading and writing is greater in sequences of a higher order of approximation than in sequences of a lower order (SUMBY and POLLACK, 1954).

In such investigations the length of the sequence used plays an important part, because if the sequence is too short, the effect of context, i.e., redundancy, is hardly noticeable. Even if we make subjects guess the gaps in a text, the process of guessing is guided by the verbal habits of the subject, or by the knowledge the subject possesses of the statistical structure of his native language. MILLER and FRIEDMAN (1957) found that, in sequences of eleven letter-symbols each, the first and last letter can be guessed correctly in fifty to sixty percent of cases, but the sixth letter, on the other hand, in 95 percent. The influence of context is effective in both the forward and the backward direction. If it was effective only in the forward direction, it should be possible to guess the final letter more easily than the sixth and the sixth better than the first. This finding leads beyond a pure Markov theory; and we shall, therefore, not pursue it for the moment.

How closely statistical factors of information content are in keeping with psychological factors in a narrower, traditional sense, can be seen when we mutilate a text in various ways. If a single letter is deleted, it can simply be omitted or be replaced by another without attracting particular attention. OLÉRON (1963) talks of varying dilutions of the same information content. The effect of these variations upon intelligibility has been clarified through a study by MILLER and LICKLIDER (1950). A speech event is interrupted to half its total duration of four minutes. But such 50 percent interruption can be distributed in various ways: it is possible to have two minutes speaking and two minutes interruption, or two seconds speaking, two seconds interruption, two seconds speaking, etc. The diagram (Fig. 35) shows that the effect upon perception is accordingly quite different.

As soon as one succeeds in identifying individual units, is it also possible to identify interrupted neighboring units via transitional probabilities. Here we should also mention the 'Cloze-procedure', developed by TAYLOR (1953). A person is tested for his skill in completing a text from which individual words have been eliminated ('Cloze' from 'closure' of configuration). With reference to the text the result gives information on redundancy, hence on the readability of the text. The procedure provides a measure of readability which is more serviceable than that developed by FLESCH. With reference to the reader it is indicative of his command of the language and his empathy with the text.

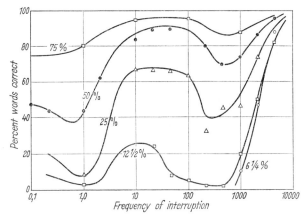

Fig. 35. Effect of interruptions of speech upon intelligibility of mono-syllabic words. The parameter is the percentage of the time during which the speech is turned on (based on MILLER and LICKLIDER, 1950, as reported in MILLER, 1951a, p. 71).

From quite a different angle similar problems were already encountered eighty years ago. According to J. McK. CATTELL (1885), in the same time span which is needed to identify four or five randomly chosen letters, it is possible to read three short words containing each four or five letters. ERDMANN and DODGE whose investigations on the reading process, round the turn of the century, became world-famous were able to show that complete words are still readable at a distance when individual letters can no longer be identified.

This is why in measuring visual acuity it is customary to use numbers because they suggest no transitional probabilities.

In direct continuation of these investigations and in parallel to the studies by HOWES (in which Thorndike values of exposed words had been varied) MILLER, BRUNER and POSTMAN displayed pseudo-words which in varying degrees approximated to the statistical structure of English words[1]. Figure 36 demonstrates the influence of statistical structure upon the threshold of perception.

What eminently practical consequences such investigations may have can be illustrated by the following study. WALLACH (1963) exposed nonsense words for brief moments to fifth-grade children. These words represented varying degrees of approximation to English. It was shown that good spellers among the children were able to recognize words of a higher order of approximation significantly faster than poor spellers.

---

[1] It should be mentioned in this context that pharmaceutical firms use a computer to compose all kinds of words of a similar type in order to select one as a new brand name for a manufactured product.

From this result it can be inferred that good spellers have acquired a knowledge of the transitional probabilities common in their language and they are able to transfer this knowledge to the solution of a new task.

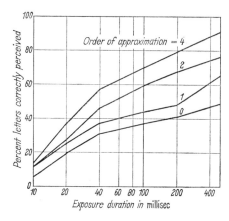

Fig. 36. Tachistoscopic presentation of eight-letter pseudowords. Curves are drawn for four different orders of approximation (based on MILLER, BRUNER and POSTMAN, from MILLER, 1951 a, p. 202)

How complex the relationships are, and how little is as yet known about the interaction with purely acoustic factors of the contextual factors we have just described, becomes evident in a most interesting investigation by POLLACK and PICKETT (1964) which takes us back to the studies of LADEFOGED and BROADBENT mentioned at the beginning of this chapter. The starting point is the fact that intelligibility of spoken text samples rises with the length of the sample. The authors now ask the following questions: Is the increase in intelligibility purely the result of an increased *structural* context (i.e., more words) or is it that in longer speech samples the increased *auditory* context provides, as it were, a clearer picture of the speaker's manner of speech so that indirectly in this way intelligibility is improved?

In the experiment subjects were given in advance all the words of a text, except the first one. The task was to guess this initial word which was masked by noise. For example, the text was: "Men and women walked slowly down the street." Subjects read the printed text: "— and women walked slowly down the street." Group 1 heard "Men" masked by noise, group 2 "Men and", and group 3 "Men and women". This means that groups 2 and 3 were acoustically offered words which were already known to the subjects as occurring in this position. In spite of that, with the addition of a second or third word, the intelligibility of the first word increased. If the structural context alone with its transitional probabilities were effective as a facilitating factor in the recognition of the first word, one would not expect an improvement from the fact that

other already known words are also presented acoustically. Instead
—LADEFOGED and BROADBENT had already hit upon that—there must
be something like an auditory context, a delicate tuning process of the
receptor mechanism to the acoustic peculiarities of this particular speaker.

The probability structures, stored in the receptor mechanism, determine to a large extent what this mechanism achieves. BROADBENT has
expressed it in a formula: if someone is supposed to reproduce what he
has read or heard, he tends to produce what he and others would have
uttered, if immediately beforehand they themselves had said what has
previously been uttered in the experiment. While the notion of verbal
habit, a concept akin to transitional probability, has thus moved into
the foreground, it must not be oversimplified. Even if the stimulus has
not been correctly understood, this does not mean that the most probable
state will automatically appear. If noise makes a word incomprehensible,
it is still possible for the number of syllables, for example, to have a co-
determining influence on the choice of what has been heard. To make this
evident, BROADBENT, following TREISMAN, assumes a series of dictionary
units. Each of these units corresponds to a given word. What actually
happens in this series is statistically determined by the units which have
just been activated and by the kind of immediate stimulation. BROAD-
BENT illustrates this approach by this example: Someone overhears in a
noisy room a political conversation and picks out the following fragment:
"I think that, at the next election Mr. Macmillan will ..." followed by a
monosyllabic word with the sound 'ite'. A position of readiness is adopted

Table 5. *(Based on* BROADBENT *in* REUCK *and* O'CONNOR,
1964, p. 85)

Words under consideration	Verb	Political context	-ite sound	One-syllable	Total
Bite	+	−	+	+	3
Stand	+	+	−	+	3
Appetite	−	−	+	−	1
Filibuster	+	+	−	−	2
Fight	+	+	+	+	4

by those units of the internal dictionary which correspond to verbs (to
satisfy syntax) and which have political significance (because of the
context). The sensory information adds to these response factors the

stimulus factors which reinforce the activity of monosyllabic units of those ending in 'ite'. The combination of these factors produces as the most probable word 'fight' and the listener will hear this word. But the decision is statistical and may be wrong; perhaps the speaker said 'bite'.

These dictionary units of BROADBENT'S are somewhat vague creations. But what is much more important for the continuation of our argument than their exact definition is the fact that in BROADBENT'S conception various factors are included in the statistical determination of a certain state: the syntactical structure of the sentence sequence and the content of the context as much as stimulus aspects.

A more accurate analysis of the differentation of these factors, however, would take us, as we shall see later, necessarily beyond the frame of a linear, left-to-right (Markov) model into the area that can with one key word be called grammar. At that point we shall have to come back to what we have just said (see chapter 13).

However, before grammar, i.e., the combinatorics of language, can be treated in a way which does not only operate with the relationship of probability linking a present state with preceding states, we have to view the word and its verbal surroundings under yet another aspect—that of 'association'.

Chapter 6

Phenomenology of Verbal Associations

From a sequential to an associationist viewpoint — The concept of association — GALTON and MARBE — Association experiments and everyday verbal behavior — Norms of association and their range of application — Group and personality factors in the differentiation of verbal habits — JUNG'S investigations and LAFFAL'S critique.

The present chapter adopts a different viewpoint from the preceding chapters, which dealt with sequential psycholinguistics. This change can be made clear by referring back to SAUSSURE. In his discussion on the arbitrary nature of symbols he says that symbols are restricted in two ways, or a speech event is determined by two groups of factors. The first group consists of the syntactical relationships which bind one link in the chain of an utterance with the preceding and subsequent ones. These are the relationships we considered in the preceding chapters; sequential psycholinguistics is concerned with syntactical and probabilistic structures which relate the constituents of a sentence to each other.

But a linguistic unit has other units not only before and after but also above and below it, so to speak; each link in the sentence chain is connected with other words, images or thoughts which are *associated* with it. As soon as a word is thought or uttered, other words simultaneously appear in consciousness or on the threshold of consciousness. According to SAUSSURE this is the second group of factors determining the speech event.

The distinction between the sequential and associative approach can be illustrated by the following example. A sentence: This man comes from Canada is a stretch in the dimension of time. As the sentence is uttered or heard, it is as if a pointer marking each moment of the utterance moved from one block to the next. Sequential psycholinguistics seeks to find the structures which link these blocks. In the previous chapter we confined ourselves to the probabilistic structures which, in the manner of a Markov model, combine a present element of the verbal sequence with preceding elements. Sequential psycholinguistics is concerned with the manifest portion of the speech event; and, as we shall shortly see, it is important to realize that sequential psycholinguistics requires no special aids or devices to make the elements among which it looks for structures visible or amenable to investigation. The material to be studied is readily available as the actual speech event.

Now supposing we stop the course of time at one point. One might almost say we shift from a diachronic to a synchronic viewpoint, although SAUSSURE, in making this distinction, thought in terms of larger blocks of time. Our question is whether in the verbal item which is just occurring there are links to latently present verbal materials in the speaker or listener.

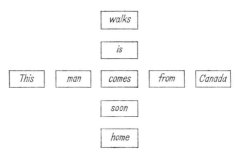

The associative approach which will occupy us in the following pages also looks for relationships but not for relationships which manifest themselves in the concrete speech event, but in the relations between a manifest unit and one (or more than one) latent or covert unit.

In discourse, in the sequence of the verbal utterance, as SAUSSURE said (Am. edition, 1959, p. 123), all elements are ordered in a linear fashion: combinations of such consecutive units are called syntagms. Outside discourse, or more precisely, between the element occurring in the utterance and the processes which simultaneously occur consciously or unconsciously in the listener or speaker, there are links of an associative character.

Syntagmatic links are relationships *in praesentia*. Associative links, on the other hand, as SAUSSURE says, bring together concepts, *in absentia*, into a potential series.

In order to be able to discover associative structures, the latent, covert *units*—as we shall call them more cautiously than if we spoke of *concepts*—must be actualized or made manifest by means of a special technique.

A technique or aid is needed to find out whether in addition to the manifest unit (the uttered word) something else is present and possibly active in the darkness of the subconscious. Such an aid is the word-association experiment which serves to transform an associative relationship which is not immediately tangible into a sequential and tangible one.

The principle of this experiment is the following: the subject is given a single unit (a word) with the instruction to respond to this unit with the first word that comes to his mind. The underlying rationale is: if no other structure determines what should follow (e.g., the intention to utter a particular sentence or the probabilistic determination derived from a particular sequence) then what follows is linked to the particular unit by association.

The concept of 'association' has certain mechanistic overtones — and for many linguistic scholars and psychologists in German-speaking countries 'mechanistic' is still a derogatory expression. Anyone who has reservations of this kind (and indeed anyone with reservations about the soulless quantitative approach in earlier sections of this book) might well consider a reflection by STENZEL who as a *philosopher* of language wrote as follows: "Even the expression at the sensory level and the combination of expressions into higher linguistic configurations are governed by certain regularities which are distinct from the freely intended meaning and yet are of greatest importance for the expressive possibilities of meanings through language. These regularities can be described as the laws of association ... An unprejudiced appreciation of the psychological study of language again reveals a basic antinomy of speech: language at each moment of its existence transcends the area of intended meaning and at the same time is still governed by the fundamentally different laws of the psychophysical plane from which it originates and from which it cannot escape. Here the power of association is the great provider of substance for expression, and objectively language, realized in the growth, life and decline of a particular idiom, is unthinkable without this primitive psychophysical foundation" (1934, p. 9).

The notion of *association* originated in Greek philosophy. Ideas, images, and thoughts are combined in such a way that the appearance of one brings to mind another *associated* with it. Such association can (e.g., according to ARISTOTLE) be brought about in two ways.

A first factor leading to such combinations consists in the *quality* of the images or thoughts. One image is associated with others which are either similar or stand in contrast to it. The word 'big' accordingly would be associated with 'huge' as well as with 'small'. This use of the notion of similarity can lead to difficulties: we associate what is similar—but, at the same time, similarity is what is associated.

The second source, from which associations may come, according to this view, is *experience*. What is experienced as simultaneous or successive is associated. If ideas *a* and *b* were once experienced as simultaneous or in close succession, idea *a* will, when it occurs in future, tend to call to consciousness idea *b*.

This view which sees the origin of association not in the inherent characteristics of the associated facts but in empirically verifiable events has remained to this day the foundation of the psychology of learning.

Above all the English school of philosophers of the eighteenth and nineteenth centuries regarded associations as the basic mechanism of the entire psychic life; HOBBES, LOCKE, HUME, the two MILLS and SPENCER should be mentioned here.

The attempt to comprehend the concept of association experimentally, previously only available in theory, is linked—like so many important events in psychology—with the name of GALTON.

GALTON simply wrote 75 words on slips of paper, put these away for a few days, then picking one of them without looking at it, put it under a book in such a way that by leaning over he could read what was written on it. As soon as he saw the word, he started a "chronograph" and stopped it again the moment two ideas in connection with this word had come to his mind. He divided the ideas which came to his mind into (a) visual or other imagery of past events; (b) histrionic representations, i.e., the re-enacting of an event or attitude, and (c) purely verbal ideas: names, sentences or quotations.

The frequencies with which these three classes appeared were 33, 22 and 45 percent. Basing himself on these experiments he expressed the following reflection in the journal *Brain:* "It would be very instructive to print the actual records at length, made by many experimenters, if the records could be clubbed together and thrown into a statistical form; but it would be too absurd to print one's own singly. They lay bare the foundations of a man's thoughts with curious distinctness and exhibit his mental anatomy with more vividness and truth than he himself would probably care to publish to the world" (1880, p. 162).

This statement by GALTON represents a milestone which is common to two, in other respects, very different lines of scientific development: on the one hand Freud's psychoanalysis, and on the other contemporary psychology of learning and psycholinguistics.

GALTON'S technique was in the first instance taken up by TRAUT-SCHOLDT (1883) in the first psychological laboratory, set up at that time by WUNDT in Leipzig, and then, above all, by one of Wundt's American doctoral candidates, J. McK. CATTELL (1886). From the beginning the studies almost always examined both of Galton's variables: first, the response made to a stimulus, and second, the time between stimulus and response. And even the instruction to the subject remained identical over the decades: 'I am going to read to you (*or in visual presentation*, 'I am going to show to you') a list of words. After each word please answer with the first word that comes to your mind.'

What this prototype of the association experiment demonstrates is regarded—as was already pointed out—as a connection resulting either from the quality of the associated words (similarity or contrast) or as a connection resulting from an earlier experience of co-occurrence of the two words. To use the modern terminology of the psychology of learning, one would say that the association experiment examines a stimulus-response bond (S-R bond) or habit by presenting to the subject a stimulus S and noting which response R is made and the reaction-time with which this R is made. That a particular R is related to a particular S is regarded as the result of an earlier reinforcement which initiated and strengthened the associative bond between S and R.

As can be seen, the study of association and its theoretical foundations brings psycholinguistics into the neighborhood of the psychology of learning (similarly, sequential psycholinguistics found a place close to information theory). This link with the psychology of learning will prove to be crucial because it connects psycholinguistics with many other fields; above all it gives access to the mechanisms of language acquisition to be discussed later.

Let us begin our presentation of the results of association studies by a relatively detailed report on some older inquiries in order to see in perspective what sort of data are produced by subjects in an association experiment.

In 1901 THUMB and MARBE published a study which to this day has remained fundamental[1]. Sixty words, one after another, were called out to the subjects; the list was made up of ten terms of family relations (father, mother ...), ten adjectives (big, small ...), ten pronouns (I, you ...), ten adverbials of place (in front of, where ...), ten adverbials of time (when, now ...) and the numerals one to ten—all these in random order. The responses of the subjects were noted as well as the time between stimulus and response.

It was found that generally terms of family relations led to answers with terms of family relations; indeed a particular stimulus-word would lead to quite a particular response. In the cases investigated by MARBE the reaction to 'brother' was always 'sister', to 'son' generally 'father' rarely 'daughter' and never 'brother' or 'uncle'. The associations called out by a stimulus-word do not consist of *any* words, but they fall into distinct classes. For each stimulus-word one can rank the frequency of occurrence of different responses. In the terminology of the psychology of learning it might be formulated as follows: if the S-R sequence in an association experiment is regarded as a habit, the habits released by a stimulus-word vary in strength. This formulation is possible, because the probability of occurrence is the principal indicator of habit-strength. Accordingly, the habit of responding to the word 'son' with 'father' would be stronger than the habit of reacting to 'son' with 'daughter'.

---

[1] Incidentally, this investigation was the result of a collaboration—rare in German-speaking countries—between a linguist and a psychologist. THUMB was a professor of comparative philology, MARBE a lecturer in philosophy at Würzburg.

If, in analogy to the psychology of learning, the probability of occurrence of a response is treated as an indicator of habit- or associative-strength, it is not far-fetched to inquire also into the other indicator of habit-strength, the reaction-time between S and R. MARBE found that in general more frequently preferred associations occur more rapidly than less preferred ones.

The curve in which MARBE related the frequency of occurrence of an association to reaction-time has found its place in the history of psychology as MARBE'S law.

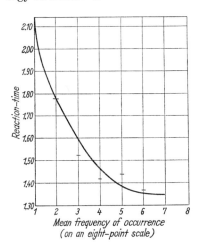

Fig. 37. Reaction-time for association as a function of the frequency of occurrence (based on THUMB and MARBE, 1901, p. 46)

On the abscissa MARBE plotted the frequency of occurrence on an eight-point scale, on the ordinate the mean reaction-times. It will be seen that "the reaction-time with increasing frequency of the responses decreases rapidly at first, then more and more slowly and finally hardly at all" (p. 46).

Continuing our discussion we interpret the THUMB-MARBE investigations as follows:

(a) Stimulus- and response-words in an association experiment are often, but not always, similar in form: kinship terms are met with kinship terms, nouns with nouns and adjectives with adjectives. The stimulus, as it were, unlocks a certain class, or touches off a certain category which thus leads to the selection of an actual response. A definite regularity of linguistic behavior is thus indicated.

(b) A given stimulus-word produces identical responses in different subjects to a marked degree. The relative frequency of certain associations is, therefore, an important starting point for further inquiries.

(c) The delay between stimulus and response or reaction-time stands in a lawful relationship to the relative frequency of occurrence of a response.

This time score, therefore, can equally be subjected to further investigation.

Historically (and logically) the first steps in the systematic advance in this area have been the following:

First, a 'phenomenology' or inventory of associations is established. Which are the most frequent associations with 'table', 'bed', 'chair', 'drive', 'work', 'long', and 'love'? With what frequency do they occur? What is the next most frequent response? In other words, the first step consists in the setting up of norms.

Secondly, certain questions result from these considerations: how widely do these norms apply? Do French speakers respond to the same stimulus-words differently from English speakers? Are the habitual verbal responses of, say, manual workers different from those of university students? Are there changes with the age of the subjects in the relative frequency of particular associations?

Thirdly, how are we to interpret individual deviations from these norms? Is the fact that someone fails to react with the most common associations significant for the total verbal behavior of that individual or even his non-verbal behavior? We can put the same question for the other index of associative strength: Can any significance be attributed to the fact that in the case of a given individual certain responses appear only after an unusually long reaction-time?

In short, our questions are concerned (a) with the general principles of organization of the fields of force underlying verbal behavior, (b) with social, cultural and developmental variants of these principles of organization and, finally, (c) with personality-specific variations which may be symptomatic only for verbal behavior, but which may also be indices of extralinguistic aspects of behavior.

Norms were established above all through the investigations of KENT and ROSANOFF, published in 1910, and based on the responses of 1000 subjects. The table below shows the distribution of responses to the stimulus-word 'needle'.

This investigation shows that a small number of responses appear relatively frequently, while a large number are produced only by single subjects. The most frequent response to a stimulus-word is called the *primary response*.

As previously, each response can be characterized by its frequency, and responses can be arranged in rank-order of frequency. An obvious step is to investigate whether these two variables obey ZIPF's law. SKINNER (1937) took up this question and—with rank order plotted on the abscissa and frequency as the ordinate on logarithmic paper—again found ZIPF's well-known straight line, an impressive hint of the regularities prevailing in this area.

8*

Table 6. *Distribution of associations with the stimulus-word 'needle'. The left-hand column indicates the number of subjects who responded to 'needle' with the word in the right-hand column.* (WOODWORTH, *1954, p. 51*)

Stimulus-word: needle

Frequency in 1000 subjects	Response-word
160	thread
158	pin(s)
152	sharp
135	sew(s)
107	sewing
53	steel
40	point
26	instrument
17	eye
15	thimble
12	useful
11	prick(s)
9	pointed
7	cotton
6	work
5	implement
5	tool
4	cloth
4	darning
4	knitting
4	sharpness
3	article
3	fine
3	metal
2 each	books, button(s), clothes, coat, dressmaker, hurt, hypodermic, industry, pricking, small, sting, thick, thin,
1 each	blood, broken, camel, crocheting, cut, diligence, embroidery, handy, help, hole, home, housewife, labor, long, magnetic, material, mending, nail, ornament, patching, pincushion, shiny, slippers, stitching, surgeon, tailor, use, using, weapon, wire, woman
$\overline{1000}$	

For the 75 words with the highest primary response frequencies on the Kent-Rosanoff list SKINNER was able to compute the frequency f with which a given association would occur in the 1000 subjects, as a function of the rank position R of this association, by applying the following formula:

$$f = \frac{300}{R^{1.29}}$$

HORVATH (1963) likewise tried to find a quantitative expression for the distribution of the frequency of associative responses to a stimulus-word. In contrast to SKINNER he did not use for his approach either the average values of responses to many stimuli or the rather clumsy rank positions. On the basis of a knowledge of the number of *different* associations (n_k) and the total number of associations in general (k), he was able to predict fairly accurately how many associations to a given stimulus-word would occur only once and how many would appear twice or three times, etc. The number of associations which occur only once can be calculated with the formula:

$$f_{(1)} = \frac{n_k}{2 - \alpha}$$

where $\alpha = \dfrac{n_k}{k}$, as parameter, describes the entire curve of distribution. The number of associations with frequencies of two, three, four etc., or i, can equally be calculated with corresponding formulae.

The example of Kent-Rosanoff norms for the word 'table' indicates the high degree of agreement between empirically determined values and those calculated according to the formula.

Table 7. *Distribution of responses to the word 'table'*
(based on HORVATH, 1963, p. 362)

Frequency of occurrence of a given response-word: i	Number of words occur-ring i times $f(i)$	Expected values according to the formula
1	28	24
2	7	8
3	3	4
4 or more	9	11

$$X^2 = 1.41, \quad p \simeq 0.7$$

Another example will show the advantage of this method of computation in comparison with one which only takes into account the primary response frequency. The primary response to 'blossom', according to the norms, has the same frequency as the primary response to 'high'. In spite of this, the distribution of responses to these two stimuli is quite different, because α is different. The word 'blossom' elicited 63 different responses and therefore $\alpha = \dfrac{63}{1009} = 0.0625$, while 90 different responses were recorded to the word 'high' which yields $\alpha = \dfrac{90}{1009} = 0.0896$. A comparison of these distributions computed with the help of these figures and distributions based on empirical evidence shows a large measure of agreement.

Before giving a relatively detailed account of word-association experiments, it is appropriate to ask a fundamental question: are the phenomena which appear in a word-association test and which can be manipulated experimentally applicable to verbal behavior outside the experimental situation? The word-association test can only serve as an instrument of analysis of verbal behavior if it is legitimate to 'apply' to linguistic behavior in general the relationships and regularities revealed in the rather restricted experimental situation.

An attempt to answer this question has been made by comparing behavior produced in an association experiment with verbal behavior of everyday life. HOWES (1957) counted the absolute frequencies with which words of certain categories appeared in both the experimental and the everyday situation. If there is a high correlation between these two frequency tables it can be argued that the verbal sampling in the experiment is stochastically equivalent to ordinary language use. It would, then, be justifiable to infer that the special conditions of an experiment do not lead to a change in the behavior which an individual normally employs in the selection of words. On the other hand, if there is a low correlation it must be concluded that verbal behavior in the association test is evidently governed by different rules from behavior in ordinary language situations and the word-association test could not be used to throw light on the dynamics of normal language use.

In practice, HOWES proceeded as follows: he compared the summed associative probability of a word, i.e., its absolute frequency of occurrence in the norms developed by KENT and ROSANOFF, with the probability of the occurrence of the word in everyday language use expressed by the corresponding Thorndike-Lorge values. This comparison gives the following picture.

It reveals a strong but not undisturbed positive correlation. HOWES succeeded with a good deal of mathematical ingenuity to subject these data to a further analysis. For Thorndike-Lorge frequencies below 800 (i.e., words which occur rarely in everyday usage) high correlations (.94) with frequencies in the association test are found. But an almost sudden change in the relationship appears at the higher Thorndike-Lorge frequencies. How can this be explained? What kind of words appear so frequently in everyday language, but are infrequent in the association studies? They are articles, conjunctions, auxiliaries, prepositions and pronouns; HOWES calls them collectively *interstitial words*, because their common function in the flow of speech is to link words of different categories. Not only do these words not occur in the associations of the subjects, they do not appear among the stimuli of the Kent-Rosanoff list. This list, therefore, in this respect cannot be regarded as a representative sample of vocabulary in general use.

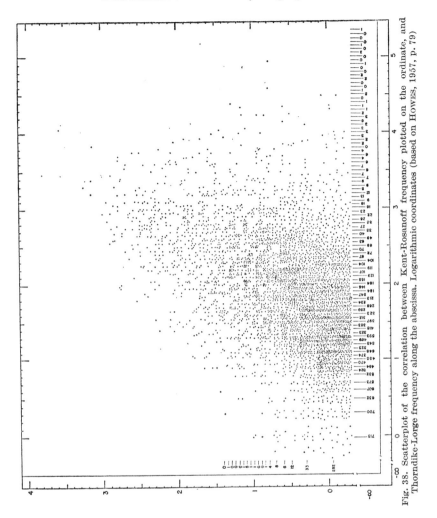

Fig. 38. Scatterplot of the correlation between Kent-Rosanoff frequency plotted on the ordinate, and Thorndike-Lorge frequency along the abscissa. Logarithmic coordinates (based on HOWES, 1957, p. 79)

If this argument is right, it would follow that by the introduction of interstitial words as stimuli in the association experiment the frequency of interstitial words would be considerably raised. An experiment along these lines was carried out by JENKINS. In contrast to the original Kent-Rosanoff experiment, the responses in this class of words rose twentyfold.

On the basis of these results HOWES reached the conclusion that verbal behavior in the association experiment was stochastically equivalent to the verbal behavior in unstructured situations.

We should mention in this connection an investigation by SAPORTA (1955b), in which the subjects were asked to use the stimulus-words of the Kent-Rosanoff list to form simple sentences. It was shown that in these sentences there was a preference for those words which in the word-association test appeared as frequent associations to a particular stimulus-word.

From these and numerous similar studies it appears possible to make successful predictions of inter-relationships in verbal behavior on the basis of the association experiment. Of course, this does not mean that such predictions can be made with certainty in each individual case.

After this digression let us now go back to our main argument. Once we have collected associations and determined their frequencies in order to gain a first impression of the psychological context in which a word is found, the question arises whether it might not be possible to order or classify such associations in a systematic way. If it were possible to find a system permitting a smooth and natural classification of associations, one might regard the structure of this system as a model of the structure of the organizing processes which occur during the associative act and which determine the result fo the association experiment. It is, therefore, entirely justifiable to try to find a good system of classification, but so far the attempt to do so has failed. Some of the proposed systems are described below.

WUNDT (1893) offers the following divisions:

Table 8. (WUNDT, *1893, vol. 2, p. 455*)

Main Form I: Outer Associations

Sub-Form I: Association of simultaneous ideas

I. Association of the parts of a single simultaneous idea 1. from whole to parts 2. from parts to whole	II. Association of independent co-existing ideas

Sub-Form II: Association of successive ideas

I. Association of successive sound percepts (principally word associations) 1. in their original sequence 2. in a modified sequence	II. Association of successive visual and other sense perceptions 1. in their original sequence 2. in a modified sequence

Main Form II: Inner Associations

I. Higher/lower-order associations 1. Association of a superordinate idea 2. Association of a subordinate idea	II. Association according to the principle of co-ordination 1. Association of a similar idea 2. Association of a dissimilar idea	III. Association according to the principles of dependence 1. causal dependence 2. purposive dependence

WUNDT himself, however, expresses skepticism with regard to such systems; he writes (*Grundzüge* III, 1911, p. 522): "(it) is ... obvious that the categories into which the results of such experiments can be classified after the event, hardly deserve the name of 'forms of association' or 'laws of association'. It is of course possible to order especially word associations (our main concern here — *The author*) according to some logical system. The simplest system of this kind is indeed the admittedly rather superficial one of the ancient four forms of associations of similarity, contrast, simultaneity and succession. The only merit of such a logical system is that, combined with statistics on particular forms, it would provide some account of the direction in which the cognitive mechanism of an individual moves subject to his natural aptitude and the influences of his social and formal education." (No small achievement, one might add from the standpoint of half a century later.)

The predominance of formal logic in WUNDT'S approach was already criticized by THUMB and MARBE. In their view WUNDT'S system is less a classification of associations than of semantic relationships of the associated words.

A psychologically more profitable classification is offered by WOOD-WORTH who distinguishes:

(1) Definitions, including synonyms and supra-ordinates,

(2) Completion and predication,

(3) Coordinates and contrasts,

(4) Valuations and personal associations.

To illustrate the application of this scheme, let us classify some responses to the stimulus-word 'needle'. We place under (1): 'instrument', 'tool', 'article', and possibly 'sewing'; under (2): 'sharp', 'steel', 'pointed', 'eye', 'work'; under (3): 'thread', 'cloth', 'pin'; and under (4): 'prick', 'hurt', 'blood', and possibly 'useful'.

The dynamic way in which WOODWORTH conceives his classification can be seen from the fact that he calls the first class the 'arriving' response, the second the 'staying by' and the third the 'jumping away' responses.

It has frequently been noted that the different classes of such a classification can also be distinguished by their reaction-times (e.g., KARWOSKI and SCHACHTER, 1948). Certain kinds of associations (e.g., contrast associations), it appears, occur faster than others. However, it remains an open question whether this finding is linked with THUMB and MARBE'S result according to which frequency of occurrence of a response determines the reaction-time.

While the investigations so far reported were concerned with accurate and serviceable descriptions of the associations of the experimental subjects, we now turn to the question of how these norms are changed or differentiated, if we do not deal simply with subjects in general, but with subjects belonging to defined groups. In other words, we are not now studying verbal habits as such, but the verbal habits of defined groups. The following discussion, therefore, lies on the borderline between psycholinguistics and sociolinguistics.

Thanks to investigations by RUSSELL and ROSENZWEIG we are now in a position to compare American, French and German groups of students. The basis of these investigations was, throughout, the Kent-Rosanoff list of stimulus-words and their translations. Table 9 below shows a part of the 100 stimulus-words with their corresponding primary responses (i.e., the most frequent associations) in each of the three linguistic groups.

Table 9. *Stimulus-words of the word-association test, primary responses in German, French and English and for each response percentage of subjects (partially reproduced from RUSSELL and MESECK, 1959, p. 196)*

German, French, English	% German	% French	% English
1. Tisch, table, table	29 Stuhl	53 chaise	84 chair
2. dunkel, sombre, dark	44 hell, e	45 clair	83 light
3. Musik, musique, music	9 Ton, Töne	16 note, s	18 song, s
4. Krankheit, maladie, sickness	15 Gesundheit	10 santé	38 health
5. Mann, homme, man	52 Frau	66 femme	77 woman, en
6. tief, profond, deep	49 hoch	12 creux	32 shallow
7. weich, mou, soft	39 hart	39 dur, e	45 hard
8. Essen, manger, eating	23 trinken	39 boire	39 food
9. Berg, montagne, mountain	35 Tal	13 plaine	27 hill, s
10. Haus, maison, house	14 Hof	14 toit	25 home
11. schwarz, noir, black	48 weiß	41 blanc	25 white
12. Hammelfleisch, mouton, mutton	7 Rindfleisch, Essen	25 laine	37 lamb
13. Bequemlichkeit, confort, comfort	15 Sessel	19 fauteuil	12 chair
14. Hand, main, hand	20 Fuß	25 pied, s	26 foot, (ee)
15. kurz, petit, short	53 lang	48 grand	40 tall
16. Obst, fruit, fruit	18 Gemüse	20 pomme, s	38 apple
17. Schmetterling, papillon, butterfly	12 Falter	11 fleur, s	15 moth
18. glatt, lisse, smooth	34 Eis	18 rugueux	33 rough
19. kommandieren, ordre, command	23 befehlen	24 désordre	20 order
20. Stuhl, chaise, chair	20 Tisch	24 table	50 table
21. süß, doux, sweet	39 sauer	11 dur, e	44 sour

In 1961 ROSENZWEIG compared the available data in American, German, French and Italian Kent-Rosanoff studies; he determined the number of cases in which the associative primary response to a particular stimulus-word was equivalent in meaning with that given to the corresponding stimulus in the other language. The response to 'table' in English is 'chair', to 'Tisch' in German 'Stuhl', and to 'table' in French 'chaise'. This suggests that there are associative structures transcending single linguistic communities[1]. The more frequently a primary response occurs in one language, the greater is the probability that the equivalent response to the corresponding stimulus-word also occurs in kindred languages.

Even more interesting than the comparison of the semantic content of the associations is a comparison of frequencies with which certain associations appear in different languages.

RUSSELL and MESECK (1959) have made the following generalization: if the primary responses to the Kent-Rosanoff list are compared, a highly asymmetrical distribution is revealed. Very large frequencies are rare; the median lies round 16 percent. A particularly striking qualitative feature is that primary responses with largest frequencies are contrast responses.

If the German and French experimental groups are compared, a high measure of agreement of the frequency distribution will be found. This, of course, does not mean that 'Fenster' and 'fenêtre' elicit *identical* responses, the agreement refers to the degree of spread of certain associations in general. But it is here that a surprising difference occurs between the French and German groups on the one side and the American group on the other. As an illustration let us take item 49 from Table 10: 'Adler', 'eagle' and 'aigle' all yield as primary responses 'bird' or their equivalents in the other languages, but among German and French students these primary responses have frequencies of 21 and 16 percent respectively, whereas 55 percent of all American students respond to 'eagle' with 'bird'. Similar trends are noted with many other responses.

Thus, in the American group there is a marked tendency to react uniformly to a stimulus-word, whereas the associations elicited by the stimulus-words in the German and French groups are much more heterogeneous. Nearly a quarter of all American associations produce higher frequencies than the most frequent German association. The difference between the mean value of the two curves of distribution is significant at the .001 level.

To sum up, in content, the associations in the three languages are very similar to each other; only quantitatively there is this surprising

---

[1] A somewhat more problematical comparison of word associations in the four European languages with the associations of Navaho Indians suggests a far greater degree of agreement among the European languages than between each of these and the Navaho language.

disparity. This result provokes speculation about national psychology. Fortunately there is empirical evidence to guide such speculations.

Table 10. *Stimulus-words of the association test, primary responses in German, English and French and for each response percentage of subjects. (Section from* RUSSELL *and* MESECK, *1959, p. 197)*

German, French, English	% German	% French	% English
49. Adler, aigle, eagle	21 Vogel	16 (l')oiseau	55 bird
50. Magen, estomac, stomach	14 Darm	8 digestion	21 food
51. Stiel, tige, stem	39 Besen	33 fleur, s	40 flower
52. Lampe, lampe, lamp	36 Licht	35 lumière	63 light
53. träumen, rêver, dream	19 schlafen	17 sommeil	45 sleep
54. gelb, jaune, yellow	12 rot	11 vert	15 blue
55. Brot, pain, bread	20 essen	11 (et) vin	61 butter
56. Gerechtigkeit, justice, justice	12 Gericht	9 juge, s	25 peace
57. Junge, garçon, boy	37 Mädchen	42 fille	76 girl
58. Licht, clair, light	22 dunkel	31 obscur	64 dark
59. Gesundheit, santé, health	35 Krankheit	19 maladie	25 sickness
60. Bibel, évangile, Bible	20 Buch	11 Dieu	23 God
61. Gedächtnis, mémoire, memory	8 Gehirn	18 souvenir, s	12 mind
62. Schaf, agneau, sheep	15 Wolle	15 brebis	20 wool
63. Bad, bain, bath	18 Wasser	16 (de) mer	31 clean
64. Häuschen, villa, cottage	17 Garten (ä)	16 maison	30 house
65. schnell, rapide, swift	32 langsam	35 train	37 fast
66. blau, bleu, blue	25 Himmel	31 ciel	17 sky
76. hungrig, faim, hungry	20 durstig	24 soif	36 food
68. Priester, prêtre, priest	17 Kirche	13 noir, e	33 church
69. Ozean, océan, ocean	34 Meer	24 mer	31 water
70. Kopf, tête, head	13 Haare	11 cheveu, x	13 hair
71. Ofen, fourneau, stove	17 Wärme	19 (de) cuisine	23 hot
72. lang, long, long	44 kurz	24 court	75 short
73. Religion, religion, religion	12 Glaube	9 prêtre, s	28 church

J. J. JENKINS of the University of Minnesota, one of the leading researchers in this area, has published a comparison of earlier American association norms with present-day norms. SCHELLENBERG'S norms for freshmen at Minnesota in 1929 are available, and in the early fifties JENKINS and RUSSELL produced new Kent-Rosanoff norms for Minnesota freshmen. While it was hitherto tacitly assumed that such norms are relatively stable over time, since the language remains fairly constant over a time span of twenty years, this comparison clearly revealed that this assumption was not justified. The frequency of primary answers had changed. The most frequent responses of 1929 were still the most frequent in 1952 but their frequency had increased by one third. The comparison with the Kent-Rosanoff norms of 1910 suggests that idiosyncratic responses (produced only by a single individual) become more and more infrequent.

In 1952 nearly all responses are identical. If in the earlier investigation the three most frequent responses to a stimulus-word made up hardly half of all the responses, in the more recent study they constitute two thirds. In other words, the communality of responses has risen.

Other results of this diachronic comparison are: the so-called super-ordinate response (red—color) are replaced by more specific ones (red—white); abstract responses decrease; concrete responses increase. The question asked by JENKINS why this change should have occurred is of some interest, because one might say quite tentatively that it looks as if the German and French results are like the American ones of 1929. JENKINS suggests that the reason for this trend towards uniformity and 'concreteness' is the growing 'outer-directedness' of society in Riesman's sense, i.e., the literally overwhelming influence of the mass media, of advertising, and the standardization of school instruction. He concludes his interpretation with the words: "If the associative processes relate to thought as we suspect they do, then the age of 'group-think' is virtually upon us" (1959, p. 584).

The method of procedure adopted here to make the group conformity of associations an object of inquiry will engage our attention once more at a later stage; at present we are continuing the discussion of differences in associative behavior between groups.

The question must be raised whether such differences occur not only between different linguistic communities and can, therefore, be accounted for by differences between the languages in question, but also whether within one linguistic community they might not follow the boundary lines between various social groups.

Investigations on this question began shortly after the turn of the century. According to WRESCHNER (1907) 60 percent of university students and professors produce associations which belong to the same parts of speech as the stimulus-words, whereas only 48 percent of workers responded in the same way. In more recent times ROSENZWEIG (1964) has made systematic comparisons between French students and workers and between American students and workmen. In the French group there are much greater differences between students and workmen than in the American group. Whereas in France only 40 percent of the primary responses are identical, in the USA 68 percent are alike. The responses of French students are more in accord with those of American students than with those of French workmen.

ROSENZWEIG tries to connect this result with the finding reported above, according to which more agreement or a higher degree of communality of responses is to be found in the USA in general. He formulates the hypothesis that American students are a less highly selected group of the total population and, therefore, perhaps reach a somewhat lower educational and intellectual level than the French students, because in the USA a higher percentage of the total population goes to college. If this difference in selection were to account for these results, one should expect that a sample of workmen would show even greater communality of response than can be found in American students. To test this hypothesis ROSENZWEIG calculated an index of communality: if the primary, secondary and tertiary responses (i.e., the most frequent, the second most frequent and the third most frequent) are taken together, the following percentages of all responses are included:

in the case of French workmen   33.3 percent

French students   37.0 percent

American workmen 54.4 percent

American students 59.1 percent

It follows that Rosenzweig's hypothesis has not been confirmed.

Using the index of communality ROSENZWEIG also calculated correlations between the groups.

Table 11. *Correlations between indices of communality of four groups of subjects (based on* ROSENZWEIG, *1964, p. 63)*

Group	American workers	French students	French workers
American students	0.756	0.646	0.150
American workers		0.777	0.279
French students			0.445

In this procedure the index of communality, i.e., the agreement of the frequency of occurrence of the most frequent associations, had been used as a measure of agreement between the groups. As was mentioned above, WRESCHNER, instead of operating with frequency of occurrence of the primary responses, used the agreement between stimulus and response with reference to grammatical category. What picture do we obtain with regard to this criterion in the case of American and French students and workmen?

The French workers responded to a total of 70 nouns 36 times with a noun, 27 times with an adjective and 7 times with a verb. If the three classes of stimuli are taken together, the result is that, in 45 percent of the primary responses of the French workers, stimulus and response agree in part of speech. In the case of the French students this agreement is much higher, i.e., 87 percent.

Table 12. *Classification of primary responses (based on* ROSENZWEIG, *1964, p. 63)*

Stimuli	French workers' responses			Stimuli	American workers' responses		
	Noun	Adj.	Verb		Noun	Adj.	Verb
Noun	36	27	7	Noun	61	5	2
Adj.	20	8	0	Adj.	4	26	0
Verb	1	0	1	Verb	1	1*	1
			45				88
Stimuli	French students' responses			Stimuli	American students' responses		
	Noun	Adj.	Verb		Noun	Adj.	Verb
Noun	63	6	1	Noun	56	6	5
Adj.	6	22	0	Adj.	5	25	0
Verb	0	0	2	Verb	1	1	1
			87				82

* Adverb

The comparison with American figures must be made with some reservation because in English it is not always perfectly clear in which grammatical category a response is to be classified (e.g., 'drink' as verb or noun).

A fact which ROSENZWEIG regards as particularly striking is that French workers only rarely respond to adjectives with adjectives, whereas among other groups the adjectival contrast associations (high-low) are particularly common. It is now known, thanks to a study by CARROLL, KJELDERGAARD and CARTON (1962-63), that these opposite-evoking adjectives in particular strongly contribute to a high degree of communality. The two trends found among French working-class subjects, i.e., low communality and few contrast associations, might well be connected with each other.

If the reported studies are reviewed, one is likely to find confirmation for ROSENZWEIG'S conclusion that subjects belonging to the same language community but to different social groups may have different verbal habits. In France where class differences between workmen and students are greater than in the USA, the differences in verbal habits are correspondingly also larger.

We started our survey on associative behavior with a description of empirical norms. We then considered the area of application of these norms, i.e., we asked ourselves whether a single set of responses or a single distribution of frequencies is adequate for a description of the associative habits of *all* members of a linguistic community. In the attempt to answer this question we found it necessary to differentiate according to sociological groupings.

We must now add other differentiations to the differences already found within one linguistic community: viz, according to sex and age of the subject. PALERMO and JENKINS (1965) compared the associations of male and female college students. Women give fewer different responses to each stimulus, respond more frequently than men with one of the four most frequent responses to a stimulus, and tend to give fewer superordinate responses.

It has been known since approximately 1915 that children have different associations from adults. But it is only in recent years—especially through the investigations by ERVIN (1961 a), ENTWISLE, FORSYTH and MUUS (1964)—that more exact information has become available.

As we have seen, adults tend to respond with the same grammatical class as that of the stimulus-word. A noun is followed by a noun, and a verb by a verb; i.e., adults predominantly give paradigmatic associations. The two words appearing as stimulus or response could be substituted for each other in a sentence frame. By way of example suppose the sentence frame is 'I can see a . . .', the empty slot can be filled by 'chair', or 'table', as well as by 'man', 'woman', 'light' or 'difference'. In another sentence frame, 'The man is walking. . .', we might add 'slowly' or 'along', but not 'table' or 'chair'. In the actual speech event we select one word from a paradigmatic set (chair, table, man, woman, light, difference . . .); the mechanism involved is called *selection* by SAUSSURE.

While adults predominantly choose paradigmatic associations, children generally make syntagmatic responses. They tend to respond to 'table' not with 'chair', but perhaps with 'sit', 'eat' or 'work'. The adult associates words like 'running' or 'standing' with 'walking', while a child produces 'about' or 'home'. In the child, stimulus and response are not related as words which can be substituted for each other in a sentence frame, but as words which in a sentence normally follow each other. The corresponding mechanism is, according to SAUSSURE, not selection but *combination*.

Selection and combination are also considered basic linguistic processes in speech pathology. JAKOBSON (1955), for example, used these two concepts in a classification of different forms of aphasia.

The difference in associative behavior of children and adults, therefore, lies mainly in the fact that children produce predominantly syntagmatic associations and adults paradigmatic ones. The change from one to the other occurs nowadays mainly between the ages of 6 and 8. This observation can be further supplemented by the following interesting diachronic study: comparable data of 1916 are available in a study by

WOODROW and LOWELL which shows that the shift from syntagmatic to paradigmatic associations occurred between the ages of 9 and 12. Once again we will have to bear in mind that the child today, because of radio and television, is much more exposed to spoken language at an early age. But it may well be a consequence of the general acceleration of development that today the verbal habits of childhood are replaced by those of the adults at an earlier age than 50 years ago.

RIEGEL and RIEGEL (1964) investigated modifications of associative behavior at more advanced ages and found an increase in variability of responses. It is interesting to note that older subjects are more inclined to respond syntagmatically than younger ones (between ages 17 to 19); this further change has not yet been adequately explained.

Next we turn to the question of whether the word-association test might not only reveal group characteristics but also indicate *personality-specific speech habits*. PETERSON and JENKINS (1957) investigated to what extent individuals with extremely high communality of response (i.e., extremely high agreement with associations of the majority) distinguish themselves from those with extremely low communality. In this study communality is treated as a dimension whose expression in a given case is characteristic of an individual. But since this investigation was strongly ideographic no generalizable results were obtained. BLOCK (1960) and others found no distinctions.

CARROLL, KJELDERGAARD and CARTON (1962-63) were able to show that communality is probably not a uniform dimension, but at least partially results from opposite-evoking stimuli in the Kent-Rosanoff list; it would be more promising to group subjects, according to their results, into those with many and those with few opposite-responses.

In connection with a search for personality-specific traits in associative behavior the studies by JUNG are particularly worth mentioning. Shortly after the turn of the century JUNG undertook word association experiments in which he employed as stimuli words which might have a special emotional significance, for the subject, i.e., words which he considered as indicative of 'complexes'. JUNG understood a complex to be a negatively toned system of recollections, images or wishes, which can, so to speak, be activated by the particular stimulus-word—even if, as is normally the case, the complex has been repressed. In JUNG'S view, such complexes become evident in an association test by a number of indicators, among which the most important one is the lengthening of reaction-time. Other symptoms are refusal of a response, stimulus repetition, deviant or echo associations ('table'—'able'). To what extent the mechanism of repression plays a role, can be seen from the following procedure: if after the test a second run-through with the same stimuli is made, it is found that just those responses to the stimuli which are apparently complex-charged have already been forgotten and must be replaced by others.

Admittedly, the reliability of the complex indicators is an open question. It is by no means certain that it is just the emotional problem which leads to difficulties in association. In the chapter on sequential psycholinguistics it was pointed out that, for example, in the area of perceptual defense the factor of emotionality can and must often be replaced by frequency factors. It is, therefore, appropriate to examine JUNG's model of associative disturbance—or the emotional influence on verbal habits—in the light of response frequency.

In studying this problem LAFFAL (1955) starts from an assumption which, in another context, will be discussed later in more detail: it is that the frequency distribution of the responses to a given stimulus-word produced by a group of subjects reflects approximately the hierarchy of responses to that word in a single subject. Since each member of the group shares approximately the hierarchy of responses of the group as a whole (with A as the strongest, B the second and C as the third strongest response, etc.), the investigation of the whole group produces the result that response A (primary response) is the most frequent and B the second most frequent, etc.

Such response hierarchies can be made evident in several ways. We have already examined HORVATH's approach. LAFFAL approaches the problem from the point of view of information theory by using the concept of average information content or *entropy*. A stimulus-word with which only a small number of different responses are associated by the group as a whole (i.e., where the small number of responses have of course a high probability of occurrence) has a response hierarchy of low entropy; on the other hand a stimulus-word to which the group gives many different responses will have a response hierarchy of high entropy.

Instead of this value which takes into account both the number of different responses and the percentage of subjects giving a particular response, it is simpler to operate with only the number of different responses to a given stimulus-word. LAFFAL employs both sets of scores.

LAFFAL relates these two sets of values to response faults in word association or complex indicators which go with a particular stimulus-word and asks this question: is there a relationship between the entropy of the response hierarchy and the distribution of response faults in word association? The result is shown in Table 13. All correlations are significant beyond the .001 level. This means that response faults in word association are determined to a large measure by the entropy of the response hierarchy which is activated by a particular stimulus-word.

Table 13. *Intercorrelations of response entropy (H), number of different responses (D), reaction-time delay, reproduction faults, and number of responses faulted (N = 100)* (based on LAFFAL, *1955, p. 268*)

Measure	Entropy (H)	Number of Responses (D)	Reaction-Time Delay
Number of responses (D)	0.925		
Reaction-time delay	0.774	0.779	
Reproduction faults	0.590	0.646	0.663
Number of responses faulted	0.737	0.789	
Multiple correlation with reaction-	🛠		
time and reproduction faults	0.733	0.798	

What strikes JUNG as a complex indicator, appears particularly frequently whenever there are many competing (i.e., approximately equally strong) possibilities of response. If, however, one response is dominant, association faults are infrequent.

This does not mean that the valence and availability of individual responses in the response hierarchy might not also be influenced by emotional factors; but the decisive point is the approximately equal hierarchy of responses in all individuals.

How important LAFFAL'S result is, not only for the correction of widespread views concerning the diagnostic value of associative studies, can be seen from the following: it was hitherto believed that words with a negative emotional connotation (and therefore words prone to associative disturbance) would be learned with greater difficulty than emotionally neutral words with undisturbed associations. (JUNG had already found that complex-charged associations are forgotten more quickly). FELDMAN, LANG and LEVINE (1959) selected from the associations of each subject some words with and some words without association disturbances and made subjects learn these words, each paired with a nonsense syllable. But, in addition, the emotionally charged and uncharged words were equal with regard to their response-frequency distribution according to LAFFAL. No difference was found between the two groups of words with regard to speed of learning. But if the LAFFAL correction is not taken into account differences in the expected direction do occur.

To recapitulate, we saw that a certain equivalence in the response hierarchy can lead to delays in association and to other disturbances. This permits a first glimpse into the structure of these processes. What happens — behind the scenes of the association experiment, so to speak — can be treated as a decision process; it must be decided which of several different possibilities, activated by the stimulus-word, is to be actualized. As is known from studies in general psychology, the timing of decision processes is strongly dependent on two magnitudes: (a) on the absolute valence or strength of the separate possibilities, and (b) on the difference between the valences of the separate possibilities. The smaller this difference, and the lower the level of strength of the alternatives, the longer is the time likely to be needed for a decision. It appears valuable to interpret the processes in the association experiment with the help of this model.

It must be admitted that this will mean moving away from SAUSSURE. Following his conception, we made the distinction above between paradigmatic and syntagmatic associations. SAUSSURE characterized the mechanism governing the paradigmatic associations as selection (from among several possibilities one is chosen), whereas the mechanism of combination accounts for the syntagmatic associations (i.e., the words which in a sentence chain have already occurred in an actual sequence are also associated in the stimulus-response sequence). The inference from the argument that has just been advanced is that syntagmatic associations should also be the result of a process of selection. Of course the choice would not be made from a set of elements which are interchangeable, but from a number of divergent sequences. The decision to be made is which of these sequences the syntagmatic association will follow. A distinct *rapprochement* between associative and sequential psycholinguistics has thus been brought about. It will become even more distinct in the next chapter where we will turn from the descriptive account of the results of the word-association process to the explanation of the process itself.

Chapter 7

The 'Mechanism' of Association

Syntagmatic and paradigmatic associations — Association and context — Strength of verbal habits — Verbal 'relatedness' as an approach to the concept of meaning — NOBLE'S attempt to quantify meaning.

In the course of the discussion of LAFFAL'S investigations, mention was made of the widespread view that the frequency distribution of responses in a group can be considered as an expression of the hierarchy of response-strength, which is similar in each member of a group of people. If 50 percent of the members of a group respond to the stimulus-word 'chair' with 'table' but only 20 percent with 'sit' it is assumed that the power of the response 'table' is approximately $2\frac{1}{2}$ times greater than the strength of the response 'sit'. In the hierarchy of responses to the word 'chair', 'table' occupies a higher rank than 'sit'.

Powerful response-strength, a well-tried habit, will result in a particular response occurring in many instances to this particular stimulus. A powerful response will also be elicited faster than a weaker one. Therefore, frequency as well as speed of occurrence of a verbal response are presumably determined by the response-strength. And this in turn means that these two variables should be highly correlated with each other.

A first indication of this relationship was already suggested by MARBE'S Law. Further and mathematically clearer evidence based on a greater number of subjects was produced by SCHLOSBERG and HEINEMAN (1950). According to their investigation, there is a correlation of -0.8 between the logarithm of reaction-time and the communality of the responses. The measure of frequency in a group (i.e., the communality) correlates highly with the time required by an individual subject, which suggests that it is legitimate to interpret frequency distribution as an expression of individual response hierarchies.

This view is further confirmed by a modification of the word association experiment attempted by ROSEN and RUSSELL (1957). Subjects were invited to respond twice in succession to the same stimulus-word but not to repeat the same association-word. If the above interpretation is correct, one would expect the second response to be one of weaker response-strength, i.e., a less frequent response for the group as a whole. The result of this investigation is: an average communality of 22.7 percent is found for the first response and 7.3 percent for the second. Two thirds of all subjects produce a second response of lower communality than the first.

A major problem for the study of association which results from what has just been described is the question of the origin of the differential response-strength.

As far as syntagmatic associations are concerned (this term is defined on p. 128), it appears that this question can be answered without difficulty. If in normal sentences of everyday-language use word B immediately follows word A, it is to be expected that in the word-association experiment stimulus-word A is followed by response B. The syntagmatic association could accordingly be interpreted as a segment from a frequently spoken sentence of everyday speech.

The question is much more difficult to answer for paradigmatic associations. In everyday-language use the verbal sequence 'table—chair' or 'large—small' are hardly ever met. How do these S-R connections come about, and what determines their strength? ERVIN (1962-63) in discussing earlier explanations offered by SAPORTA (1955b) argues approximately as follows. According to the results of sequential psycholinguistics, the receiver of a verbal message must anticipate what is likely to come next. Such anticipations make comprehension possible even under adverse conditions; however, they can hardly ever lead to the anticipation of a definite word; instead they prepare almost always for a number of possible words fitting into a sentence frame which can be expected to complete the portion of the sentence that has already been heard. Supposing the frame is 'I can see the . . .' the continuation might be 'man', 'boy', 'bird', 'difference', 'heel', etc. Whatever is likely to occur in a particular sentence structure in the same position belongs to the same paradigm. If the sentence begins with 'I can see the smiling . . .' one might add 'person' or 'child', but 'difference' or 'heel' would no longer be possible; it is a smaller paradigm.

What we have discussed gives us a brief glimpse of a problem which we will treat more fully at a later stage. We have tried to answer provisionally the question of what guides the choice of a particular paradigm by using the notion of 'anticipation'. A closer look will show us that this 'anticipation' can be analyzed into two components: on the one hand there are the probabilistic relationships by which preceding sentence elements lead up to the point in question (Markov model); on the other, there are grammar rules according to which even sentence elements actualized at a later stage have a determining influence on the selection of an element at a given moment. This raises the question of the psychological reality of grammar, which will be discussed in more detail in chapter 13.

The more frequently two words are combined in a single paradigm, the more frequently the hearer experiences a connection between the anticipated possibilities and the word actually used by the speaker. And as the frequency of this 'experience' increases, so the paradigmatic association is strengthened. This is to say that the larger the number of sentence patterns into which the stimulus- and response-words might fit, the closer is the link.

Experimental investigations by ERVIN (1961 a) and MCNEILL (1963) have *prima facie* confirmed ERVIN'S hypothesis. One possibility of explaining syntagmatic and paradigmatic associations by means of a mediation model will be considered later in connection with the discussion of this model (see p. 181).

It is therefore possible to consider a pair of words from the point of view of the number of sentence patterns in which either one or the other might fit. Thus it is hardly possible to imagine a sentence in which the word 'big' is appropriate where 'small' might not equally have occurred. If in a concrete utterance 'big' occurs, it is likely that, almost in every case, 'small' is also available. On the other hand, there is hardly ever a sentence in which the choice would have been made between, say, 'heel' or 'sour'. Accordingly, 'big—small' have many sentence patterns in common, 'heel—sour' hardly any. It is possible to order pairs of words along a continuum which ranges from 'many sentence patterns in common' to 'no sentence patterns in common'. And if we ask what this continuum is, it appears *prima facie* as the dimension of similarity. When considered from this point of view, 'big—small' are more alike than 'heel—sour'. This similarity, defined more precisely, can be described as *similarity of meaning*.

Thus, we have reached a highly interesting and important point, where associative behavior and the problem of meaning are linked. It is commonly agreed among students of psycholinguistics today that a psychological approach to the concept of meaning (a philosophical concept in the first instance) must presumably be made, in one form or another, through an analysis of associative verbal behavior.

Let us once more examine the juncture at which the connection with meaning as a notion and as a phenomenon had become visible. Paradigmatic associations happen because the verbal stimulus is a word that occurs at a position in a sentence where a particular word and other similar ones are available. Associations with a particular stimulus-word are, therefore, (to a large extent at least) determined by the context in which the word that is used as stimulus appears in everyday use. This applies to syntagmatic associations where the context is given through the real sequence of words actually occurring in normal use. But it applies also to paradigmatic associations where the potential occurrence in a single paradigm can be treated as context. Here words are associated with one another because they are available simultaneously as possible continuations of one and the same speech event.

This fairly convincing explanation of the genesis of paradigmatic associations has, however, one weakness which should be pointed out. An association of the type 'table—chair' has a habit-strength expressed in the frequency norm. For example, 50 percent of all subjects produce 'chair' as an associate response to 'table'. If 'chair' now is used as stimulus-word we may find that 20 percent or 80 percent of the subjects, as the case may be, respond with 'table'. This means that the associations between 'chair' and 'table' in the two directions differ from each other in strength. This fact remains unexplained by the model we have just presented. If common availability were the only factor to account for the occurrence and strength of a paradigmatic association, there should be no distinction in the habit-strength between the associations in the forward or reverse directions. An additional directional factor must therefore be introduced.

A further complication results from a finding by RUSSELL, (Minnesota Conference, 1955).   Under certain circumstances response-stimulus associations which are generally quite weak can manifest themselves with a strength which does not differ from the corresponding stimulus-response association. But these are psychological problems of learning rather than language. Let us now pick up again the main thread of our discussion.

Associations are determined by the context in which the stimulus-word is used in everyday speech. If this view is correct, it should be possible to guide verbal associations in an association experiment by giving the stimulus-word not singly (as in the experiments employed so far) but in a context.

Such a context can, first of all, be provided by giving more specific instructions. In the classical association experiment the subject is asked to utter the first word that comes to his mind when he hears the stimulus-word. For a 'controlled' association more precise specifications are added; e.g., the subject is asked to make a response which expresses a whole-part relationship to the stimulus-word; or a month is to be responded to by a corresponding season, or a verb by a fitting noun (e.g., swim—fish). Such 'controlled' associations are usually faster than 'free' associations. This can be explained in terms of the decision theory already referred to. As a consequence of the instructions the range of possibilities from which a selection is to be made is restricted in advance. Hence time-consuming conflicts between competing responses are less frequent.   There are, however, difficulties in obtaining clear-cut results because controlled association involves the use of previous knowledge: hence numerous other factors come into play.

The directing influence of different instructions upon associative behavior has been —as is well-known— the starting point for important theoretical development advanced by the so-called Würzburg School of the psychology of thinking.

What is even more interesting from a psycholinguistic point of view than the effect of the context provided by the instruction to the subject is the study of the influence of words preceding the stimulus-word. As Fig. 39 shows, a hierarchy of responses goes with each stimulus-word;

OSGOOD (1954) calls it a divergent hierarchical habit family. Every, or nearly every, response can, in turn, be evoked—although with varying degrees of probability—by quite different stimuli (Fig. 40). If this is so, the question now arises how these associative connections of varying strength are combined in a concrete individual case assuming that the choice of the response is determined not only by one but by several S-R bonds or verbal habits.

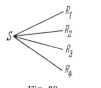

Fig. 39

Fig. 40

An investigation by HOWES and OSGOOD (1954) attempted to answer this question. Instead of giving subjects, as usual, a single stimulus-word, the stimulus-word was preceded by three other words. For example, if an association to the word 'book' was to be evoked, the experimenter said perhaps 'toy, come, wretched, book'. The responses produced in this manner were analyzed by HOWES and OSGOOD with the help of exceedingly complicated mathematical procedures. The intention was to find out the probabilistic relationships between S and R, between the preceding words and R, and between S and R under the influence of the preceding words.

The effect of the words preceding the stimulus-word proper, is clearly evident: the response-strengths in the hierarchy of S-R connections are modified, as an example from this study can demonstrate. Associations of varying strength occur between the word 'dark' as stimulus and different responses (Fig. 41). In the habit hierarchy the association 'dark-light' takes first place; it is the strongest; normally 'light' will appear as the most frequent association to 'dark'. Weaker associations link 'dark' with 'night', 'gloomy' and 'hell'. HOWES and OSGOOD now gave to different groups of subjects word-sets such as:

Fig. 41

devil—eat—basic—dark

devil—fearful—basic—dark

devil—fearful—sinister—dark

The result is that the associative effect (i.e., the frequency) of 'dark—hell' is increased with the number of words, preceding the stimulus-word, which themselves have associative connections with 'hell'.

Here is another example: three groups of subjects each are given the following series:

skin, wind, mountain, rough

mountain, skin, wind, rough

wind, mountain, skin, rough

The result is that the probability of the occurrence of the response 'hands' to the stimulus-word 'rough' rises as the distance between 'skin' and 'rough' becomes shorter. The directing influence of the word 'skin' upon the habit-strength of 'rough—hands' is a function of the distance between the influencing word and the stimulus-word itself.

COLEMAN (1964a) arrived at quite similar results. If, for example, 'moon' is offered as stimulus in a series such as 'elephant, hall, whale, stadium', i.e., words which normally evoke the response 'big', the association 'moon—big' is momentarily strengthened so much that the response 'big' will appear and not the words that are normally high in the response hierarchy, such as 'sun', 'night' or 'star'.

What brings a word to consciousness depends on the verbal context in which it is spoken. Earlier in the discussion a brief and quite tentative reference was made to the fact that the *meaning* of a word has something to do with the associations evoked by this word. It is in this way that we have come to speak of *associative meaning* of a word which has become a key concept in modern psycholinguistics; in this area the investigations by HOWES and OSGOOD and by COLEMAN lead to the conclusion that the context of a word can influence the meaning of that word inasmuch as certain associations of the word are momentarily strengthened by this context, while others recede and become less available.

FREUD'S magnificent analysis of slips of the tongue has shown that parts of the context influencing the associative process can lie in the unconscious.

How complicated one must imagine the effect of context to be has been made clear through an investigation by COFER and FORD (1957). In this investigation, like in the study by HOWES and OSGOOD, other words preceded the stimulus-word, either a neutral word with no connection to the stimulus-word or a synonym of the stimulus-word. The reaction-time between stimulus and response was measured. To the surprise of the investigators it was found that the reaction-time was longer when a synonym preceded the stimulus-word. They had expected a shorter reaction-time on the grounds that a synonym would suggest a response which, subsequently, would be evoked by the stimulus-word.

To explain this finding it may be necessary to fall back once more on the conflict-theory already referred to. A synonym calls into play a verbal habit which is similar to the S-R association in question, without being identical with it. Similarity of habits, however, leads to time-consuming conflicts. This phenomenon might also be regarded as a case of interference or of refractoriness. Similar interference phenomena have also been noted by PODELL (1963) in convergent associations.

To put it differently, the verbal association experiment does not reveal an unmodifiable static structure which underlies verbal behavior; instead, the structural relationships between verbal elements are in a state of dynamic change. The word-association experiment uncovers dynamic processes behind the manifest speech events in which the stimulation of the experiment is interposed as an added directing and modifying factor.

The underlying dynamics of this process appear with particular clarity in the process which, following BOUSFIELD (e.g., 1953), has been described as clustering. If the subject is given the task of thinking of names of flowers and musical instruments, the items do not occur in random order, but relatively systematically, e.g., six flowers, followed perhaps by four instruments, then again five flowers, and so forth. In other words the subject produces clusters of related words.

The same phenomenon occurs when words in random order are read aloud to the subject and recalled by him after a lapse of time. What the subject recalls is more ordered than what he was given.

The link between these observations and the word-association experiment was demonstrated by JENKINS and RUSSELL (1952). They selected 24 stimulus-words from the Kent-Rosanoff list along with their associated primary response-words and arranged all 48 words in random order. This list was read aloud to the subjects with the instruction to subsequently write down any words they remembered without regard to the order in which they had been presented.

The authors' hypothesis was that words which in the Kent-Rosanoff norms are closely associated as stimulus and response should also be recalled as pairs or at least in close proximity. While 'table' and 'chair' were separated by 20 other words in the list, as it was read out, these two words, which according to the Kent-Rosanoff norms are closely associated with each other, should have been reproduced in close succession during recall. This hypothesis was confirmed with a significance beyond the 0.001 level of confidence.

This result has meanwhile been corroborated by several studies. ROSENZWEIG (1957) found in a French group of subjects a correlation of 0.57 between the frequency of associations in the group and the frequency with which these words, having been heard in random order, were again clustered together in recall. RUSSELL and MESECK (1959) obtained similar results with German-speaking groups.

These investigations have taken us beyond the field we have so far considered. While in the studies which had been reported earlier we referred to associations between a word which explicitly functioned as stimulus and another word explicitly functioning as response, associations in the reproduction phase of a clustering experiment are evoked between responses; the word 'table' is uttered by the subject (and not by the experimenter) as well as the word 'chair'. This extension of the concept of association, which henceforth comprises not only the association between stimulus and response, but also between response and response, is—as we shall see later—important for the further development of the problems we are discussing.

The investigations by JENKINS and RUSSELL and the numerous studies by BOUSFIELD and his students can also be regarded as confirmation for the view that associative verbal relations are effective in areas which need not be considered as strictly verbal or linguistic—as here, for example, in the study of memory.

According to these investigations, associative- or habit-strength is a determinant of the clustering phenomenon. Next, however, it can be demonstrated that the degree of cohesion between the related words is not stable. At the beginning of the reproduction the tendency to recall related words rises; after one third of the total list it begins to fall again. This observation has led BOUSFIELD (1953) to look for a second factor besides habit-strength as an explanation for clustering, because if habit-strength is to be considered a function of the frequency with which the two members of an association have hitherto occurred together, it should remain stable over a time-span. This second factor to account for clustering he has called 'relatedness increment'. He imagines the effect of this factor as follows: if a certain word is reproduced in the recall test all other words with which this word has associative relations are made available; they are, so to speak, 'warmed-up'. A momentary increase in habit-strengths of these words makes this possible so that these words are 'lifted over the threshold', i.e., recalled more easily.

Approaching this problem from a totally different angle, i.e., from the point of view of neurophysiology of co-ordinated automatized movement, LASHLEY has used the somewhat similar concept of 'priming'. He regards it as the "subthreshold activation of a whole system of associations" (1960 p. 498). Movements and activities which are executed with great rapidity and quite automatically (speech is a case in point) are, according to LASHLEY, only possible if the anticipation of the next link in the sequence leads to an activation or anticipation of the necessary structures.

There is only a short step from LASHLEY to HEBB whose model appears particularly appropriate for the processes we are discussing. According to HEBB a habit can be said to be based on a phase sequence or functional assembly of neurons which can easily be inter-connected. The relatedness increment, advanced by BOUSFIELD, would occur because the phase sequences, corresponding to related words, have partial paths in common.

In Fig. 42 the phase sequence representing word A consists of the neurons a_1 to a_6. As this phase sequence is activated, parts of the phase sequences belonging to B and C are also brought into action so that only a slight additional impulse is needed for these phase sequences also to be fired. The fact that one phase sequence has just been run off facilitates the activation of neighboring phase sequences.

These formulations should be valid not only for the phenomenon of clustering but apply more generally to retention and recall. A word W should be retained all the more easily the more words there are available in its vicinity to facilitate W, i.e., the more other words can serve as 'cues' or release mechanisms of W. ROTHKOPF and COKE (1961) investigated this problem experimentally. They defined the cue number of word W as "the number of words in the learning list for which W is normally given as an association response in a word association test." It was found that a word is retained particularly well if it

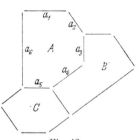

Fig. 42.
Diagram of phase sequences

appears, according to the table of norms of the association experiment, as a frequent response to many other words in the list.

ROTHKOPF and COKE, therefore, argue that clustering and retention can be explained with the help of a single model: at each point in time of a retention test one particular word which has not yet been reproduced has the greatest superthreshold habit-strength and as a consequence will be reproduced next. The fact that this word is 'lifted across the threshold' means that the habit-strength of all words associated with it are thereby increased. Consequently, such revalued words change their position in the habit hierarchy. They move up in the hierarchy and are therefore more easily reproduced, which manifests itself—depending upon the experimental set-up—as an increase in recall frequency or as clustering.

According to this view, associations form a structure which determine, what is associated (and reproduced)[1]; but at the same time this structure is changed by the process of associating or reproducing. SCHWARTZ and ROUSE (1961), in an investigation strongly oriented toward depth psychology, speak of associative priming: a word, a thought, an image of which a person is conscious primes or activates a constellation of other words or thoughts with which the priming word is connected. According to these writers, dream events, for example, are determined by associative priming.

Psychopathology can provide confirmation for factors of this kind: PÖTZL (1917) and SCHILDER (1924) had already described patients with organic cerebral

---

[1] More recently TULVING (1969) has advanced the view that forgetting can be explained as a consequence of absence of appropriate retrieval cues, rather than as a consequence of any changes in the originally stored information.

lesions, who were no longer able to name a well-known object, but were still capable of responding with a word which was associatively connected with the word they looked for. On this observation SCHILDER based a conclusion of psycholinguistic interest: words which are evoked by such associative processes form the substructure of normal, healthy thought-processes. Conscious, ordered thought-processes are preceded by preconscious stages in which associations are activated, examined, accepted or rejected. This phase-theory of verbal thinking and verbal behavior proposed here by SCHILDER has great similarity to the theory of 'Aktualgenese' (microgenesis) developed in the so-called 'Leipzig School' of SANDER with particular reference to the field of perception.

This theory of microgenesis was taken up and applied especially to word association by RAPAPORT (1945-46) and by FLAVELL, DRAGUNS et al. (1958). A brief account of the investigation by the last-named authors must be given.

In the early phases of the associative process which occur in the experiment between the moment of perception of the stimulus-word and the utterance of the response-word, latent or covert responses demand expression.

These responses are less logical and do not obey the consciously held standard of normal thought processes. Unless a subject of the word-association experiment is under pressure or suffers from a psychopathological disturbance, these tentative responses never see the light of day because they are replaced by associations which are produced later and accord with higher standards. In the case of schizophrenics, however, or of normal subjects under time pressure, such immature and prelogical responses should occur more frequently. Investigations in this area (besides the above named study by SIIPOLA, WALKER and KOLB, 1955, among others) have produced somewhat contradictory results which may well be a consequence of the vagueness implicit in the concept of microgenesis.

On the other hand, the success which BRUNER, POSTMAN and others have had with a quite analogous interpretation of the process of perception, suggests that in the process of association there might also be different phases, e.g., an analyzing phase followed by a synthesizing one; in this second phase the association selected from among the activated associations will be the one which, according to the subjects' standards, fits best in the given situation.

These arguments can be related to BROADBENT's theory (see pp. 107 f.) concerning the selection of the most appropriate dictionary units in speech perception. These dictionary units were discussed in the context of a Markov model applied to the *receptive* side of speech. The present discussion has familiarized us with association and associative activation as further factors which may have a determining influence also on the selection of such units at the *productive* end of the speech process.

Associative activation may, therefore, be assumed whenever the occurrence of event A increases the probability of the occurrence of event B which is associated with A. Here we can clearly see the close relationship between the associative approach to language and the probabilistic approach treated in chapter 5.

In the investigations discussed here, the concept of 'relatedness' between words plays an important part. Frequency of association is used again and again as an indicator of such relatedness, which manifests itself as frequency of occurrence of a certain S-R bond in the word-association experiment.

The work of BOUSFIELD as well as that of ROTHKOPF and COKE has shown that the relations between words are likely to be more complex than is expressed by simple frequency norms of single S-R connections. The question now arises whether it is possible to come closer to the structure of the system of relationships underlying verbal behavior and expressing itself through it, by looking for further, quantitative values rather than by looking upon the relationship between two words as simply a matter of the frequency with which B follows A.

JENKINS and COFER (1957), and BOUSFIELD, WHITMARSH and BERKOWITZ (1960) have developed an index which they call *mutual frequency score* or *measure of relatedness*. It comprises *all* responses which are common to two stimulus-words; i.e., it is the overlap between the associations of two stimulus-words in relation to the total number of responses:

$$\frac{\Sigma Rc}{\Sigma R}$$

It can be illustrated by the following constructed example. The stimulus-words 'black' and 'white' evoke the following responses in 200 subjects:

Table 14. *Mutual frequency score*

| Responses | Stimuli | | Rc |
	Black	White	
Black	[200]	*30*	*30*
White	*50*	[200]	*50*
Sleep	20	10	10
Night	30	0	0

Rc is the number of responses common to both stimuli. This consists for the moment only of 10 (the response 'sleep'). However, this is not yet satisfactory; the fact that the stimulus 'black' evokes the response 'white' 50 times, and the stimulus 'white' the response 'black' 30 times, is equally to be taken into account in the index of relatedness. The authors, therefore, make an important additional assumption: the very first response to a stimulus-word is a subvocal repetition of the stimulus-word; it is called *representational response*. On hearing 'black', the subject first of all repeats 'black' quietly to himself, without of course voicing it, because such repetitions of the stimulus-word are not permitted according to the instructions of the association experiment. These implicit responses are also entered into the table [200]; moreover, the 30 'black' responses to the stimulus 'white' and, equally, the 50 'white' responses to the stimulus 'black' may now also be counted as overlap, and may therefore be entered in the column *Rc*. The index in this example has the value of $\frac{90}{200}$.

The index of inter-item associative-strength, used by DEESE (1959a), has a certain similarity to this index. DEESE was interested in the learning and reproduction of word lists with reference to the degree of organization found in these lists.

Again and again he came across the fact that words appeared in the subject's reproductions which the subject said he remembered, but which, in fact, were not on the lists to be learned. DEESE hypothesized that such intrusions resulted from associative relationships between the words in the list and others not contained in the list. If a list consists of words A, B, C, D, E, F and G, and if the words B and F have a strong associative bond with the word X, then it is X that will appear in the reproduction of the list. The point in question is similar to the problem studied by ROTHKOPF and COKE. In order to be able to predict the extent of these intrusions, DEESE developed an index of inter-item associative-strength which he defined as "the average relative frequency with which all items in a list tend to elicit all other items in the same list as free associates" (p. 305).

In this study it is the first time that not only two words but all words of a list are brought in relationship to each other. But in contrast to the previously mentioned index of JENKINS and BOUSFIELD, only direct (and no indirect) associations are included.

The usefulness of DEESE'S index has been tested in experimental investigations. DEESE constructed word lists of widely different inter-item associative-strength and he tested how well they were retained. The correlations obtained between the index and the number of words recalled was 0.88, and between the index and the number of intrusions the correlation coefficient was -0.48. The closer the words in a list are associated with one another, the more, therefore, they mutually support each other, and the better they are retained. Each word is sustained by its neighbors and consequently preserved from being forgotten. It would be interesting to relate this observation to AUSUBEL'S subsumption theory of learning. But we cannot pursue this line of thought; instead we will turn to a study which, from a psycholinguistic point of view, is more relevant because it points again to the concept of meaning.

The discussion of associative links in linguistic structures was concerned with those habits which in the habit hierarchies display greatest strength. This associative- or habit-strength expresses itself in frequency of occurrence and in the rapidity of the S-R connection. Next to the strength of the primary association, the investigations we have discussed above have shown the importance of the *number* of associations which link a word with neighboring words. At this point the experiments undertaken by NOBLE (1952 and after) are relevant because they are designed to define meaningfulness and to make it evident as a variable.

The impetus for NOBLE'S work came from the psychology of learning. It had been found again and again that, for learning and retention of verbal material, meaning, sense and significance play an important role. In order to exclude this variable, EBBINGHAUS, as is of course well known, had invented the nonsense syllable. However, it had been discovered that not all nonsense syllables were equally difficult to learn. Consequently it was necessary to give up the sharp distinction between sense and nonsense and to replace it by a continuum. This meant that the attempt was made to express sense or meaningfulness in terms of a graded scale.

We have already come across one of these attempts in MILLER'S approximations to genuine language. A different attempt, which is connected with the names of GLAZE (1928), HULL (1933) and finally NOBLE, does not set out, as MILLER did, from the sequential aspects, but approaches it from the aspect of association. Thus GLAZE determined the association value of 'nonsense' syllables by finding the percentage of subjects who within three seconds could think of a meaningful word as an association to the nonsense syllable. The syllable 'ful' is by definition nonsense because it cannot be found in an English dictionary, but nearly all subjects immediately think of the meaningful word 'full'; the syllable 'ful', strictly nonsense, has a high associative value. Syllables with high associative value are learned faster and retained better than those with lower associative value.

This is the point at which NOBLE'S work must be considered; he treats under meaningfulness not only the associations of what are formally nonsense syllables, but he understands the meaningfulness of words as the number of associative relations of a word to other words. He argues as follows: "Meaning is a relation between terms" (1952a, p. 422), i.e., roughly speaking, a connection between two data. He assumes a stimulus-element S_x, a class of conditioned responses R_1, R_2 ... and a series of habits linking S_x with individual R's, H_1, H_2 ... (Fig. 43).

The origin of this model in HULL'S theory of learning is evident. NOBLE now defines meaningfulness as the number of habits existing between S_x and the various R's taken together. Each H is a special meaning of S_x. All these special meanings together yield meaningfulness. The system $_sH_R$—as HULL designates the habit linking stimulus and response—is isomorphically equivalent to 'A means B'.

Meaning and habit-*strength* are, however, by no means identical. Habit-strength increases the more frequently a particular R follows a particular S; meaningfulness, on the other hand, increases with the number of different S—R links.

The index developed by NOBLE is

$$m = \frac{1}{N} \Sigma R_s$$

where S is a certain verbal stimulus, R the response, and N the number of subjects. Subjects receive the following instruction: 'This is a test to see how many words you can think of and write down in a short time. You will be given a key word and you are to write down as many *other* words which the key word brings to your mind as you can.' The subject is given one minute for each stimulus-word. The index m defines the average number of different associations which are evoked in a subject by a given stimulus-word.

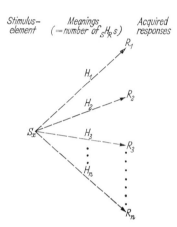

Fig. 43. Schema illustrating the development of meaningfulness (from NOBLE, 1952a, p.422)

In this manner NOBLE succeeds in emptying the basically qualitative concept of meaning of all colorful content and in reducing it to a single quantitative, formal variable. What is lost by this procedure? Or looked at more positively: what does this approach achieve in the analysis of the relationships under consideration? In other words, we are asking whether NOBLE, with the help of this index, really grasps that kind of meaningfulness which determines speed of learning, as he had intended to. It turns out that m does indeed meet this requirement: the higher the m-value of the words to be learned the more steeply rises the learning curve. Slow learners are more sensitive to differences in m-value than fast learners.

It follows from these results and from several others of particular interest to learning theory that NOBLE has succeeded in distilling, so to speak, the formal quantitative extract from the qualitative profusion of meaningfulness and its relationships. In doing so—he makes no bones about the origin of his views—he follows an earlier behavioristic trend to banish completely from psychology the concept of meaning, with its connotations of introspection, subjective images, and so forth and to replace it by exact behavioral data. NOBLE'S question is behavioral: how many verbal responses does a particular verbal stimulus produce?

Despite the value of NOBLE'S contribution to empirical research, we may perhaps hesitate to go along entirely with this development:

Meaning as association,

Meaning as associative habits,

Meaning as numbers of such associative habits.

Yet, if we examine this development closely and, at the same time, attempt to view it in a wider perspective, we will come to recognize that we have not been led into a blind alley of which NOBLE'S thesis would constitute the extreme position. On the contrary, it will be seen that this trend of thought is in part an expression of major changes that have occurred in linguistics and in the philosophy of language. Before advancing from NOBLE'S approach to other attempts which have been made to understand the nature of meaning psychologically as association, let us therefore digress in order to sketch in broad outline the philosophical background against which the concept of meaning has been discussed in the past decades.

Chapter 8

The Philosophical Background to Modern Psycholinguistics

Meaning as inherent bipolar connection — The designating function of language — *Adaequatio rei et intellectus* — Language and meta-language — Empiricist criteria of truth — Pragmatism and operationalism — Between-world of meaning — Meaning as context — Role of language-user — MORRIS — Meaning as behavior.

"The fundamental change in the relationship between philosophy and language," which distinguishes "the twentieth century from previous ones, might well be said to consist in the fact that language is no longer treated purely as a subject for philosophical inquiry. For the first time in history, language is viewed as the prerequisite which makes philosophy possible. 'Philosophy of language' is no longer simply a philosophy *of language* ... Instead, it does today what, after KANT, epistemology had done once before. It has taken the place of ontology. In a way, linguistic analysis has pushed the Kantian critique of knowledge to its radical conclusion as a critique of language" (APEL, 1964, p. 22).

The present chapter is not intended to describe this development in full detail or in historical sequence. Instead, by highlighting a few decisive moments we merely want to indicate the horizon within which modern psycholinguistics has studied the concept of meaning. As we shall make several overlapping approaches to psychology from the standpoint of 'pure' philosophy, a certain amount of repetition can hardly be avoided.

Among recent German writings on linguistic philosophy the work of APEL is most noteworthy; the following presentation is largely based on it.
Perspectives in psychology from different philosophical positions are indicated in this chapter by indentation.

The first concept of importance for our discussion is that of *logos* in Greek philosophy. What we regard today as the confusing ambiguity of this concept—broadly speaking, 'word' *and* 'true idea'—is in Greek thought a unity which guarantees that language is 'right' or 'true'. But this self-evident view soon gave way to a question: how can language be 'true', i.e., 'mediate' an external world ? A first superficial answer to this question is: because words and sentences mean something, i.e., have a reliable relationship to the objects in the extra-linguistic world. The next question is: how does this relationship to the extra-linguistic world come about ? In philosophy this raises the problem of linguistic truth and in psychology the problem of the acquisition of linguistic meanings.

The Platonic answer to this question is that there is a natural and necessary link between linguistic and non-linguistic facts. In *Cratylus* we find that names are not conventional but natural; they are equally true and right for Greeks and barbarians, and they transcend individual languages. The truth of language, therefore, lies in the sound pattern of individual words. In this conception truth means that names follow things.

> This conception is reflected in linguistics in the treatment of onomato-
> poeia and popular etymology, and in psychology as 'word magic' and
> sound symbolism. It is rejected by General Semantics (cf. chapters 12
> and 15).

The view that words are naturally *(physei)* related to things outside language implies a very simple structure of that relationship which can be called 'meaning': linguistic and extra-linguistic facts are naturally and necessarily linked without any intervening psychological mechanism. Meaning is a bipolar or dyadic relationship which has come into being naturally without human beings having any part in it. Such arguments can be found down to the present era; as late as 1960 GADAMER said that things speak for themselves, and language, in the last resort, is the language of things (GADAMER, 1962).

The Aristotelian conception is quite different. The link between language and extra-linguistic reality does not consist in factual necessity *(physei)* but is put there by man *(thesei)*. Man can grasp the world or the way things are apart from language. Things, which thus are already known to man, are afterwards named by him with the help of arbitrarily chosen words. This conception of the designating function of language reaches from antiquity via OCKHAM and Scholasticism right into the present era. The decisive characteristic of this view is not the appropriateness of the sound pattern but the unambiguousness of the designation. In this approach the demand that language should be true becomes much more problematical than in PLATO because the order of language must now reflect the order of the world. As early as the twelfth century attempts were made to link grammar, i.e., the structure of language, with the structure of reality. According to BACON there is only *one* grammar for all languages—*licet accidentaliter varietur*. In Scholasticism there was much discussion of the theory of supposition, i.e., of the relationship between the word and the object designated by the word. The triad particularly noted was *supponentia* (designations), *supposita* (the designated objects or individuals) and *supponere* as a process (i.e., the act of substituting designations for things).

This implies that man participates in establishing the meaning relationship and that it is, therefore, inherently arbitrary.

The discussion of the various *modi significandi* leads from a dyadic to a triadic scheme of the meaning relationship in the work of MORRIS. The idea of supposition, i.e., the substitution of the designation for the thing, becomes of renewed modern interest as the problem of verification in logical positivism and in the conditioning theory of meaning of WATSON and PAVLOV.

In contrast to the scholastic procedure the mystics attempt through contemplation to enter into direct contact with this world and the transcendent world, undisturbed by the arbitrariness of words invented by man.

If the Aristotelian-Scholastic view is adopted as a basis, then truth is the *adaequatio rei et intellectus*, the agreement between things and mind. The structure of a language can, if it is logically correct, reflect the structure of the world. But how can one be certain that language is logically right and that the *adaequatio rei* has been reached?

A further question was later added: what happens when *res* and *intellectus*, thing and language, are not regarded as independent of each other, i.e., when, in contrast to the earlier assumption, language is said to influence our view of reality? This is the issue which HUMBOLDT, SAPIR and WHORF have discussed.

In OCKHAM'S conception the *adaequatio rei et intellectus* is, moreover, guaranteed by the fact that the world of things in its whole qualitative richness is treated as the effective cause of our propositions (cf. on this point APEL, 1963).

In modern scholarship a similar cause-effect relationship reappears in the philosophy and psychology of language as a stimulus-response connection as, for example, in the work of OGDEN and RICHARDS, BLOOMFIELD and SKINNER.

Another approach which has been attempted to reach *adaequatio* and, thereby, to guarantee the truth-function of language reduces to syntactical relationships the whole qualitative and intangible substance.

It is in this way that LEIBNIZ has come to view words as tokens and to operate with them according to the rules of a formal calculus.

"In the use of language it must also be considered that words are signs for things, and that we need signs not only to convey our thoughts to others, but also to help us to think. For just as in large centers of trade, in games, and so on, one does not always pay with money, but instead makes use of slips of paper or tokens, in the same way the mind uses representations of things ..." The mind is content "to put the word in place of the thing ... And just as a master of arithmetic who refuses to write a number which he could not carry in his mind would never complete his calculation, in the same way we would have to speak very slowly or remain silent, if in speech or even in thought we attempted to use a word without forming a clear picture of its meaning ... That is why words are often used as cyphers or counters in the place of images of things, until step by step the sum total has been attained and thus only at the logical conclusion the thing itself is reached" (translated from *Unvorgreifliche Gedanken* as quoted by STENZEL, 1934, p. 62).

In a similar manner HOBBES does not see the truth or untruth in the agreement between judgment and reality but in the use of words, i.e., the relation between the signs. Accordingly, we read in *Leviathan*: "verum et falsum attributa sunt non rerum, sed orationibus".

From this position a direct line leads to logical positivism. For example, CARNAP, too, ignores the content; his aim is to construct a logical syntax of language in general, without recourse to meaning, as a kind of algebra of language. In general terms, it is a basic tenet of logical positivism that language cannot communicate substance but only structures; it is up to the receiver to put substance to the signs or, in other words, to interpret them according to the situation.

Information theory is, in a certain way, akin to these views. Also MOWRER'S thesis belongs here: according to MOWRER, during speech meanings are not carried from one person to another, but within one person from sign to sign. The importance of interpretation is particularly stressed in the work of OGDEN and RICHARDS.

The logical structure of language as a guarantee for the capacity of language to be true is found again in BERTRAND RUSSELL'S work and even in WITTGENSTEIN'S *Tractatus*: "The configuration of objects in a situation corresponds to the configuration of simple signs in the propositional sign" (i.e., in the sentence) (3.21).

New difficulties—and consequently a further development—can be seen in RUSSELL'S well-known contradiction of the lying Cretan. A Cretan says: "All Cretans are liars." If this sentence is true the speaker must also be a liar; consequently, the sentence is false if it is true. RUSSELL solves this contradiction by proposing a logical principle: if a judgment is made about all judgments which belong to a certain class, this judgment no longer belongs to this class. This theory of logical classes is the so-called 'theory of types'.

General Semantics would distinguish here judgment$_1$ from judgment$_2$.

According to this view sentences on the logical form of language could not be expressed in the language itself but would be formulated in a language of a higher order, a meta-language. In meta-language, statements can be made about language, in the meta-meta-language, statements about the meta-language.

> The separation into language and meta-language is called into question by the empirical observation that in everyday language metalinguistic components occur, e.g., such phrases as 'Do you follow?', 'What do you mean?', 'Have I made myself clear?'. This is done to ensure that both partners use the same code (on this point cf. AMMER, 1961, pp. 63 ff.).

If we do not want to continue to apply the notion of meta-language ad infinitum, we face the necessity, as CARNAP has done for instance, to use in the construction of a logical syntax of a language some basic concepts already formulated in that language, such as 'and', 'not', 'if ... then'.

It follows that syntactical structure, without reference to semantic content, cannot simply be regarded as a mirror of the structural order of the world. The consequence is that the "decision on the criterion of meaning has shifted from the realm of logic to an empirical critique of everyday language" (APEL, 1965). This question of empirical verification is in the center of neo-positivistic thought on the analysis of language. Thus SCHLICK points out that verifiability by immediately available empirical data is a criterion for regarding a sentence as meaningful.

But what constitutes 'immediately available empirical data'? When does a sentence truly represent a record of experience? This question can no longer be answered by referring to a criterion which in the last resort is metaphysical, such as the thesis of the reflection of the structure of the world in the logical structure of language. In the last resort, all that remains in order to decide this issue is the 'consensus of recognized scholars' or the confirmation through use in everyday language. WITTGENSTEIN in one of his later writings says: "Asking whether and how a proposition can be verified is only a particular way of asking 'How d'you mean?' The answer is a contribution to the grammar of the proposition" (*Philosophical Investigations*, § 353). "Grammar tells what kind of object anything is" (§ 373); i.e., grammar is the totality of rules, according to which the given word or given sentence is normally used in practice.

Thus, a completely new position on the concept of truth is reached. Truth is now no longer something of absolute validity to be expressed through language. Instead, regarding the external world as given means that a decision has been taken to speak a certain language because of its usefulness (CARNAP, 1950). The designating function of language —since ARISTOTLE the leitmotif—is abandoned. Language is no longer the means of representing a pre-existing world already previously perceived by other means. Symbolizing is no longer an act of grasping an existing 'sense', but an act of establishing sense. The beginning is *not* the symbol followed by its use; instead, it is everyday behavior from which gradually—to use the linguist's abstraction—symbolizations are formed. WITTGENSTEIN introduces the notion of the language-game, which is intended to emphasize that *"speaking* of language is part of an activity, or a form of life" (*Philosophical Investigations*, § 23). "We may say: only someone who already knows how to do something with it can significantly ask a name" (§ 31). In linguistics LEISI, for example, on the basis of WITTGENSTEIN's philosophy, compares language with custom. The description of the word-content is an indication of the conditions under which the use of a verbal form or, more precisely, the performance of the verbal utterance is possible and appropriate (LEISI, 1961). WITTGENSTEIN himself has expressed it even more succinctly: "To understand a language means to be master of a technique" (§ 199). "The meaning of a word is its use in the language" (§ 43).

The development which has just been broadly outlined has been summarized by APEL in these terms: "At the beginning, the logical order of the world was explicitly used as the theoretically given yardstick of all linguistic order, and the dependence of the categorial world order upon language was disregarded. At the end of this historical evolution, we find WITTGENSTEIN's philosophy of analysis of language which claims to find, in the pluralism of language-games and their approach to situations, a guide to problems of logical categories" (APEL, 1962, p. 205).

It must be remembered that the search for a guide to all "problems of logical categories" is only one factor in the historical trend which is of interest in this connection. Another is the pragmatic view and mode of thought which was established by PEIRCE[1]. We now follow the second line of development in the evolution of present-day linguistic philosophy. American pragmatism has led to an intensification of interest in questions of linguistic philosophy. While logical positivism was more interested in logic, mathematics and physics, pragmatism leans more towards biology, physiology and sociology (cf. NEUBERT, 1962).

According to PEIRCE a scientist understands meaning as follows: if a definite instruction for an experiment is possible and is executed, it will be followed by a definite experience.

---

[1] It should be remembered that we are not concerned with exact priorities of chronological sequence in the history of philosophy; it is, for example, very likely indeed that the later works of WITTGENSTEIN would not have been possible without the preceding work of PEIRCE.

This is a statement of decisive importance for the whole of modern psycholinguistics.

Meaning, as interpreted here, is a process. The meaning of a sign, or a word, lies in what happens in terms of stimuli and responses in its environment—the real events, which precede the utterance of the word, and the real events which follow the utterance of the word. The decisive thing for the pragmatist is the practical effect elicited by the symbol within an interpersonal context (NEUBERT, p. 61).

Here is also the basis for the operational mode of procedure and definition, initiated by BRIDGMAN, according to which a concept is defined as an instruction to carry out a given set of procedures; e.g., a rat is 'hungry' if it has not been fed for 48 hours.

Even prior to the formulation by BRIDGMAN this technique has achieved its greatest success in Einstein's theory of relativity. This theory was the outcome of the consistent pursuit of the question of which measuring operations could define the concept of simultaneity.

In this connection language appears as the continuation of action by different means. BRIDGMAN himself sees the difference between language and experience in the fact that "language separates out from the living matrix little bundles and freezes them" (1964, p. 24).

This view is close to BLOOMFIELD'S conception according to which 'acts of speech' are elicited by 'practical events' and lead to 'practical events'. If reliability of communication matters, the verbal bridge linking practical events is reinforced by the addition of further speechless occurrences. The more the demand for reliable communication increases, the more it is necessary to add non-verbal operations. This reciprocal relationship is also expressed in WEIZSÄCKER'S proposition on language and science: "Precision in the object permits imprecision of language" (1960, p. 139).

Accordingly, linguistic meaning is closely connected with human activity and with the situation in which the particular word is uttered.

The inclusion of situational context means, among others, a decisive rejection of the traditional dyadic model, according to which meaning is the relation between word and object; for in this relationship the situation is of no importance. Let us now go back once more and follow up the third strand, the development of the dyadic model, up to the point we have just reached, i.e., up to the inclusion of the situational context in the interpretation by the sign-user.

SAUSSURE'S scheme was still entirely dyadic, but it was no longer a crude juxtaposition of words and things. The sign *(signe)* constitutes a firm link between *signifiant* (the sound pattern) and *signifié*. And *signifié* is not the object itself but the idea or concept of the object, nor is *signifiant* the actual physical event, but the idea of this event (cf. MALMBERG, 1963).

ULLMANN, in a similar way, contrasts 'name' and 'sense', where 'name' is the acoustic shape, and 'sense' the mental content. WEISGERBER, equally, speaks of 'concept' in contrast to the 'sound pattern'.

What for a long time has been a stumbling block to psychologists becomes particularly evident in WEISGERBER'S views: "One of the most important results of human self-consciousness is the understanding of the separation of the world of the mind from the world in which we move physically. The world of real life in all its wealth and fullness cannot enter consciousness directly" (1962a, p. 38). Instead, it enters a 'mediating sphere' *(Zwischenwelt)*. Where we meet verbal manifestations we can "in every case assume a mental mediating sphere" (1962a, p. 58). This separate existence of a world of meanings can also be found in STENZEL'S writings: "The meaningful signs of verbal expression acquire in turn objectivity which stands between the consciousness of the speaker and the signified object ... separating them ... and yet making the connection between them possible" (1934, p. 35).

In this conception the world is duplicated so that we have a world of objects and, connected with it, an intermediate world of meanings. This conception no doubt has a Platonic element: a word or thought can be communicated and in the course of a conversation can retain its identity; the word and its meaning cannot be a purely subjective construct; it must have an existence of its own.

In contrast to this view most psychologists because of their somewhat anti-Platonic outlook have certain hesitations to hypostatize such abstract intangible entities.

This cautious attitude is demonstrated by the behavioristic tendency to do altogether without the notion of meaning. Thus, SKINNER says: a speaker does not express ideas or images; he simply utters words.

An element of Platonic idealization is also contained in HUSSERL'S view of the nature of language. Man always 'means' something; he always relates his thoughts to something which—if a subject-object division is to be assumed—can be described as the 'object signified' *(das Bezeichnete)*. As we speak we always carry out an act of meaningful intent which merges with words and, so to speak, breathes life into them (1929, p. 20). As HUSSERL here employs psychological notions in quite an unpsychological way it is not surprising that his extraordinary influence on philosophy is not matched by a similar influence on psychology. The fact that in this formulation intentionality, i.e., a mentalistic act *par excellence*, is central can hardly have appealed to a behavioristically oriented psychology, which, with its mechanistic concepts, is certainly less sophisticated but epistemologically more consistent. Corresponding to STENZEL'S fascinating formulation: "The breath of meaning defines the sentence" (1958, p. 53), we find in psychology ACH'S interpretation. According to ACH'S view, the meaning-giving act results from a signifying *Einstellung* or set, i.e., an unconscious determining tendency to invest new objects with a name. No doubt, also in ACH'S theory, association is the meaning-giving mechanism, but association is not viewed as mechanical, rather it is seen as an unconscious drive or tendency.

In psycholinguistics the reification of a definite mediating sphere of meanings is as unacceptable as the use of such 'mentalistic' explanations as intentionality or *Meinen* (i.e., the act of investing with meaning). Yet, the *kind* of relationship implicit in the dyadic model has been adopted; it is a reciprocal relation (in contrast to HUSSERL'S notion of intentionality); i.e., either pole can 'evoke' the other; in other words, meaning is viewed as association.

One of the most prominent representatives of this point of view in psychology is TITCHENER: "Meaning, psychologically, is always context; one mental process is the meaning of another mental process if it is that other's context. And context, in this sense, is simply the mental process which accrues to the given process through the situation in which the organism finds itself" (1910, p. 367).

Meaning as connection or context became more and more accepted and has maintained itself as a basic feature of psycholinguistics, though not in the concrete form in which it was viewed by TITCHENER; for, in TITCHENER'S theory, the second added mental process is the image. The word 'dog' has meaning because the perception of the word evokes the image of a dog. The sign which is heard or read has meaning because it evokes in the receiver a 'corresponding' image.

NOBLE cites TITCHENER as chief witness to the effect that meaning can be understood as association. This is fundamentally correct; but TITCHENER was concerned with the context of conscious ideas, while for NOBLE, the *quantity* of associations elicited in the experiment was the decisive factor.

In these interpretations, too, the bipolar, dyadic model is basically maintained, although in TITCHENER'S theory the inclusion of situation indicates the possibility of a widening conception.

The limitations of this model were transcended by OGDEN and RICHARDS whose book *The Meaning of Meaning* (first published in 1923) was very influential from a philosophical, linguistic and psychological point of view. The starting point for their critique is the view, implicit at least in the dyadic scheme, i.e., that a word has always only one fixed meaning: the relationship to the corresponding object or the connection with the one corresponding idea. From this view has originated, since the beginning of mankind, the argument about the 'true' or 'genuine' meaning of words. What is the real meaning of 'God'? What do 'freedom', 'democracy', 'love' or 'happiness' *really* mean? COPERNICUS and GALILEO were threatened with ultimate penalties because they questioned the traditional meaning of the word 'earth', i.e., earth as the center of the universe[1].

The conviction that every word must have *one real* or *true* meaning, driven to its logical extreme, leads to the appearance of 'word magic'. The practice of many magic formulae and incantations originates in the primitive opinion that the name *is* the thing, and even in the fairy tale there is someone who is happy that no one knows that his name is Rumpelstilskin.

In contrast to these views ERDMANN, around the turn of the century, already remarked: "Everywhere there are bitter fights which would soon be found to be completely futile if a few preliminary terminological questions had been settled" (Preface). "Words are signs for rather vague complexes of ideas which are more or less loosely connected ... The boundaries of word meanings are blurred, vague and fluid" (p. 5). Therefore, "... the boundary of the meaning of a word can figuratively only be represented by a network of lines" (p. 8).

Let us compare with this view WITTGENSTEIN'S words about the concept of a game, written 35 years later: "Can you give the boundary? No. You can *draw* one; for, none has so far been drawn" (*Philosophical Investigations*, § 68). By contrast, the question, raised by R. and H. KLAPPENBACH as late as 1965, appears almost anachronistic: "What characteristics are necessary for the definition of a word to be grasped in its *full* meaning?" (1965, p. 54). General Semantics has as its great mission to show that meanings are arbitrary or man-made and that they must be recognized as such, if we want to be guided by reality and not by language.

OGDEN and RICHARDS reject every fixed name-object relationship. Their conception is much more dynamic: what meaning really is can only be grasped if the process which occurs during a verbal exchange is understood. Words have no meanings as such; they get meaning by the way they are used by individuals. Language is a means not "of *symbolizing references*" ... but "for the *promotion of purposes*" (p. 16).

The pragmatic element and closeness to the later writings of WITTGENSTEIN are clearly indicated.

---

[1] Note the link between this view and the earlier discussion of the question of the truth-function of language.

Instead of the well-known relationship between word and object OGDEN and RICHARDS propose a triangular model. As, for example, WELLS (1961) has pointed out, this tripolar scheme represents the combination of two dyads: sign—interpreter (or sign-user), and interpreter—object. In the sign-user occurs a process (interpretation) which is what is normally understood by meaning. The authors describe the nature of this process as follows: "... the peculiarity of interpretation (is) that when a context has affected us in the past the recurrence of merely a part of the context will cause us to react in the way in which we reacted before. A sign is always a stimulus similar to some part of an original stimulus and sufficient to call up the engram formed by that stimulus" (p. 53).

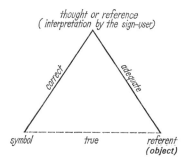

Fig. 44. Schema of the relationship between symbol, reference and object (based with slight modifications on OGDEN and RICHARDS, 1952, p. 11)

These sentences reveal the intermediate position taken by OGDEN and RICHARDS between the older view—meaning as connection with images or engrams—and the newer conception, according to which what goes on in the language-user is a third constituent (besides sign and referent) in the meaning relationship.

Moreover, for the further development of psycholinguistics it has been important that OGDEN and RICHARDS have interpreted the two dyads (word—language-user, and language-user—object signified) as a cause-effect or stimulus-response relationship. This goes back to PEIRCE who, as early as 1878, had written that in order to understand the meaning of a sentence all one had to do was to observe what habits it evoked.

By treating 'meaning' as 'stimulus' and 'response' it becomes accessible to that type of psychological enquiry which seeks information not through introspection but through observable behavior. At the same time, meaning, understood as well-practiced connection between stimulus and response, or as 'habit', places it into the area of the psychology of learning. But even for a philosopher, such as TELEGDI, meaning is a generalization, accepted by society, which "manifests itself through action and through the use of the word, which implicitly expresses the rule governing this action" (1961, p. 210; cf. p. 277.).

Morris, basing himself partly on Peirce and partly on Ogden and Richards, tried to bring logical positivism and pragmatism together. In this way he hoped to do justice to the logical, biological and empirical aspects of the symbolic process and at the same time to confine himself to statements which are controlled by rules of operation and which express verifiable predictions (1938, 1946). In his *Foundations of the Theory of Signs* (1938) he attempts to produce a three-dimensional schema of 'semiotic' (i.e., the science of signs) which integrates "a logico-empirical linguistic analysis with a basic pragmatic conception" (Apel, 1965). This schema will now be briefly described.

A necessary presupposition for the existence of signs is the goal-directed behavior of the sign-user. The essence of the sign does not lie in an abstract or ideational sphere; it lies in the fact that it is interwoven in a tissue which covers more than language, viz, the goal-oriented behavior of the sign-user.

This close connection between sign and action is also seen by Wittgenstein; his "'language-game' (is) the whole of language and the actions into which it is woven" (§ 7). For Bloomfield speech events are embedded in practical events. In Russian psychology (e.g., Vigotsky), too, it is emphasized that the beginnings of infant speech lie in the activities of the infant.

A sign establishes relations in three dimensions:

  (a) the 'syntactical' dimension relates signs to one another;

  (b) the 'semantical' dimension relates signs to the objects to which the signs are applicable; and

  (c) the 'pragmatical' dimension relates signs to human beings who use them.

Whereas Bühler holds that a sign can be analyzed as signal with regard to the receiver and as symptom with regard to the source, Morris saw the pragmatic dimension not as one of several others but as fundamental to the function of the sign. "It is precisely the interpersonal meaning of signs of a language system—however much its treatment in semantics may abstract from the concrete situation of language-use— which cannot be grasped without presupposing an act of interpreting situations as part of behavioral activity" (Apel, 1963, p. 30). Conversely, the use of signs is the major feature which distinguishes human from non-human behavior. Signs are the most powerful bonds humans have forged as well as the most useful instruments for the liberation of the individual and for the creation of societies.

A practical application of these arguments, developed by Morris, is found in Korzybski's and Hayakawa's General Semantics.

APEL has rightly pointed out that it is just this pragmatic element in MORRIS' procedure which leads to a humanistic integration and realization of linguistic structure. "Syntactical inter-relationships among signs and semantic relationships of signs to facts make sense as indicators of substantive truth only because they act as mediators in human behavioral settings" (1959 a, p. 176).

According to MORRIS meaning is, so to speak, at the intersection of the three *modi significandi*. Meaning, which in its dyadic form was treated as a purely philosophical problem, has become interesting for psychology because it takes the language-*user* into account and, as we have seen, it is the business of psycholinguistics to analyze linguistic events in relation to the language-user.

Thanks to PEIRCE, WITTGENSTEIN and MORRIS the notion of meaning, originally conceived in purely philosophical terms, has been viewed in the context of practical activity and goal-oriented behavior; it is in this way that a relationship to psychology had been established. As a consequence general developments in psychology have, in turn, come to exercise their influence on this border-area between a psychology of language and linguistic philosophy. In the next paragraphs we shall outline these influences.

Among psychological theories of meaning, that of TITCHENER was dominant for quite some time: the extra-linguistic reality with which linguistic signs are associated consists in mental processes or images. TITCHENER was famous for his extraordinarily lively mental imagery. For example, when he heard or read the word 'cow' he visualized a longish rectangle with a marked facial expression suggesting an exaggerated pout (1910, p. 529). On the other hand, other equally known psychologists reported that hearing, reading or thinking evoked different images or even no imagery at all.

These psycholinguistic arguments are akin to those of the psychology of thinking of the Würzburg School.

The research worker who wants his statements to be compelling and exact is likely to object to the 'private' and introspective character of one side of the dyadic meaning-relation. It is further questionable whether general, categorial images are at all possible. An image of my spaniel Jimmy is no doubt possible—but what image goes with 'dog' or, at a more general level, with 'animal' or 'creature'—has it fur or feathers and so on ?

In linguistics psychological terms such as 'image' or 'thought' have been used much longer than in psychology. As late as 1961 LEISI felt obliged to warn that "We have even less knowledge of the psychological facts and there is a danger of circular definition, e.g., 'thoughts and images = elements of consciousness', 'consciousness = the totality of thoughts and images'" (1961, p. 11).

The reference to images, ideas and thoughts or, in more general terms, to states of consciousness, which dominated in psychology around the turn of the century, gave rise to three opposing trends: (a) Gestalt psychology, because it mistrusted the mechanism of association linking states of consciousness; (b) psychoanalysis, because it could not find in the conscious states a common motivational thread and searched for it in the unconscious; and (c) behaviorism, because it rejected, on epistemological grounds, introspection as a method, and the appeal to states of consciousness as an explanation of psychic phenomena; but both psychoanalysis and behaviorism retained the mechanism of association.

Of these three 'revolutions' the first—Gestalt psychology—has had relatively little direct effect upon psycholinguistics, because it paid less attention to learning than to perception—and language was viewed as being acquired by learning.

It should, however, be pointed out that indirectly Gestalt psychology has contributed a great deal to modern psycholinguistics by uncovering the weaknesses of orthodox behaviorism and thus forcing it to develop further.

The second revolution, depth psychology, has yielded as its most brilliant contribution to psycholinguistics FREUD'S analysis of slips of the pen and tongue.

The third, the behavioristic revolution, became decisive for the more recent developments in psycholinguistics.

Thanks to behaviorism the endless search for the inner processes or states corresponding to verbal utterances was abandoned; as BROWN (1958a, p. 93) expressed it, WATSON mercifully closed the bloodshot inner eye of American psychology. "From the behaviorist's point of view", writes WATSON, "the problem of 'meaning' is a pure abstraction. It never arises in the scientific observation of behavior. We watch what the animal or human being is doing. He 'means' what he does. It serves no scientific or practical purpose to interrupt and ask him while he is in action what he is meaning. His action shows his meaning. Hence, exhaust the conception of action—*i.e.*, *experimentally determine all of the organized responses a given object can call forth in a given individual, and you have exhausted all possible 'meanings' of that object for that individual*" (WATSON, 1924, pp. 354-355).

Meaning equals behavior; i.e., it equals the behavior which leads to the word, and the behavior which is elicited by the word—this is the leitmotif of all present-day efforts to grasp the concept of meaning. It should be remembered that PEIRCE (before WATSON) had said that meaning is a kind of instruction to the sign-user to act in a certain way. MORRIS (after PEIRCE and WATSON) moved pragmatism into the foreground, i.e., the embedding of signs into the goal-directed behavior of sign-users, and WITTGENSTEIN (after PEIRCE, WATSON and MORRIS) gave this advice: "Don't ask for the meaning, ask for the use". The behavioristic treatment of language—as LOHMANN pointed out in 1960 (1962)—in a certain way has drawn the ultimate conclusion from the Saussurian conception of language as a system based on formal distinctions.

However, this agreement is by no means perfect. For the orthodox behaviorist the pragmatic dimension does not yet exist, at least not in its relativistic function concerning the dyad, sign—object signified. For him a sign operates as stimulus for the same behavior that originally was elicited by the object signified. The origin of this substitution is quite simply explained by WATSON through a Pavlovian conditioning theory: if a conditioned stimulus (i.e., a sound pattern) is perceived several times in temporal contiguity with an unconditioned stimulus (i.e., the object), the conditioned stimulus will soon evoke the same behavior as hitherto the unconditioned one.

This view of the replacement of objects by signs or words has of course not originated with PAVLOV or WATSON; it can, for example, already be found in SWIFT's *Gulliver's Travels*.

Gulliver visits an Academy and asks for an explanation of the research projects of the Faculty of Philosophy. One of these projects aims at the abolition of words. As speaking diminishes the lungs by corrosion, the professors made the following proposal: since words are the names for things it would be better to carry about the things needed for discourse. Unfortunately foolish women protested against this scheme, yet several most learned men adhered to it so that Gulliver was able to report that he saw some of these sages almost sinking under the weight of the packs they carried, going to debates where they opened their sacks to converse with the help of the objects they laid out.

The point that is made here is that the transition into the verbal medium is less troublesome and requires less effort (cf. GEHLEN, 1950). The same point is made in the following illustration by BROWN (1958a); we will have occasion to refer to it again later.

Suppose someone is quite familiar with the phenomenon of *rain* but has no name for it. If he is outside when it starts raining, he may open an umbrella or look for shelter. If he is at home when the rain begins, he is likely to put a coat on or, perhaps, decide not to go out. When this person learns that this event is called 'rain', he will in future behave at the sound of the word 'rain' as if he had felt or seen the rain. His 'rain behavior' which so far was evoked by the stimulus rain is now also

evoked by the stimulus-word 'rain'; what has occurred is the characteristic transfer of behavior from one stimulus to another, which is familiar
as the essence of the conditioning process (p. 94).

The key position accorded to conditioning in this theory has formed
the focus of a decisive critique which will be referred to in detail later in
this book.

Now that the discussion of the development of modern linguistic
philosophy and of the interaction of this philosophy with behavioristic
approaches has enabled us to place studies such as those by NOBLE
into a wider context, we shall return to empirical investigations of
meaning within the framework of associationism.

Chapter 9

The Field Concept of Meaning

Concept of a lexical field — TRIER — PORZIG'S 'essential relations' — The conceptualization of associative meaning — DEESE'S investigations.

As we have seen, meaning as connection can be understood in two ways: it can be the connection of the word to extralinguistic behavioral events (BLOOMFIELD'S 'practical events'); but it can also be understood as the connection of the word to other words which constitute its verbal environment. We have become acquainted with the latter in the experiments on word meaning which studied the associations which words evoke. Closer inspection will show that the distinction between these two approaches to meaning as connection is not very great; in both cases it is a question of behavior, practical or associative, and again in both the meaning of a word is viewed as a response evoked by it.

NOBLE had completely concentrated on one formal characteristic of the associative connection, i.e., the number of associations which a word evokes in the unit of time. This extreme behavioristic and formalized attempt to interpret meaning prompted us to digress and to explore the background in linguistic philosophy to the problem of meaning.

Taking up the discussion again at this juncture, we will find that modern linguistics has contributed a concept which we must now consider, i.e., the lexical field. This concept extends the dyadic scheme on which, at its origin at least, associationism was based. It originated in the twenties under the influence of Gestalt or holistic psychology. In 1924 IPSEN talked about the 'semantic field' and understood it as a group of words which together form a semantic unit. He cites as an example the Indo-Germanic words for sheep and sheep-rearing. Such words do not necessarily belong together from an etymological point of view, nor are they inevitably linked by association. They are—contrary to holistic conceptions—viewed as close to each other like the stones of a mosaic and divide up a field of activity of the ancient Indo-Europeans into semantic areas (IPSEN, pp. 224f.).

The field concept introduced by TRIER has become even more important and more influential than that of IPSEN. In contrast to a psycholinguistic approach, TRIER investigates language as *ergon* or, in Saussurian terminology, as *langue*. "Existence is given to us through the intermediate world of language" (1934, p. 428). This statement defines the position from which he starts[1].

TRIER'S conception of the lexical field can best be put in his own words: "Every language confronts reality as a system of selection of a kind which always creates a completely closed and rounded image of that reality. The manner in which language constructs its image of reality, which is a complete whole with no gaps, yet, at the same time, selecting, restricting and dividing, can best be described with the concept of structure. The linguistic substance is not simply copied from reality; instead, the ordering structure of language projects upon reality a view which creates the linguistic-conceptual forms of its wholes and parts, its links and divisions" (p. 429).

HUMBOLDT'S influence is evident: language orders the world—a point of view which will be examined later. "In saying this we recognize at the same time that there is nothing isolated in language. Since structure is the essence of language, each individual item results from structuring; it is determined in its nature and function by its position in the structure, its place in the whole of language" (TRIER, p. 429).

Whereas scholars who operate with the concept of association view context as a synthesis of fundamentally independent elements, TRIER proceeds in the opposite direction. Following a holistic approach according to which the whole is prior to the parts, he argues: "If the essence of language is a structure and organization of the whole, the field approach moves downward from the whole to the part and not upward, gathering separate items into larger units" (p. 449). "The word exists only because it is part of the organized whole of lexis. This organization of the whole determines the significance of each part. Every act of speaking and listening is orientation within this structure ..." (p. 429).

The meaning of the word is, therefore, determined by the reality of the field as a whole which is available to the speaker and the listener. This theory reinforces the point of view represented in this book according to which sequential and associative determinants must be treated as closely related.

To cite one example: "a word such as 'intelligent' certainly relates to the totality of the lexis, but not directly; in the first instance it forms part of the smaller partial group to which belong, besides 'intelligent',

---

[1] We recognize clearly the reduplication of the world to which psychology with its anti-Platonic approach is opposed.

such words as 'wise', 'clever', 'smart', 'cunning', 'learned', 'experienced', 'knowledgeable', 'educated', etc." (TRIER, p. 430). "Fields are the linguistic realities intermediate between the single word and the total lexis" (p. 430). In this formulation, again, the individual word without the field would not be meaningful; thus the field is regarded as a reality of a special kind.

TRIER'S lexical field-theory, which has been upheld vigorously, has exercised a great influence on German linguistics (e.g., on WEISGERBER). It must, however, be noted that this concept in no small measure derives its prestige from a rather imprecise analogy with field-theoretical arguments in physics and, as already mentioned, in Gestalt psychology. ÖHMAN has, for example, pointed out that it is not clear what the lines or points of force are in a lexical field.

Another field concept in German linguistics developed by PORZIG (1934) stands in contrast to TRIER'S. It is less widely known but is closer to psycholinguistics. PORZIG starts out from the essential semantic relationships between verbs and nouns or adjectives and nouns. The verb 'walk' presupposes 'legs' or 'feet'; it is therefore a predicate which implies a subject; 'grasp' presupposes 'hand', and 'blond' presupposes 'hair'; the verb 'bark' implies 'dog'. "Evidently, therefore, all items belonging together semantically within such necessary relationships are interchangeable or could be substituted for one another" (p. 73). A Porzig field is built up from below, i.e., from the individual word, a word pair, or its inter-pair relations.

These ideas on the field concept expressed in German linguistics have been formulated in a manner which is not particularly congenial to present-day psychology. This explains why there has been hardly any cross-fertilization. If we contrast the linguistic field concept with investigations by DEESE and thus resume the discussion begun in chapter 7, it will become clear that it is possible to reach similar viewpoints by starting out from entirely different positions and by employing entirely different procedures.

Fig. 45

The starting point for DEESE is the phenomenon of 'clustering' already referred to; i.e., in a memory experiment, words to be learned, presented in random order, are not recalled randomly but ordered according to categories. There are forces at work which bring together words that belong together. Such associations seem to form well-organized networks or clusters.

NOBLE did not assume a network of relations but a constellation: all connections link *one* stimulus with a number of responses (Fig. 45).

DEESE now discards this simple S-R model because it has been found that two stimulus-words, although they fail to evoke each other as responses, can have a number of responses in common. Thus, 'piano' does not evoke 'symphony' as an associate, nor does 'symphony' elicit 'piano'; but 'music', 'note' or 'orchestra' are responses which are evoked both by 'piano' or 'symphony' as stimulus-words.

This observation prompted DEESE to attempt to come to grips with associative meaning by describing the relations which exist between responses to different stimuli. "If the associative meaning of a stimulus is given by the distribution of responses to that stimulus, then two stimuli may be said to have the same associative meaning when the distribution of associates to them is *identical*. Two stimuli overlap or resemble one another in associative meaning to the extent that they have the same distribution of associates" (1962, p. 163). The connection between associative responses is the associative meaning of the stimulus concerned.

DEESE gives common associations a weight corresponding to their frequency. In order also to include pairs of stimulus-words which evoke each other as responses but have no other response in common, DEESE makes use of the concept of 'representational' response already referred to (cf. p. 144); i.e., he assumes that, to begin with, each stimulus-word evokes itself as response.

For his empirical investigation DEESE selects stimulus-words in a specific manner: he chooses words which, he assumes, somehow belong together. In this way he is able to study whether his concept of associative meaning and the operational definition of this concept can make evident relationships which are known to us from a prescientific linguistic insight. If this is the case it is possible to make use of this operationally defined concept even in cases where prescientific linguistic insight has no ready answers. In the following illustration DEESE uses words as stimuli all of which, according to Kent-Rosanoff norms, appeared as responses to the word 'butterfly'. In other words, DEESE makes use of a Trier-type word-field.

These words are presented to 50 subjects as stimuli in a word-association experiment (Table 15).

Afterwards the frequency of occurrence of a given word as response to these stimuli is calculated. The response 'moth' is given twice to the stimulus-word 'insect', once to the stimulus-word 'bug', 8 times to 'cocoon' and 7 times to 'butterfly'. The similarity of associative meaning

Table 15. *Frequencies of associates in common to 19 words based on responses of 50 subjects* (based on DEESE, 1962, p. 166)

Responses (associated words)	Stimulus-words (the numbers correspond to the first 19 response-words)																	
	1	2	3	4	5	6	7	8	9	10	11	12	13	14	15	16	17	18	19
1 Moth	50	2						1	8										7
2 Insect	1	50			3				3										6
3 Wings	2		50	4															5
4 Bird			25	50	4			1	2				9				2		4
5 Fly	10	9	12	15	50			2			1		1				1		4
6 Yellow						50	2				1			4					3
7 Flower						2	50				1	2	1		10		1	2	2
8 Bug		24			4			50	5			1							2
9 Cocoon								50	50										2
10 Color						5				50	6								
11 Blue				1	1	2	2			8	50		1		40				
12 Bees		1					2	2				50							
13 Summer	2								1			1	50	1	1				
14 Sunshine													1	50				12	
15 Garden						6									50				
16 Sky					1						6			1		50			
17 Nature																	50	1	
18 Spring													3					50	
19 Butterfly	1								8										50
20 Light	4				1									4					
21 Pretty							3												2
22 Ant		3			1		5												
23 Bright										1				4					
24 Airplane			4		1														
25 Feather			2	3															
26 Flight			1	2															
27 Tree				2	1									1			6		
28 Plane			2		5														
29 Red						6	1			16	13								
30 White						1				5	2								
31 Green						5	2				4		1		3		2		
32 Sun						2													
33 Beetle		1						1											
34 Spider		1						1											
35 Gold						1					1		1						
36 Black		1				1				8	2								
37 Winter													17					4	
38 Warm													3	8					
39 Plant						2									5		1		
40 Gray						1				1	2								
41 Brown						1				1									
42 Vacation													2					1	

of two stimuli is determined in the following way: DEESE relates the number of responses which are common to these two stimuli to the maximally possible number of common responses to the same two stimulus-words.

In the above table 'moth' and 'insect' have 12 responses in common: the response 'moth' occurs 50 times in response to the stimulus-word 'moth' (this is the implicit response), and twice in response to the stimulus-word 'insect'; therefore two responses are common. The re-

Table 16. *Overlap coefficients for common associates between the 19 words in Table 15*
(Decimals omitted) (from DEESE, 1962, p. 167)

Stimulus-words	Stimulus-words																		
	1	2	3	4	5	6	7	8	9	10	11	12	13	14	15	16	17	18	19
1 Moth	100	12	12	12	11	02	00	05	11	00	00	02	02	05	01	01	01	01	15
2 Insect		100	09	09	17	01	01	33	10	01	01	03	00	00	00	00	01	00	12
3 Wing			100	44	19	00	00	03	02	00	00	10	00	00	00	00	03	00	13
4 Bird				100	21	01	00	03	02	01	01	10	00	01	00	01	05	00	12
5 Fly					100	01	01	08	06	01	02	06	00	03	00	02	04	00	11
6 Yellow						100	07	00	00	17	23	02	02	07	05	02	04	03	05
7 Flower							100	02	00	03	07	02	01	06	18	02	06	02	04
8 Bug								100	07	00	00	05	00	00	00	00	02	00	04
9 Cocoon									100	00	00	04	01	01	01	00	02	00	22
10 Color										100	32	00	00	02	00	08	00	00	00
11 Blue											100	01	02	04	04	46	03	02	02
12 Bees												100	01	02	03	00	04	02	07
13 Summer													100	05	02	00	01	10	00
14 Sunshine														100	02	03	02	15	04
15 Garden															100	00	04	02	02
16 Sky																100	00	01	00
17 Nature																	100	02	03
18 Spring																		100	02
19 Butterfly																			100

Table 17. *Rotated centroid factor loadings of stimulus overlap coefficients presented in Table 16.* (Decimals omitted) (from DEESE, 1962, p. 169)

Words	Factors					
	I	II	III	IV	V	VI
Moth	44	03	−27	−01	−03	−32
Insect	50	01	−33	01	−34	11
Wing	52	01	45	01	29	−07
Bird	52	02	46	01	29	−07
Fly	48	03	32	01	−28	−03
Yellow	01	44	−03	34	−32	−02
Flower	01	39	−03	−32	03	44
Bug	41	01	−34	00	−14	37
Cocoon	40	01	−35	00	25	02
Color	−02	42	−04	44	04	−04
Blue	−02	57	−04	52	23	−04
Bees	36	04	34	−02	−30	00
Summer	−01	31	−03	−34	−02	−34
Sunshine	02	37	−04	−33	−03	−35
Garden	00	35	−02	−34	−03	44
Sky	−01	41	−03	43	38	−07
Nature	04	31	29	−02	01	34
Spring	−01	35	−03	−37	−02	−36
Butterfly	48	06	−29	−01	26	01

sponse 'insect' is given once to the stimulus-word 'moth' and 50 times to 'insect' as stimulus-word; one response is common. The response-word 'fly' occurs 10 times with 'moth' as stimulus-word and 9 times with the stimulus-word 'insect': accordingly 9 responses are common. The two stimuli 'moth' and 'insect' have $2+1+9 = 12$ common responses. The maximally possible number of common responses would be 100; it would occur if each of the stimulus-words would only evoke the other as response. The coefficient of similarity of the associative meanings of these two stimulus-words in this case amounts to $\frac{12}{100}$ or 0.12. DEESE calls this value the 'overlap coefficient'.

After these values have been entered on a matrix, they are subjected to factor analysis to find out mathematically how many factors can account for these relationships (Table 16). DEESE is aware of the fact that the factors to be extracted are in this case determined by the special selection of the words employed. The resulting factor loadings have been set out in Table 17.

It is evident that the separation into factors has been fairly successful; approximately half the words have positive loadings on Factor I and nearly zero loadings on Factor II; the results are reversed for the other half. Factor I appears in words which suggest animal creation: moth, insect, wing, bird, fly, bug, cocoon, bees, butterfly. Factor II loadings refer to non-animate items: yellow, flower, color, etc. Factor III has zero loadings on the non-animate words and appears to order animate items on a bipolar dimension: positive loadings on such words as wing, bird, fly and bees, and negative ones on bug, cocoon and moth. Factor IV makes a bipolar split of the non-animate words: summer, sunshine, garden, flower and spring on the one hand, and, on the other, blue, sky, yellow and color.

A comparison of factor profiles for pairs of words is particularly instructive; e.g., 'blue' and 'yellow'. Both are alike in that they share common loadings with summer, sunshine, color, etc. On one factor they diverge: in factor V 'blue' goes with sky, butterfly, wing and bird, while 'yellow' goes with insect, fly, bug and bee.

The result of factor analysis, therefore, is a division of the lexis into lexical areas—exactly what TRIER had attempted to achieve with his field concept. But whereas TRIER invents a purely subjective, intellectualistic structure, DEESE'S procedure is based on the actual verbal behavior of an entire group of speakers.

How unsatisfactory the subjective, 'invented' construction (or reconstruction) of semantic fields often is, is suggested by the following example. WEISGERBER divides the lexical field 'misdemeanor—crime' in the manner indicated in Table 18. What is postulated here as difference, for example, between 'Tölpelei' ('clumsiness') and 'Flegelei' ('loutishness'),

Table 18. *The Field* "Vergehen —Verbrechen *Misdemeanor —crime*"
(adapted with approximate English translations in italics from L. WEISGERBER, 1962 a, p. 262)

Verstoß gegen welche Norm: / *Offence against standards of:*	Grad der Verantwortung / *Degree of responsibility*						
	ohne Wissen und Willen (reine Feststellung). *without knowledge and without intent (pure statement of fact), inadvertently*	Wissen möglich. *knowledge possible*	Verpflichtung zu Wissen. *knowledge required*	Ansatz des Wissens. *beginnings of knowledge, "inkling"*	Aufhören des Nichtwollens. *acting almost deliberately*	mit Wissen und Willen. *deliberately, with intent*	aus Anlage. *acting out of natural disposition*
Was zweckmäßig ist / *appropriateness*	Versehen / *oversight*	(Bock, Lapsus) / *(slip, lapse)*	Gedankenlosigkeit / *thoughtlessness*	Unbedachtheit / *hastiness*	Unüberlegtheit / *rashness*	Sinnlosigkeit / *senselessness*	Torheit / *folly*
Was sich gehört / *acceptability*	Fehler / *mistake*	Schnitzer / *bloomer*	Unschicklichkeit / *unseemliness*	Ungehörigkeit / *impertinence*	Unfug / *prank*	Böswilligkeit / *maliciousness*	Tölpelei / *clumsiness*
Was vernünftig ist / *reasonable conduct*	Irrtum / *error*	Fehlgriff / *blunder*	Dummheit / *stupidity*	Unbesonnenheit / *recklessness*	Unvernünftigkeit / *unreasonableness*	Verrücktheit / *madness*	Narrheit / *foolishness*
Was sich gebührt / *propriety*	Entgleisung / *faux pas*	Mißgriff / *hooler*	Unziemlichkeit / *unseemliness*	Ungebührlichkeit / *impropriety*	Unverschämtheit / *impudence*	Gemeinheit / *meanness*	Flegelei Lümmelei / *loutishness uncouthness*
Was Satzung ist / *statutory law*	Verletzung / *breach*	Zuwiderhandlung / *contravention*	Überschreitung / *infringement*	Übertretung / *violation*	Widersetzlichkeit / *insubordination*	Vergehen / *misdemeanor*	(Rebellion) / *(rebellion)*
Was recht ist / *right*	Verfehlung / *misguided action*	Fehltritt / *serious lapse*	Übergriff / *encroachment*	Übeltat / *offence*	Missetat / *misdeed*	Verbrechen / *crime*	Schurkerei Schuftigkeit / *roguery villainy*
Was zur sittlichen Ordnung gehört / *ethics*	Verirrung / *aberration*	Untat / *misdeed*	Schandtat / *infamy*	Ruchlosigkeit / *felony*	Frevel / *outrage*	Sünde / *sin*	Teufelei / *devilishness*

or between 'Fehlgriff' ('blunder') and 'Irrtum' ('error')—to name only a few—expresses WEISGERBER'S opinion; but it certainly does not reflect accepted usage to such an extent that everyone would unquestioningly agree with it.

In this presentation WEISGERBER expresses his personal intuitions on what constitutes a field, i.e., something that in a particular language is 'objectively' given. By contrast it is possible to study objectively (i.e., by counting or measuring) the subjective field structure of an individual speaker. In other words, it is possible to investigate which words or topics go together in the verbal behavior of a particular person, and draw conclusions, e.g., as to the emotional state or the value structure of this speaker. In this approach the aim is not to discover lexical field structures in a language as a study in semantics, but to discover field structures in a speaker as a study of personality. In this case these relationships are exploited for clinical diagnosis rather than for linguistic study. The interest is not directed to structures in the language or in speech, but in the speaker. Certain approaches to content analysis should be mentioned here, which—as OSGOOD (POOL, 1959) says—use verbal utterances to draw conclusions about characteristics of the speaker. One might mention as an example the evaluation of GOEBBELS' Diary to study the thought structure of its author.

Returning now to psycholinguistics in the narrower sense, let us add the result of one other of DEESE'S investigations as a counterpart to WEISGERBER'S semantic fields. DEESE extracted from the ALLPORT-VERNON *Study of Values* (a questionnaire concerned with value orientation based on SPRANGER) words which refer to religious values. These words were submitted as stimuli to students who, according to the ALLPORT-VERNON questionnaire, had been found to have a marked religious value orientation. The factor loadings calculated from the matrix which had thus been produced are represented in Table 19.

It will be seen that the words arrange themselves into two groups: divine, spirit, prayer, worship, reverence, religion, faith and devotion in one group, and hope, soul, love, inspire, service, sermon and clergyman in the other. The two fields might perhaps be described as the institutional-theological and the human-individual respectively.

DEESE'S use of the concept of associative meaning and of similarity of associative meaning between two words has affinity with certain views of SAPORTA and ERVIN to which we referred in the discussion on paradigmatic associations. The greater the similarity of associative meaning between two words the greater is the probability that these words occur in the same situational and verbal context. And vice versa: the more sentence frames there are in which words A and B can be slotted into the same position, the greater the similarity of meaning. Since for SAPORTA and ERVIN the criterion of similarity is of course the substitutability within equal sentence frames, their approach is complicated by the fact that sequential and grammatical determinants are at work and therefore leave relatively little manoeuvrability for similarity of meaning to manifest itself, whereas in the word-association experiment such grammatical constraints do not exist and therefore similarity of meaning can be demonstrated with greater ease.

Table 19. *Factor loadings of the overlap coefficients for 15 stimulus-words with religious reference.* (Rotated centroid factors; decimal point omitted) (from DEESE, 1962, p. 171)

Words	Factors					
	I	II	III	IV	V	VI
Sermon	03	43	38	−10	04	33
Clergyman	11	42	05	−47	00	26
Religion	54	03	−02	−34	−03	−36
Service	−01	40	−02	−43	37	−16
Worship	57	04	33	−05	−30	−02
Reverence	55	04	36	02	27	−03
Prayer	54	03	34	−03	−01	−34
Soul	06	38	−02	34	03	39
Spirit	39	00	−37	05	39	05
Divine	50	00	05	35	34	04
Faith	52	08	−36	−04	−35	01
Inspire	03	40	−01	33	−01	−41
Devotion	49	10	−33	02	00	34
Love	03	38	00	35	36	05
Hope	06	37	−41	−01	−04	−45

With the help of the free association method, past concrete speech situations show up as a kind of 'deposit'; or, to use another metaphor, the landscape of associations surrounding a particular word reflects the climate which has prevailed at this particular syntactic, semantic and pragmatic juncture in the development of the individual and his language.

Chapter 10

Mediation Theories of Language Processes

Chains of associations — Semantic generalization — Mediating associations — BOUSFIELD's mediation theory — The mediation process in relation to classification and differentiation — OSGOOD's model — Emotional components of meaning — Semantic differential — Application and critique of the semantic differential — Denotation and connotation.

In neobehavioristic psycholinguistics meaning is viewed basically as that form of behavior which follows as a response to a verbal stimulus whose meaning is to be ascertained. On the basis of the word-association experiment it is generally assumed that the correlate of a verbal stimulus is *verbal* behavior. Thus, DEESE defines the meaning of a word as the distribution of *verbal* responses to this stimulus. Meaning in this conception is equated with a network of verbal associations.

In this way an important role is accorded to *verbal* associations. In the present chapter we intend to investigate to what extent the view can be sustained that the association between *words* is decisive and to find out at what point it must be replaced by another view in which association is not specified in this manner.

Similarity and contrast, contiguity in time and space have for over 2000 years been recognized as the laws of association. However, similarity and dissimilarity are largely subjective categories accessible only to introspection and therefore not amenable to a behavioristic procedure; the result is that all the emphasis has been laid on contiguity or co-occurrence.

However, a number of experiments in the psychology of learning are known in which processes seem to be associated with one another which hitherto have not occurred together and to which the categories similar-dissimilar are not applicable either. This connection can best be illustrated by the so-called SHIPLEY example: tapping the cheek elicits eye blink as an unconditioned reflex. A weak light-flash is presented several times at the same time as the tap; as a consequence the flash elicits eye blink as a conditioned reflex.

Next the tapping is paired with a pain stimulus to one finger which elicits the withdrawal of the finger. Once the connection

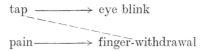

is well established the light-flash alone is offered to the subject, and although hitherto neither light and finger-withdrawal nor light and pain have occurred together, the light-flash elicits the withdrawal of the finger:

light ————→ eye blink + finger-withdrawal

The explanation lies in the fact that in the second step of the described conditioning process the finger-withdrawal is 'hooked' onto the eyelid reaction evoked by tapping.

If we attempt to formulate this more precisely the finger-withdrawal does not become attached directly to the eyelid reaction but to the perception by the subject of his own response, in other words to the proprioceptive stimuli produced by the response. Since the light in the first phase of the conditioning experiment can elicit the eyelid reaction, in the second phase the light also evokes the finger-withdrawal mediated by the eye blink.

Thus a chain has been created by interposing a connecting link as mediator between light and finger-withdrawal, which hitherto have not occurred together; or, expressed in more general terms, if two elements A and B which have no connection with one another are each separately linked to C, they, in turn, become linked by way of C.

In the above example a connecting link is assumed as an explanation of the fact that a stimulus evokes a response with which it has hitherto not occurred. A second approach to this problem can be made by asking how it is that two different stimuli can evoke the same response. A preliminary answer is provided by numerous Russian investigations on the second-signal system. These investigations have been based on the following design. To begin with, a conditioned response to a particular stimulus-object is acquired. If the subject is subsequently presented with a word which designates this object this word also evokes the reaction. Thus, for example, the response 'press lever' can be conditioned to a light signal. Once this conditioned response has been established, the word 'light' alone can also evoke the response.

That this phenomenon is a case of generalization (i.e., a response hitherto evoked only by a particular stimulus is now also evoked by a second 'similar' stimulus) can be further clarified by the experiments which, for example, RAZRAN has undertaken to study the phenomenon of the so-called 'semantic generalization'. If, for instance, a saliva secretion response is conditioned to the word 'style', the same response can be evoked, although more weakly, by the semantically similar 'fashion'. The less similar to the original stimulus-word the meanings of the words subsequently offered as stimuli are, the more reduced is the response. It is interesting to note, that in these cases semantic similarity is more influential than phonological similarity: generalization is surprisingly more marked for synonyms than for homophones. If in the given example 'style' is not followed by 'fashion' but by 'stile', it evokes hardly any response.

What mediates between the first and the second stimulus, between 'style' and 'fashion'? Are both unconsciously brought in contact with a *genus proximum*? Whereas in the SHIPLEY experiment the subject after the tap on the cheek is still blinking when he retracts his finger and therefore the blink as a mediating link is quite overt, in the case of semantic generalization the mediating link is entirely hidden.

The question of the origin and nature of these connecting links and the mechanism of mediation is today in the center of a great deal of psycholinguistic work. These studies will now be considered.

Chain formation (SHIPLEY) and semantic generalization can only be explained by an S-R theory if a mediating device between S and R is postulated. Following the behavioristic orientation this mediating mechanism is not regarded as thought or as a cognitive state ('knowledge') which does not directly manifest itself as behavior; it is viewed as an association. In contrast to the immediate associations discussed in the preceding chapter, this one is labelled the 'mediate' or 'mediating association'.

This construct can be traced back to HULL (1930) who argues that there are acts whose sole function it is to serve as stimuli for other acts. He calls them pure stimulus acts. HULL was aware of the significance of this argument: he describes these pure stimulus acts as the "organic basis of symbolism".

How should we imagine these pure stimulus acts? It may be illustrated by one of OSGOOD's examples (1953, pp. 400 f.), which—although not taken from psycholinguistics—explains the principle: the sequence of acts of tying a shoe lace. If we consider such a sequence in a five-year-old child who requires all his skill and attention to complete this task, it will be recognized that an initial situation describable in physical terms S_1, i.e. seeing the loose laces, is followed by the associated response R_1, grasping the laces with both hands. This response R_1 changes the situation for the child: hands and laces are seen in a new position S_2. This new stimulus S_2 must now be followed by the next response R_2, the movement of crossing and twisting the laces. This again changes the stimulus situation, so that we now have S_3 and so on.

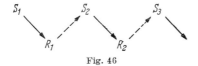

Fig. 46

How does this series of almost isolated stimuli and responses become the unitary sequence which an adult can execute without paying direct attention and even in darkness? The external stimuli which in the early stage in the child guide the action must lose their significance. Their role is taken over by proprioceptive stimuli. It is no longer necessary to see the laces; the feedback of hand movements is sufficient. All that is needed are the kinesthetic and sensory-motor input of the individual's own responses.

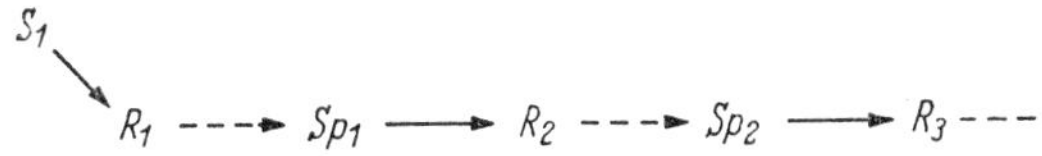

$$S_1 \searrow$$
$$R_1 \dashrightarrow Sp_1 \longrightarrow R_2 \dashrightarrow Sp_2 \longrightarrow R_3 \dashrightarrow$$

Fig. 47

Response R_1 is fed back and perceived as proprioceptive stimulus S_{p1}. Each response has at the same time stimulus value, and this stimulus value is associated with the next response, so that the feedback of the completion of one response serves as the stimulus for eliciting the next response.

As already mentioned previously, LASHLEY drew attention to the fact that the feedback of the individual's own action would require too much time to guide in this way very rapid sequences, e.g., piano playing. Consequently, HEBB has moved this organization from a combination between peripheral and central areas entirely into the central area. HEBB's phase sequence achieves the spatio-temporal organization here referred to. For our present purposes the following arguments are, however, more important than a detailed neurophysiological specification.

It was seen in the most diverse areas of psychology that it is essential to postulate, between the initial stimulus and the terminal response of an action chain, intermediate links which assume the role of mediator, i.e., which are to be understood as being at the same time response *and* stimulus. These mediation theories, which are widely recognized today, frequently appear remarkably close to linguistic processes, even where

—e.g., in the psychology of thinking—they have been used outside the area of psycholinguistics proper.

Having formulated the principle of this theory in terms of general psychology and theory of learning, let us now discuss the psycholinguistic implications of this approach.

An experiment by RUSSELL and STORMS (1955) was intended to study the effect of such mediational processes upon the acquisition of linguistic material.

From the norms of the word-association experiment it is known that the response to the stimulus-word 'stem' is most likely to be 'flower'. If 'flower' is presented as stimulus-word, the primary (i.e., the most frequent) response is 'smell'. 'Stem' hardly ever elicits 'smell' directly, but it can be assumed that a chain leads from 'stem' to 'flower' and from 'flower' to 'smell'. Accordingly, an experiment was devised to find out whether such a chain with a mediating response had any influence on learning. One group of subjects learned a pair consisting of a nonsense syllable and the word 'stem': 'CEF-stem'; the second group was not given this learning task. Later, both groups were asked to learn pairs of the type 'CEF-smell'. The result was that those who had learned 'CEF-stem' learned 'CEF-smell' more quickly.

> In more general terms the design of this experiment is as follows:
> The norms show: A—B; B—C;
> the subjects learn: X—A;
> they are tested for speed of learning of the pair X—C.

Mediating associations, therefore, create a relationship between the two acts of learning. This relationship manifests itself as positive transfer or as facilitation of learning the second task.

A number of investigations are available which were able to produce evidence for the effect of such mediating processes on learning, retention and on availability of verbal material. In addition, they provide information—of greater interest to learning theory than to psycholinguistics—on the effects of details of design and execution of such experiments. Among these studies mention should be made of those by CRAMER, DUNCAN, HOUSTON, MARTIN and DEAN, PETERSON, PETERSON et al., RUNQUIST and FARLEY.

In the experiment reported above, a covert verbal mediating association is assumed as a link between a verbal stimulus and a verbal response. The fact that the mediating link is supposed to be of a verbal nature constitutes further specification of a general mediation theory of learning which, in its original form, had only stated that the mediating link was not cognitive in character but purely a response-stimulus unit.

On the basis of this general mediation theory two constructions of psycholinguistic interest have been built. They differ from each other in that in the first the character of the link—as in the study just mentioned by RUSSELL and STORMS—is specified as a *verbal* association, whereas in the other the mediating unit is an *emotional* link. UNDERWOOD and RICHARDSON, GOSS and DEESE adhere to the first view; their case is particularly clearly stated by BOUSFIELD. The principal representative of the other view is OSGOOD. The debate between these two opposing schools of the mediation family has provoked such a wealth of ingenious experimentation that this may well be considered as one of the most interesting and most fruitful areas of psycholinguistics today. Without going into the details and subtle distinctions of the argument, let us at this point attempt to understand the two basic models.

BOUSFIELD sets out from the strictly behavioristic conviction that meaning is such an elusive concept and is so closely bound up with philosophical implications that it would be best to avoid it altogether in psychology. But since this notion—because, as BOUSFIELD has said, of able and influential friends—has penetrated into psychology, the least one can try to do is to link it to operations. The meaning of a word—as it appears as a factor of a speech event—is the behavior correlated with that word, which results whenever this word occurs as a stimulus. Verbal stimuli and verbal responses are given; the mediating associations which are required for an S-R analysis in behavioristic terms are also conceived as verbal in nature, analogous to overt verbal associations.

BOUSFIELD assumes that repeated stimulation leads to the development of a representational sequence. Such a sequence (the order of presentation should be noted) consists of a representational response and a representational stimulus.

The representational response, which has already been mentioned in a different context (cf. pp. 144, 167), is a specially stable part of the total reaction system to a stimulus and is particularly conditionable. In the cases of interest to us here, the representational response is generally identical with a silent repetition of the heard stimulus-word. This implicit repetition of the heard word has in turn also the character of a stimulus:

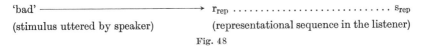

'bad' ⸺⸺⸺⸺⸺⸺⸺⸺→ r_{rep} .... s_{rep}
(stimulus uttered by speaker)   (representational sequence in the listener)

Fig. 48

r_{rep} is the response part and s_{rep} the stimulus part of the representational sequence. s_{rep} is conditionable.

How can this model serve to explain the development of a meaningful response to a verbal stimulus ? BOUSFIELD illustrates it with the example of how the meaning of the word 'evil' develops. How does a child learn what 'evil' means ?

12*

The developmental sequence begins when the small child hears the word 'bad' and at the same time is given a slap on his hand. This is interpreted as a conditioning process: the pain is the unconditioned stimulus US; it prompts also a representational response R_{rep}. The conditioned stimulus CS is the word 'bad' uttered by the adult; it, too, is followed by a representational response r_{rep} whose proprioceptive stimulation is s_{rep}. As CS and US are almost simultaneous, s_{rep} is being conditioned so that in future s_{rep}, when the word 'bad' is heard, is capable of evoking the representational response to pain.

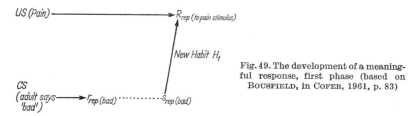

Fig. 49. The development of a meaningful response, first phase (based on BOUSFIELD, in COFER, 1961, p. 83)

By running through this sequence several times a habit has been created which we call H_1.

At a later point in time the child hears the word 'evil', which so far has been unknown to him, and, immediately after, the word 'bad' with which he is already familiar. He might, for example, have asked his parents what 'evil' means; or both words have been applied to him. The word 'evil' here functions as CS which has its representational consequence. The word 'bad' is the US which elicits the representational sequence belonging to 'bad' as well as the habit H_1, acquired through earlier conditioning, so that the representational response to pain is evoked.

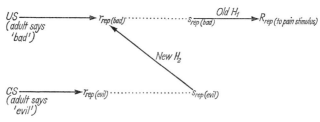

Fig. 50. The development of a meaningful response, second phase (based on BOUSFIELD, in COFER, 1961, p. 83)

If the child at a later stage hears 'evil', we should expect that he should say 'bad' either implicitly or, at least, think it associatively. Thus the habit H_2 is established by the new conditioning process.

r_{rep}('evil'), then, evokes the entire representational sequence of 'bad'; i.e., it leads as far as the R_{rep} (pain).

In BOUSFIELD'S model the representational response r_{rep} constitutes the mediating link between a relatively new stimulus and a response evoked earlier by another stimulus. r_{rep} is a mediating response. BOUSFIELD'S interpretation is a mediation theory of the acquisition of meaning.

In the course of the use of language and as a result of such use, a certain equivalence of stimuli is created. Such acquired equivalence can also be regarded as the formation of classes of stimuli which is caused by the mediating function of the intermediate links.

To test such a mediating theory let us consider once more a problem we discussed earlier (p. 135): how can it be explained that children have largely syntagmatic associations (e.g., go—home), whereas adults tend to form paradigmatic ones (e.g., go—come). JENKINS (in ROSENBERG, 1965) argues as follows. Let us assume a child repeatedly encounters two different words in the same context, e.g., A-B-C-X-D and A-B-C-Y-D. This should lead first of all to syntagmatic connections: C should elicit X and Y, and X as well as Y should elicit D. If these sequences are repeated often enough and if other contexts are available in which X and Y play similar roles, then X and Y (resulting from the common mediating links C and D) should become members of the same class and should thus have the capacity to elicit one another. If X still evokes D in the child, in the adult X would elicit Y.

Careful consideration will show that in this case the mediation model has achieved even more than just to explain the difference in associative behavior between adults and children. For the first time an interpretation is offered of how a class of words (and indeed a grammatical class) is formed. Hitherto we had merely taken note — with some astonishment — of the fact that grammatical classes appear in associative behavior; e.g., verbs as stimuli produce verbs as responses, and nouns nouns, without discussing it in greater detail. We are now getting to know a mechanism which enables us to account for such grammatical classes which evidently have also psychological reality. We shall take up this argument again at a later stage (cf. chapter 13).

Mediation theories also play an important role in explaining concept formation, a problem halfway between the psychology of language and cognition. KAMINSKI (1964) describes concept-forming mediation in an analogous manner to BOUSFIELD'S model.

How do we learn that apples and bananas are collectively referred to as 'fruit', and cucumbers and cabbages as 'vegetables'? How does a person who knows the names of the different sorts acquire the class concepts 'fruit' and 'vegetables'? The sight of apples is stimulus US_1, the sight of bananas US_2, that of cabbages US_3 and of cucumbers US_4. CS 'fruit' is conditioned to US_1 (apples) and equally to US_2 (bananas). This means that the representational sequence following CS is the same for apples and bananas, and that the s_{rep} for apples and bananas are identical. The result is that—if one may use this expression—the total impression of apples (to which, besides US_1, $s_{rep\ fruit}$ also contributes) becomes somewhat more similar to the total impression of bananas ($US_2 + s_{rep\ fruit}$).

On the other hand, the CS 'vegetable' with its representational sequence containing s_{rep} is conditioned to US_3 and US_4. This $s_{rep\ vegetable}$ brings cabbages and cucumbers closer to each other because it occurs with both of them. At the same time $s_{rep\ vegetable}$ is an additional means of distinguishing US_2 from US_4. Even if a particular banana might look very much like a cucumber, they will both be categorized differently, because US_2 evokes $s_{rep\ fruit}$ and US_4 the quite different $s_{rep\ vegetable}$[1].

The conceptual aspect (i.e., the 'fruit-ness' and the 'vegetable-ness') is contained, in Bousfield's manner, in the communality of naming or the proprioception of naming. It is the connecting *verbal* link which creates the communalities and generalizations. To put it differently the *genus proximum*, in this view, is not a categorial entity on a higher level of abstraction, but a connecting link in the shape of a *word* which has been introduced by a process of conditioning.

OSGOOD'S model to which we are now turning is different from BOUS-FIELD'S in that it looks for a mediating connection in the emotional rather than in the verbal domain.

For OSGOOD—perhaps even more than for BOUSFIELD—mediation is the central concept for grasping the psychological aspect of meaning. In his view the psychologist must concern himself, in a very large measure, with studying the mediating process which takes place in the organism during encoding and decoding. OSGOOD, too, conceives this mediating process as a covert response which serves as stimulus for what finally appears as the manifest response.

The introduction of this *emotional* factor, which so far has not been considered in the attempt to come to grips with the psychology of the problem of meaning, necessitates a brief digression.

Traditional theories of language (from ARISTOTLE to WUNDT) have tended to place in the foreground the rational or functional aspect of language. The expressive and emotional aspect was considered merely in connection with the evolution of speech from the prelinguistic state (e.g., STEVENSON). Following the Scholastic distinction between various *modi significandi* and somewhat outside the main stream of historical

---

[1] *Translator's note.* The reader may be interested to note that in the German text the author contrasts apples and pears as examples of fruit with tomatoes and cucumbers as examples of vegetables, and that the distinction between an apple that looks like a tomato or a tomato that looks like an apple is helped by the different verbal classification. In English this point would have been lost, because it is customary to classify tomatoes as fruit!

development, a distinction was introduced between denotative and connotative meaning. 'Denotative' is understood as the factual content of a concept. The denotative meaning of 'moon', accordingly, would be 'a heavenly body circling round the earth, partially illuminating the night of the planet earth by means of reflected sunlight'. Denotation can, therefore, perhaps be equated with semantic meaning, i.e., the relationship between sign and object signified and, equally, with BÜHLER'S symbol function. Connotative meaning refers to evocations which occur when the word 'moon' is uttered or heard, e.g., night, cold, longing.

The 'intellectualism' of most theories of language is further shown by the fact that semantic meaning is the approximate equivalent to denotation, whereas connotation has no such corresponding equivalent.

A more differentiated division is offered by ERDMANN, one of the few scholars who has repeatedly stressed that words are more than just signs for concepts. He distinguishes in a word (a) the conceptual content, (b) the associated meaning, and (c) the affective value or emotional content. He understands under 'associated meaning' all accompanying and supporting ideas evoked by a word; and under 'affective value' or 'emotional content', he understands all emotional reactions or moods evoked by a word.

STENZEL sees a particularly close connection between emotion and meaning: "'Fundamental meaning' often lies in the emotional stratum which maintains a certain tension between the conceptual parts. From the emotional stratum different meanings derive a more precise conceptual content. But orienting impulse or emotive gesture is primary" (1934, p. 94). The experience of emotional set (the *Anmutungserlebnis* in the psychology of LERSCH), the human tendency towards experiencing meaningfulness, and ACH'S latent signifying disposition appear, in STENZEL'S conception, as the meaning-substratum of words: the "incandescence of thought" has as its sole basis "the autonomy of affect" (STENZEL, p. 34).

We reach firmer ground and come closer to OSGOOD'S model, which prompted us to digress, if we examine empirical investigations in the attempt to understand the role of emotive meaning. A consistent emotional set may establish similarity of meaning. As evidence we can cite, from a long series of mainly Russian studies, one by VOLKOVA (1953). In a conditioning experiment salivary secretion was conditioned to the utterance of the word 'good'. Subsequently, sentences were presented to a subject, some of which, according to the author, implied 'good', others implied 'bad', and others still were neutral. It was found that a transfer of the salivary secretion occurred in the case of the 'good' sentences.

There are various methodological objections to this experiment. In another experiment with a much better design ACKER and EDWARDS (1964), using a bipolar semantic scale, were able to demonstrate transfer of vasoconstriction.

In these experiments an emotive and evaluative meaning dimension acts as mediating link which makes transfer possible. It is not, as in BOUSFIELD, a covert *verbal* association. We are now ready to discuss OSGOOD's mediation model.

A stimulus S invariably and reliably evokes a particular behavior pattern R_T. A neutral stimulus Ⓢ, the sign-to-be, is now repeatedly associated with this stimulus S. In this way the neutral stimulus Ⓢ is connected with a *part* of the total behavior pattern R_T; this part is designated as 'mediating response'.

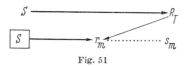

Fig. 51

At first sight this appears to be an orthodox conditioning process. But there is a decisive difference: the mediating response r_m, which follows sign Ⓢ as a representational mediating process, is not identical with R_T following the original stimulus S (the object or significate). r_m consists only of parts of R_T, in particular, of those parts which are most easily subject to conditioning (i.e., attachable to signs), require little effort and do not disturb ongoing processes of behavior of the organism. These are, above all, glandular and emotional components of R_T when elicited by S; hence, those parts which make R_T easily recognizable and readily distinguishable from other responses by the individual.

OSGOOD (in BRUNER et al., 1957, p. 94) gives the following example: the object is a ball. S designates those stimulus characteristics of the object (its shape, its resilience, its weight and so on), which regularly lead to a particular behavior pattern R_T (eye movements, grasping, squeezing, bouncing, as well as the pleasurable associations of play-behavior). According to OSGOOD's hypothesis the easily conditionable part of this total response is conditioned as r_m to the sign Ⓢ for ball. This mediating link has also a stimulus aspect s_m which elicits the further behavior prompted by the sign.

This process can be called 'representational' because the response r_m following the sign Ⓢ is part of the behavior R_T which is elicited by the designate S. The process can also be called 'mediating' because the proprioceptive stimulation s_m which originates in r_m can, in turn, be associated with the most varied instrumental acts R_x, one of which will manifest itself as most appropriate for the object designated and for the particular situation. The entire schema could be represented as in Fig. 52.

OSGOOD, too, divides the total sequence between initial stimulus and terminal response into two parts. The associations between the sign Ⓢ

and the mediator r_m he designates 'decoding habits', while the associations between the mediator and the manifest instrumental response (i.e., $s_m - R_x$) are described as 'encoding habits'.

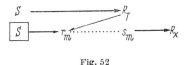

Fig. 52

Osgood defines the meaning of signals, seen from the decoding end, as significance; from the encoding end, as intention.

In principle, Osgood's model is as behavioristic as Bousfield's. The difference between the two theories is the following. According to Bousfield's view the representational response to the heard verbal signal consists in a subvocal or voiced repetition of this word. Osgood rightly criticizes this conception, for a model of sign learning should also be equally valid for the infant at a prelinguistic stage when he is not yet capable of repeating a word. Bousfield's theory is basically a refined version of the old substitution theory, according to which a sign acquires its meaning by a process of conditioning which enables it to evoke those responses which originally were evoked only by the object signified. The word 'evil' has meaning because it evokes in the child the same sequence as 'bad', and this means the identical sequence in every respect from the verbal associations right up to the possibly non-verbal terminal response. In other words, 'evil' is meaningful because its representational verbal response is, on the stimulus side, conditioned to the response following the US pain. Osgood rightly raises the objection that even in classical conditioning the conditioned response is not identical with the unconditioned response; e.g., Pavlov's dog secretes saliva upon the bell-tone but he does not really feed. Therefore it is not a case of simple substitution.

Osgood's counter-argument now runs as follows. Signs do not become meaningful because they are linked with associated words, but—and this above all—because they are also connected with emotional and dispositional states. What a certain word means for a given individual, we learn not only through verbal associations which this word evokes in him but through his facial expressions, his gestures, his expressions of joy or of distress.

The most important function of the representational mediating process is, according to Osgood (1954), to provide mediation in generalization and transfer. If different sign stimuli (or more precisely, future signs) accompany the same significate, they become linked to a common mediation process; i.e., they acquire common meaning.

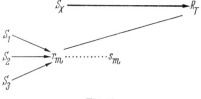

Fig. 53

This is called a convergent hierarchy of signs.

In the first phase of an experiment on mediated associations BLÖSCHL (1961) made subjects learn paired associates, e.g., 'Italy—cuckoo'. In the second (free-association) phase 'Rome' was offered as stimulus and subjects again responded with 'cuckoo'. This generalization shows that S_1 (Italy) and S_2 (Rome) are connected in some way, i.e., activate a common mediator.

Similarly, a given sign or a group of signs can be connected with quite a number of manifest responses R_1, R_2 ... (Fig. 54).

Fig. 54   Fig. 55

They form a divergent hierarchy of signs associated with a mediator. A dog's furious bark, his threatening appearance, and a call 'mind the dog' are signs for danger; they converge towards the meaning 'danger'. The mediator 'danger', in turn, is associated with a divergent hierarchy of possible acts: running away, calling for help, freezing, etc. These instrumental acts are likely to have varying habit-strengths. Which of these possibilities is selected, depends on habit-strength and the situation.

A sign can also be associated with a divergent hierarchy of mediators, e.g., when the same sign is associated with several different meanings: the sign 'woman' may evoke household, sex, anger, and so forth (Fig. 55).

These different hierarchies enable a human being to adjust himself in the flexible manner and in keeping with his experience and the situation as in fact he does.

If we relate OSGOOD'S model to BLOOMFIELD [1], we recognize that the representational process is in exactly that area in which BLOOMFIELD places meaning. But whereas in BLOOMFIELD'S conception meaning is viewed as the connection between behavioral events before and after the speech

---

[1] "... the *meaning* of a linguistic form (is) the situation in which the speaker utters it and the response which it calls forth in the hearer" (1933, p. 139).

event, in Osgood's view, meaning is to be looked for in the fractional *implicit* emotional and physiological responses which accompany the occurrence of a word.

The question now arises: are these conditioned phenomena associated with a sign as differentiated as the vocabulary of a language ? According to Osgood, there could be no greater number of different meanings than the differentiations of mediating responses permit. To express it in another way, how effective is Osgood's model which treats connotative, rather than denotative meaning as central ? This question of the efficiency of Osgood's model can indeed be answered, because Osgood, on the basis of his model, has developed a technique for the measurement of meaning, which we shall now consider. It has been designated by him as 'semantic differential'.

If we ask someone to say what a word means, the answer naturally consists of a verbal output. This spontaneously produced output will vary considerably from subject to subject in quantity and subtlety. Consequently, the answers to the question of what a given word means are not easily comparable and therefore do not lend themselves readily to an exact empirical investigation of word meanings.

Osgood now draws the following conclusion: the subjects who are asked to give the meaning of a word should have at their disposal a standardized sample of verbal responses from which they can then make a selection. The number of such responses is not left to the subject; and the response possibilities offered must be representative of the dimensions along which meanings can be distinguished.

In practice, Osgood presents to the subject a series of bipolar, adjectival scales which refer to the word whose meaning is to be defined. The subject's task is to differentiate semantically the word in question, that is, to make judgments about it by allotting to it a position on each of the scales.

An example will illustrate the procedure:

Father

happy	—— —— —— —— —— —— ×—— —— —	sad
hard	—— —— —— —— —— —— ×—— —— —— ——	soft
slow	—— ×—— —— —— —— —— —— —— —— ——	fast
. . . . . .		. . . . . .

The subject sees 'father' as rather sad, fairly soft, fairly slow and so forth.

In Osgood's view, the semantic differential represents a combination of controlled association and scaling procedures. The direction or, in more precise terms, the dimension of the associations is prescribed, but the subject is free to determine its strength.

OSGOOD aims at determining the functioning of the mediating processes which manifest their trends through these bipolar scales. As the number of such scales for a given word presented to the subject is determined by the experimenter, the question arises: how many dimensions are needed to differentiate the meaning of a word semantically in an adequate manner? Or, putting the question in another way: along how many independent dimensions can the mediating processes vary?

The answer to this question can be reached by the following consideration: anyone who classifies the word 'sin' as 'wicked', is also likely to regard it as 'ugly' and not as 'beautiful'. If this happens with many words and with a high measure of agreement among subjects, the scales *good—evil* and *beautiful—ugly* evidently measure the same dimension. Therefore, the intercorrelation of the different scales may give information as to the number of dimensions needed to order the mediating responses—or, putting it in more sophisticated terms, to define the dimensions of the semantic space.

To uncover these dimensions OSGOOD has carried out numerous factor analyses. These have shown that, for example, *good—bad, fair—unfair, beautiful—ugly,* and *sweet—sour* correlate highly with one another and can therefore be comprised in a single factor, labelled 'Evaluation' by OSGOOD. The correlation of the scales *strong—weak, hard—soft, difficult—easy, masculine—feminine,* etc. yields a 'Potency' factor; and the correlation of the scales *active—passive, fast—slow, excitable—calm, sharp—blunt* produces an 'Activity' factor.

These are the three factors of the semantic space. There are not just three because the space could not have any more, but because the analyses hitherto have not produced any more dimensions. Every concept or every word scaled by the semantic differential is allotted a place along these three dimensions, dependent on what ratings for 'good' or 'strong' and so forth had been made.

As an example let us cite an investigation in which different groups of voters of different party affiliations before the 1952 American presidential election were studied by means of the semantic differential (see Fig. 56a and b). Among the concepts presented to them were the following: Stevenson (3), policy in China (4), Churchill (5), federal spending (6), Stalin (11), Truman (13), atom bomb (18) and McCarthy (19).

Figure 56a and b clearly shows how the 'meaning' or in this case perhaps the 'image' of different personalities varies from group to group.

As the example indicates there are numerous possibilities for the application of the semantic differential. Thus, it is possible, for example, to compare or correlate the profile, resulting from the ratings of a concept

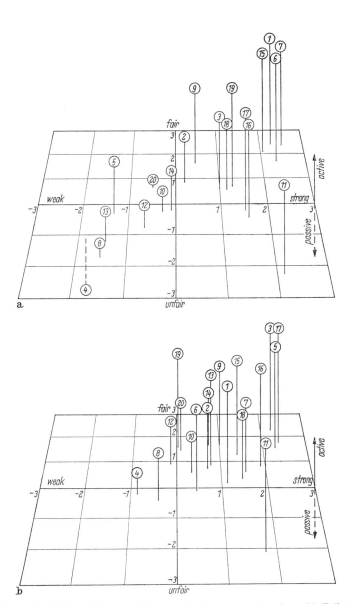

Fig. 56a and b. Models of the semantic spaces for two groups of voters: (a) Taft voters, (b) Stevenson voters. The rated concepts are, for example: Taft (1), Stevenson (3), policy in China (4), Churchill (5), federal spending (6), Stalin (11), Truman (13), atom bomb (18), McCarthy (19), United Nations (20). The base of the projection indicates the position of ratings on the scales *fair — unfair* and *strong —weak*. The length of the projection corresponds to the ratings on the scale *active — passive* (from OSGOOD, SUCI and TANNENBAUM, 1957, pp. 114 and 115).

or word on the 20 scales (the number usually applied) of the semantic differential, with the profile of another concept on the same scales. It must be remembered that the rating of a concept on these adjective scales is regarded as an expression of the representational mediating process corresponding to the meaning of this word. Similarity of ratings between two words (expressed in the profile-correlation index D), accordingly, is an expression of the similarity of the mediating processes corresponding to these two words.

To illustrate this once more by a few examples: 'red' is often called the color of love; i.e., 'red' is vaguely felt to be semantically similar to 'love'. HOFSTÄTTER who calls the semantic differential 'polarity-profile' (*Polaritäts-Profil*) has pursued the question whether what is called meaning here is identical with the meaning aspect expressed in the semantic differential. If so, 'red' and 'love' should lead to similar profiles. Indeed, the correlation between the two profiles is .89. Thus the semantic differential offers a technique of giving a solid foundation to color symbolism—often the happy hunting-ground for speculation.

HOFSTÄTTER is also the author of another interesting study on the effect of grammatical gender of the words 'sun' and 'moon'. In German 'sun' (*die* Sonne) is feminine, and 'moon' (*der* Mond) masculine, while in French and Italian it is the other way round. Has the fact that grammatical gender in one language is masculine, in another feminine, an influence on the meaning of the particular word ?

In other words, does the masculine German noun 'der Mond' evoke different associations or attitudes from the feminine Italian or French nouns 'la luna' or 'la lune' ? The poet RILKE (as quoted by HOFSTÄTTER) said he could hardly get himself to say 'die Sonne'[1]; if we adopted the Whorfian hypothesis (to be discussed in detail at a later stage), we would not be surprised to find that gender colored the meaning of a word.

HOFSTÄTTER asked German students to rate 'die Sonne' (sun) and 'der Mond' (moon) on a polarity profile. Italian students were given the translation of the same scales to rate 'sole' and 'luna'. The comparison of the average of the profiles for 'Sonne' and 'sole' revealed an extraordinarily high correlation (r = 0.92); the results for 'Mond' and 'luna' were of the same order. From a psycholinguistic point of view this finding leads to the interesting observation that we would read too much into language if we regarded grammatical gender as equivalent with psychological experience[2].

---

[1] *Translator's note.* i.e., to use a feminine noun in contrast to the French masculine 'le soleil'.

[2] RILKE'S experience does not affect this conclusion; psycholinguistics is more concerned with language-users in general than with an individual poet.

To give a further instance of the versatile possibilities in the application of the semantic differential, let us, finally, refer to an investigation in which BOUSFIELD himself, taking up once more the BOUSFIELD-OSGOOD controversy, interestingly finds confirmation for the OSGOOD model.

YAVUZ and BOUSFIELD (1959) asked their subjects to respond to unknown Turkish words with known English ones which apparently represented a translation of the Turkish ones. A week later they examined how much the subjects had retained by giving them the Turkish words to translate. Subsequently, the subjects rated the Turkish words on the *good—bad* scale of the semantic differential. The result was that the subjects were able to reproduce the good—bad connotations of the Turkish words which these words had acquired by being linked with the corresponding English translations even if the subjects had not remembered the translation of these words. This suggests that the 'meaning' captured by the semantic differential was still present, although the mediating verbal link had been lost. The mediating response cannot be equated with a latent word association.

Thus, besides the cognitive aspect of meaning, prominent, for example, in DEESE'S studies, and also in the field concept of German linguistics, we find an emotional aspect. Thanks to the semantic differential, the notion of a *cognitive* map (in TOLMAN'S sense), in which the position of a word is located by reference to other related and associated words and is thereby defined in its meaning, can be matched by an *affective* map into which emotional fields are drawn which relate the word to the language-user[1].

Having considered what the semantic differential can achieve we must—before resuming our principal argument—give due place to criticisms that have been made of it as a technique of the measurement of meaning.

CARROLL (e.g., 1964a), in a most thoughtful and therefore serious criticism, has asked whether, in view of the necessarily limited number of scales and concepts rated with their help, it is at all possible to establish two or more independent dimensions of the semantic space.

The presupposition for the claim that two dimensions can be considered as independent is that the points which are said to determine the dimensionality by their position must represent an adequate sample of this space. However, in OSGOOD'S technique, the rated concepts are not a representative sample of the vocabulary of a language, nor are the scales employed a representative sample of all possible scales. If OSGOOD had not only used the red—green scale, for example, but also pink—turquoise, orange—pale green, strawberry red—moss green and had asked his subjects to rate the concepts cheek, grass, forest, tulip and glowing coals, his semantic space would have a fourth red—green dimension.

---

[1] This is perhaps the map for the 'mountains of the heart' and the 'farmsteads of feeling' of which the poet RILKE speaks!

Another critic, WEINREICH (1958), has represented the point of view of the lexicographer, i.e., of someone whose business it is to grasp the unique meaning of the individual word, whereas OSGOOD—in common, by the way, with nearly all other modern psycholinguists—is concerned with 'meaning' as similarity of meaning, such as similarity between different words or similarity of mediating responses. In particular, WEINREICH questions the results of OSGOOD's factor analyses, arguing that a too limited proportion of the total variance is accounted for by the extracted factors. This objection, however, is hardly apposite. An argument which would seem much more decisive to us would have been to question whether it is right to attempt to reduce the dimensions to the smallest number (the only condition under which factor analysis is the suitable method), or whether it would not have been better to find out the largest number of dimensions which could just about be distinguished in the semantic space.

In the construction of tests, factor analysis is employed in order to operate with the most economical number of qualities needed to classify the responses of subjects; small differences between two variables are ignored and two slightly different variables are treated as equal.

WEINREICH'S critique culminates in the accusation that with OSGOOD's procedure the meaning of a word is related to "the infinity of *I's* and *today's*" (p. 350) and that the semantic differential grasps subjective and not objective meaning. But if we examine this objection more closely it turns out to be a compliment; for OSGOOD is primarily not a linguist but a psychologist, and as such interested in the interaction between language and language-user. Moreover, his concern with language-user and situation is entirely in keeping with the rejection, in the newer linguistic philosophy, of 'pure' semantics as a dyadic relationship between sign and object signified.

In more general terms, OSGOOD's procedure has been criticized for calling 'meaning' what at best is only a partial aspect of the total meaning of a word, namely connotation. This objection is no doubt justified, and OSGOOD, taking note of it, has in fact modified his position. He has now come to speak of an "affective mediating system which is biologically determined and capable of some limited number of gross, bipolar discriminations. This is the system the semantic differential technique is assumed to tap primarily; I have referred to the aspect of meaning indexed as *connotative*" (1962b, p. 26).

Thus we come back again to the distinction between denotation and connotation. CARROLL defines as denotative meaning "the properties or patterns of stimulation which are essential—that is, criterial—for the socially approved use in the speech community" (1964a, p. 40). But an individual does not only react to the "criterial" characteristics of stimulation, but also to the less essential ones. These appear regularly in conjunction with this stimulation, but do not govern reinforcement by the speech community; such noncriterial attributes form the connotative meaning (CARROLL, 1964a).

If we add to this definition MALMBERG'S view, according to which connotation is decisive for the choice between synonyms (e.g., whether one speaks of 'Father', 'Dad', 'Daddy' or 'Old Man'), it will be seen that CARROLL'S juxtaposition is too rigid. The social context is particularly decisive for such choices. Whether one uses 'Father' or 'Pop' is indicative both of the sign-user and of the person signified, but equally it depends on the context in which the sign appears (e.g., in a biographical description the word 'Pop' would be unlikely to occur). This, in fact, means that a triadic, post-Morris conception of the sign no longer permits the neat separation between denotation and connotation. This interpretation does not invalidate the criticism that OSGOOD'S approach is restricted, but it eliminates the argument that what OSGOOD has studied is not 'real' meaning. OSGOOD'S semantic space may be extremely sparse in its dimensions, nevertheless it has three more dimensions than had previously been known.

Chapter 11

The Conditioning Theory of Meaning: Its Achievement, Weakness and Further Development

Experimental modification of meaning — Semantic satiation — Model of bilingualism — MOWRER's theory of the sentence — The negation of the meaning problem in SKINNER — Operant conditioning of verbal behavior — CHOMSKY's critique of SKINNER — Meaning as disposition — BLOOMFIELD's conception of meaning as stimulus and response — A non-behavioristic cognitive conception of meaning.

The models presented in the preceding chapter regard meaning as a conditionable, mediating response. If this view is correct, meaning should be amenable to conditioning even in an experimental situation; and it should be possible to modify experimentally the meaning of a verbal sign.

Observing changes of meaning presupposes that meaning can be measured accurately. This is precisely what the semantic differential (within its limited sphere) enables us to do, and it is also the reason why we can only now, after the discussion of the semantic differential, do justice to the following investigations.

Experimental investigations on the changing and establishing of meaning which are of interest to the mediation model have been made above all by ARTHUR and CAROLYN STAATS (1957, 1958 and later). If meaning is a conditionable response it should be possible to associate with another simultaneous stimulus the meaning response ($r_m \ldots s_m$) elicited by a word. If a nonsense syllable is presented and immediately followed by a meaningful word, several repetitions of this process should make it possible to invest the nonsense syllable with the meaning of that word by a process of conditioning.

There is of course a danger that the pairing leads to a direct association between the word and the nonsense syllable, i.e., that in future the nonsense syllable as stimulus will evoke a particular word as response. According to the BOUSFIELD model, this process would be described as establishment of meaning. The two STAATS, as adherents of OSGOOD, however, hold that in that case this would not be conditioning of meaning but conditioning of a word; and meaning, in OSGOOD's formulation, is not the same as the covert repetition of a word as a representational response. The two STAATS, therefore, argue as follows: if the nonsense syllable is paired in close succession, not with a single word but with several words (with a similar meaning component), it is likely that the nonsense syllable will acquire this similar component of meaning without being strongly associated with any one particular word.

The semantic differential should lend itself particularly well to a demonstration of this 'similarity of meaning' between the different words. The STAATS' experiment in more than one respect offers the opportunity of reexamining the validity of OSGOOD'S postulates.

In this experiment nonsense syllables are presented to the subjects visually. Immediately after the exposure of the nonsense syllable on the screen the experimenter utters a meaningful word. The nonsense syllables appear several times in random order and each time are paired with another word. Thus YOF is presented with 'beauty', 'win', 'gift', 'sweet', 'smart', 'rich', 'friend', 'happy', 'pretty', etc., i.e., words with high loadings on a positive evaluative factor. For another group of subjects the same syllable YOF is paired with words of a high activity loading.

The subsequent ratings of the nonsense syllables on the semantic differential indeed indicate that they have acquired the meaning-tone of the words offered in the conditioning experiment.

This result could not have been predicted had the Bousfield model been applied because it would have led to the expectation that the different verbal responses conditioned to the nonsense syllable should cancel each other. OSGOOD'S model, on the other hand, is ready to offer an explanation: the US 'beauty' evokes a meaning (or mediating) response with an emotional or evaluative component which conditions the nonsense syllable. The US 'win' elicits a differently composed meaning response, but it includes an evaluative emotional component which is similar to that of 'beauty'. As a result of the repeated linking with this common emotional meaning component, the nonsense syllable gradually acquires this meaning aspect, whereas the divergent components (i.e., those which distinguish 'win' from 'beauty') cancel each other.

In later experiments the STAATS used the same method to modify the meaning of meaningful words, for example, the 'meaning' of a nationality term—an experiment of interest from the point of view of social psychology. One reservation of importance to our subsequent discussions is suggested by the investigations by COHEN (1964) and HARE (1964). Both authors noted that the method employed by the STAATS of conditioning emotional meaning leads to the expected results only when the subjects are sophisticated and are aware of the conditioning process. The question of the role of awareness of meaning, which is thus raised, will be more fully discussed at a later stage (see pp. 273ff.).

Whereas the experiments devised by the STAATS had been based on the more immediate implications of a conditioning model of establishing meaning, another group of investigators has studied other, somewhat less obvious consequences: if meaning is something that can be conditioned to a sign, it should be possible also to study with similar means the phenomenon of extinction. This group of studies is generally summarized under the title of 'verbal (or semantic) satiation'. The basic hypothesis, as already mentioned, derives from conditioning theory: a constant repetition of a word alone without any possibility of reinforcement should lead to the extinction, or gradual loss, of meaning. Outside the framework of conditioning theories TITCHENER already, on the basis of introspection, reported similar experiences; they have been studied experimentally by LAMBERT and JAKOBOVITS.

In these experiments selected words are first given ratings by the subjects on semantic differential scales. In the second phase of the experiment the subject pronounces the word repeatedly for 15 seconds and immediately makes his ratings once more on a semantic differential scale. Then he utters the word again for 15 seconds and subsequently makes his ratings on another scale and so forth. If the ratings before the satiation phase are compared with those after satiation, it is found that the ratings become more neutral and the meaning of the word loses color.

LAMBERT and JAKOBOVITS explain these results entirely in OSGOOD'S terms: meaning is a partial component of a total response. In the satiation phase this meaning response is evoked again and again, producing a reactive inhibition which temporarily reduces the availability of this response, i.e., weakens its meaning[1].

Although JAKOBOVITS and LAMBERT (1962a and b) were able to show (i) that satiation of a mediating link in a chain impairs learning of an association mediated by this link and (ii) that satiation of a number prolongs the time needed for additions with this number, the whole problem appears more complicated than the original experiment led one to believe. For example, YELEN and SCHULZ obtained contrary results.

However artificial the satiation process may appear, the experiment demonstrates a phenomenon familiar in everyday life: the continuous use of a word without the reinforcement of an objective reference transforms the word into a meaningless hollow shell.

While semantic satiation is a phenomenon which it was possible to predict by consistently applying a conditioning theory, the conditioning theory of meaning in its more generalized form has been used as a basis for two other areas of inquiry to which we shall now turn. One of these is the second-language area or, more precisely, the problem of bilingualism; and the other is MOWRER'S theory of the function of the sentence. We shall now consider the first of these.

---

[1] HULL calls 'reactive inhibition' the growing tendency to discontinue a habit produced by frequent repetition of this habit.

A bilingual is a person who expresses himself as efficiently and fluently in two languages as others usually express themselves in their native tongue. The learner of a second language ideally becomes bilingual. That is why the answer to the question 'what mechanism underlies the linguistic behavior of bilinguals?' is of fundamental interest even in cases where a second language is not mastered to the extent that it satisfies the suggested criterion. Genuine bilingualism generally occurs in children who grow up in a bilingual family, e.g., speak German to the mother and English to the father, or in situations where a child, through contact with a foreign nurse or servant, learns a second language from infancy. For example, British rule in India produced a considerable number of bilinguals in this way.

In the analysis of the psycholinguistic problem of bilingualism, ERVIN and OSGOOD (1954) have introduced a fundamental distinction. If one starts from the assumption—as is commonly done in foreign language instruction in school—that the *same* object is referred to by two designations, a so-called 'compound' system prevails. One representational mediating process $r_m - s_m$ corresponds to the sign stimuli in decoding (S_A from language A, and S_B from language B) and two verbal responses in encoding (R_A in language A and R_B in language B).

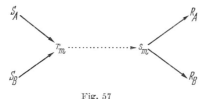

Fig. 57

Such a compound system develops above all when, as in the school setting, a sign in language B is associated with a meaningful sign in language A. This system also develops in a child who lives in a parental home in which two languages are used indiscriminately, i.e., without separation of person and situation.

In the coordinate system, however, linguistic signs and responses in language A are combined with one mediation process ($r_{m1} \ldots s_{m1}$), whereas the signs and responses in language B are combined with a somewhat different representational mediating process ($r_{m2} \ldots s_{m2}$). This is 'typical' or 'genuine' bilingualism which occurs when, for example, a child speaks language A with his parents and language B in school. Language A occurs in different situations from language B.

This theory of bilingualism leads to certain consequences which can be tested experimentally. The most important argument, perhaps, runs as follows: if in the case of bilingualism—to put it crudely—two words are available for each object, learning theory would lead us to expect negative transfer or mutual interference. This should be particularly so in the case of compound bilingualism, because here the same mediating processes lead to alternative verbal responses; the decision whether a response belonging to language A or language B should occur is determined by purely attitudinal or situational factors. Anyone who masters a second language knows quite well that often the second-language response dominates (i.e., suppresses the native-language response), if the second-language response has been evoked with greater frequency by the particular mediator.

According to ERVIN and OSGOOD'S theory, the ratings of equivalent words (e.g., 'house'—'maison') on a semantic differential scale should produce more divergent results in the case of coordinate than of compound bilingualism, since in the compound system only one representational mediating process is present and since the semantic differential is supposed to tap particularly the mediating processes. LAMBERT, HAVELKA and CROSBY (1958) have empirically examined this hypothesis and found it confirmed.

Another attempt to test the distinction between the two types of bilingualism experimentally has been made by making use of the concept of semantic satiation. If in compound bilingualism (e.g., English/French) the word 'house' is repeated several times, meaning impairment should also extend to 'maison'. In coordinate bilingualism 'house' and 'maison' have not the same but only similar mediating pathways, and therefore satiation in one should not lead to satiation in the other. JAKOBOVITS and LAMBERT (1961) found, in compound bilingualism a confirmation of this hypothesis, but in the case of the coordinate systems they found unexpectedly, a strengthening of meaning in one language if the equivalent word in the other was satiated.

The process of translation is also likely to be different in the two types of bilingualism. In the compound system a genuine cross-cultural translation should hardly be possible because there is only one carrier of meaning (belonging to one particular culture) which is encoded in two different languages. In the coordinate system, however, the two related meaning carriers run parallel, but are not identical. According to this model, several pathways of translation (from A to B) are possible (Fig. 58).

However, as no empirical investigations are available, we shall not discuss these possible distinctions any further. The problem of second languages and bilingualism will be approached from quite a different angle in the chapter on linguistic relativity (chapter 15) where the cultural and linguistic relativity of thought and world-view will be considered. It will be particularly important at that stage to recall that, within a limited sector of this field, ERVIN and OSGOOD have operated with a precisely formulated theoretical model.

The conditioning theory of meaning has found a further most elegant elaboration in the work of MOWRER. MOWRER (1954) asked: what happens in a sentence? According to a widespread view, meaning is communicated in a sentence by the speaker to the listener; it is thus trans-

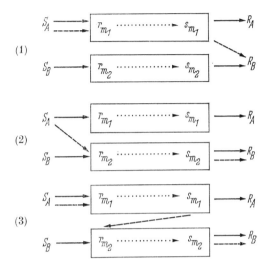

Fig. 58. Possible pathways of translation from language A to language B

ferred. However, the preceding discussion has shown that meaning is not something existing in its own right which could be transferred from the source to the receiver by means of sound waves. It is a process which occurs either in the source or the receiver. MOWRER has formulated this alternative theory in the following manner.

As we speak, meanings are not transferred from person to person, but within one person from sign to sign. In order to communicate with another person, the receiver must already possess the meanings with which both operate. The essence of the communicative act is to modify the signs which carry a given meaning. With the help of words the speaker evokes a certain meaning in the listener. To give an example: John tells Charles, 'Tom is a thief'. This sentence can have the effect upon Charles, desired by John, if Charles already knows who Tom is and what a thief is. The sentence, 'Tom is a thief', is a kind of conditioning process (of a somewhat higher order than a Pavlovian one); 'thief' is the US which evokes in the listener a response such as 'take care, an unpleasant fellow, be on your guard'. If the US 'thief' is preceded by the word 'Tom', the expectation will be that the response evoked by the US attaches itself equally to the CS 'Tom' so that later the receiver will react to 'Tom' as he had previously reacted to 'thief'.

In the communicative act certain meanings in the listener are touched off and reorganized by the speaker so that they are combined in new and informative ways. The sentence is not a chain of containers of meanings but a device to recondition meanings of one sign in relation to another (e.g., subject in relation to predicate).

The same thing could also be expressed in the language of logic. Accordingly, a sentence would be one premise of a syllogism, whereas the other premise would lie in the meanings already available in the receiver.

Minor premise (the sentence): 'Tom is a thief.'

Major premise (meaning or definition): 'Thieves cannot be trusted.'

What previously was called conditioning is here the conclusion to be drawn from these two premises: 'Therefore, Tom cannot be trusted.' This conclusion changes the definition of 'Tom' by taking Tom out of the class of 'honest men' and placing him among the 'dishonest ones'.

It can easily be seen that MOWRER'S view coincides with the views derived from information theory where it is also assumed that the lexicon of signs was present both in the source and the receiver. Communication in the sense of information theory consists in a process of selection, undertaken by the listener in keeping with the signals received from the source, *plus*—as we must now add following MOWRER—an organizing process which operates with already available meanings.

Thus MOWRER'S view and information theory together blur BÜHLER'S distinction between symbol and signal (cf. pp. 18 ff.). A symbol does not have meaning because of the inherent relationship between the sign and the object signified, but because it acts as an instruction (i.e., as a signal) directed to the receiver to establish such a relationship[1].

The conception of a word or sentence as a 'releaser' of already available meanings or as an instruction to establish and reorganize meaning responses offers a phylogenetically interesting prospect if it is related to the concept of releaser usep in ethology (e.g., by LORENZ or TINBERGEN) —a line of thought which cannot be developed here.

We have seen that the difficulties in making *meaning as idea* amenable to exact inquiry have led to the view of *meaning as response;* or, to put it more precisely, meaning has come to be seen as an individual response learned by conditioning, which can henceforth be evoked by the sign, as well as it was previously evoked only by the object signified. Meaning as response is fundamentally a behavioristic approach, although admittedly a moderate one. The attempt to view the meaning-giving process as conditioning, carried now to its ultimate conclusion, leads to the denial of the concept, and indeed of the problem of meaning altogether, as we

---

[1] In our view it is possible to specify even further this process of establishing the relationship, a point to which we shall return later.

shall see in the following brief sketch of this orthodox behavioristic trend in psycholinguistics.

It starts with WATSON himself for whom the problem of meaning is "a pure abstraction". HUMPHREY (1951) admittedly views as a problem the question of how it is possible that a cluster of sounds emitted by A can evoke a certain reaction in individual B, but he regards the process as a learning problem, and in his view this learning problem should not be further complicated by giving it another name, i.e., 'meaning'.

The tempting simplicity of orthodox behaviorism and of an approach from learning theory can be witnessed nowhere more clearly than in SKINNER'S *Verbal Behavior* (1957). In the first place, the importance of this work lies in the fact that SKINNER has attempted to design a psychology of language which, in view of the difficulties presented by the concept of meaning, dispenses with 'meaning' altogether. The fixation on this notion, it can be argued, has led to stagnation in psycholinguistics. It is therefore justifiable to assume that a rejection of all mentalistic notions could lead to rapid advances in this area just as much as in other areas of psychology.

SKINNER'S approach is, secondly, of significance because his learning theory (in his view no 'theory' at all), which naturally also permeates his psychology of language, has become widely known as a basis for programmed learning.

In his entire book SKINNER avoids terms such as 'language', or even 'language behavior', or 'linguistic behavior', because it suggests the notion of a linguistic 'community', hence of something supra-individual, approaching SAUSSURE'S *langue*. Language for SKINNER is no entity; he recognizes only behavior, and verbal behavior as a particular form of behavior. His aim is—as TIKHOMIROV (1959) expressed it—to show in what respect verbal behavior and other forms of behavior are alike[1].

SKINNER intends to present a functional analysis of verbal behavior; the variables determining verbal behavior are to be identified and their interaction to be described. The mode of description must be objective; as far as possible operational definitions are to be used, hence such terms as 'stimulus', 'response' or 'reinforcement' are employed. This functional analysis has achieved its object if, in this way, the verbal behavior of a speaker can be predicted on the basis of other observable behavioral or situational elements. The correct prediction, hence the control, of this behavior is the criterion of success of such an analysis. The search for variables determining verbal behavior is concentrated upon actual stimuli and earlier reinforcement, whereas the inherent

---

[1] It will be remembered that in the introductory chapter of our book we were concerned with showing in what way linguistic behavior is different from other forms of behavior.

structure of the language or structural elements within the speaker play no part in this analysis because they cannot be equated with behavior.

Although SKINNER endeavors to analyze verbal behavior in terms of the same determinants as other forms of behavior, he discusses in detail why it is justifiable to treat verbal behavior separately from other forms of behavior. Behavior normally changes the environment of the behaving individual by means of mechanical operations. When I pick up a glass of water, it comes closer to me. Someone who is afraid of a dog and runs away increases the distance between himself and the dog. If someone slays the dog, the latter changes from a living creature into one that is dead.

Verbal behavior is different. If I don't go to the water tap but request a glass of water, such verbal behavior does not affect the environment directly, but indirectly through the intervention of another person. If I eventually receive a glass of water, this result is no longer directly or mechanically dependent upon my own physical action, i.e., the production of sounds.

Verbal behavior, therefore, is distinguished from other forms of behavior by achieving its object through the intervention or, as SKINNER puts it, the 'mediation' of other persons.

In principle at least, only the listener makes it possible that verbal behavior achieves a goal. In this way the items of behavior carried out by the speaker and listener can be summarized in what SKINNER calls a speech episode. Such an episode contains nothing that is more than the sum of the items of behavior of the participating individuals.

In order to be able to recognize the full weight of this last proposition, let us contrast it with the following: "Language is the thought-forming instrument. Intellectual activity—entirely mental, completely inward, proceeding, one might say, without a trace—manifests itself in the sounds of speech and thus can be perceived by the senses" (HUMBOLDT, 1949 edition, pp. 52f.). HUMBOLDT's view represents in every word the extreme opposite to SKINNER's behaviorism. In HUMBOLDT's view, language has an existence transcending the concrete act of speech; it has power over the human being.

SKINNER vehemently opposes this view. He argues that previously it was customary to 'explain' verbal behavior as an expression of ideas; but are ideas more than words? A speaker does not utter ideas, images or thoughts—these are purely subjective notions; what he utters are nothing more than words. SKINNER's procedure is consistent. He rejects not only such notions as 'idea' or 'image', but also 'meaning' and 'information'.

Let us now look again at another of SKINNER's propositions: verbal behavior is behavior reinforced by the mediation of other persons. Thus, greatest importance is attributed to the element of *learning*. Human speech—in contrast to other forms of communication in the animal world—is learned; hence its acquisition and maintenance must follow the general laws of learning.

Laws of learning determine why, in a given situation, these and no other verbal utterances occur. SKINNER (who does not claim to have a theory of learning) regards laws of learning as descriptive accounts of the events and of the conditions under which these events occur. This description is what he calls a functional analysis which, in his case, is inevitably made in terms of stimulus-response aspects of the present situation and earlier reinforcements.

Stimuli are parts of the environment which regularly evoke certain responses. According to SKINNER, responses can be divided into two large classes: first, those which the organism appears to produce spontaneously, 'emitted responses' or 'operants', and which only on the basis of certain learning processes are linked with certain stimuli; and, second, those which from the start are elicited by certain stimuli ('elicited responses').

If responses show any regularity at all, they are under the control of a stimulus (thus SKINNER's terminology) or—in more precise terms—under the control of a certain stimulus-quality of an object. If an armchair is described as 'red', this response occurs under the control of the 'redness' of the armchair.

SKINNER finds these different types of responses reflected in the types of verbal behavior. Thus, a 'mand' is a verbal operant response which is reinforced by certain consequences. Mands are therefore commands, wishes and threats. A command is a command because it is obeyed; and a wish becomes a wish because it is fulfilled.

A 'tact' occurs whenever a certain response is evoked by a certain object or by particular qualities of that object. If mands are determined by the consequences, tacts are defined by the stimulus.

While, traditionally, the occurrence of an utterance was explained by referring to its 'meaning', SKINNER accounts for the occurrence of a word ('pencil') by asking what the stimulus situation must be like to elicit the response 'pencil' in the speaker.

That a particular stimulus evokes a particular response is the result of a conditioning process. Whether the response is 'emitted' or 'elicited' it has become attached to a stimulus in a predictable manner because of the reinforcement of the S-R sequence. What acts as reinforcement? Broadly speaking, praise, approval, confirmation, success.

Thus we reach a group of empirical studies which—in addition to numerous investigations by SKINNER's students on simple learning tasks— offer the most important evidence for the heuristic value of SKINNER's interpretation for an analysis of verbal behavior. These studies can be summarized under the title of 'conditioning of verbal behavior'.

In order to understand what is meant by that, the following situation should be imagined. Two persons are engaged in conversation. One of them has the intention of bringing a certain aspect of the verbal behavior of the other under his control by increasing the frequency of occurrence of this feature. For example, let us assume he wants to cause the other person to include in his talk expressions of opinions such as 'I mean', 'D'you see', 'I believe', or 'I feel', we can achieve this by reinforcing each appearance of such a phrase, by an expression of approval such as 'mmm-hmm', 'right', or 'yes'.

In an investigation by VERPLANCK (1955) it was possible to multiply the occurrence of such phrases considerably, without any awareness even on the part of the subject that an experiment was in progress, let alone that the subject was aware of the fact that a modification of his verbal behavior had occurred. But even in experimental situations openly described as such, it is possible to modify verbal behavior by means of operant conditioning (to use SKINNER'S technical term). Thus GREEN-SPOON (1955) was able by means of a 'mmm-hmm' of approval to increase significantly the use of plural forms, and in the same way, by means of what might be described as 'negative reinforcement', 'huh-uh', to lower it again. The greater the prestige of the experimenter the clearer the results. Probably there are also relationships between personality structure and the conditionability of the subject, i.e., the ease with which his verbal responses can be brought under the control of a verbal stimulus.

It is today beyond any doubt that it is possible to bring verbal behavior under control by means of such external direction of the learning mechanism and in this way to exercise a determining influence upon it. The verbal response can be attached to a certain verbal stimulus, and since the response is dependent upon the verbal stimulus, it is therefore also possible, given a knowledge of the stimulus qualities of the situation as a whole, to predict the verbal response.

But SKINNER'S claim that verbal behavior is always and in every situation under the control of the stimulus overstretches the applicability of this theoretical construct. The claim has had fateful consequences for the entire theory as has been clearly demonstrated by CHOMSKY (1959). CHOMSKY'S critique deserves to be reported in detail as a corrective to the claim of orthodox behaviorism in psycholinguistics.

When verbal behavior is conditioned it is possible (just as in a Skinner-box experiment) to define the stimulus independently, e.g., the 'mmm-hmm' of the experimenter, or the light signal in the Skinner-box. This stimulus is linked with a response by means of a well-known regular relationship; a response is what is evoked by a stimulus in accordance with a precise rule. If I talk about my friend Jack and therefore use a proper noun, this is, according to SKINNER, "a response under the control of a person or thing". What does it mean in this context to say "under the control of" ? The presence of a stimulus should increase the frequency of occurrence of the response. But we are likely to talk about friend Jack more frequently in his absence. Let us illustrate the point we are making by another example. Someone sees a red chair and says 'red'. According to SKINNER, this verbal response is under the control of the stimulus aspect of the color red. If that same person says 'chair', this response is made under the control of the stimulus aspect of the chair qualities. If, instead, he says, 'Thank goodness, I'm tired of standing', the corresponding stimulus aspect is comfort-seeking or the like. It is quite clear that for every response the corresponding stimulus aspect is invented. The stimulus is inferred from the response and consequently has lost its objectivity which was so highly valued.

In SKINNER's approach the essential dependent variable, i.e., the variable which is reinforced, is response-strength, defined as the probability of occurrence (and intensity) of a response. SKINNER illustrates it by the following example: if we are shown a work of art and exclaim, 'Beautiful!', the speed and intensity of our response are likely to influence the owner of the work of art. But if we take SKINNER's definition of response-strength literally—and this is what we ought to do if we say that his experimental investigations on simple learning tasks have psycholinguistic implications—a person who is particularly impressed by the work of art would exclaim, 'Beautiful!' in a loud voice and as often as possible.

CHOMSKY further selects the concept of reinforcement to show how SKINNER attempts to give the psychological study of language the reputable aura of objectivity which notions such as 'stimulus' or 'response-strength' have acquired in the field of learning without at the same time ensuring that the concepts are used with the same rigor.

According to SKINNER, reinforcement is the presentation of a certain stimulus in a temporal relationship either to another stimulus or to a response. The 'mmm-hmm' of the experimenter acts as reinforcement because it follows immediately the response to be confirmed. If we examine the use of the concept of reinforcement in *Verbal Behavior*, it appears that a person talks to himself because this is 'reinforcing' for him. A child imitates sounds it has heard because such imitation 'reinforces'. The speaker's verbal behavior is reinforced by the behavior of the listener—in short, a speaker says what he would like to say because it is 'reinforcing' for him. The presence of reinforcement is inferred from the fact that verbal behavior occurs. This means that the concept of reinforcement has lost its meaning[1].

The application of concepts taken from learning theory has led to difficulties here, because these concepts have lost their operational anchorage. The fact that SKINNER uses the same terms in the psychology of language as in the psychology of learning creates "... the illusion of a rigorous scientific theory with a very broad scope, although in fact the terms ... may be mere homonyms ..." "The magnitude of the failure of this attempt to account for verbal behavior serves as a kind of measure of the importance of the factors omitted from consideration, and an indication of how little is really known about this remarkably complex phenomenon" (CHOMSKY, 1959, pp. 30 and 28).

With regard to the problem of meaning, SKINNER shares with nearly all empirically oriented psychologists a disinclination to appeal to states of consciousness and other subjective experiences. This was the starting point for his psycholinguistic *tour de force*. There was a feeling of being on safer ground if one spoke only in terms of behavior and explained the causation of such behavior according to the well-tried model of learning theory.

Fundamentally SKINNER's approach belongs to the substitution theories of meaning. All of these start out from the fascinatingly simple assumption that the conditioned stimulus 'word' serves as a substitute for the unconditioned stimulus 'object' to evoke those responses which hitherto were evoked by the object.

This view gets into difficulties on two sides, even ignoring SKINNER's overextension of certain concepts for which he was already criticized. On the one side, the reality of the object is being questioned and, on the other, the kind of response which was previously elicited by the US and which is now evoked by a CS.

What object is replaced by the word 'justice' for example? What object is substituted by the word 'or'? These examples show that, with the application of the substitution model, the sign or word is treated as a name, and thus the fact is overlooked that the entire vocabulary of a language cannot be fitted into this scheme. Admittedly, this accusation can be equally directed against linguistic philosophers with no behavioristic orientation: when GADAMER (1960) writes "language is the language of things", he is in trouble with such words as 'or', 'not', 'if' and 'against'.

The difficulties which a view of *meaning as image or idea* had run into led, as a reaction, to the view of *meaning as response*. And within the framework of substitution theory, this was interpreted as a conditioned

---

[1] This is quite different from the use of the same concept in the work of HULL, PAVLOV, GUTHRIE or THORNDIKE where the definition of reinforcement has remained independent.

single response which, after a period of learning, was evoked by the CS (the sign) in exactly the same manner as it was previously evoked by the US (object or *designatum*). But which single response is evoked by the word 'rain' in the same way as by the object rain itself? It is evident that there is no single or certain response either to the object rain or the word 'rain'. What follows the object or word depends to a large extent—although not exclusively—upon the situation in which they occur. From this results the difficulty that, as long as meaning is equated with the overt behavioral response to an object or sign, it becomes something quite unstable.

Moreover, which response is evoked if, for example, the reader of a novel encounters the word 'rain'? No visible behavioral response at all is evoked. Yet, the behaviorist will hardly be inclined to say that in this case, therefore, the word has no meaning. WATSON'S stop-gap solution was the 'implicit response', which was not observable in external behavior, but which would in the future be identified by means of special techniques of investigation, such as incipient movements of the speech apparatus, innervations and so forth.

Another solution which made it possible not to abandon the simple conditioning model was to shift the responses which 'correspond' to meaning to the associations which the given word as a stimulus evokes (NOBLE, BOUSFIELD, DEESE). The implicit response also forms the basis for the mediation theories of BOUSFIELD and OSGOOD. Especially in the work of OSGOOD, who identifies meaning as an emotional part-response, the behavioristic conditioning theory has found its last refuge. The meaning-carrying response is so deep in the central nervous system that—just like the ideas and images of old—it can hardly be found any more.

It is now conceivable that one rejects the substitution aspect of the theory and yet conceives meaning as response to a sign. In that case it must be shown (BROWN has emphatically drawn attention to this point) what the relationship is between the response to the object signified and the response to the sign.

This suggests the assumption of different but similar and interconnected responses—a Hullian habit-family hierarchy. This hierarchy can be brought into action by the sign as well as by the object signified. It then depends on the situation as to which response in fact occurs. Real rain will evoke responses which will lead to taking shelter, whereas the word 'rain' is likely to be uttered before the actual event and leads to actions to avoid getting wet.

It is clear that the search for the response evoked by the sign leads to the rejection of a rigidly dyadic scheme and to the addition of the situation —a pragmatic moment one might say— as a qualifying factor.

In this conception, represented above all by MORRIS, continuity between the object designated and the behavior evoked by the sign is
established with the help of the argument that the sign does not evoke a
single response but a *disposition to respond*. Additionally, the *situation*
must be taken into account so that the disposition can manifest itself in
actual behavior.

Thus, MORRIS in a very logical way comes to grips with one of the
greatest difficulties presented by the theories of meaning as response.
If meaning, as BLOOMFIELD, for example, has it, consists in a sign being
followed by a definite mode of behavior—how is it that the phrase, 'It's
raining', is at different times followed by taking a rain-coat, or shutting
a window, or running quickly, or sometimes even by nothing at all ? Does
this imply that, 'It's raining', has various meanings ? MORRIS' answer is
that the uniform meaning of a word does not rest in behavior but in a
disposition to behave, evoked by the word. The sign (or word) is a
preparatory-stimulus which influences the behavior evoked by other
stimuli.   A preparatory-stimulus—MORRIS adopted this concept of
MOWRER'S—influences a response which the organism may make to
another stimulus. Suppose a motorist asking the way is given the direction, 'When you come to the white building, turn left'. This sentence,
although it does not immediately evoke a response, is a preparatory-
stimulus (and therefore meaningful), because it influences the behavior
of the driver which will be evoked by the sight of the white building.

In this way, MORRIS obtains a uniform correlate of meaning to which
to relate the multiplicity of modes of behavior which follow signs without
being fully determined by them. This also solves the great difficulty
presented to theories of meaning as response by the act of reading because there is no visible response in behavior. "Whether a sign does or
does not lead to overt behavior depends upon whether or not certain
conditions of motivation and environment are fulfilled" (MORRIS, 1955
edition, p. 51).

The *uniformity of disposition* corresponds to the *uniformity of meaning*,
whereas the multiplicity of behavioral responses comes into existence
through the influence upon this disposition of the particular situation.
The perception of the sign, i.e., of the stimulus, is simply not the only
cause for subsequent events, the behavioral responses. And conversely,
differences in behavioral responses do not necessarily imply the presence
of different dispositions. In this way, MORRIS—and following him, for
example, also STEVENSON (1944)—attain the desired constancy of
meaning.

This of course to some extent changes the character of meaning: meaning as
response was a dependent, directly observable variable; meaning as disposition,
however, is an intervening variable, i.e., something that must be postulated (hence
is not directly observable) as intervening between stimulus and response.

MORRIS' theory —meaning as disposition— may also be said to include the distinction made by FRIES between linguistic and sociocultural meaning. Linguistic meaning is the result of all constituents and of sentence structure; sociocultural meaning is the stimulus value for behavior. The sentence, 'The window is open', in one case uttered by someone in winter, in another as a stage direction, has in both cases identical linguistic meaning but different sociocultural meaning (cf. GREEN-BERG, 1957, p. 84). According to MORRIS, in both cases, the same disposition would be activated, but the determining influence of different situations would lead to different responses.

While disposition as a carrier of meaning in MORRIS' theory can still be considered as a kind of response to a preparatory-stimulus (the sign), in BROWN'S theory the response notion has still further moved into the background. BROWN writes (1958a, p. 103): "When one comes to understand a linguistic form (i.e., a word or sentence) his nervous system is partially rewired (in the sense of changes in synaptic resistances or neurone process growth) so that one is disposed to behave appropriately with regard to that form. For the psychologist meaning is not any particular response. It is the disposition to behave in varying ways with regard to the form as the contingent circumstances are changed. The disposition has no substantial character other than the structure of the nervous system. ... It is a response potential. A disposition is discovered by creating various contingencies and observing responses."

The last sentence implies that a disposition theory of meaning must concern itself with masses of overt behavioral items, because the disposition as meaning-carrier is bound to manifest itself in quite different ways in accordance with the other factors determining the manifest behavior. In order to analyze the disposition it will be necessary to discover an identical component in many different modes of behavior. BROWN consoles us by saying that the concept of 'attitude' in social psychology, which is conceived in quite a similar way because it is also a disposition to behave, can—in spite of this complication—become a legitimate subject for psychological investigation.

In the course of the development outlined above, which advanced from a substitution theory to a complicated stimulus-response theory, its behaviorism—as BROWN (1965, p. 79) says—has faded into the promise of a program, and the theoretical statements have lost their vulnerability. The view that prevails is that meaning could be discovered through an analysis of the circumstances surrounding the use of the word: an analysis of the processes leading in the speaker to the utterance of the word and an analysis of the processes in the listener who perceives it. In other words, meaning is conceived as a kind of stimulus-response relationship in which the word is inlayed as a 'habit'—as S-R links are called in learning theory. Thus, JESPERSEN (1964, p. 7) says that the only incontrovertible definition of the word is that it constitutes a human habit, and LEISI views acts of speech as composed of a series of microscopic habits. The word is a communal habit or usage. In the exercise of the speech acts the speaker must conform to rules of society. Each speech act is normally subject to two sets of conditions: the extra-linguistic and the intra-linguistic conditions which result from the accompanying acts of speech (1961, pp. 13ff.). BLOOMFIELD, whose work has been influential, offers as a definition of meaning the situation in which the speaker utters the linguistic form and the response which it calls forth in the hearer (1933, p. 139). The behavior sequence in which linguistic behavior occurs normally begins with a practical event and leads via an act of speech to another practical event. BLOOMFIELD gives this illustration: when Jill sees an apple, her speechless response can be represented as follows. The seeing of the apple (stimulus S) leads to grasping (response R). If this simple action is not possible (because, for example, the apple hangs too high), the sequence is as follows: Jill sees the apple (S) and says something (r) which causes Jack (s) to pick the apple (R); $S \rightarrow r \ldots s \rightarrow R$ is the model of a response mediated by speech. S and R are practical events; $r \ldots s$ is the speech act itself. The partial sequence $S \rightarrow r$ occurs in the speaker, and the partial sequence $s \rightarrow R$ in the hearer.

Here once more we come across the notion of 'mediation', which has already been discussed in detail. $S \rightarrow r \ldots s \rightarrow R$ is a reaction mediated by speech. The speech act links the behavior sequences of speaker and hearer.

BLOOMFIELD'S model is found again in the theory of FRIES, who lays particular emphasis on the habit aspect. The analysis reveals first that a sequence of sounds fits into a "pattern of recurring sames"; i.e., it is not an arbitrary but quite specific sequence of sounds which have already been repeatedly perceived. Secondly, the "recurring sames" of the stimulus situation, which appear concurrently with these sound sequences, are recognized. And thirdly, the recurring sames of the practical responses which are evoked by the sound sequences are perceived. "A language, then, is a system of recurring sequences or patterns of sames of vocal sounds, which correlate with recurring sames of stimulus-situation features, and which elicit recurring sames of response features" (1954, pp. 64-65). This recognition of identities will engage our attention again later as a process of classification.

Similar, but somewhat less differentiated, is GREENBERG'S view (1954), according to which meaning must be described as a rule of use formulated in situational terms. Even for STENZEL, a linguistic philosopher without any behavioristic leanings, each word singly has infinitely graded shades of meanings which become clearly determined only "by being predicated upon the meaningful context of concrete speech situations" (1934, p. 16).

Naturally, BLOOMFIELD had already acknowledged the fact that the total situation of the use of a word can not always be identical with a second use of the same word; only definite traits in these situations are repeated, which FRIES has called the "recurring sames". In his search for these common traits even a behaviorist like BLOOMFIELD will have to have recourse to non-observable features.

In the endeavor to grasp meaning in psychological terms it is probably timely not to be impeded by too narrow a conception of stimulus, association and response or by the atomistic methodology of behaviorism.

The obstinate clinging to an S-R conception of meaning can be explained as resulting from a fundamental conviction that the cause of behavior must lie in events and not in a state extended over a period of time. This basic conviction has compelled the theorist to bridge the temporal separation between S and R by creating intermediate links which, in turn, have the characteristics of events or behavior.

However, it is an essential trait of language that in language the chain of events can, so to speak, be lifted out of the flow of time; it can be stored in memories, plans or wishes and can be dropped again into the temporal stream of behavior. A theory of meaning must not ignore the case of signs which have meaning *without* resulting in behavior.

There are other arguments against the conditioning model which, in principle, underlies even the latest versions of the mediation theories. One argument to be substantiated in detail in a later chapter (chapter 14), runs as follows. The way a learning-theory model predicts the acquisition of meaning does not coincide with what genetic or child psychology really observes. But more specifically, one further argument has critical significance: if meaning is acquired through a process of conditioning, then some form of reinforcement is required. Either, following PAVLOV, this reinforcement can be found in the simultaneity of US and CS, or, following THORNDIKE and HULL, it can be seen in the fact that the response produces a pleasurable state for the organism. If this reinforcement is absent—and in many verbal situations there is no evidence of such reinforcement—this should necessarily lead to extinction or wiping out of meaning. RAPAPORT (1957) above all has raised this objection: a conditioning theory is unable to account for the stability of meaning.

If the concept of reinforcement is not to be abandoned—and there are indeed good reasons for maintaining it, because through it the link with learning theory is established—a modification would have to be introduced to overcome this inconsistency.

Accordingly, we propose the following hypothesis. The meaning of a sound sequence does not lie primarily in the fact that it is associated with other events. In the use of signs the decisive moment is not that this link is created or that it exists; what is decisive is that we are aware of it. Meaning is not association but knowledge of an association.

This hypothesis clearly requires further specification of the term knowledge. We mean by 'knowledge' what, admittedly somewhat vaguely as yet, may be described as 'cognitive availability' in the sense that connections and relations are capable of being more or less consciously perceived.

A cognitive, hence non-behavioristic, concept is introduced because of a conviction that behavioral concepts are not adequate for the conceptualization of meaning. As MERLEAU-PONTY expressed it, "exprimer, pour le sujet parlant, c'est prendre conscience" (1952, p. 99).

This does not mean that the concept of mediation, which has proved its worth over a wide area, should be completely discarded. It can readily be conceded that the representational response (r_m) maintains the character of the representational, but the response itself must be viewed somewhat differently. While the older conditioning theory spoke of responses in the sphere of behavior and the more recent ones of MORRIS and BROWN speak of responses in the sphere of disposition, we speak of a response which has moved into the sphere of cognition.

If we want to maintain not only the concept of response, but also the concept of reinforcement—we have seen that this was possible only at the cost of watering it down considerably—we must accord to this cognitive element, i.e., the cognizing of an association, the character of a fundamental drive or need. What this achieves is that meaning as a representational response which reaches into the sphere of cognition is not subject to extinction. The knowledge of meaning is a pleasurable state and, in THORNDIKE'S or HULL'S sense, a reinforcement.

Such an inclusion of cognitive processes into the reinforcement concept is suggested also by developments in quite a different sector. In the psychology of motivation BERLYNE, HARLOW and others have recognized that curiosity, the wish to explore, the "desire for knowledge" have the character of needs whose satisfaction has reinforcement value (1954b, 1953). The role of awareness in the STAATS' experiments has already been pointed out.

Cognition is not an event which—in the manner of $r_m \ldots s_m$—has on one side response and on the other side stimulus character. In cognition, or knowing, the linear sequence of events in time is broken by a quasi-timeless state. This view admittedly has somewhat disturbing philosophical implications: thus, the transition from a *state* of awareness into a *sequence* of behavioral events leads us into the vicinity of the notorious problem of free will because a new chain of events starts without any visible cause. On the other hand, the mechanistic conception, on which our discussion has been based so far, though philosophically less problematical, has disturbing *psychological* implications.

The possibility that the cognitive function has the capacity to generate stimuli is suggested not solely by our approach which ascribes to knowing a representational and at the same time 'temporal' function; but RAPAPORT (1957), too, has pointed out that the conception of attention which, particularly in psycholinguistics, is unlikely to be fully replaced by probabilistic constructs inclines, in quite a similar manner, towards a stimulus-generating consciousness.

In the approach to meaning as knowledge of a relationship, which we have here proposed, the genesis of this knowledge may have to be imagined as of a schematic nature. The 'schema'—a concept used by BARTLETT, PIAGET and CHURCH—is a principle which organizes experience. The schema retains common features of similar impressions; perception functions in a schematic way; when we grasp meaning our knowledge has the essential features of a schema.

Functionally, the 'knowledge of a relationship' can be most readily compared with TOLMAN'S cognitive map. In this map the 'if ... then' structure of the sequence of events is indicated; it answers the question: 'What leads to what ?' When the meaning of something is understood we know what to expect.

The knowledge of relationships may well also include knowledge of certain emotional concomitants. On the other hand, meaning may equally have emotional concomitants of which we are not aware. If such unconscious emotional aspects are to be included in the definition of meaning (and the results of OSGOOD'S semantic differential suggest that they might), it would require a modification of our cognitive definition of meaning.

In borderline cases, modes of behavior which in the sequence of events occur later may originate solely from a state of awareness; in this respect meaning is frozen action. Generally, however, the knowledge of relationships intervenes as a steering device in the organization of the 'practical events' by means of which the individual strives to achieve his goals. Looked at in this way meaning is disposition.

To sum up: meaning is the knowledge of a relationship evoked by a sign.

Chapter 12

The Imitation of Sounds and Sound Symbolism

Imitation of sounds as the germ of human speech — HUM-
BOLDT'S dichotomy — Evolution of onomatopoeia — Traces of
sound symbolism in linguistic behavior — 'maluma' and
'takete' — Matching experiments in the mother tongue and
an unknown second language — Concept of physiognomy —
WERNER'S theory of symbol formation.

In the preceding chapters meaning as response has been discussed in
detail. Depending on the particular theory in question, this conception
has been, to a varying extent, based on the assumption that the connection
called meaning is 'hooked up' to the sign by a conditioning process. *What*
meaning is conditioned to *which* sign is basically quite arbitrary. Therefore, there is an element of randomness or absence of logical necessity in
the relationship of sign and object signified.

However, this last statement can be questioned and in chapter 8 this
problem was touched upon from another angle: at that point we asked:
what is the basis for claiming that language is actually the true expression
of the world as it is ? PLATO was cited and we referred to the controversy
on the relationship between sign and object: does it originate in the
nature of things *(physei)* or in human invention *(thesei)* ? Starting from
this debate we followed the 'winner', ARISTOTLE, and traced the anti-
Platonic position down to the neobehavioristic psycholinguistics of our
own day.

In modern psycholinguistics it is still possible to discover a refined
version of the other, the *physei*, conception, which will be considered in
the present chapter. The question is to what extent the meaning relationship between sign and object can contain an element of necessity or non-
arbitrariness. We must occupy ourselves with "the belief, deeply rooted
in our natural feeling for language, that meaning lies directly in the
sounds of words; this belief is sustained by a peculiar feeling that it is
self-evident, which certainly constitutes a very important experience in

the mother tongue and in any other language of which we have a reasonable mastery" (STENZEL, 1934, p. 92).

This feeling of self-evidence and of an inevitable link between sign and object forms the basis of those phenomena which range from word magic—of interest to ethnologists—to the phenomena discovered by the General Semanticists (KORZYBSKI and HAYAKAWA). They are clearly illustrated, for example, by such remarks as: "Pigs are called pigs because they are so dirty."

A full discussion of the problems raised by the so-called sound (or phonetic) symbolism must be prefaced by a few remarks to show the deep rift which almost completely separates this complex of ideas from the prevailing view among present-day psycholinguists.

It may be regarded as certain that most linguists today (and most psycholinguists in their train) operate with the distinction between phoneme and morpheme. The phoneme is a unit of sound; the morpheme a unit of meaning. The meaningful morpheme is composed of phonemes which in themselves do not mean anything. Therefore there is a boundary between morpheme and phoneme: on one side of this boundary there is meaning; on the other there is not.

The existence of this boundary—and with it the phoneme-morpheme distinction—is called into question if meaning is already ascribed to the individual sound. In principle this applies even if the meaning value attributed to the sound is regarded as vague and purely suggestive.

Besides, the meaning value of the individual sound need not necessarily point to an object in the external world; it may well be an indication of a state of mind in the speaker. BÜHLER's distinction between symbol and symptom, of which one is reminded (cf. chapter 2), may be phylogenetically and ontogenetically more advanced.

If even a single sound is meaningful, e.g., if, in all Indo-European languages right from the River Ganges to the Atlantic Ocean, the sound cluster 'sta' designates the notion of standing and the sound cluster 'plu' the notion of flowing (CURTIUS, 1858), we are led to the fascinating thought that the collection, comparison and analysis of such fundamental meanings may open up the possibility of reconstructing the original language of mankind *(lingua Adamica)*. No lesser authority than LEIBNIZ pursued this idea. In more recent times, RIMBAUD, RUDOLF STEINER and ERNST JÜNGER—to name only a few—have speculated about the meaning content of speech sounds.

In PLATO the idea of words following things guarantees that language can and does represent world. LEIBNIZ finds the key to man's original language in the universals of sound symbolism which transcend national differences. Although HUMBOLDT does not adhere to such views, he gave close attention to the relationship between speech sound and object.

His exposition provides in a preliminary way the major division of this problem area.

"The advantages of language with regard to its sound system rest particularly in the relationship of this system to meaning ... it seems certain that a connection between a sound and its meaning exists." HUMBOLDT then distinguishes various possibilities.

(1) "Direct imitation occurs whenever the sound produced by a resonant object is copied inasmuch as articulated sounds are capable of reproducing unarticulated ones. These signs can be likened to pictures" (1949 edition, p. 78).

"Since the copy in these cases always refers to unarticulated sounds, designation and articulation are, so to speak, in conflict with one another. This is why this kind of sign is little in evidence wherever there is a strong natural sense of language and gradually disappears in the advancing evolution of language" (p. 79).

This first possibility distinguished by HUMBOLDT is the imitation of sounds, which today is generally known as onomatopoeia. In this case an original is copied.

(2) The second possibility, sound symbolism, is different: here the speech sound does not copy an original; it symbolizes it. To cite HUMBOLDT once more, here we are not concerned with "a directly imitative sign but a sign which imitates a quality which the sign and the object have in common. This sign can be called symbolic. To designate objects it selects sounds which partly independently and partly in comparison with others produce an impression which to the ear is similar to that which the object makes upon the mind; thus '*stehen*' ('stand'), '*stetig*' ('steady') and '*starr*' ('stiff', 'rigid') create the impression of firmness ... '*nicht*' ('not'), '*nagen*' ('gnaw'), '*Neid*' ('envy') create the impression of slicing or sharp cutting. In this way words pertaining to objects producing similar impressions have predominantly identical sounds, such as '*wehen*' ('wave', 'flutter'), '*Wind*' ('wind') and '*Wolke*' ('cloud') in all of which the vacillating restless, and random movement—confusing to the senses—is expressed by the 'w' which has solidified out of the naturally hollow and dark 'u' sound.

"This kind of sign process which is based on the particular meaning of each individual letter and whole groups of letters has undoubtedly exercised a prevailing, perhaps even exclusive, influence on primitive word-formation. Its natural consequence has been a certain likeness of word-formation throughout all languages of mankind ..." (p. 79)—a consequence which will engage our attention later.

HUMBOLDT, however, concludes these reflections with the warning that this pursuit of language to its origins is "an altogether slippery path" (p. 80), because it is so hard to say which sound was the original one and what its original meaning was.

The term 'sound symbolism', which so far in this chapter has been employed in a global fashion, represents a dimension ranging from onomatopoeia at one end to the freely chosen abstract sign at the other. What varies along this unnamed dimension is closeness of connection between sign and object and the degree of cogency in the relationship, whether subjectively felt or objectively present.

In linguistics it is quite common to talk in this connection about the 'motivation' of a sign. Accordingly, a scream would be emotionally 'motivated', whereas the use of representational words would be 'unmotivated'. 'Motivated' in this context is almost equivalent to BÜHLER'S 'expressive'; 'unmotivated' to his term 'representational'. This is a good illustration of an unfortunate use of psychological concepts, which is not uncommon in linguistics.

Let us now, following HUMBOLDT'S division, look at this whole problem from a psychological point of view and attempt to analyze the determinants or, perhaps more modestly, some contributing factors.

The origin of such words as 'tinkle', 'rattle' or 'buzz' as an imitation of noises is immediately apparent; yet, they have been part of the language for a long time and have therefore been subject to the general historical development of all words so that the original relationship, 'meaning as imitation of an object', is no longer quite so obvious. The question can therefore be asked whether the genesis of these words will reveal something about this connection. The German linguist WISSEMANN (1954) undertook a study of the creation of onomatopoeic words from noises. Various noises were presented to the subjects, who were not able to observe the manner in which the noise was produced; the instruction was to invent or select names for the noises.

The noise in experiment No. 2, for example, was described in the following manner: "A lacquered wooden ball of 4 cm. diameter, weighing 20 gr. was rolled by the experimenter down a plywood board, 121 cm. long, inclined at an angle of 13° to the horizontal. At the lower end of the board was a square metal box with sides 23 cm. long, fixed so that the falling distance of the ball from the lower edge of the plywood board to the bottom of the box was equal to the side of the box (i.e., 23 cm.)" (pp. 12f.).

WISSEMANN'S experiments produced a large number of results, but an inadequate research design makes them hard to interpret. When subjects were asked why they gave preference to particular sounds in making up new words, it appeared that vowels served to represent the pitch and qualitative features of the noise. The /i/ sound is used to imitate a high-pitched, spiky noise, and /u/ for a low, dark noise. The evaluation of the words produced by subjects showed that the number of syllables in the word inventions was not proportional to the length of the noise; it reflected, rather, sections of the noise sequence. A noise with an abrupt beginning (e.g., when a tower of building blocks collapes) is described by a word beginning with a voiceless plosive (/p, t, k/). A gradually starting noise is generally given a word beginning with /s/ or /ts/.

According to BROWN (1958a, p.116), it follows that the initial sounds of onomatopoeic names copy the stimulus gradients of the noises they designate. At a closer inspection this will already reveal the limits of pure onomatopoeia. The details of the noise are not imitated; instead, a *formally* similar sound sequence is assigned to *formal* characteristics of the time extension of the noise sequence, e.g., its suddenness. In CASSIRER'S terminology (1953 edition) this case would be described as one of transition from mere 'mimetic' to 'analogical' expression; according to HUMBOLDT it is the boundary area between the imitation of sounds and sound symbolism. If we look at this boundary from the other side, it will be even more clearly seen.

GABELENTZ, in a book on linguistics which appeared in 1901, described the language of a child which contained a private word for 'chair'—a feature which is not uncommon among children of a certain age. 'Chair' was 'lakeil'; a little doll's chair was 'likil'; and the huge grandfather chair 'lukul'. Here the speech sound does not imitate a noise; it cannot be called onomatopoeia.

Another child calls a large bowl 'mum', a plate 'mem' and little stars 'mim'.

In the Ewe language of Africa most words have a high-tone and a low-tone form; the former describes small things, and the latter large ones (KAINZ, II, p. 206). If a small specimen of a class of usually large objects is referred to, a word generally spoken in a low tone is uttered with a high tone. In another language the word 'creep' is expressed by 'džarar', creeping of a small animal by 'džirir', and of a large one 'džurur'. In German 'teeny-weeny' is expressed by 'klitzeklein'. In certain Sudanese languages high-tone words are used to express long distances or high speed, low-tone ones to express proximity or slowness. "And purely formal relations and oppositions can be expressed in this same way. A mere change in tone can transform the affirmative into the negative form of the verb" (CASSIRER, 1953 edition, p. 194).

The development from sound imitation to phonetic symbolism becomes even clearer if we study another basic device of word formation, *reduplication*. CASSIRER (p. 195) points out that reduplication first of all appears to have, as its purpose, the reproduction of certain objective characteristics of the referential object or process. Objects with the same feature occur several times or an event in time is composed of a sequence of equivalent phases; this is where 'reduplication is most at home' (p. 195).

In these cases, therefore, there is something more than pure onomatopoeia; reduplication does not only occur to refer to repetitive noises, but to designate repetition in general.

This particular line of development can be pursued even further. 'Repetition in general' becomes 'plurality in general'. In that case the repetitive element is not contained in the temporal succession of the *appearance* of the objects but in the *perception* of the objects. 'Plurality in general' can further be analyzed conceptually into the expression of 'collective' and 'distributive' plurality. Some languages have a highly developed notion of such distributive plurality. The distinction is made between an act as a whole or an act which is composed of several individual acts. "If the latter is true and the act is either performed by several subjects or effected by the same subject in different segments of time, in separate stages, this distributive division is expressed by reduplication" (1953, p. 195).

The developmental trend which CASSIRER'S example here illustrates provides evidence for the importance of onomatopoeia and sound symbolism as components in the evolution of speech. The interest of a lawful relationship between word and thing does not lie in the fact that in everyday life we always imitate or symbolize things in a direct fashion, but in the observation—to paraphrase BÜHLER'S words (1934, pp. 29 f.)—that, in the historical prelude to the matching of word and object, sound symbolism is likely to have played a role of which slight traces can, from time to time, be found even in our own speech.

We shall now address ourselves to those psychological experiments and theoretical approaches which are intended to explore how these less obvious determining factors operate.

The most impressive of these experiments is one described by KÖHLER (e.g., 1947).

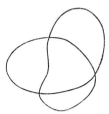

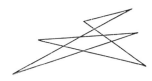

Fig. 59a   Fig. 59b

Two nonsense line drawings as well as two nonsense words are presented to the subject who is asked to decide which word matches which drawing (Fig. 59a and b).

Looked at purely rationally, it is completely immaterial whether 'maluma' is used for the round or the angular figure. If the designation is arbitrary, one would expect a random distribution of matchings, and approximately 50 percent of the subjects should assign 'maluma' to the rounded figure and 50 percent to the angular design.

In fact the overwhelming majority of all subjects assign 'maluma' to the round figure and 'takete' to the angular one. This result has not only been found in Germany and USA (HOLLAND and WERTHEIMER, 1964), but, for example, also in Tanganyika (DAVIS, 1961). It is as if there was a strange parallel or similarity between the visual and auditory shapes. WERNER calls such similarities, transcending different sense modalities, 'physiognomic' similarity; the theoretical conceptualization of this notion will be discussed in some detail below.

One of the first psychological investigations going beyond anecdotal evidence for the existence of such sound-symbolic relationships was undertaken by SAPIR (1929). More than 500 individuals were asked to imagine that the syllables 'mal' and 'mil' mean 'table'; but one of the syllables refers to a large table, and the other to a small one. Which refers to the big one, which to the small one? Of all subjects 80 percent, i.e., a majority far greater than chance, agreed that 'mal' fits better for the large table. Even more precise are the indications to be derived from an investigation by BENTLEY and VARON (1933): /a/sounds are felt to be larger than /i/sounds in the proportion 4 : 1, /i/ is three times as angular and twice as hard as /a/.

Accordingly one would expect that terms for large objects contain /a/sounds rather than /i/sounds. A corresponding systematic sampling of a dictionary (NEWMAN, 1933), however, has not confirmed this expectation.

These arguments and investigations are all, implicitly or explicitly, based on the assumption that the causal relationship expressed by the term 'sound symbolism' is naturally given. A general Gestalt principle of organization operates equally in things and in sounds, hence the 'similarity' between thing and sound. The presence of such a Gestalt principle is a universal human characteristic and occurs in all humans alike. It is not the result of experience nor is it influenced to a varying degree by the acquisition of different languages.

On the basis of this argument the psychologists who have studied phonetic symbolism have always attributed considerable importance to the proof of *universality*, i.e., the universal spread and applicability of sound symbolism, as we shall see from the following studies.

TSURU and FRIES (1933) have undertaken a matching experiment in the manner of KÖHLER'S 'maluma' study; but instead of using nonsense material they operated with verbal data. This experiment has become the prototype of a whole series of studies. Lists of pairs of opposites in two different languages are prepared (e.g., big/small — groß/klein) and presented orally. Subjects who are speakers of only one of these languages are invited to match the corresponding words in the other language. Does an English speaker who has never heard or learned German identify 'klein' as the translation of 'small' or 'big' ? If correct choices exceed the 50 percent chance level, this would indicate a sound symbolism which is universal and therefore is not tied to a particular language.

According to TSURU and FRIES, English-speaking undergraduates who have never heard a word of Japanese can identify the meaning of Japanese words with a certainty exceeding chance.

Objections to such investigations have inevitably led, by a highly interesting process of elimination, to the exclusion of more and more possible sources of error. A first objection, expressed, for example, by BROWN (1958a), was the following: authors operating with this type of study search for the words to be employed, having a full knowledge of both languages. Since in every language the number of phonemes is limited, it is possible that by pure chance similar phoneme sequences occur in both languages in words with equal meaning. Unconsciously the experimenter selects from the usually available series of synonyms a word which structurally (i.e., in its phoneme sequence) resembles the corresponding word in the other language. This would lead the subject —equally guided by the idea of structural similarity, matching A with A— to assign words correctly with greater than chance probability; but sound symbolism has nothing to do with this.

ALLPORT was the first to correct this weakness. BROWN, BLACK and HOROWITZ (1955) have followed. The experimenter selected only English words and asked scholars of the particular languages to translate these into Chinese, Czech and Hindi. The results of the subsequent experiment correspond to the earlier studies: the matching of English and foreign words is successful.

Another objection is difficult to formulate but can best be explained with the help of the experiment which has led to it. MALTZMAN, MORRISETT and BROOKS (1956) carried out an experiment on phonetic symbolism in the already familiar way: the matching of English-Japanese and English-Croatian succeeds with more than chance probability. The authors now argue: if it is really the result of a universal phonetic symbolism that enables us to guess the meaning of unknown words, it is of no consequence whether or not the subject knows one of the two languages. It should therefore be possible to match the words of two languages unknown to the experimental subjects. The test of this argument —American subjects match a Croatian and Japanese list of words—yields a result which is not above chance expectancy.

What does that mean ? In KÖHLER'S experiment the hitherto unknown nonsense words were matched with a nonsense drawing. It is argued that this was possible because of the isomorphism in auditory and visual organization. This, however, is apparently not operative in the experiment of MALTZMAN, MORRISETT and BROOKS. The factor which accounts for the negative result in the matching between two foreign languages becomes somewhat clearer in a subsequent experiment of BRACKBILL and LITTLE (1957): in contrast to many other investigations, the matching does not succeed if a Chinese word is juxtaposed with an English word and the subject has to decide whether it means the same as the English word or the opposite.

The difference in results has evidently something to do with the change in the method of investigation. What is possible when the first-language word pair is juxtaposed with the second-language word pair is no longer possible when the word pairs are in two foreign languages or when only a single word of the native language is to be matched with one in the foreign language. This leads to the conclusion that the native-language word pair offers hints for matching which, in the other cases, are either totally absent or are at least not present to a sufficient degree.

This argument is analyzed further in an excellent investigation by BROWN and NUTTALL (1959). It is known as a result of the experiments by SAPIR and others that the vowels /o/ and /u/ appear physiognomically 'bigger' than /i/ and /e/; the consonants /b/ and /d/ bigger than /p/ and /t/; polysyllabic groups appear bigger than monosyllabic ones. If it is assumed that experimental subjects possess this knowledge—without obviously having consciously formulated it—the method of paired comparison between native and foreign language is the only one which enables the subjects to employ this 'knowledge' for guessing the meanings of words in a foreign language. When the subject inspects the word pair in the mother tongue (e.g., 'tall—short'), he knows that the lexical dimension is 'size', and he can now make use of his knowledge according to which this dimension can be symbolized by vowel contrast or by the monosyllabic-polysyllabic contrast, and so forth. If the subject is asked to match word pairs from two unknown languages, he does not know what dimensions are offered. He is likely, therefore, to make use of phonetic similarities which in the two languages are not necessarily linked in an equivalent manner. A certain semantic dimension (e.g., size) can, as is already known from empirical investigations, be symbolized by several sounds and sound contrasts. And, vice versa, the same sound may—according to the context in which it occurs—have different meanings; a /p/ may in one instance symbolize smallness, in another speed or suddenness.

If the influence of phonetic symbolism is to be experimentally demonstrated, the possibilities of choice open to the subjects must be restricted. WILDE (1958), in a related study of matching terms of emotions with drawings representing these emotions, came to similar conclusions. If drawings in which one group of subjects have expressed certain emotions (anger, anxiety, etc.) are submitted to other subjects with the request to write down freely their impressions, 'correct' interpretations are hardly ever made. On the other hand, if subjects are given a list of terms of emotions from which to select the nearest approximation to the one expressed in the design, nearly all the expressive drawings are correctly identified. Quite similar conclusions were later reached by MÜLLER, a student of WILDE, in an investigation on the emotional expression of the speaking voice. These studies indicate the transition from sound symbolism to expression: the expectation is that somewhere the graphic or vocal expression of anger, grief, etc. turns into a symbol of anger or a symbol of grief. It is regrettable that WILDE was no longer able to explore more fully this borderland between the two fields.

Certain formal properties of the graphic or vocal expression normally evoke a particular impression in the receiver. WILDE had intended to base a psychology of art on these relationships. In the investigation by MÜLLER speakers were invited to utter the alphabet with varying emotional expression, e.g., with sadness, anger, yearning. The tape recordings of these speech samples were then submitted to subjects who were asked to state which emotion had been represented in each instance. It was found that some of these emotions can be identified by listeners with a high degree of assurance, whereas others cannot. Of course, a speaker who is supposed to express sadness, anger and so forth in his speech tends to employ a strongly conventionalized form of utterance, because he is not really sad or angry. What he utters could be described in BÜHLER's terms as half-way between symptom and symbol.

One way of narrowing down the possibilities in the phonetic symbolism experiment is to offer to the subject a word pair in the mother tongue in order to enable him to recognize the dimension in question. Another possibility is to influence the subject's decision by offering him associations with meaningful objects: if it is known that the topic is 'tables' correct matching is facilitated (WEISS, 1964b). Once the experimental subject is familiar with the dimension or topic he can make use of sound symbolism to make accurate localizations along the dimension or within the area in question.

ERTEL and DORST (1965), modifying this technique in an interesting manner, have found confirmation for expressive sound symbolism in twenty-five languages. They asked native speakers to make tape recordings of terms of emotions in the different languages. Judges who listened only to these tape recordings had to decide whether the sound sequences had a 'positive' meaning valence (lovely, good, sweet, right, loving, pleasant, joyful, happy) or a negative valence (ugly, bad, bitter, sad); whether they meant strength or weakness, movement or rest. Therefore the subject had only to make a decision on the feeling tone (i.e., a dimension of OSGOOD's semantic space); and such matching succeeded in all languages with a probability of $p < 0.01$.

Thus, it has been possible in the course of the past decades to overcome various methodological objections to the experiments which had been carried out in the attempt to elucidate the problem of phonetic symbolism.

A further confirmation—different from the usual matching experiments—for the existence of a universal phonetic symbolism has been given by OSGOOD who reported on experiments in which American and Japanese subjects were presented with nonsense syllables composed of sounds which appear in both languages as phonemes. These syllables were rated on the semantic differential. It was found that the various phonemes were rated almost equally by Americans and Japanese. For both groups front consonants (e.g., /p/) are more pleasant than back consonants (e.g., /g/); high frequency sounds are associated with smallness and impotence (1962b).

OSGOOD'S results suggest a universal sound symbolism. But it cannot be denied that, even today, there is no agreement whether the 'physiognomic' expression inherent in a word in a foreign language is identical for members of different language groups, or whether the development of sound symbolism is not, perhaps, to some extent determined by elements of learning, therefore leading to the expectations of differences in sound symbolism[1]. Hence the question: 'What is phonetic symbolism and where does it come from?' is still open.

BROWN (1958a) has put forward an elegant theoretical solution: what is mysteriously named 'physiognomic' (and we shall see shortly how confused this term is!) is a result and consequence of a simple act of learning. In everyday experience there is a correlation between certain physical attributes of objects and the noises produced by these objects. A large object, for example, is more likely to produce a deep sound than a small object when it is pushed or when it falls. This relationship between size and deep sounds can therefore be learned; equally a connection between sharpness and high frequency and between roundness or bluntness and low frequency.

Such relationships are therefore neither 'prehistoric' nor physiognomic, but simply learned.

Whether this theory can account for all phenomena subsumed under 'phonetic symbolism' appears questionable; but it is the most reasonable that so far has been advanced.

The success with which OSGOOD has made use of the method of the semantic differential in the study of phonetic symbolism prompts reflections which are long overdue. Most inquiries on sound symbolism select the linguistic material to be presented to subjects somewhat arbitrarily from the everyday vocabulary. But it is not to be ruled out that sound symbolism has certain preferred fields of manifestation, i.e., words with

---

[1] See the controversy between TAYLOR (1963) and WEISS (1964a).

which a language expresses emotions. Perhaps it is not denotation but connotation which is the main field of action of sound symbolism (which in that case had better not be described as a *symbolism* of sounds). STEVENSON remarks that the tone of a word may be 'physiologically fitted' for the expression of certain emotions; this fitness and conventional factors together form a unified determinant.

ERTEL (1964, 1965), who has expressed thoughts along these lines in his studies, has in a very logical way translated them into the experiments we have already reported. Deeper insight into the causation of sound symbolism can be expected from further studies in this direction.

This trend of thought has also given the impetus to a theory developed by WERNER, to which we are now turning. His theory of symbol formation, especially by introducing the notion of physiognomy, has given a new lease of life to the problem of sound symbolism, but quite generally it has introduced a completely novel element into the psycholinguistic debate. It forms a link between the area of phonetic symbolism and the developmental psychology of language.

In the primitive perception of animals, of children, and even of adults in a state of fatigue or illness, there is no categorical separation between the individual and the objects in the environment. But even at higher levels of evolution "at a stage where the object forms no longer an inseparable part of a psychophysically undifferentiated vital and total situation and is therefore distinct from the individual, we are still not simply in a sober world of objective facts; for objects are intimately interwoven with affective and motor activity" (WERNER, 1953, p. 45). Things participate in the dynamic acts by which they are perceived; they also play a part in emotional and motor behavior. This is why they appear totally different to an animal, a child or a naive adult from the way they appear to an adult with a purely factual and rational orientation. "Things are not treated objectively, but physiognomically, i.e., as if they expressed an inner life and had a mind" (p. 45).

Thus, a landscape may be 'cheerful', the contour of a mountain 'threatening', a sloping pasture 'melancholy' and a cup on its side 'tired'.

These assumptions supported by a wealth of examples from animal psychology, child psychology and psychopathology, are offered by WERNER as presuppositions for symbol formation in general and, hence, also for sound symbolism.

If we relate WERNER's approach to our earlier discussion, it will be particularly interesting to note how this approach brings language and expression closer to each other (cf. p. 25). This link has been stressed in psychopathology particularly by GOLDSTEIN, who, with reference to certain cases of motor aphasia, found that after the representational function of language had disappeared the expressive function of language alone had remained intact.

WERNER, who believes that growth and decline of psychic functions move along identical paths, has made use of such findings to support his genetic theory. What constitutes a symbol is explained by WERNER in terms of an account of its formation. His theory—developed fully in the work *Symbol Formation*, published jointly with KAPLAN in 1963—is therefore a genetic one.

Objects are expressive. Physiognomic quality or dynamic properties are as inherent in objects or events of our perception as are their geometrical or technical features. The head-lights of an automobile are not only round and brilliant; they also look like threatening eyes.

Identical dynamic-expressive features may be perceived in different objects or events. The contour of a rock or a musical passage may be equally 'threatening'. This transcendence of expressive qualities, as WERNER and KAPLAN have called this feature, does not only form the basis for analogies, metaphors and similes; but it is also the basis for seeing similarities in such fundamentally unrelated things as rounded shapes in a drawing and the word 'maluma'.

Two remarks should be interposed at this point: a first objection to be raised is that this interpretation is utterly unsatisfactory as an explanation. Whereas all earlier theories had attempted to answer *why* the same expressive qualities appear in parallel in different sense modalities, in other words, why it is that these qualities transcend *one* sense modality, WERNER covers up this problem by asserting that this transcending of expressive qualities happens because expressive qualities possess transcendence.

Secondly, the importance of metaphor in the genesis of genuine symbols must be stressed; it has, above all, been developed by WEGENER and, following him, by LANGER (1963). Every new experience with things prompts immediately some metaphorical expressions. If someone says for the first time, 'The brook runs swiftly,' the hearer is forced by the context of 'running' to forget that 'legs' are originally included in the use of the word 'running' (PORZIG, cf. p. 176). In sentences such as, 'The rumor runs through the town', or, 'The fence runs round the barnyard', the distance from the original metaphor becomes greater and greater: "constant figurative use has generalized its sense" (LANGER, p. 140). The metaphor has developed into a predicate. This transformation of a metaphor into a predicate is a process which, no doubt, runs parallel to the 'transcendence of expressive qualities'.

Different factual processes can, according to WERNER, be physiognomically similar; they may have the same expressive qualities. But an act of intentive and denotative reference must be applied to the factual process, i.e., an act of decision to interpret one similar objective process as a symbol for the other. Two hitherto equal objective processes are separated into a symbol carrier or vehicle (e.g., a sound pattern) and an object to which the symbol refers.

This aspect of intentionality which is emphasized in this act may philosophically be referred back to HUSSERL and psychologically to ACH. In ACH's work the 'latent, signifying set' plays an important role, but this set is a factor in a framework of thought which, in general, has a more associationist orientation. According to ACH the meaning-giving act is a process of fusion or "concrescence"; according to WERNER it is a process of differentiation. WERNER's view, therefore, comes closer to that of MERLEAU-PONTY than to ACH's.

Our account so far may easily have given too static a picture. The act of denotative reference is not projected upon two given independent objective states. Neither the symbol carrier nor the external object are finished products. (Without this proviso, WERNER's thesis would come suspiciously close to associationism, which he rejects.) Latent expressive qualities in the symbol carrier and the object are first made apparent through the referential act, which is directed towards them. These are "*twin form-building processes*, one directed towards the establishment of meaningful objects (referents), the other directed towards the articulation of patterns expressive of meaning (vehicles)" (1963, p. 22). WERNER names this directional, regulative, form-building process *dynamic schematization*. The semantic correspondence between sign and object has been established when the word, as well as the object, is rooted in similar or equal organismic states[1].

Symbol formation is conceived here quite differently from the theories with an associationist orientation. It does not consist in the linking of two originally independent ready-made sets of data[2], but in the gradual shaping and singling out of two factual processes from the common physiognomic fundament.

Two factual events take place: one leads to the formation of the symbol carrier or vehicle, and the other to the thing or referent. What is, literally, object of (or juxtaposed to) the word originates in the same act of creation in which the word is also created. This idea is again mindful of the great Humboldtian thought of language as *energeia* which transforms the world into the property of the mind. STENZEL speaks of "the primal phenomenon of the crystallization, from the buzzing confusion, of an object by means of the word. The word is so powerful that without it the object would not exist for the mind, but once the mind has a word it seems to be able to do with it what it likes ... Mental activity which

---

[1] This argument should be compared to OSGOOD's!

[2] Without such independence the possibility of postulates arbitrarily invented by man would not exist.

15*

reaches awareness only through language helps to define more clearly the essential qualities of an object in all its manifestations ..." "As a result (the word) now becomes an inherent part of the object and expresses it, and must henceforth be used to refer to it" (1934, p. 38).

An advantage of WERNER'S theory lies in the genetic priority it offers of the whole over the parts. The construction, implicit in the concept of association, of a comprehensive whole arrived at by a process of synthesis of separate elements has been questioned in various quarters. In the introduction to a work on the Kavi language of Java, HUMBOLDT writes: "In fact, speech is not produced out of words which precede it; on the contrary words are produced out of the totality of speech" (1907, p. 72). Likewise, BLOOMFIELD'S approach (language develops out of speech events which are scattered within the total context of practical events) suggests an analytic direction. All signs in a speech event allude to an overriding total meaning (MERLEAU-PONTY).

A second advantage of WERNER'S theory of symbol-formation in comparison with other theories on the same problem is that it offers the possibility of grasping psychologically the world-forming, rather than the world-reflecting, function of language. Thus, a link is created to another field of inquiry, i.e., 'linguistic relativity', a field which we associate with the names of HUMBOLDT, CASSIRER, SAPIR, and WHORF (cf. pp. 310 f.).

In view of the merits of this theory, the lack of clarity and other deficiencies of WERNER'S theory are all the more disturbing. The semantic correspondence between symbol and object, according to WERNER, comes about "through the operation of schematizing, form-building activity which shapes the pattern on one hand and the referent on the other" (WERNER and KAPLAN, 1963, pp. 23-24). What is meant by "schematizing, form-building activity"? Let us attempt to clarify this statement with the help of an illustration given by WERNER and KAPLAN.

An individual is confronted by a configuration which has a "sitting tone" in UEXKÜLL'S sense; i.e., this configuration instigates in him a postural-affective state which is schematically organized as "something there to sit down on". This activity and this state cause the individual to apprehend the configuration as a 'chair' rather than as a 'table'.

WERNER now assumes that the same schematizing activity leads to the lexical item 'chair' whenever a dynamic, intonationally molded sound /čɛr/ is articulated into a production whose expressive features parallel those contained in the percept 'chair' (p. 25).

The present author must admit that this example, too, does not help him to find an answer to the question how it is that just the word 'chair' comes to designate the object chair. WERNER stresses again and again (with particular emphasis, for example, on pp. 205-206) that this connection between sound and object does not come about through association. He argues that, neither in the more restricted field of sound symbolism, nor in the wider one of symbol formation in general, could anything so arbitrary and unstable as an association have such decisive results.

WERNER'S ctitique has undoubtedly a certain force. Yet, what he offers as an alternative to the association mechanism, is not clear even if he employs the prestige terms of the Leipzig School: 'organismic', 'genetic', 'patterning', 'globality', 'form-building', or 'structurization'.

The merit of WERNER'S approach is threefold: it lies, firstly, in the suggestion of the importance of expressive and emotive processes in the genesis of word-object relations; secondly, he rightly draws attention to the fact that this relationship is rooted in the total state of the language user; and thirdly, he recognizes the necessity of seeing the development of linguistic events not only synthetically, but also analytically.

The model of association—basically plain common sense—is certainly too simple to be able to account for the creation, stability and dynamic force of semantic relationships. But WERNER'S approach is too 'physiognomic' to serve as an alternative theory.

Chapter 13

The Psychological Reality of Grammar

Limits of the Markov model — Concept of grammaticality —
Linguistics and psycholinguistics — Effect of syntactical
structure upon learning and retention — What functions as
a unit ? — Temporal characteristics of speech perception and
speech production — Syntactical and lexical selection —
Role of generative grammar in psycholinguistics — JOHN-
SON'S hierarchical model — LASHLEY'S view of the temporal
organization of speech events — Plan and *Impulsfigur* —
The concept of recoding — MILLER'S studies of transformations.

A wide gulf separates the subject matter of the present chapter from
that of previous ones. We have considered at length the relationships
that bind single speech events to other speech events. These 'other speech
events' may either precede the single event or be latent and simultaneous
with it. The former relationships are probabilistic, the latter associative.
Basically one kind can be transformed into the other.

The presentation of the consequences and mode of functioning of
associative processes repeatedly led us to results which made it clear that
there is an additional factor beyond the observed relationships. For example, the observation that most responses in the word-association experiment belong to the same word class (noun, verb, etc.) can, up to a
point, be explained by a mediation model (see pp. 180f.), but it is equally
the consequence of a system which operates above the word level—
this system is called grammar in linguistics.

The assumption that such a system does operate is further suggested
by the argument (as pointed out by LASHLEY, 1951) that the combinations of word associations—and nothing else has so far been considered—are not sufficient to account for the structure of the largest
linguistic pattern constituting a unit, i.e., the sentence. The order of
words in a sentence cannot be accounted for in terms of associations
which exist between the words in the sentence.

This peculiar relationship between words and sentence exists at a lower level between phoneme and word. As we utter a word a sequence of specific movements of the vocal cords, tongue and jaw occurs. The elements of this sequence have almost no associative interrelationships, because, when we utter another phoneme or another word, the same tongue movement can be combined with a different positioning of the vocal cords and a different shape of the oral cavity. Therefore, the order of the elements of articulation cannot be derived from a directly associative combination of these elements; instead it seems, so to speak, to be imposed from above.

One might now be inclined to compensate for the inadequacy of the associationist model by employing a Markov model.

When language is considered as a Markov process, we adopt—as is already familiar— the point of view that speech event A (phoneme, letter or word) at the producer or the receiver end is dependent upon which events $(A-1, A-2, A-3...)$ have preceded it.

As was seen previously this approach has been particularly useful in explaining a great deal in the area of speech perception; for, as we receive a single speech event, the only additional aid at our disposal is what we have already received. Starting from what we have just heard, we have to draw probabilistic inferences as to what speech event will follow.

However, even the Markov model, which like the associationist mode of explanation is a finite-state model (see p. 97), has its inadequacies. Let us take one of these points to develop gradually what may perhaps be described as the 'psychological reality of grammar'.

The investigation by MILLER and SELFRIDGE on the connection between order of approximation and retention of linguistic material showed —it will be remembered—that the curve of retention after the fifth approximation no longer rises. This result was confirmed by a whole series of subsequent studies. Only combinations up to six words play a part in retention (and also, incidentally, in guessing omitted words, according to DEESE, in COFER, 1961a).

In certain studies, however, a surprising observation was made: at the seventh, eighth or tenth order of approximation not only does the curve not rise any more, but it declines again. This observation was made by COLEMAN (1963) the subject of an investigation in which he attempted to answer the question: do the transitional probabilities with which we operate when the order of approximation is raised constitute in fact a uniform factor?

His conjecture was that another factor should be separated from this one, one that is *not* probabilistic in character, i.e., a factor of grammaticality (or grammaticalness).

The concept of grammaticalness has been used, above all, by CHOMSKY (1961). His famous illustration consists in the comparison of these two sentences:

a) Colorless green ideas sleep furiously
b) Furiously sleep ideas green colorless

Both sentences are nonsense, but (a) is certainly 'well-formed' in a sense that (b) is not. What makes (a) superior to (b) is that it has a grammatical structure which is independent of the meaning of the words and of the sentence. "The degree of grammaticalness is a measure of the remoteness of an utterance from the generated set of perfectly well-formed sentences" (CHOMSKY, 1961, p. 237). This concept of grammaticalness has already been encountered earlier (see pp. 47f.).

COLEMAN submitted to a group of twelve linguists, who were not familiar with 'order of approximation', sequences of varying degrees of approximation and invited them to rank the sequences according to the degree of grammaticalness.

It was found that the degree of grammaticalness did not rise beyond the fifth order of approximation. In other words, approximations of a higher order do not offer a higher degree of agreement between subject and verb, or between verb and object. On the contrary, one gains the impression that to make up a sixth-order approximation more unusual constructions are used than, for example, to make up a second-order approximation. The procedure for making up these approximations should be remembered (pp. 100f.): at the sixth order a person is given six words and is asked to add a suitable seventh. In order to find a continuation for "humble because they have no electricity", one must no doubt think of something more unusual than if one searched for a continuation of "humble because".

HERRMANN (1962) undertook syntactical investigations on the immediate recall of strings of words and equally came to the conclusion "that the exclusive concern with the expectancy structure basically does not offer an adequate psychological explanation for the immediate recall of verbal strings." Besides factual content, i.e., the semantic meaning, and the motivational context of the words to be remembered, the grammatical regulation of the sentences is always a factor to be taken into account.

Although grammaticalness—like order of approximation—is independent of meaningfulness in the semantic sense (cf. CHOMSKY, 1961, p. 231) grammaticalness is not to be equated with order of approximation. According to Coleman's investigations it appears that, for example, the amount of material retained on the lower levels of approximation is in keeping with the degree of approximation (and at this stage still rises with the degree of grammaticality), but after a certain point has been reached, the score of retention is more in keeping with grammaticality, which no longer increases, and less with the order of approximation, which continues to rise. In other words the retention score, too, does not improve any more.

Further evidence for grammaticalness as an influence beyond transitional probabilities is found in a study by SALZINGER, PORTNOY and FELDMAN (1962). In sequences of different orders of approximation, words to be guessed by subjects had been deleted. According to expectation the percentage of correctly guessed words rose with the order of approximation. Then the results were re-scored on a more sensitive scale; i.e., the correctly guessed words were counted separately from those in which the grammatical category only had been guessed correctly (e.g., suppose the word omitted was 'oven', and the guessed word was 'table', only the grammatical category was scored right, not the actual word). It was found that the two scores do not run parallel. Whereas the percentage of the correctly guessed categories rises most markedly between zero to third order of approximation with only a relatively small increase after that, the percentage of correctly guessed words continues to rise steadily beyond the third level. This again can be regarded as an indication that behind the probabilistic structure lies grammar as a further causal factor.

The investigations we have outlined demonstrate an influence which is not identical with either association or transitional probability. We have assigned this factor—perhaps somewhat prematurely—to that system which in linguistics is called grammar. That is to say, we have accorded a certain psychological reality to the concept of grammar, a concept which does not originate in psychology. Grammar is something that determines verbal behavior.

Close investigation of this psychological reality may enable us to conceptualize a model which still includes the associative factor and transitional probabilities, but goes beyond them. However, such a model must take note of the way linguistics has conceptualized grammar. As we know, linguistics—as LEES and MACLAY, according to JOHNSON (1965, p. 31), have pointed out—describes *what* must have been learned when we can speak a certain language; psycholinguistics, on the other hand, aims at exploring *how* this something has been learned. This means that psycholinguistics, to a very considerable extent, has to rely on linguistics— at least for its 'raw material'[1].

MILLER (1965) has expressed the same line of thought in the following manner. A description of the rules which are applied in the use of a language is not identical with the description of the psychological mechanisms which are involved in the use of these rules; it is the task of the psycholinguist to design performance models for the language user,

---

[1] On several previous occasions we have referred to this kind of interaction between psycholinguistics and linguistics, e.g., in the discussion on the 'psychological reality' of the phoneme.

but the exact specification of what the language user uses must be supplied by the linguist.

In linguistics, however, there are widely differing conceptions of what constitutes grammar[1]. We will have to choose a model in which grammar is conceived *linguistically* in a way which corresponds most adequately to the kind of constructs developed by psychology. Thus we are confronted by a somewhat peculiar interdisciplinary situation. Linguistics must tell psycholinguistics *what* to investigate, but the linguistic offerings are so heterogeneous that the student of psycholinguistics is in a position to select, and indeed is forced to select, a theory which he finds especially congenial, and in its mode of operation particularly suitable for psychological inquiry.

But before we can take this decision and can say: "*This* is the linguistic system whose acquisition and functioning we must explain in psychological terms", we need further guidance and information on how to understand better the psychological reality of grammar, which, so far, is still very vaguely conceived.

In the first instance, a much clearer separation of the influence of semantic meaning, grammaticalness and transitional probability or association must be attempted. Investigations by EPSTEIN (1961, 1962) on the effects of syntactical structure had this objective in mind.

Table 20. *Learning materials* (from EPSTEIN, 1962, p. 122)

Category	Sentence
1*	(1) A haky deebs reciled the dison tofently um flutest pav. (2) The glers un cligs wur vasing un seping a rad moovly.
2	(1) deebs haky the um flutest reciled pav a tofently dison (2) cligs seping a wur rad un moovly glers the un vasing
3*	(1) Wavy books worked singing clouds to empty slow lamps. (2) Helping walls met eating trees from noisy poor lines.
4	(1) worked clouds slow empty to wavy singing books lamps (2) noisy trees walls from lines helping eating poor met

* It should be noted that the 'sentences' in categories 1 and 3 begin with a capital and end with a period.

In order to isolate syntactical structure as a variable, EPSTEIN produced categories of materials consisting each of two sentences (Table 20). The 'sentences' in category 1 are nonsense-syllables mixed with the two

---

[1] This is well illustrated by a volume of studies on German grammar edited by MOSER (1965) and significantly entitled *The Struggle for a New German Grammar (Das Ringen um eine neue deutsche Grammatik)*.

function words 'a' and 'the'[1]. Additionally, the grammatical tags 'ed', 's', 'ing', 'ly' and 'est' are appended to the nonsense-syllables. In this way sentences are made up which are nonsense but still have a certain measure of grammaticalness in CHOMSKY'S sense.

Category 2 contains the same words but in random order.

In these two categories 1 and 2 there is neither meaning in the usual sense (i.e., with object reference) nor are there statistical dependencies in the form of transitional probability because the 'words' in these sentences have never been met before by the subjects and consequently cannot have been encountered in this particular order. The difference between categories 1 and 2 is purely the presence of the empty syntactical structure in 1.

Categories 3 and 4 consist of sentences with meaningful words, composed as patterns making up nonsense 'sentences'. Transitional probabilities should be extremely slight. In category 3 words are arranged in such a way that a syntactical structure is produced, whereas in category 4 the same words appear in random order.

The subject's task is to learn these sentences. The results are presented in Table 21.

Table 21. *Results.* (Both sentences combined for each category) (based on EPSTEIN, 1962, p. 122)

Measure of learning	Category 1		Category 2		Category 3		Category 4	
	M	SD	M	SD	M	SD	M	SD
Trials to criterion	7.29	2.87	8.87	3.37	2.62	1.12	3.78	1.87
Errors to criterion	23.95	9.89	35.54	9.48	4.75	2.72	10.00	3.74

M = mean

SD = standard deviation

If one compares the number of repetitions needed to learn categories 1 and 2, it will be seen that at work here is a sequential factor (1 and 2 are distinguished *only* by the order of words) which can have nothing to do with transitional probabilities or associations, for neither can be present since the subject has met them here for the first time. Meaningful words are learned more rapidly than nonsense words (compare 1 and 3), but even in the nonsense combination of meaningful words we can see the influence of an empty but syntactically correct sequential structure.

---

[1] 'Function words' are articles, conjunctions and prepositions. Their function is purely to structure the sentence; they have no referential 'meaning' outside the sentence.

Characteristically, EPSTEIN's findings apply only as long as the subject can read the sentences as units, as would normally occur when they are in a book. If the same sentences are presented in the form of a serial learning experiment, i.e., a word every two seconds, the influence of the syntactical structure is no longer present. All one finds is the usual serial position effect in the learning of nonsense-syllable lists.

What conclusions can we draw from these results of EPSTEIN's investigations and similar results obtained by MILLER and ISARD (1963) and MARKS and MILLER (1964)? Syntactical structure operates as a comprehensive whole, characterized, for example, by a definite speed of occurrence.

In contrast, probabilistic and associative determinants are always attributes of a single unit, e.g., an individual word. For example, NOBLE describes how many associative relationships a single word possesses; the order of approximation tells us how many preceding words have to be taken into account in the choice of a single word.

The next step in the analysis of what can here be called comprehensive structure consists of investigations by GLANZER (1962). Here, too, the distinction made by EPSTEIN, between function words (articles, prepositions, conjunctions, etc.) and content words, which have a correlate in reality, plays an important role. Function words are few in number, but they have existed in the language for a long time; they form the 'skeleton' of the language. Content words are a huge open class; new words are added every day and old ones are discarded; they are the 'meat' of the language. Function words are always frequent, content words less so.

GLANZER now raises the question whether this linguistic distinction has a psychological correlate. To answer this question, he divised a learning experiment in which nouns, verbs, prepositions and conjunctions were associated with nonsense syllables (e.g., food — YIG, church — NIV, think — HUC, grow — FEP, of — TAH, with — SEB, and — KEX, if — NED). It was found that the association of a noun and a nonsense syllable was learned more rapidly than the association between a preposition or conjunction and a nonsense syllable.

It was fortunate that GLANZER was not satisfied with this first confirmation of his hypothesis, for he attempted to find a more convincing explanation. Function words, he argued, can only be regarded as separate words in a restricted sense; perhaps they are only complete if they appear in a context within which they can function as 'function words'. Content words, on the other hand, ought to be less affected by isolation. To express it differently: in the case of content words the addition of a context should therefore have less influence upon ease of learning. To put this argument to the test, GLANZER asked his subjects to learn the following:

YIG — food — SEB

MEF — think — JAT

TAH — of — ZUM

WOJ — and — KEX

The order of learnability is indeed changed now. Whereas previously nouns were learned fastest, and prepositions or conjunctions slowest, the order is now reversed. Similar results were obtained by ROSENBERG and BAKER (1964, in ROSENBERG, 1965). GLANZER draws the conclusion that isolated function words are psychologically incomplete as units.

If this argument is taken further, it can be said, following GLANZER (p. 313): an utterance consists of a series of signals or units: some of these units are single words, but some of them are sets of words. Content words, in this sense, are one-word units, whereas multiword signals contain a function word embedded in them.

This result immediately reveals a fundamental difference between psycholinguistics on the one hand and nearly all other branches of psychology on the other. Whereas in general psychology or in personality research the psychologist has an almost completely free hand in what he wants to choose as a unit of investigation, the student of psycholinguistics must find out empirically what the language user in fact uses as a functional unit and base his psychological investigation upon it.

GLANZER'S study and the inquiries previously reported are almost at the end of a line which begins with SKINNER who tried to explain verbal events without ever leaving the plane of behavior. But a verbal event is structured in a lawful manner. It might be said that this structure has an independent existence; in any case, it can become the object of scientific investigation.

One such attempt to grasp these determining structures operates with the concept of transitional probabilities, the Markov model. Transitional probabilities are relations between units which are always on a particular level, e.g., between phonemes, or between letters, or between words. As we can now see and as, for example, CARROLL has repeatedly pointed out, these units are again organized into a more comprehensive whole; this organization is such that it cannot be reduced to transitional probabilities. What matters is not only which word follows another in a sequence, but also which function a particular word fulfills in this sequence. Grammar creates relations within a sequence which do not coincide with probabilistic relations.

If, for example, we operate in the framework of a Markov model of language at word level, each word is considered a unit which is linked to the following unit, and the one after, etc. by certain transitional probabilities. We now recognize that a word is sometimes the psychologically relevant unit and can therefore be considered as the base line for transitional probabilities. But, at other times, the single word does not constitute a psychologically relevant unit; it must be combined with other words. It is quite thinkable that the simple sentence, 'There are men and women', should not be considered as a Markov chain consisting of five units; instead it should be represented as follows:

'Men' and 'women' on the one hand are complete units; on the other the 'and' between them becomes a complete unit only if it is preceded and followed by a content word. This indicates that in the analysis of linguistic events it is necessary to operate with units on more than one level.

We can now formulate the principal objections to language as a Markov model. This conception enables us, perhaps, (even though with certain reservations) to make an adequate description of the decoding process at the receiving end of messages; it is not adequate for the description of the encoding process at the source. As the receiver hears a text he undoubtedly makes use of transitional probabilities in order to understand it. The speaker, however, already 'knows' what he wants to say and what he is going to say. If the determining aspects of speech production were only of a probabilistic order, diversions of the speaker would be much more frequent: for example, a slight accidental slurring of a phoneme would change the direction of the sentence, and it would not be possible to explain real diversions (slips of the tongue) as meaningful in the Freudian sense.

"The distinctive elements, the phonemes which the listener recognizes, lead him to the grammatical form and the understanding of meanings. Here the probability factor plays an important part. What helps us to perceive a text ... are above all the transitional probabilities. For the speaker the rank order of the levels of language is reversed: he proceeds from the sentence down the hierarchy of immediate constituents and morphological units to the sound form which completes it. In the verbal exchange both orders co-occur, and their interrelationship rests—as BOHR would say—on the principle of complementarity" (JAKOBSON, 1962, II, pp. 55 f.).

If the linear probability model lays emphasis on the conception of sending and receiving as a process of selection in which transitional probabilities determine which event is chosen as the next one, the importance of this selection process is not diminished as a result of the above considerations. Sending and receiving messages are indeed selective processes, but the question now is: what determines the time sequence of the command to select? It is by no means always a simple matter of preceding speech events determining subsequent events.

Even looked at from the angle of the perception of speech, the view that the speech event is structured on several hierarchical levels has received valuable confirmation. LADEFOGED (1959) assumes that the receiver, too, even if he had been specially asked to pay attention to these segments, would have difficulties in grasping the speech event at each single moment of hearing as if it were composed of small segments. In one experiment, the word 'dot' was superimposed upon a spoken sentence. Subjects were asked to indicate the exact place in the sentence at which the superimposed word had begun. In many cases 'dot' was located by the subject two or three words ahead of the place where it had actually occurred. This observation led LADEFOGED to the conclusion that the processing of ongoing contextual information has different temporal features than the processing of isolated stimuli; ongoing speech events result in complex time patterns which have to be grasped as a whole. "... items of speech such as syllables, words, phrases, and even some sentences, have a perceptual unity; and any theory which attempts to explain the perception of speech in terms of the sequential identification of smaller segments is likely to be unsatisfactory" (1959, p. 402).

From this vantage point it is of interest to glance back to the motor theory of speech perception (LIBERMAN, cf. pp. 63ff.) on the one hand and to BROADBENT'S dictionary units (cf. pp. 107f.) on the other. It will be remembered that 'dictionary units' were postulated because the process of recognition in the hearer was seen as an act of comparison. The fragments of the percept are complemented in accordance with the most fitting pattern of the inner repertoire; or to put it differently: what is perceived coincides with an already existing pattern. The difficulty of this conception of the process of speech perception lies in the assumption that the input must be compared in a fraction of time with an infinite number of such patterns.

As we know, one restriction of this infinite number is provided by transitional probabilities. In spite of that, it is hard to imagine that a huge number of dictionary units and a vast number of sentences can be stored as patterns.

To solve this problem, HALLE and STEVENS (1962) have advanced the hypothesis that these internal patterns against which the input is matched might be created only at the moment of receiving the message in accordance with the same rules of a generative grammar which the hearer would follow if he himself were the speaker.

The comprehension of the input, according to this view, begins with guesswork or a hypothesis. On the basis of this hypothesis the hearer generates an internal pattern of comparison to which to relate the input. Discrepancies in this comparison lead to the creation of a second pattern for comparison, matching better with the input. As soon as the match is judged to be satisfactory, the message is accepted or 'recognized', which does not mean that it is necessarily 'correct'.

In the theory of HALLE and STEVENS the comparison of the input with a repertoire of possible patterns plays a role, but these possible patterns are not all stored singly, they are created at the moment of perception according to the rules of generative grammar.

LIBERMAN'S motor theory offers a parallel in that the hearer's production is decisive for the perception of what he hears. But, different from LIBERMAN (hence circumventing the objections to his theory), what is produced by the hearer does not in HALLE and STEVENS' theory consist of an actual, if only covert, articulation. The hearer need not articulate what he hears; what he does is to activate the program which could generate the sentence which enters as input.

Time markers in speech (as was clearly seen in EPSTEIN'S study) serve as indicators of the underlying structure of an utterance. As one would expect, the study of time features in the *production* of utterances will reveal this with particular clarity. Such studies were made by GOLDMAN-EISLER (1964) in the form of detailed analyses of pauses in speech sequences.

GOLDMAN-EISLER used as a measure for pauses—always in spontaneous speech—the proportion of the length of the pauses to the number of words in the utterance. It was found that pauses take up approximately 40 to 50 percent of the total time of utterances. Pausing regulates nine-tenths of the speed of speech, while the rate of articulation itself is remarkably constant. This can be explained by the fact that the articulatory performance constitutes the real 'art' of speech, whereas pauses represent that part of the total event in which 'verbal planning and selection' occur and in which, therefore, information is created. Pauses are related to the information content of subsequent words; fluency of speech is related to redundancy. The information content in these studies was measured in terms of transitional probabilities. In this context it became apparent that the linear Markov model cannot be satisfactory: the relationship between information content and length of pauses became significant only when the transitional probabilities were estimated both in the reverse as well as the forward direction. The speed of an utterance, therefore, is determined by the probability structure of subsequent as well as preceding speech. That means that, at least as far as the production of speech is concerned, there must be a plan which, in the moment of event A takes into account not only the preceding events (A−1), (A−2), etc. but also future events (A+1), (A+2), etc.; this view will later be considered in detail.

Moreover, GOLDMAN-EISLER was able to prove that a subject who has to fill blanks in a text as he reads it can complete this task successfully only if he makes the same pauses as the speaker who originally produced the particular sentence. This suggests the importance of time factors in the selection processes which are basic to the speech event (cf. LASHLEY). If a speaker describes the significance of an event, pauses are more than twice as long as when he gives a description of the event itself. During the repetition of previously narrated sentences, pauses are reduced. This is to say that length of pauses apparently is not only related to the information content of the utterance itself, but also to the creative activity of the speaker. GOLDMAN-EISLER draws the conclusion that pausing indicates that, in the course of speech, information is being generated and an act of verbal planning is taking place.

MACLAY and OSGOOD (1959) were able to make an even more differentiated study of pause phenomena because they had GOLDMAN-EISLER'S work as a basis to build upon. They interpreted their results in approximately the following way. The speaker operates with units no smaller than words. But words always involve a syntactical and lexical selection; immediately before the 'final common path', i.e., before articulation, it must be assumed that a kind of 'mixer' enters into action. It is as if, on a lower level of encoding, a 'pool' of heavily practiced, tightly integrated word and phrase units were available, from which a choice is made as a result of the simultaneous action of lexical and syntactical determinants.

We have now come to the point where it should be possible to sketch out a preliminary model of the structure we are looking for which, in linguistics, is referred to as 'grammar'. The organization of encoding occurs on two levels. The first of these may be described as the 'lexical' level, and the second as the 'syntactical', 'structural' or 'grammatical' level.

Support for this kind of conception had already appeared in MILLER'S earlier investigations, in which the view was advanced that the context preceding a word had the effect of limiting or defining the number of possible decisions as to which words to receive at a particular moment. In the light of these considerations, which have been briefly referred to earlier, MILLER (1962b) already raised the question of how to imagine the mechanism limiting the possibilities of selection in accordance with the probabilistic view. It must be remembered that the recognition of words and sentences demands additionally a segmenting activity. If the listener is supposed to make a decision for each word, or even each phoneme, the review of all the possibilities and the selection of appropriate ones must take place extremely rapidly, too rapidly to make the assumption of so many decisions plausible. To be sure, the context of a sentence reduces the number of possibilities for each sentence; but, additionally, the context enables us to organize the flow of speech into larger units, consequently to reduce the number of possible decisions and thus to have time to make these decisions. The decisions, which are noticeable at pauses, are made on two levels: (a) on the grammatical level where they involve the selection of a particular construction down to the choice of form classes, and (b) on the lexical level where they require the selection of particular words which fit into the construction of the sentence as a whole (cf. CARROLL, 1964a).

A further support for the assumption of this simple model can be found in the everyday observation that a speaker, beginning a sentence, often hesitates immediately before a lexical choice. It is as if he had already selected the syntactic structure which he wants to employ, but not yet the lexical item which the realization of this structure requires at this particular point[1].

A two-stage model, consisting of a syntactical and a lexical level of organization, at closer inspection, however, proves to be unable to cope with all the requirements which arise from the interpretation of studies so far reported. For example, GLANZER'S results demand a more differentiated model. The insufficiency of such a two-stage model becomes clearer still if one uses it to analyze the following kind of sentence: 'He slew the man with the club.' The lexical meaning of the single words is completely clear, but the meaning of the whole sentence is ambiguous: the club can be the instrument the killer used; it may equally be a descriptive characteristic of the man who was murdered. The only way to grasp the meaning of the whole sentence consists in treating words that belong together as units which lie between the unit word and the unit sentence.

Or to put it in another way, the plan for the production of a sentence, within the area of syntax, must include more than one level. To illustrate it once more with the example given, this plan demands that 'with the club' must either be bracketed with 'he slew' or with 'the man'. We must look for rules which prescribe what goes with what.

The consequence is that the kind of grammar which psycholinguistics requires as a working basis must be a generative grammar in CHOMSKY'S sense. It must operate with units which have psychological reality.

---

[1] An investigation by WISSEMANN, reported at the 16th International Congress of Psychology held at Bonn, 1960 (1962), was also based on a two-stage model of grammar. He showed that the comprehension of sentence meaning is, to a much greater extent, dependent upon lexical, than upon syntactical or grammatical factors.

While the grammarians should be able to account for *what* is being learned, it is the task of the psycholinguist to explain *how* such learning takes place (cf. p. 45). A generative grammar, which describes a language by developing the rules which in the language lead to the production of grammatical sentences, is, therefore, a congenial partner for psycholinguistics.

The reader should refer back to the account of CHOMSKY'S approach on pp. 45 ff. In more recent work CHOMSKY'S model of a generative grammar has been further refined.

The basis of CHOMSKY'S model is a syntactical component. Its output is 'interpreted', first, by a semantic component and then by a phonological component. In more recent studies the output of the syntactical component has been further differentiated into (a) what is produced by the phrase-structure sub-component and (b) what results from applying transformation rules to the 'string' generated by (a).

This view is the basis of the currently common distinction between 'deep' structure and 'surface' structure of a sentence. Thus, for example, the two sentences: (A) 'The book was taken by a thief' and (B) 'The city was taken by surprise' have identical surface structure, but different deep structures. Likewise, in the analysis of the previously cited example, 'He slew the man with the club', it would have been useful to make the same distinction.

The following discussion on the application of generative grammar to psycholinguistics is based on the earlier version of CHOMSKY'S theory. The merit for having recognized the fruitfulness of this approach for psycholinguistics belongs to G. A. MILLER. MILLER has not only been active in initiating the interpretation of speech events in terms of a Markov model; he has equally been a leading exponent of the further development beyond the finite-state model towards the inclusion of grammatical structures.

Some years ago, JOHNSON (1965) offered a very clear analysis of the relations of CHOMSKY'S theory to the psychology of language behavior. His argument runs roughly as follows. The analysis of language behavior, which leads to the production of sentences, presupposes four levels. The lowest is formed by the unstructured lexicon of the particular individual. On the next level is a system of word classes into which this individual reservoir is sorted; here, for example, is the class of nouns (N), verbs (V), etc.[1] The third level is formed by phrase-structure rules (e.g. $NP \rightarrow D + N$). The highest level is represented by transformation rules, e.g., the negative transformation (see p. 47).

On the lowest level, one problem for psycholinguistics is, for example, how morphemes or words of which the lexicon is composed are acquired. How does a child learn to produce a particular sound sequence ? And how does he learn the meaning of the sequence ? In this context, conditioning and similar concepts will appear in the discussion.

On the second level, the psychologist must demonstrate that the fairly numerous form classes are 'real', not only linguistically but also psycho-

---

[1] Cf. the account of CHOMSKY'S view in chapter 3.

logically, i.e., in terms of behavior. Word-association and substitution experiments show that words belonging to the same class are more closely related in the sequence of language behavior than words of different classes. Certain morpheme classes have formal characteristics (e.g., 'endings') which give our thinking and perception quite a definite direction.

The third level, that of phrase-structure rules, leads the psychologist to ask the question of how these rules are learned and how their function manifests itself in language behavior. Developmental psychology has begun to understand the changes in syntactical rules during the growth of the child. The pauses in the flow of speech, too, can be regarded as further clues to the process of reorganization.

The transformations, forming the fourth level, again raise the problem as to what it means, in terms of psychology, to 'know' a rule and to act in accordance with it. But the empirical study of the behavioral correlates of such transformations is still in its early stages.

To return once more to the question which, after so much preparatory discussion, had eventually led us to generative grammar: what must the rules be like according to which the sequence of words is organized to generate grammatical sentences? The help which generative grammar can give in answering this question is illustrated by BRAINE'S investigations (1963a, b).

BRAINE examined the speech and vocabulary of early childhood with the help of generative grammar. This is to say he has attempted to sketch a grammar which describes what sentences a child in a given period will or will not produce. Detailed records of the utterances of Steven, aged 23 months, were kept over a period of several weeks so that a survey of his linguistic repertoire was established.

Asking the question, '*What* can appear *where*?' (i.e., by establishing the 'privilege of occurrence'), BRAINE, was able to define two word classes: 'X-words' and 'pivots'. There are only a few pivots; they appear in various combinations, mostly however in position 1 (P_1); only 'do' occurs in P_2. X-words are a large open category, comprising the entire remainder of the infant's vocabulary. If the classes of the sentence constituents are defined in this way, it is possible also to describe the syntax or arrangement in which these constituents occur. Steven's syntax has two rules:

$$P_1 + X$$
$$X + P_2$$

Following CHOMSKY it is now possible to predict which sentences Steven at this stage of his linguistic development can and will produce, or which ones he cannot produce. Thus, it is possible to predict that 'want candy' or 'want truck' could occur, but not 'Baby want'.

Table 22. *Verbal utterances of a 23-month-old child* (based on BRAINE, 1963b, p. 7)

want baby	it ball	get ball	there ball	that box
want car	it bang	get Betty	there book	that Dennis
want do	it checker	get doll	there doggie	that doll
want get	it daddy		there doll	that Tommy
want glasses	it Dennis	see ball	there high	that truck
want head	it doggie	see doll	there momma	
want high	it doll	see record	there record	here bed
want horsie	it fall	see Stevie	there truck	here checker
want jeep	it horsie		there byebye car	here doll
want more	it Kathy	whoa cards	there daddy truck	here truck
want page	it Lucy	whoa jeep	there momma	
want pon	it record		truck	bunny do
want purse	it shock	more ball		daddy do
want ride	it truck	more book	beeppeep bang	momma do
want up			beeppeep car	(want do)
want byebye car				

Other utterances:

bunny do sleep	baby doll	find bear	eat breakfast	
Lucy do fun	Betty pon	pon baby	two checker	
want do pon	byebye car	pon Betty	Betty byebye car	
want drive car	Candy say	sleepy bed	Lucy shutup Lucy	shutup Lucy

Following JENKINS' argument (see p. 181) the formation of such a word class can be thought of as a mediation process.

BRAINE'S investigation shows that it is possible to interpret the linguistic behavior of a child, before he has full control of his language, as the manipulation of function classes by means of phrase-structure rules.

This successful procedure leads to the question of whether the word sequences determined by phrase-structure and transformation rules are identical with those functional units into which the language user divides the speech event. Or, in other words, to what extent can the psychological reality of phrase-structure and transformation rules be discovered by studying the functional units in which the total speech event is structured during encoding?

This is the question which JOHNSON (1965) has raised. We report his investigations in detail because, in our view, these studies—together with those by MILLER to be discussed later—constitute the growing edge of psycholinguistic research.

If the language user structures the speech event into relatively large units, the composition of these units should occur *before* the sentence is in turn composed out of these units. When, for example, a sentence is to be memorized, the subject is likely to learn to move from one word to the next within one unit before he learns to combine one word of the last unit with the first of the next. Mistakes (i.e., the occurrence of a wrong word after a right one) should, according to this view, be less frequent within a unit than across units.

To test this hypothesis JOHNSON had his subjects learn sentences of the following kind: 'The tall boy saved the dying woman.' A grammatical analysis divides this sentence Σ into subject S and predicate P; subject S is composed of article T plus modified noun MN; MN is adjective A plus noun N. Finally A designates a certain form class of words. This sequence can be represented in the manner which is usual in phrase-structure grammar:

$$\Sigma \to S + P$$
$$S \to T + MN$$
$$MN \to A + N$$
$$\ldots\ldots$$
$$A \to \text{tall, blue, lively} \ldots$$

This constituent structure of the sentence can also be shown as a tree diagram.

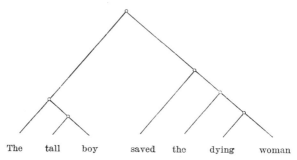

The   tall   boy   saved   the   dying   woman

Fig. 60. 'Tree diagram' of a sentence (based on JOHNSON, from ROSENBERG, 1965, p. 48)

Errors of the kind we have described are possible at six points, i.e., at each transition from one word to the next. According to the hypothesis they should occur, above all, at transition point 3, which lies between the two units into which the sentence is divided.

Or in more precise terms, in a tree diagram it is possible to rank the nodes, at which the division into constituents occurs, according to height: e.g., the node between 'the' and 'tall boy' lies higher than the node between 'tall' and 'boy'. The rank order arrived at in this way correlates significantly with the frequency of errors. The profile of error frequency reflects the sequence of the constituent analysis (Fig. 61).

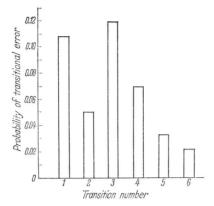

Fig. 61. Pattern of transitional error probabilities obtained when subjects learn the sentence: 'The tall boy saved the dying woman' (based on JOHNSON, from ROSENBERG, 1965, p. 49)

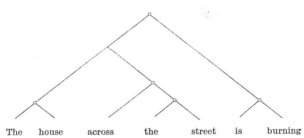

Fig. 62. Tree diagram of a sentence (based on JOHNSON, from ROSENBERG, 1965, p. 48)

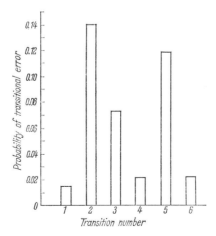

Fig. 63. Pattern of transitional error probabilities obtained when subjects learn the sentence: 'The house across the street is burning' (based on JOHNSON, from ROSENBERG, 1965, p. 50)

A differently constructed sentence (Fig. 62) correspondingly produces a similar error pattern (Fig. 63).

By adopting the concept of the 'depth' of the node at the place at which a particular structuring of the constituents occurs, the linear model of speech production (such as the Markov model) is eventually discarded and replaced by a hierarchical arrangement. Broadly speaking, in a hierarchical model a speech utterance is viewed as generated from 'top to bottom' and not from 'left to right'. Only the terminal coding process in each case leads to concrete words; the preceding processes, which according to the model are recoding processes, do not yet lead to concrete manifestations in the form of words.

To make these ideas more explicit we must once more review JOHN-SON'S approach against the background from which it has evolved: considerations, derived as much from general psychology as from psycholinguistics, have inevitably led to such notions as the *planning* of behavior processes or the *integration* of molecular behavior units into larger sequences.

A very clear but quite inadequate answer to this problem was the reflex chain theory. This theory, which originated in the early part of the century and was to a very large measure adopted by WATSON in the development of his psychology of 'behaviorism', assumes that the occurrence of each single reflex serves as the stimulus for eliciting the next reflex. The kinesthetic and auditory sensations which the articulation of a speech sound produces evokes the articulation of the next speech sound.

This view, represented also, among others, by WASHBURN, has distinct similarity with the conception of the speech event as a Markov process. In both theories the event which has just occurred determines the event which is about to occur next.

Towards the end of the twenties LASHLEY'S investigations showed conclusively that this theory is unable to account for the temporal arrangement of behavior. Thus, rats, for example, which have learned to run a maze are able to run the maze faultlessly, even if, as a result of surgical extirpation, they are forced to activate different muscle groups in quite different temporal patterns in order to reach their objective. Later, LASHLEY was also able to demonstrate, at the hand of linguistic examples, that a linear model is inadequate and that comprehensive integrating structures must be assumed (cf. p. 140). Here, then, is a first link to the notion of *plan*.

The historically second approach, following the reflex chain theory, was the Würzburg School, operating with the concept of 'determining tendency', as it was evolved by KÜLPE and later by ACH. The arrangement of a sentence, for example, constitutes a mental set (*Bewusstseins-*

lage) in which the temporal sequence is not yet recognizable as such. Pick, for example, has drawn attention to the processes which occur in translating from one language into another with a different sentence structure. Suppose an English-speaking reader reads a German sentence and expresses it in a free English translation. As he moves from German to English, the German sentence must, in a certain way, be taken out of the time dimension and after that put back into it as an English sentence but in a different serial order. A speaker of several languages—at an international conference, for example—can express the same thought in different languages and in doing so change several times from one word order to a totally different one. This again suggests that the preconceived organization of thought does not necessarily contain a temporal organization.

How complicated the factors involved may be was shown by Lashley with reference to the phenomena which psychoanalysis has studied as 'slips' of the tongue and pen, etc.

Suppose a typist writing the word 'manner' accidentally fails to double the middle 'n' and writes 'maner'; she crosses it out and at her second attempt writes 'maaner'. This means that the command to double the letter was carried out, but the instruction evidently had not included a sufficiently precise indication of serial order[1].

Lashley (1960, p. 515), too, is finally led to postulate hierarchically organized levels: the order of articulatory movement as a word is uttered, the order of words in a sentence, the order of sentences in a paragraph, the order of paragraphs in a discourse.

We thus already approach a more differentiated conception: the order of words in a sentence is not on a single level, but is itself in turn the result of a hierarchy of factors.

In this connection, Lashley lists the following problems requiring explanation: (1) the activation of the expressive elements (e.g., of words); (2) the determining tendency, idea, or set; and (3) the syntax of the act, which can be described as a habitual order of relating the expressive elements. This order can be imagined as an integrating generalized schema covering the multiplicity of specific acts. The hub of the problem of a serial order lies in the existence of generalized schemata of action, non-specific dynamic patterns determining the sequence of specific acts which themselves—both independently and in association with each other—lack temporal valence.

It is now conceivable that these generalized schemata of action can be looked upon as analogous to phrase-structure rules of a generative grammar.

---

[1] In Hull's psychology of learning this would be described as an anticipatory goal response; it is interesting to note here the fragmentation of a complex response.

The explanation, particularly of speech *production*, demands the assumption of an orienting device which permits a view of things to come. The speaker does not only know what he has just said; he knows equally what he is going to say. He unfolds the sentence according to a plan anticipating future events.

This notion of a plan, which is intended to overcome the weakness of a purely probabilistic conception of speech, is central to a theory developed by MILLER, GALANTER and PRIBRAM (1960). A plan is "any hierarchical process in the organism that can control the order in which a sequence of operations is to be performed" (p. 16). A plan is to the organism what a program is to the computer.

This modern analogy must not lead us to overlook the fact that what MILLER, GALANTER and PRIBRAM understand as 'plan' is exactly the same as what ALLESCH described twenty-five years ago as *Impulsfigur* ('dynamic pattern' or 'directive configuration'). The *Impulsfigur* is a plan compressed into the formula of a program or a list of instructions.

The probability structure we discussed previously is a sequential structure on a single level. The assumption of a hierarchical plan as the organizing principle of the speech event takes into account the viewpoint that the speech event is simultaneously organized on several levels. It is important to recognize the distinction between a sequential and a sequential-hierarchical structure.

When a sentence is uttered, a motor plan must exist which regulates the sequence of articulating speech movements. This event remains on a single level and can be described in probabilistic terms. Behind or above the motor plan, however, there must be a process which generates or selects the motor plan. In other words, above the level of the motor plan, other plans influence or direct the motor plan. MILLER, GALANTER and PRIBRAM refer to these collectively as the 'grammar plan'. It is made up of the hierarchy of general grammatical rules which come into play in sentence formation in the particular language. CHOMSKY'S influence is evident here.

Theoretically, the motor plan could be an inherited feature or it could be acquired. It is obvious that motor plans for the speech event must be learned. The number of motor plans which it is possible to learn is smaller than is required for the command of a particular language; a motor plan cannot be composed of prefabricated parts; hence it must be possible to construct quickly afresh a motor plan by applying a restricted, manageable and learnable set of *general* rules. This is the function of a higher-level plan, i.e., the grammar plan which has the motor plan as its goal or product[1].

---

[1] In CHOMSKY'S model, the order is reversed: there is, first, a syntax-generating device, the output of which is then semantically interpreted and, finally, transformed into the motor pattern of articulation.

The grammar plan tests the sentence quality of the preliminary motor plan, or, in CHOMSKY'S terms, the grammaticalness of the motor plan, and having tested it, passes it, as it were, as fit for articulation. For the notion of 'feedback' distinctly suggested here, MILLER, GALANTER and PRIBRAM postulate a special functional unit which tests, modifies, re-tests and executes. They refer to it as the TOTE unit (test-operate-test-exit).

A TOTE unit has a certain affinity with the concept of the reflex arc—with the important distinction, however, that the TOTE not only carries impulses, i.e., energy, but also information or control.

In the view of the authors a complex plan, e.g., the grammar plan of a sentence, consists again of a hierarchy of such behavioral TOTE units; and the feedback mechanism which—as already mentioned—is also one of the features of this model serves to recognize and correct deviations from a standard.

This feedback mechanism cannot be of a purely sensory nature. From investigations on delayed speech feedback, it is known that sensory feedback plays an important part in the auditory control of the speaker's own productions. But the plan with whose help the grammaticality of a sentence to be uttered is tested is of a different order: it cannot merely consist of a sensory feedback device, because the corrections must be made *before* the utterance takes place. It is clear that, in the area of the *production* of speech, problems present themselves which are much more difficult to investigate than the problems which occur in the *perception* of speech.

The model we are considering still lacks a mechanism through which the plan is put into effect. The concept of 'recoding' constitutes this mechanism. Introduced by MILLER into the psychology of memory, it is meant to identify a process by which data to be remembered for the purpose of storage are converted into more economical form, into a kind of shorthand, so to speak. Such shortened units may further be gathered into more comprehensive units; i.e., they may be encoded at the next level up. At recall these compressed units are decoded again or reconverted into the original longhand.

This process of decoding downwards from a higher level of generality to the concrete units has been equated by JOHNSON with the downward progression of sentence production (Fig. 64).

The first step in the process of generating sentence Σ, viewed as a unit, is to decode it into subject S and predicate P. The subject S is then further decoded into article T plus modified noun MN, etc. In this version of a tree diagram the nodes indicate encoding units and the lines decoding operations. It can be seen which words are determined or 'dominated' by a certain encoding unit. When a terminal response has taken place, i.e., a word has been pronounced, the broken line indicates the next step in the sequence. JOHNSON, therefore, sees the production of a sentence as a series of decoding steps in which high order encoding units are reduced to units of a lower order. It is as if the speaker decoded his own products in the downward direction. In this process each encoding unit is reduced to one or several subunits. While the first subunit continues to be decoded the others are stored in the immediate memory.

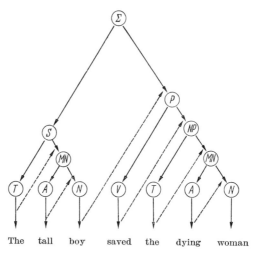

The   tall   boy   saved   the   dying   woman

Fig. 64. Tree diagram of sentence generation showing decoding processes (based on JOHNSON, from ROSENBERG, 1965, p. 54)

Σ is divided into S + P. P is stored in the immediate memory while S is further decoded into T + MN. While T leads to the terminal response, i.e., the utterance of the word 'the', MN remains stored in the immediate memory. As soon as 'the' has been pronounced, the last stored unit, MN, is taken out of the store and decoded into A + N. N is stored until A has led to the pronunciation of the word 'tall'. Once N has also been led to the end response, the only unit stored in the immediate memory, P, is in turn decoded into V + NP and so forth.

The higher the level of the unit, the more operations are needed to decode downwards to the word level. We can now account for two empirical findings which have so far guided our procedures: (a) on pp. 246ff. we presented an error profile for sentences of this type: the greater the number of decoding steps above a certain node, the greater is the probability of an error; and (b) we reported the observation that hesitations between words reflect the structuring of the subunits of a sentence: decoding processes take time; the greater their number, the longer the pauses.

The model that is outlined here, then, is much more differentiated than the one based on an association process.

It should be added that, in JOHNSON'S theory, associations also have a part to play, but here they are associations between decoding operations, not between words. This is the least developed part of the theory.

This model does not take into account the role of meaning (of a word or sentence) in the construction and process of the sentence[1]. Yet, for the time being, it is the best model of the psychological events of what in linguistic terms are phrase-structure rules.

As is known, phrase-structure rules are not the final stage of CHOMSKY'S grammar. Above it, a level of *transformations* is to be assumed in which kernel strings, which are constructed according to phrase-structure rules, are transformed into kernel sentences, negative sentences, passive sentences, questions and so forth.

JOHNSON has demonstrated the psychological reality of the phrase-structure model; MILLER has done the same for the transformation model. In an inquiry by McKEAN, SLOBIN and MILLER reported in MILLER (1962b) the subjects were given a list of simple structure sentences ('kernel sentences') which they were asked to transform in accordance with definite instructions: kernel sentences (K) were to be transformed into negative (N), passive (P), and passive-negative (PN) sentences. If these four sentence types were psychologically independent of each other, the transformation of K into P would require approximately the same time as from K into N or K into PN. According to CHOMKY'S transformational theory, a somewhat different result is to be expected: the six relationships, represented in the accompanying diagram (Fig. 65), can be reduced to a single pair of transformations: one transformation

Fig. 65   Fig. 66

for the affirmative-negative aspect and one for the active-passive aspect. If CHOMSKY'S hypothesis has psychological relevance, it follows that two steps are needed to transform K into PN, i.e., first, a transformation into the negative and, second, a transformation into the passive, or vice versa. Moreover, the transformation from N to P should require two steps: first into affirmative-active (K), then into affirmative-passive (P), or first into negative-passive and from there into affirmative-passive (P). Therefore,

---

[1] Generative grammar at that time overemphasized its independence from semantics and pragmatics.

in place of the schema depicted above, the pattern according to Fig. 66 is to be expected, if the conception of transformation in CHOMSKY's sense is to be employed.

Transformations—so argued MILLER and his collaborators—require time. Can one deduce from the different times required by the subjects for these transformations how many steps are involved?

Table 23. *Mean numbers of sentences matched correctly by the experimental group (with transformations) and by the control group (without transformations).* This *figure is used to estimate the average transformation time per sentence* (based on MILLER, 1962b, p. 759)

Test condition	Mean number of sentences correct		Time for average subject (secs.)		Estimated transformation times (secs.)
	Experimental group	Control group	Experimental group	Control group	
K : N	7.5	8.7	8.0	6.9	1.1
P : PN	5.5	6.4	10.5	9.3	1.2
K : P	8.1	10.1	7.4	5.9	1.5
PN : N	6.7	8.5	8.9	7.1	1.8
K : PN	6.9	10.0	8.7	6.0	2.7
N : P	5.6	8.4	10.7	7.2	3.5

Without going into detail (the experiments included some complicated comparisons with the control group), the inspection of the final column (Table 23) suggests the following conclusion: transformations into the negative require the least time. Transformations into the passive and from the passive require more time. However, times recorded are very much higher for those transformations which, according to the model developed above, involve two transformational steps (K:PN and N:P).

Further information on the processes involved in transformations of this order have resulted from an investigation by another of MILLER'S students, MEHLER (reported by MILLER, 1962b), who presented to his subjects sentences such as the following:

The typist has copied the paper. (kernel sentence)
The student hasn't written the essay. (N)
The photograph has been made by the boy. (P)
Has the train hit the car? (query: Q)
Hasn't the girl worn the jewel? (negative query: N Q)
The passenger hasn't been carried by the airplane. (PN), etc.

The order of the sentences was changed after each presentation. Subjects noted what they had remembered. An error analysis is offered in Fig. 67.

As is to be expected in a learning experiment, omissions decline from series to series. Other errors, such as intrusions of strange words or mixing up of two sentences, remain approximately constant. But the mass of errors is syntactical in character. Although the subject remembers the semantic content of the sentence, he changes its syntactic form so that a passive sentence, for example, appears as an active one.

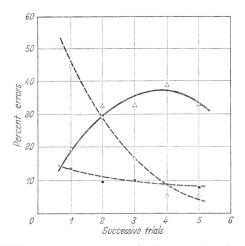

Fig. 67. Course of different error curves. △: syntactic errors, ○: omissions, ◉: other errors
(based on MEHLER, from MILLER, 1962b, p. 760)

MILLER relates this finding to the concept of 'recoding' which JOHN-SON previously had used to explain the processes which take place on the phrase-structure level. MILLER assumes that the experimental subject remembers each sentence as a kernel sentence plus the footnote in which the syntactic structure of the sentence occurred. For example, the sentence, 'Hasn't the girl worn the jewel?' would be stored in the memory as, 'The girl has worn the jewel', plus some kind of implicit code 'negative-interrogative sentence'. The code represents the command to transform. According to the results of the investigation, kernel sentences and annotations are stored separately from each other and apparently are also forgotten independently of each other. This finding should perhaps be expressed in more precise terms as follows: the independence in the act of forgetting suggests that a functional separation can be made between the kernel sentence and the command to transform. MILLER himself (1963) has advanced the following hypothesis: when the experimental subject learns the sentences, he analyzes them into a semantic component (the fundamental carrier of meaning) plus a syntactic correction. This is why it is so much simpler to retain the general content of a message than its exact text.

As is now known, this explanation is too simple; not everything that occurs below the level of transformation can be described as semantic component. JOHNSON, two years after MEHLER, was able to show that, even on the level of the phrase-structure rule, coding processes occur which determine the syntax.

However, the conception that a transformed sentence is encoded as a kernel sentence plus annotation links up in a highly interesting way with certain observations in general psychology, which should at least be noted at this point.

Thirty years ago, WOODWORTH—probably inspired by BARTLETT— expressed the view that memory might work according to the principle: schematization plus correction. When we have seen a particular house we do not remember details, but fit these details into a BARTLETT schema; in other words, we recode them into such a schema, and add to this generalized schema outstanding features as a correction, e.g., that it was a house with green shutters[1].

MILLER-MEHLER'S psychological application of Chomskian thought is certainly impressive; nevertheless, it is not entirely convincing. The assumption that the organizing activity of the human memory follows precisely the lines indicated above cannot be sustained. For example, take the sentence, 'The train was no longer reached by the traveler'; according to MILLER and MEHLER, first, the *semantic* component 'train-traveler-reach' and, second, the *syntactic* instruction 'passive-negative' would be stored. Among the reproductions of this sentence one is likely to find with a high degree of probability the sentence, 'The traveler hasn't reached the train any more', i.e., an active instead of a passive form. But it is most unlikely that under normal circumstances the version, 'The train was reached by the traveler', would appear, thereby converting a negative into a positive sentence. Included in the general coded data stored by the memory is certainly also the overall positive or negative coloring of the sentence. MILLER'S investigations in this area have no doubt suggested the probability of the psychological functioning of transformations, but so far there is no adequate evidence as to which aspects of a sentence are handled and produced on the level of phrase-structure rules, which on the level of transformation, and which in more general semantic terms.

A further objection to the present form (not to the principle as such) of MILLER'S procedures, which was made by CARROLL (1964a), should be added. If a speaker, instead of a simple statement, 'It's getting stuffy

---

[1] It is possible to note here something approaching a dialectical movement between two sets of data which anyone with philosophical training might identify as *genus proximum* and *differentia specifica*.

in here,' chooses the question form, 'Isn't it getting stuffy in here?' this may be regarded as a linguistic transformation, but is it also a psychological one? Likewise the question, 'Would you mind opening the window?' is certainly so current in this form that it need hardly be transformed in one or even two steps from, 'You would mind opening the window' (cf. p. 50).

If we now review the foregoing chapter, what conclusions do we reach? There is clear evidence of the need to conceive speech production in accordance with a model which demands organization and unit formation on several levels. This need arises particularly at those points where the explanatory force of the associative and probabilistic conception of the sequential sentence order breaks down. A generative grammar in CHOMSKY'S sense is at the present time the best available to describe those structures which determine the psychological events involved in generating sentences. The weakness of this approach lies in its relationship to semantics. Many linguists claim that the structure of a sentence is already given in advance as a result of phrase-structure and transformation rules, and therefore the production and interpretation of a sentence can be explained by the fact that these syntactic structures are selectively directed upon a semantically ordered lexicon. However, it is questionable whether, as CHOMSKY (1965) thinks, the features introduced by syntactical categorization rules really always dominate over those features which are determined by the semantic selection rules of the lexicon. When we speak of coding processes, it is hard to imagine that there is a complete separation (and consequently also a separation in time) between the syntactic and semantic aspects. ALLESCH'S conception of 'general feature' (Allgemeingegebenheit), which is less based on the assumptions of information theory, could fruitfully come into use in this connection. Coding processes lead, not only to changes in the degree of compression of linguistic units, but also to changes in the degree of awareness with which the linguistic units are held. Such cognitive aspects of the processes which lead to speech production are no doubt very difficult to grasp empirically (because of their very short duration), but they cannot be overlooked—here no less than in the analysis of meaning.

What the foregoing chapter has shown is that psycholinguistics, which had originated in behaviorism, has turned away from behaviorism. The body of data whose interaction is under investigation no longer consists of directly observable stimuli; nor are the responses directly observable, for they can only be studied by the effects they produce. The cognitive processes whose organization was considered are *real* events even if they do not manifest themselves directly and completely in behavior. What happens in a sentence cannot be explained without reference to cognitive processes and structures.

Chapter 14

Genetic and Child Psychology as a Testing Ground for Psycholinguistics

Trial and error as a principle of language acquisition — MOWRER'S autism-theory — 'Mama' — Language as part of the total dynamics of the child — Language as a link between practical events — The interaction of language and total situation — Language and thought in the work of VIGOTSKY — The role of consciousness — Meaning as awareness of constancy — Classification processes in language acquisition — The word as a 'lure to cognition' — Genesis of predication — The acquisition of linguistic rules — The role of imitation.

The discussion of the concept of meaning led us to an intensive study of the process of association. It was seen that the principle of association can serve in the explanation of narrow semantic relations, but it cannot account for the relations among words within a sentence. Probabilistic models take us a step further, but they, in turn, prove to be too simple. In the previous chapter it was shown how a grammar which bases itself on CHOMSKY'S theory leads to hypothesis which are fruitful for the explanation of linguistic behavior.

In our discussion of the associative, probabilistic and syntactic-structural models we have operated with the concepts and modes of thought of general psychology. Such models can be examined in the first instance for their inherent explanatory power. This is what we have attempted to do in the preceding chapters. But there is another important testing ground of their value for psycholinguistics, i.e., genetic or child psychology, because findings in this area provide a kind of external criterion for the usefulness of these models.

From observations and studies of children at different age levels, a number of facts of psycholinguistic interest are known. To what extent are these facts, e.g., the order of appearance of different stages of linguistic development, compatible with the explicit or implicit postulates of the views discussed hitherto?

It is, of course, not enough merely to test the validity of these genetic models and to make comparisons. What we hope to do is to define our own theoretical position more clearly by placing the theories in a wider context.

We begin once more right at the beginning, i.e., with verbal association. The associationist has fundamentally two possibilities of interpreting language acquisition: either, following PAVLOV, the conditioning process can be said to produce a *stimulus* substitution so that the designated object is replaced by the sign, or, following THORNDIKE, conditioning leads to *response* substitution so that a less economical response is replaced by a verbal one.

Both conceptions have weaknesses which reveal themselves whenever the attempt is made to explain language acquisition as a conditioning process. The commonly applied concept of reinforcement is unable to account for the speed of acquisition or for the stability of meanings thus acquired.

The difficulties arising from the Pavlovian view have already been discussed in detail (cf. pp. 206, 211). We must now take a second look at THORNDIKE's view because its further development has led in HULL's work to the most sophisticated theory of learning and in SKINNER's work to the most radical conception of verbal behavior.

According to THORNDIKE the organism spontaneously produces many different modes of behavior. Among these occurs accidentally a certain mode of behavior which corresponds to the requirements of the stimulus-situation and therefore leads to a state which satisfies the organism. This satisfying state acts as a reinforcement of the immediately preceding mode of behavior, which then is more likely than before to occur again in the same stimulus situation. In THORNDIKE's view, trial and error leads to the selection of the mode of behavior which is followed by reinforcement. The organism must do something; and this act must be followed by reinforcement for an association to be formed between the S (situation) and the R (this mode of behavior), so that, in other words, learning takes place. Similarly, in SKINNER's conception, a mode of behavior is learned if its execution is followed by reinforcement. It is singled out, by a process called 'shaping', from among the mass of unnecessary and undesirable modes of behavior.

Now, even the psychology of learning recognizes a number of phenomena which indicate the possibility of learning without doing: latent learning explored by TOLMAN, latent extinction, learning with insight, and so forth.

17*

Such phenomena are particularly common in language learning. The parents of a child do not wait for the chance appearance, among the random vocalizations, of a word or a word-like sound sequence and then reinforce it by a reward. Language learning is not based on the principle of trial and error. Nor are these vocalizations accidental pre-forms of words produced spontaneously by the child and then remolded by a gradual Skinnerian shaping-process. A child does not produce a vast number of random sound sequences, nor does it live in an environment constantly handing out differential rewards; consequently, the view of language acquisition as a selection process can hardly be justified. The model of a selective learning process in the sense of THORNDIKE or SKINNER is too artificial to serve adequately as a model of language acquisition.

But there are further reasons why this model must be rejected. According to others who represent this view, the child learns those combinations of sounds with which he can control his environment (BROWN and DULANEY, 1958; BROWN, 1958a). But the child also learns elements or aspects of language (such as allophones) which have no sign function and which therefore do not, as these theories claim, have instrumental function. And, at least for the early stages of language acquisition, it is valid to say that the infant could manage without the instrument of language. He will be fed even if he does not speak and only screams and therefore fails to utter any conventional signs.

The model of *language acquisition through selective reinforcement of utterances*, which goes back to THORNDIKE, and is upheld today above all by SKINNER, must therefore be discarded for a variety of reasons. The babbling child is in a prelinguistic sound contact with his environment (a phenomenon still to be discussed below); suddenly he utters his first word. It is obvious that the child must have learned something before he produced the sound himself. In other words, it is, no doubt, a case of so-called latent learning. TOLMAN describes latent learning as a learning process which occurs under the following conditions: the organism does not execute the response to be learned; there is no differential reinforcement (BLODGETT, 1929; TOLMAN, 1959), and the learning process can only be identified at a later stage by the effect it has produced. Although the possibility of such latent learning is indisputable and language acquisition in infancy is one of the most significant proofs for its existence, yet there is little that can be added to what has already been offered in rather negative terms in the above definition.

Another approach may take us further. If there is no gradual shaping of words out of random preformations and if it is unnecessary to assume that the child must already be a speaker in order to learn to speak — what then can be the foundations and basic elements of speech?

The presently most satisfactory answer to this question is offered by MOWRER, who argues that the infant learns to speak by imitation.

This is not exactly a new idea. MOWRER'S theory can be regarded as a reformulation of BALDWIN'S 'circular reaction' (1895), which was also accepted by BEKHTEREV, STERN, KOFFKA and others. What is new is that MOWRER was able to give a theoretical explanation of this process without having recourse to an *ad hoc* construct, such as an instinct or drive of imitation; his explanation is compatible with known facts of child psychology and of the psychology of learning. We shall now consider this theory which MOWRER treated principally in his work *Learning Theory and the Symbolic Processes*.

Like all learning psychologists MOWRER likes setting out from animal experiments; in his case the experimental animal was not the rat but the parrot. How does a parrot come to copy a word that someone has said to him? He must hear this word repeatedly in a pleasurable situation. This pleasurable situation is a reliable primary reinforcement. A specific feature of MOWRER'S theory is that the word heard in this situation assumes secondary-reward or reinforcement value. When the parrot at a later stage produces a similar sound, the hearing of this sound acts automatically as reward.

The great weakness of THORNDIKE'S and SKINNER'S approach is that it presupposes an external reward-giver. SKINNER goes so far as to define language as behavior which is 'reinforced through the mediation of other persons'.

The imitative acquisition of speech by the infant follows the same principle as that of the parrot. The secondary reinforcement, conditioned to the word uttered by the adult, generalizes to the sound sequence emitted and heard by the child, whenever this sound sequence is similar to the word pronounced by the adult. Imitation here is, so to speak, an automatic trial and error process which is only indirectly dependent upon reward by an adult. The infant acquires the habit of producing a word, not only by uttering it himself, but, even before that, when he hears it uttered by others. Here, then, is a case of latent learning, which is confirmed by the child psychologist's observations of speech development, but which the theories of PAVLOV, THORNDIKE and SKINNER were unable to explain. What the organism (the child) is to learn as response (the word) impinges upon the organism in the first instance as stimulation (produced by others). Since this stimulation occurs in a pleasurable situation; i.e., it occurs together with a pleasant primary stimulus, it acquires the characteristics of a secondary reward. This is the Pavlovian aspect of MOWRER'S theory. When the learning organism succeeds in giving himself this stimulation, it is automatically rewarded. The basis of language learning is not so much the organism's own activity as it is the coincidence of timing between a certain acoustic (and possibly articulatory) stimulation and reinforcement.

The way a dog learns to 'shake hands' is not that his master waits for the right position to occur accidentally and then (following THORNDIKE) to reward it; what the dog's master does is to bring the paw into the desired position, thereby producing a particular proprioceptive stimulation of the dog which he then rewards.

The early word-like combinations of sounds are produced by the child because the child has heard these sounds in situations of being fed or soothed, and therefore these are pleasurable sounds.

At this point MOWRER'S theory needs supplementation. The purposeful production by the infant of certain sound combinations (acting as secondary reinforcement) presupposes that such sound combinations are already available to the child. A sound expressing satisfaction can only be uttered in a different neutral (or generally non-satisfying) situation if it is no longer dependent upon the close link with the pleasurable context within which it had previously occurred. There must be awareness of the possible availability of speech sounds as such. And if we ask how this availability of speech sounds is practiced by the infant, the clue to it is found in the phenomenon of *babbling.*

'Babbling'—as our later discussion will show in detail—represents an essential, preparatory and transitional stage of all speech development. To set it going and to keep it up, it must be assumed that there is a driving force, such as is provided by the concept of BÜHLER'S 'function pleasure' *(Funktionslust)*, a concept which does not easily fit into the framework of learning theory. It is, however, worth considering whether the notion of function pleasure ought not to be associated with MOWRER'S secondary reinforcement.

Returning at this point to MOWRER'S arguments, we will see that the infant—in teleological terms—wants to represent his mother by means of the imitations of heard sounds because she provides pleasurable situations. This representation, at this stage of development, does not occur, as it will later, by means of a conventional word ('Mother'), but through the imitation of sounds heard in the mother's presence.

MOWRER calls his theory an 'autism theory of word learning'. The child (re-)produces a word because of the autistic, indirect comfort which the hearing of the sound has provided. This theory brings the acquisition of speech into the vicinity of wishes, in particular, of day-dreams and fantasy. It accounts above all for the earliest verbal utterances, i.e., modes of speech behavior in which imitation and latent learning are clearly evident. At this point, a theory which operates only with externally provided differential reinforcement of accidental sound-response sequences is necessarily inadequate.

A first test of the validity of MOWRER'S theory is suggested by one of its implications: if it is supposed to be an adequate theory, it should be found that a child's earliest words should refer to pleasurable states.

MOWRER recognizes this test for his theory but disposes of it in a somewhat cavalier fashion (1960, pp. 85f.): he argues that the child learns negative words because it soon recognizes the usefulness of speech in general. This means that MOWRER offers an answer which is outside his theoretical framework. In fact, however, the question whether the first utterance of 'Mama' occurs in a situation of comfort or discomfort is entirely relevant to this theory. What empirical investigations are available on this issue ?

BIXLER and YEAGER (1958) have published a paper entitled "It may have begun with 'Mama'". They note, first of all, the fact that in the most varied cultures and epochs 'Mama' has been used by children to refer to the mother or nurse. According to the 'happy mama theory of the origin of words', this sound sequence would be the first word because it is produced by infants in pleasurable situations.

The first objection to it is that in such situations plenty of other sounds and sound combinations are also produced, e.g., /dedede/, /mimim/, /gugu/, etc.

The second objection is that experience shows—the authors of the study cite in support the work of GESELL and LEWIS—that 'Mama' is uttered especially when the child cries and is obviously unhappy. GESELL found that children at the age of approximately seven months, when whimpering, begin to make an m-m-m sound. LEWIS refers back to an old Darwinian observation according to which the undifferentiated total reaction to disturbing stimuli includes a contraction of facial muscles. The resulting compressed sounds /ε/, /w/ and later a frontal nasal/m/. LEWIS describes clear /a, o, u/ and /g, k, r, p/ as comfort-sounds.

A forced nasal 'mama' would accompany states of discomfort. In the view of BIXLER and YEAGER, this sound complex attains its meaning of designating the mother as a person by a process of Skinnerian operant conditioning; the sound sequence fetches the mother.

LEWIS (1963) adopts a consistently Darwinian and physiological point of view: the 'nucleus' of 'mama', the angry/m/, is first produced when the lips during sucking are shut tightly; consequently, vocalizations are nasal. This sound is subsequently produced in anticipation (HULL would call it an anticipatory goal response) as the infant approaches the breast, sees the bottle or even as soon as the bib is fastened. This sound sequence, then, acquires its referential function not through a selective SKINNER-type reinforcement, but rather as a case of Pavlovian stimulus-contiguity.

JAKOBSON (1960), who holds that the 'atoms' of the phonemes, the distinctive sound features, are acquired in a definite order, represents the same view as LEWIS. The nasal tight-lipped mumbling, anticipating feeding, develops into a kind of manifestation of wanting to be fed and generalizes to every unfulfilled wish. On the other hand, a 'pointing' function is first acquired by the designation of the father (pa...). The preoedipal mother-child unit—just because there is a close identification— does not allow an objectifying referential designation to develop. The designation of father, then, "heralds just the transition from affective expression to designative language" (JAKOBSON, 1942, p. 58).

If we now return to the question at issue, it can be said: according to empirical findings, the first verbal utterances of the infant are not always, nor predominantly, bound up with pleasurable situations. This is a first argument against MOWRER'S autism theory.

A counter-argument could, of course, be formulated as follows: the infant utters the words which he has heard in pleasant situations whenever he finds himself in an unpleasant situation and wants to improve the latter. But this counter-argument does not lead very far. If a sound (originally heard in a pleasurable situation), is uttered in an unpleasant situation, and does not quickly lead to a state of comfort, and therefore to a primary reinforcement, this sound must rapidly lose its value as a secondary reinforcement. The phenomenon of secondary reinforcement is much too unstable to explain the use in unpleasant situations of words acquired in this way. In general terms, it may be said that this instability which conditioning processes entail is probably the greatest weakness of all conditioning theories of language acquisition, including MOWRER'S.

An investigation by FOSS (1964) also argues against the role of autistic satisfaction through imitation. FOSS noted that parrots imitate sounds even if the imitation is not followed by reinforcement. Against the leading role of imitation in general, we refer once more to the pathological case, described by LENNEBERG (1962), of a child who could not produce language himself but was able to understand it.

A last objection is directed less against the mechanism postulated by MOWRER'S theory than against the range of application of such a theory. The autism theory is exclusively concerned with the emotional component of speech acquisition. It ceases where the instrumental character of speech begins, i.e., where the child no longer produces speech for his own autistic gratification, but where he employs it for the mastery of problems of communication. Too much communication is involved in speech for a theory such as MOWRER'S to represent any more than a partial answer.

By drawing attention to the weaknesses and insufficiencies of MOWRER'S theory, we must at this point abandon the attempt to establish a theory of language acquisition with the help of the psychology of learning and its sophisticated apparatus. The alternatives to a theory operating with 'reinforcement', 'association', 'mediation', or 'conditioning' offer perhaps something more appealing which displays fewer deficiencies or incompatibilities. But these advantages are bought at the price of precision of thought and evidence; and this is indeed one of the most troublesome features of present-day psycholinguistics.

As a transition to a new level of theorizing, we cite a statement by MILLER: "It is difficult to imagine how children could acquire language so rapidly from parents who understand it so poorly unless they were already tuned by evolution to select just those aspects that are universally significant. There is, in short, a large biological component that shapes our human languages" (1965, p. 17).

Here maturation is contrasted with the learning aspect which had hitherto alone been stressed. It is true that CARMICHAEL (1964), in a comprehensive survey, had already shown that the anatomical and physiological basis of the receptor and motor mechanisms of speech are ready to function at birth, but that the actual functioning of these mechanisms was still dependent upon further cerebral maturation after birth. Not until then, says CARMICHAEL, does the infant reach the state of 'speech readiness' which is the precondition for the acquisition of meaningful linguistic patterns.

This emphasis on the biological and developmental aspect comes out particularly clearly in MILLER'S account of causative factors in language acquisition:

"He learns the language because he is shaped by nature to pay attention to it, to notice and remember and use significant aspects of it" (1965, p. 20). The child is capable of abstracting, for example, grammatical structures from the incoming flow of speech and to learn these because he pays attention only to a restricted number of possibilities.

The process of selecting linguistically significant details from the flood of other events which in the past was supposed to find an explanation in differential reinforcement, is now looked upon as a biologically given fact which cannot be reduced any further.

In this connection we might remind ourselves of a pronouncement by LENNEBERG, cited at the beginning of this book (p. 2), which stated that the capacity to acquire and use a human language does not depend on the fact that the organism is intelligent or has a large brain, but that it is a human organism (1964 b).

From the atomistic and therefore associationist theories of language acquisition, we move into a more biological and more holistic climate of opinion.

A modern work on child language begins with the sentence: "A child is born a speaker and born into a world of speakers" (LEWIS, 1963). (a) The infant utters sounds from the first days of his life; (b) he responds to the human voice; (c) the mother responds to the child's voice; and, (d) she speaks to him. These are the four fundaments on which later speech development is based. If one of them is absent, the whole structure of later linguistic growth is imperilled. From the very beginning, even before speech proper, constant use of speech characterizes the child's environment. Long before the sound utterances of the child have any definite meaning, they serve — though imperfectly — the same goals as the skilled language use of the adult.

Therefore, it is false to think in terms of the child facing a world to be depicted and to be named by him; instead, one must think much more of a dynamic whole comprising the two poles: child and world.

A powerful interpretation of the infant's situation is to be found in BLOCH'S *Tübinger Introduction to Philosophy*:

"A self alive does not yet mean awareness of self — and least of all awareness of its activities. All the creature feels is hunger and want ... All is centered around this non-aware self; yet it is not self-sufficient; ... its wants make it dependent on the outside world; its own hunger takes it beyond itself. 'I want' is the first glimmer of awareness" (pp. 12 f.). The infant is inevitably a part of this dynamic unity. "Even to sense its own existence the creature must reach for something beyond" (p. 11).

The experience of this dynamic reality — and with it the experience of being part of it — can, according to CHURCH, be characterized by three components: realism, phenomenalism, dynamism. This is to be understood as follows. All events are equally real; as yet there is no distinction between doing and wishing, or between fear and pain. All events are accepted as they appear. The closer in time two events appear, the closer appears their 'causal' relationship. The infant sees his world as endowed with energies which make him — through the phenomena of animism, anthropomorphism and magicalism — subject and object of active processes.

Perception and action, looked at from 'inside', are hardly different. Both involve, as CHURCH says, total mobilization of the organism.

Under the concept of 'mobilization' CHURCH subsumes what, on the stimulus side, is referred to as 'attention' and, on the response side, as 'set'; it is therefore a form of directed concentration upon an activity.

Out of the dynamics of the total situation which comprises speaker and listener, action and vocalization the child's situation attains its organization. Originally, action and sound are not distinguished in their meaningfulness. The question, therefore, is not how a primarily meaningless combination of sounds becomes meaningful (this has been the problem of all associationist theories of meaning); the question now is how, out of the flow of stimuli and modes of behavior, some which are collectively referred to as speech are singled out.

It appears, therefore, that the infant does not first learn to understand and use words; what happens is that in the total stream of behavior the verbal aspect becomes more and more clearly differentiated. Well before speech sounds have established unambiguous and socially binding relationships to other events, and therefore have acquired semantic meaning, they already have functional value in the totality of behavior.

From this point of view, we should once more consider a model previously discussed (p. 210), BLOOMFIELD's diagram of the speech event. The usual behavior sequence leads from stimulus (S) to response (R): S→R. Jill sees an apple (S), grasps and eats it (R). If this simple sequence meets an obstacle, e.g., the tree is too high for Jill to reach the apple, a change in the behavior sequence occurs. Jill sees the apple (S), says something (r) that causes Jack (s) to pick the apple and to give it to Jill (R): S→r ... s→R. For Jill the direct action (R) is replaced by a verbal one (r); for Jack a direct stimulus (S) is replaced by a verbal one (s); in Jill's case it is a Thorndike response substitution; in Jack's it is a Pavlov stimulus substitution. The simple S→R sequence, the 'speechless reaction', occurs within one person; it becomes a verbal reaction which links two persons with each other—a reaction which as, BLOOMFIELD said, is "mediated by speech".

BLOOMFIELD's mediation is an interpersonal event; it becomes—as we shall see later—through a process of internalization, an intrapersonal mediation in VIGOTSKY's sense as, for example, in OSGOOD's theory.

In BLOOMFIELD's conception the speech act is the mediating link between two practical events. But from the point of view of our previous discussion, it is important to remember that the speech act does not link two separate practical events; on the contrary, in the 'preverbal' stage these practical events were contiguous members of the dynamic structure of a behavioral unity.

The speech act does not link what previously had been apart. (This is the reason why the concept of association cannot be the main key to the speech event.) The speech act makes it possible to part what previously had been combined. Speech makes it possible to pull practical events apart.

The relationship between practical events and speech events is repeated on a higher level in WEIZSÄCKER's conception of the relationship between language and formula. "A formula makes sense only through the connection which has been established by words." "There is always a known area of shared knowledge within which comprehension is quite adequate enough to make it possible to use this common ground for an advance upon new fields" (1960, pp. 144 and 152).

The practical events can be seen to be distributed upon conduct in two directions: the speaker's and the listener's. The more these two forms of conduct are pulled apart, the more reliance must be placed on the speech act.

Speech bridges practical events and is crystallized out of the behavioral totality. This point of view can be related to the tendency to fall back on non-verbal behavior whenever verbal communication is inadequate. The scientist, for example, uses 'operational' definitions; he reverts to operations or actions.

And, vice versa, the more clearly defined the business of practical events is, the less care need be taken of the verbal link. "Exactitude of the object ... permits inexactitude of language" (WEIZSÄCKER, 1959, p. 139).

To summarize we can say: language is the continuation of action with other means.

This proposition is to be further clarified by the following discussion. To begin with, BLOOMFIELD's definition of meaning should be recalled. Meaning of a word is the situation in which a speaker utters it plus the response it calls forth in the hearer. We recognize now that this definition is to be interpreted as far less 'primitive' and 'associationist' than BLOOMFIELD presumably had intended it to be understood. The word whose meaning is in question is, at first, no independent element to be regarded as distinct from the stimulus-response sequence of the situation and as labelling the sequence. The child, to begin with, does not understand what a word as such means, but he does understand what a person talking to him means (CHURCH, 1961, p. 61).

Three very different authorities can be cited to corroborate this viewpoint. Firstly, RÉVÉSZ describes the imperative as the basic form of language, i.e., a form of utterance which arises in quite a primitive way in a situation of social action.

Secondly, HEIDEGGER argues: "Calling is fundamentally not naming; it is the reverse; naming is a kind of calling in its original sense of 'calling hither' or 'summoning'" (1954, p. 151).

And, thirdly, WITTGENSTEIN regards the command call which the individual directs to his situational partner as the nucleus around which an emerging language-game becomes crystallized.

This point of view, i.e., the origin of the sign in the dynamics of the total situation, makes it comprehensible why the philosophy of language had so little relevance to the psychology of language until PEIRCE and MORRIS had introduced a pragmatic element. Looked at in this light, language does not appear as the sum of basically separate parts; and further, the concept of association loses its explanatory power. To sum it up in HUMBOLDT's terms: "Speech is not put together out of words that precede it; on the contrary, words are singled out from the totality of speech" (HUMBOLDT, 1907 edition, p. 72).

How very much the comprehension of utterances of early childhood is dependent upon the support of the total situation is indicated by SHERMAN's experiments. A number of subjects, mothers and nurses, were asked to state what caused an infant, lying behind a screen, to cry. The actual causes of the cries were varied: hunger or pain, etc. The observers were unable to distinguish between the cries and to identify their 'meaning'.

And looking at the problem from the other side, we cite a case to demonstrate how much the situation which surrounds and accompanies the speech event in the narrower sense is the carrier of meaning: MEUMANN asked his little son in German (his mother-tongue), "Wo ist das Fenster?" and the child pointed in the right direction. He then asked him in French, "Où est la fenêtre?" Again the child pointed to the window; equally so in response to the English question, "Where is the window?" MEUMANN went on and asked him in German, "Where is the door?" and the child again pointed to the window! The child did not react to the meaning of individual words but to the dynamic configuration of the total situation.

The close interaction between word and total situation becomes clearer through LURIA's experiments (1959) on the directive function of speech. A child at the age of approximately $1;3^1$ is shown a toy fish.

The experimenter said, "Give me the fish"; the infant followed the instruction. Next, a toy cat was placed between the infant and the fish. The experimenter said, "Give me the fish." The infant reached towards the fish but, as his hand passed near the cat, seized the cat and handed it to the experimenter. In a dynamically unambiguous situation the word can already perform its directive role. But as soon as there is a possibility of conflict in the dynamics of the situation, the child cannot yet resist the orientational pull of the situation. The forces determining the dynamics of the situation do not lie in the words on the one side and the stimulus configuration on the other, but partly also in the 'mobilization' of the infant as determined by the immediately preceding modes of behavior. In another series of experiments, LURIA placed before the child a tumbler and a cup. A coin was hidden under the cup; the child lifted the cup and picked up the coin. Having repeated this sequence four times, the experimenter placed the coin under the tumbler within sight of the child and asked again, "Find the coin". If the child is immediately allowed to pick up the coin, most subjects (aged $1;4$ to $1;6$) go straight for the tumbler. However, if a pause of 10 seconds is introduced between instruction and action, the motor habit, i.e., the old mobilization, is dominant: the child reaches for the cup.

In a third experiment, after the coin had regularly been placed under the tumbler, it was placed under the cup without the child seeing this. The experimenter said: "The coin is under the cup". The child, following the dynamics of the situation, reached for the tumbler. To put it in

---

[1] *Translator's note.* In this notation the figure before the semi-colon indicates years and the figure after months, i.e., $1;3$ reads "one year three months".

different terms: the word achieves an independent status only gradually and relatively late, and its dominance over the dynamics of the situation, comprising both child and situation, is an end phase.

To what extent reliance upon the total situation can delay the developmental differentiation of language can be illustrated by the speech development of twins. Twins, as siblings of the same age who may even be monozygotic, find themselves in similar situations. We recall what was said earlier (pp. 2ff.) about the interaction between spontaneity and life space. If twins grow up together, they share common life experiences to such an extent, and patterns of behavior fit together so well, that additional verbal guidance is hardly necessary. The mutual understanding can still be carried entirely by the parallel structure of practical events. Correspondingly, language development of twins in comparison with only children is delayed (DAVIS, 1937; FORCHHAMMER, 1939; and ZAZZO, 1960). This delay can be even more marked in one of the twins if the other assumes the role of 'ambassador', making contact with the environment (thereby normalizing his own speech development) and transmitting to the other twin the verbal signals of the external world in form of behavioral clues. Frequently the speech development in the last named partner, in comparison with speech development of his contemporaries, is seriously retarded.

LURIA and YUDOVICH (1959) have thrown further light on the close interaction between speech and total situation in a detailed study in a pair of neglected twins. The vocalization of these children had meaning only in concrete-active situations. Verbalization was closely interwoven with the rest of the activities; sometimes the word functioned as grammatical object whereas the subject remained on the level of concrete activity. (This distribution between verbalization and activity has already been mentioned previously.) LURIA, who called this use of language 'synpraxic', meant more or less the same as what BÜHLER had previously called the 'empractic' use of language.

The twins' verbal comprehension was confined equally to concrete situations. Since language here was not yet distinct from actions, the child was unable to arrive at generalizations and, consequently, at abstractions. Any ordering of concrete individual objects and events into classes, hence a "new principle of nervous activity" (1959, p. 91), was not yet possible. Corresponding to the primitive use of language, therefore, the organization of activity had still remained equally primitive at the level of direct action.

This raises the question of the influence of language on cognitive development, which VIGOTSKY has described in detail (English edition, 1962). VIGOTSKY treats the formation of the first meaningful words as analogous to the intellectual operations which KÖHLER'S chimpanzees had to perform. "Words enter into the structure of things and acquire a certain functional meaning, in much the same way as the stick, (has meaning) to the chimpanzee" (p. 123). To be true, the analogy does not take us very far; thinking in relation to the use of tools can be related to the use of speech only in man, but not in any animal. According to VIGOTSKY, anthropoids have some speech components of a phonetic, emotional and social kind, but these components never form a language because the component of a specifically human intelligence is absent. If we wish to lay as much emphasis on the evolution of thought as VIGOTSKY has done, it is possible to detect, in the phylogeny of thought and speech, a prelinguistic phase of the development of thought and a preintellectual phase of the development of speech.

Crying, babbling and perhaps even the early autistically acquired words, just as much as the social contact with persons in the environment, are the preintellectual roots of speech.

⌊Up to a certain point in time, thought and speech develop separately; at this point they meet and thought becomes verbal and speech rational (VIGOTSKY, English edition, 1962, p. 44). We shall return later to the localization of this stage.

We should note in parenthesis: if the lines of thinking and speaking run independently of each other for long stretches this has important negative implications for the WHORF thesis of linguistic relativity to be discussed in the next chapter.

For the following ideas VIGOTSKY makes use of PIAGET's notion of egocentric speech. According to PIAGET, the child up to about the age of seven does not use speech with social intent; he uses it egocentrically because his thinking is still egocentric.

At this point we might recall MOWRER's autism theory, which also claims that the child's speech is 'egocentric'.

This theory undoubtedly lays too much stress on the intellectual component and too little on the social component of the total behavior. But more important for VIGOTSKY than the theory itself is one obvious observation, i.e., that the child frequently talks to himself. Why does he do it and on what occasions? VIGOTSKY's answer is: he always starts talking to himself when his activities meet obstacles. The combinations of thought needed to help him across a difficulty and the reorganizations of earlier experiences are made in the medium in which these experiences (in abstract and generalized form) are stored: in the medium of language.

BLOCH (1963, p. 14) says: "Necessity is the father of thought." We may add: Necessity is the father of speech. The "naked self", which reaches for something beyond itself in order to become aware of its own existence, seizes what it can most easily manipulate: the fabric of sounds, language.

But in VIGOTSKY'S theory such 'speech for oneself' originates through differentiation of the originally social function of 'speech for others'. The so-called egocentric speech is "a phenomenon of the transition from inter-psychic to intrapsychic functioning, i.e., from the social, collective activity of the child to his more individualized activity — a pattern of development common to all the higher psychological functions. Speech for oneself originates through differentiation from speech for others" (1962, p. 133). At the early stage of its development to inner speech, egocentric speech is still very much like the speech used for social, inter-individual com-munication. Gradually a tendency emerges towards abbreviating, and towards phonetic and syntactic 'economy'. Nevertheless, according to VIGOTSKY, the origin of inner language functioning as the vehicle of thought always remains clear; it derives from socialized external speech and, therefore, in the last resort, from the activities of man. Thus the sentence, "In the beginning was the Deed"[1], even applies to speech development if one lays stress on the word 'beginning'[2].

The connection between language and thought, which VIGOTSKY so convincingly describes, is not only an important topic in the language development of the child; it is also important at the 'opposite' end, the pathological deficit and loss of speech. Neurologists assumed for a long time that definite anatomical centers within the central nervous system corresponded to the organization of speech so that the loss of such a center would entail the disturbance of a particular psychological element of speech. This view has been abandoned almost everywhere. Instead, the attempt is made to explain in phonetic and psychological terms the significance of the functional disturbances which appear in the different forms of aphasia.

From this point of view it can easily be understood that the connection between thought and speech and the various possibilities of its disturb-ance play a large part in the discussion of aphasic pathologies. Thus, GOLDSTEIN, for example, has attempted to explain a certain group of these diseases as a disturbance of the capacity to categorize, i.e., as a disturbance of cognitive ability. The change in verbal behavior is the manifestation of a loss of VIGOTSKY'S 'inner speech'.

However, the way in which both VIGOTSKY and GOLDSTEIN operate with the concept of 'inner speech' and the connection between thought and language reveals a difficulty which is inherent in such views. The diagnostician, in these cases, makes it necessarily his business to find out whether the capacity to categorize is impaired or whether 'only' that act

---

[1] *Translator's note.* i.e., Faust's reply to the Biblical "In the beginning was the Word" (GOETHE, *Faust*, English translation, Part I, l. 889).

[2] More than a hundred years ago, SETCHENOV had already described thinking as a "reflex with an inhibited end."

is affected which translates categorizing activities into speech. But in practice there is no possibility, as TEUBER (1964) emphatically pointed out, to grasp thought processes and their results without reference to linguistic processes.

To put it in more general terms, the problems of the relationship between thought and language are immeasurably confused (or may even have been created) by the circularity of the definition of language and thought as well as by the methods used to study these relationships.

After this necessarily sketchy digression into the psychopathology of linguistic behavior, we now return to the main line of our argument.

In the beginning was the Deed. Necessity is the father of thought. Necessity is the father of speech. But soon speech detaches itself from the motor of need, for "the hunger of humans, unlike that of animals, is not easily satisfied. What he eats gives him a taste for more" (BLOCH, p. 15). It is not necessity alone that stimulates speech; at an early stage questioning and wonder appear on the scene as well. Next to the cry, 'I want to eat', another call is heard, first feebly, then stronger and stronger and more and more frequently: 'I want to know'.

We thus come to an aspect which most theories viewing the differentiation of speech from the totality of behavior have tended to neglect: in speech, consciousness plays a part which must not be underrated. When we discussed the concept of meaning (pp. 211 ff.), we drew attention to the necessity of taking this fact into account: meaning is knowledge of a relationship. The urge to know is directed towards language; the possession of knowledge requires language; the achievement of knowledge serves as reinforcement in learning language and meaning.

The next question is at what point of speech development does the role of consciousness become evident? In our view this point can be located with the help of LEWIS' theory of the development of imitation.

LEWIS (1951) distinguishes three stages of imitation. In the first, which comprises the period up to approximately the fourth month of life, the infant responds with vocalization to human sound utterances. Then follows a pause in vocalization or at least a marked reduction. A third stage around 8 or 9 months is characterized by increased vigor, frequency and accuracy (1963, pp. 23-24).

According to LEWIS (1963) this revival of vocalization coincides with the observation that, at that time, the child is beginning to understand what is said to him.

PREYER (1900) held that imitation was not possible before understanding; the STERNS (1907) held the opposite view.

LEWIS offers an explanation of the second stage, i.e., of the period of marked decline of vocalization; he says that the child becomes more attentive to the circumstances in which the sound event occurs. The sounds—as it might be formulated—have become sufficiently detached from the total situation that the infant can perceive them as independent entities. This enables him to relate sounds to practical events—a fundamental feature of all language. Since the infant's attention span at this stage is, however, still very limited, he is unable, while watching, to vocalize imitatively at the same time.

Following LEWIS, we assume that in this second stage of imitation, a silent latency phase between the fourth and eighth month of life, a new consciousness factor becomes effective: the infant, so to speak, 'gets the point' of language.

STERN (1st ed., 1914; 6th ed., 1930) expressed a similar view. Between the ages of 1;6 and 2;0 the child makes the most important discovery of his life, i.e., that everything has a name. This is viewed in *too* intellectualistic a fashion by STERN and, therefore, chronologically placed too late.

During LEWIS' vocalization pause, a new psychic function emerges in a preparatory way, a function which decisively intervenes in the development of speech and of the human being generally: we call it the symbol function. Man has a biologically given tendency—hence a tendency not derived from experience—to make and use symbols. The principle of symbolism is, one might say, the key to the specifically human world[1].

And yet, traces of this evolutionary trend can be found among lower organisms[2]. The mouse which has learned to avoid an electrically charged grid screams 'hysterically' when it accidently touches the grid, even though it is not electrically charged. The rat which has reached a crossroad in running a maze at this point 'thinks' about which way to go and makes, while sitting, tentative movements in the different possible directions; it is as if the animal 'mentally' tried the various possibilities. TOLMAN refers to this activity as 'vicarious trial-and-error' (VTE). By executing a quasi-symbolic behavior the rat gathers, so to speak, information on what it would be like to carry this or that possibility into effect.

Here a point of view gradually emerges which should not be overlooked in the discussion of the symbolic function and the principle of symbolism; symbolizing is a means for achieving control of tension. With this consideration in mind we might ultimately be led to KENNETH BURKE'S view of poetry as 'equipment for living'.

The early vocalizations of the infant are always part of the total behavior of the infant. Their motivation is 'orectic', as LEWIS calls the

---

[1] See on this point KAINZ, 1943, II, pp. 27ff.

[2] In chapter 1 it was seen how valuable it can be for our orientation to indicate such hypothetical lines of evolution.

mixture of affect and conative strivings which characterize the early period; striving and emotion are, so to speak, the devices by means of which the infant is inducted into the dynamics of the total situation. The dawning symbolic awareness, which makes speech out of these orectically motivated vocalizations, is a result of attention which briefly arrests the fleeting moment of the flow of events. Thus, certain events become detached from their context and are thrown into relief. This process initiates a trend whose characteristic development LANGER noted (1963, pp. 116-117); i.e., genuine symbols have a dissociated character and are produced without practical motive.

If we regard the early directed vocalizations as autistic wish-fulfillment, and if we assume that speech develops through a process of differentiation from the flow of behavior comprising two individuals, consciousness has the task of imposing 'constancies' upon the flow of sounds and events. Man's symbolizing capacity is identical with his ability to discover constancies in the flow of events. The beginning of this most human of all capacities lies in the exclamation which WILLIAM JAMES expressed so aptly in the telling phrase: "Hallo—thingumbob again."

We must make it clear that there is more to this phenomenon than the crystallization of permanencies; even an animal is capable of guiding behavior by making use of generalization from many similar situations. JAMES' exclamation indicates, however, not only the process of detachment of common features in similar situations but, at the same time, it indicates the *awareness* of communality: the common features have become part of our knowledge, or the 'beam' of cognition has picked them out.

The combination of sounds produced by the adult and heard by the infant is, to begin with, part of the total situation. The various situational aspects may change, the speakers may change, the orectic characteristics may change also—yet there is something that is not lost. Included among these permanencies and recurring features is a complex of sounds. The awareness of a relationship—transcending the here-and-now of every moment—between constancies in the sound combinations and constancies in the situation, in other words, the act of taking note of this relationship—however dim and ill-defined it may be—is at the root of the experience of verbal meaning.

There is a case on record in the psychological literature where this experience has been described with unusual insight. In this case it did not occur in an early phase of childhood, when it is no longer accessible to the adult's memory, but at a later stage. HELEN KELLER, who grew up blind and deaf, described it in her memoirs.

HELEN KELLER became deaf and blind when she was about one-and-a-half years old. She grew up without speech, until, at the age of nearly seven, she had a teacher, ANNE SULLIVAN. Miss SULLIVAN soon began to teach her the finger alphabet. The child liked the game without knowing of course that these were letters—she did not know anything of words or language. Eventually she was able to imitate letter sequences without grasping that they had a constant relationship to an object. Her teacher wrote: "... 'mug' and 'milk' had given Helen more trouble than all the rest. She confused the nouns with the verb 'drink' ... (She) went through the pantomime of drinking whenever she spelled 'mug' or 'milk' ... We went out to the pump-house, and I made Helen hold her mug under the spout while I pumped. As the cold water gushed forth, filling the mug, I spelled 'w-a-t-e-r' in Helen's free hand. The word coming so close upon the sensation of cold water rushing over her hand seemed to startle her. She dropped the mug and stood as one transfixed. A new light came into her face. She spelled 'water' several times. Then she dropped on the ground and asked for its name and pointed to the pump and the trellis, and suddenly turning round she asked for my name. I spelled 'Teacher'" (KELLER, *The Story of my Life*, 1905, p. 316). And HELEN KELLER herself wrote: "I knew then that 'w-a-t-e-r' meant the wonderful cool something that was flowing over my hand. That living word awakened my soul, and gave it light, hope, joy, set it free! There were barriers still, it is true, but barriers that could in time be swept away."

"I left the well-house eager to learn. Everything had a name, and each name gave birth to a new thought. As we returned to the house every object which I touched seemed to quiver with life. That was because I saw everything with the strange, new sight that had come to me ... I learned a great many new words that day ... words that were to make the world blossom for me ..." (*op. cit.* pp. 23-24).

We therefore assume that meaning is the perception of constancy. Viewed from this aspect, meaning has close similarity to what cognitive psychology calls 'concept'. CARROLL (1964 b), above all, has drawn attention to this close relationship: "... concepts are properties of organismic experience—more particularly, they are the abstracted and often cognitively structured classes of 'mental' experience learned by organisms in the course of their life histories ... One necessary condition for the formation of a concept is that the individual must have a series of experiences that are in one or more respects similar; the constellation of 'respects' (references) in which they are similar constitutes the 'concept' that underlies them" (pp. 180f.).

Accordingly, a concept is formed whenever a constant feature is picked out from the flow of events; and thus, we might add, the precondition for the formation of meaning is given.

The question, thus raised, of the relationship between meaning and concept can be looked upon in a variety of ways. In CARROLL's view, meaning is the interpersonally binding aspect of a concept, expressed in a word. TELEGDI sees the genesis of meaning differently: "With meanings an individual is in possession of generalizations which are akin to concepts; meanings are early forms of concepts. Generalizations in form of meanings are tied to the overt or covert use of speech. Meanings develop into concepts whenever we learn to consider them independently outside any immediate relationship to reality." "... in the meaning, a socially acquired universal is present, which, to begin with, is an activity, i.e. the application of a word as an implicit rule of that activity" (1961, I, p. 210). MEIER, somewhat less precisely, has stressed the need to distinguish between the linguistic term 'meaning' and the 'gnoseological' term 'concept'. It is true that both terms are linked through the use of language, but the genesis of a concept is independent of language (1964, II, pp. 244 f.).

In CARROLL's conception, the "experiencing of similarities" has still a rather passive character. We should like to view this process somewhat more actively. The similarities are not only and not always contained in the events from which the individual abstracts them, but they may equally, at least sometimes, originate in the individual and may be imposed by him upon the events. The notion of 'abstracting' does not mean a passive subjection to impressions; it is a psychologically active process. There is a natural human trend to arrest the flow of events and to capture the ephemeral character of concrete events in images which man himself created. CASSIRER comments upon this as follows: "Another indication that the creation of the various systems of sensuous symbols is indeed a pure activity of the mind (and not merely a passive reflection—*the author*) is that from the outset all these symbols lay claim to objective value. They go beyond the mere phenomena of the individual consciousness, claiming to confront them with something that is universally valid." This claim in itself "belongs to the essence and character of the particular cultural forms themselves ... It is characteristic ... that they do not clearly distinguish between the content of the 'thing' and the content of the 'sign' ... the mere word or image contains a magic force through which the essence of the thing gives itself to us ... For consciousness the sign is, as it were, the first stage and the first demonstration of objectivity, because through it the constant flux of the contents of consciousness is for the first time halted, because in it something enduring is determined and emphasized" (CASSIRER, *The Philosophy of Symbolic Forms*, I, 1953 ed., pp. 88-89).

The part the language-user plays in establishing order in the world will occupy us in greater detail later in the discussion of the WHORF hypothesis. But even before that a similar trend will be met in certain views expressed by BROWN.

Man, as JESPERSEN has put it (1964, p. 388), is a "classifying animal";
it may be said that the entire speech process is nothing but the distribution of various phenomena upon different classes, and this distribution is
made according to perceived similarities and dissimilarities.

The establishment of constancy occurs at two different points, i.e., at
those points (once these distinctions are clearly made) where later we
speak of 'sign' and 'referent'.

Thus the child must learn to recognize the repetition of vocalizations
as identical. This means he must learn to ignore variations in intensity
of the sounds which are caused, for example, by varying distances of the
speaker, or by varying frequency spectra of different speakers. He must
recognize that 'dog' uttered in a low and deep voice is equivalent to 'dog'
uttered in a loud and high voice. He must learn—even on the acoustic
side—what are 'criterial attributes' in BROWN'S sense, i.e., attributes on
which depends the decision whether a sound belongs to this or that
category. He must learn to ignore 'noisy attributes' which are irrelevant
in subsuming a sound to a certain category (the intensity of a heard word
is a 'noisy' attribute in establishing meaning). The child must further
learn to employ the criterial attributes, not only for word recognition, but
also for word production (BROWN, 1956 and later).

The acquisition of language and speech involves categorizations and
the establishment of constancies, not only in this direction (acoustic or
vocal categories and constancies), but also in the other direction, which,
following BROWN, we shall describe as the 'reference category'.

We do not only summarize a large number of different-looking
quadrupeds as 'dogs' but a variety of percepts, changing in time, as 'the
landlord's dog, Prince'. This aspect is of greatest importance because it
demonstrates a link with other branches of psychology and therefore
establishes the universality of the principle: even the individual object
or thing in this sense is a *category*. We comprise a series of very different
retinal images under the class 'this table'. The designation 'this table' is
not the verbal label of one particular retinal image but the correlate of
a constellation of slightly varied, but similar, retinal images. In accordance with a profoundly human tendency, we project upon this constellation a unitary and unifying designation.

As the introductory chapters of this book have stressed again and
again, this setting up of constancies is a fundamental psychological
feature, a tendency which manifests itself in the psychology of perception
as constancy of objects or as size constancy and reaches right into social
psychology where it accounts for such phenomena as prejudice and
stereotyping.

As the constancy of the sign as well as of the referent establishes itself,
the situational context gradually loses its function as the meaning car-

rier in the act of speech. It loses this function only gradually and never completely; but the growing constancy of the sound pattern on the one hand and of the reference category on the other reduces the importance of the dynamic pattern of the context as a determiner of meaning. The activity of the language user in establishing constancies enables him to abandon his role as link in the meaning process. One might say a de-pragmatization occurs; a 'pure' science of semantics, i.e., a scientific study of the relationship between sign and referent, disregarding the sign user, comes close to realization—and with it also the possibility of writing dictionaries.

If the development of constancies of reference categories is examined more closely, two processes—according to BERKO and BROWN—may be distinguished: (a) identification and (b) definition.

(a) The process of *identification* has been examined in detail, among others, by PIAGET who—looking at it more from a cognitive than from a psycholinguistic point of view—was concerned with the following questions: from which stage of development onwards can the child identify new cases of 'size', 'quantity', or 'velocity'? By way of illustration we may mention the well-known example which PIAGET describes under the heading of 'conservation of quantity (or volume)'. In an adult's ordinary language, the use of a statement about the quantity of a liquid is determined by the relationship between the size of the vessel and the level of the liquid in the vessel. If the liquid is poured from a tall vessel with a narrow diameter into a wide receptacle, the adult expects the level of the liquid to fall. The child centers his attention on one or the other of the two variables; his statement about quantity is determined only by either the size of the vessel *or* the level of the liquid, but not the relationship between the two. The adult observes 'contingent' rules; the child acts according to 'uncontingent' rules. BERKO and BROWN explain this phenomenon by referring to the particular kind of verbal experience which children of this age have had hitherto[1].

A child is generally taught the vocabulary of quantity with simplified examples in which *one* variable (either size of vessel *or* level of liquid) is held constant and which, therefore, does not appear relevant to the child. Now, if the child—as for example in a Piagetian experiment—faces a more complex situation, he acts according to his rule, which, measured by the adult's standard vocabulary, is too simple. The child has hitherto experienced a too limited scatter of positive cases for the category

---

[1] PIAGET, on the other hand, accounts for this phenomenon almost entirely in endogenous terms as being determined by the given stage of development. AEBLI (1963) who, in contrast to PIAGET'S biological approach, offers a more empiricist point of view, argues that the state a child's thinking and verbalization has reached is equally dependent upon previous learning experience,

'quantity' and for the meaning of this term (CARROLL), so that he treats a case, deviating from this norm, as a negative instance and as not belonging to this category: if he takes note of the variable 'level of liquid', he will say, when the liquid has been poured into a flatter dish, that the liquid had become less, or that the quantity had been changed.

It follows that a concept or the meaning of a word can evolve; it can become more differentiated until the degree of complexity which is accepted in a given language has been reached. The word 'weight', for example, is still used by a child without attaching importance to the attribute of constancy. Even an adult uses the word 'size' or 'simultaneous' in a way which, in its degree of complexity, does not do justice to the demands of the theory of relativity.

(b) This leads us to the second kind of reference formation, *definition*. As the individual grows up and becomes familiar with his language, he is given a catalogue of verbal rules which have to be obeyed in the use of certain linguistic forms. Whenever a piece of land surrounded by water is talked about, the word 'island' may be used; when a railless motor vehicle with at least two axles is the subject of discourse, the word 'automobile' may be employed. The definition delimits verbally what belongs to a class and is supposed to be constant.

An investigation by WERNER and KAPLAN (1952) shows that even in this process of definition which, logically, appears so obvious both analysis and synthesis are involved. The two investigators gave children between the ages of eight and thirteen artificial words embedded in defining sentences and they asked their subjects to guess their meaning.

1. a CORPLUM may be used for support;

2. CORPLUMS may be used to close off an open place;

3. a CORPLUM may be long or short, thick or thin, strong or weak;

4. a wet CORPLUM does not burn;

5. you can make a CORPLUM smooth with sandpaper;

6. the painter used a CORPLUM to mix his paints.

The child is presented with these sentences one after another; he is supposed to indicate what the meaning of CORPLUM might be. The results suggest that younger children cannot distinguish between the meaning of a word looked for and the meaning of a whole sentence ("CORPLUM means that you can close off an open space"). Although the higher age groups appear to distinguish between sentence meaning and word meaning, the latter is still quite vague and wide: more precise definition remains dependent upon the dynamics of the situation which originally was the only carrier of meaning. Constancy of vocalization and reference is developed only gradually out of a dynamic background.

Constancy of the vocal pattern and of reference are preconditions for the establishment of meaning. Meaning is present whenever a constant relationship is cognized between a constant sound pattern and a constant referent. But the development of this constant relationship between a constant sound pattern and a constant referent is not a third chronological phase following previous phases of establishing constancy; the three tendencies interact closely.

Further, it should not be assumed that the knowledge of this relationship must necessarily occur immediately and at all times on a high level of intellectual awareness and insight. The most basic form of recognition or awareness of a constancy relationship is—as CHURCH (1961, p. 36) had already pointed out—what HEAD and BARTLETT have called a *schema*. "... a schema is an implicit principle by which we organize experience. Psychologically, the schema has two faces. On the environment side, we become sensitive to regularities in the way things are constituted and act, so that we perceive the environment as coherent and orderly ... On the organismic side, schemata exist in our mobilizations to act and react" (CHURCH 1961, pp. 36-37). Without going into further detail about related notions in PIAGET and TOLMAN ('cognitive map'), we can simply say that a schema is a summary reduced to bare essentials. The schema, as a communicating agent, establishes a permanent link between the vocal constancy and the constant reference category. And as a permanent pattern it links past, present and future.

What has here been called 'schema' has been named 'characteristic mass' by the Polish scholar ZAWADOWSKI (1961). More particularly, according to him, a correlation exists between the characteristic masses of the textual elements (i.e., 'signs') and the characteristic masses of extra-textual elements (i.e., 'referents').

The chronological process of integrating constancies, whose early phases have been referred to here as schema, has also a correlate in associationist psychology. According to MOWRER, a hitherto neutral stimulus which coincides in time with drive increments or with drive satisfaction acquires the capacity to arouse fear or hope in the organism and thus to provide the organism with 'memory of the past' and 'knowledge of things to come' (MOWRER, 1960, p. 124).

In MOWRER's approach, the term 'knowledge' lies outside the boundaries of his system; but we are not inhibited by any behavioristic self-denial from comprehensively referring to memory and premonitions as 'knowing' which turns mere association into meaning.

It was pointed out above that the development of a constant relationship between sound pattern and reference category and the conscious awareness of this relationship should not be viewed as a subsequent appendage to the existing constancies. All the processes we have analyzed should be imagined as closely interwoven. How close these inter-relationships are is shown by the high correlation of many descriptive terms which are clearly distinguished in their meaning in the language of adults. Most things which are described as 'big' are also 'heavy'. What is 'long' is generally also 'taller' than what is called 'short'. This means that a high correlation in terms of empirical occurrence exists between these words, which in their meaning are quite different. This is why a child, as he acquires his language, has difficulties in grasping what should be constant from one situation to the next so as to justify the use of a particular term.

It is to be expected, as ERVIN and FOSTER (1960) have pointed out, that this correlation makes it hard for children to distinguish between such descriptive terms. For example, words such as 'good', 'pretty', 'clean' and 'happy' correlate so highly with each other that they appear to children at first as synonymous or, perhaps more accurately, as completely undifferentiated. ERVIN and FOSTER presented to six-year- and twelve-year-old children pairs of objects in which size, weight and strength varied independently. For example, the two objects might be of different size and yet have the same weight. The younger children said with significantly greater frequency than the older ones that the objects differed on other dimensions in addition to the attribute actually contrasted. More than half of the six-year-olds used 'good', 'pretty' and 'happy' as interchangeable synonyms in the description of pictures.

These results are interpreted by the authors as follows: the descriptive terms whose denotative meanings are not yet distinguished by the small child are identical with those descriptive terms which are linked connotatively in metaphors even in the adult. Or to express it in different terms: in the semantic differentials of adults (see pp. 187 ff.) those descriptive terms which the child has not yet learned to distinguish are associated with one another[1].

The semantic differential can be said to indicate what, by omissions and additions, the adult has created out of the undifferentiated mass, which, in the early stages before the separation into denotation and connotation, was simply the full meaning for the child. CARROLL (1964a) rightly expresses the view that the semantic differential should more accurately be called an 'experiential differential'. The uniformity of the physical and biological environment of man has caused the words related to it to generally represent conceptual invariants: 'sun', 'moon', 'day', 'animal', 'to fall' have in nearly all languages identical meaning. However, in society, technology and culture there are greater

---

[1] WEGENER has drawn attention to the role of the metaphor in language development (cf. LANGER, 1963, pp. 139 ff.).

differences in the experiences which human beings grasp through word meanings; in these areas we must not expect universal agreement in relation to the attributes which are regarded as critical for a concept of the meaning of a word; ratings on the semantic differential bring to light differences between individuals.

From this point of view we can detect connections with the problem of the dependency of concept formation on language, which was referred to previously (cf. pp. 271 f.).

Looked at in another way, the findings by ERVIN and FOSTER offer other interesting insights: they show that what is called 'word' in the developed language had been formed out of a less differentiated ground, which also contained non-linguistic elements; the word does *not* develop by a process in which a circumscribed meaning is conditioned to a sound complex.

As we have seen, a verbal sign is a category defined by specific acoustic and kinesthetic attributes. The meaningful vocal pattern also acts simultaneously as an attribute of the reference category because the occurrence of a case belonging to this reference category evokes as a response the vocal or sub-vocal enunciation of the verbal sign. The term or name X belongs to a series of distinctive responses which are evoked by the occurrence of a case of class X; the term X—like all distinctive responses evoked by this case—contributes something to distinguish this case from others. This function of the name as an attribute of the reference class can be illustrated by an example (following LEWIS, 1963). SHIPINOVA and SURINA gave infants between 13 and 31 months tasks involving the learning of discriminations: a red box always had a sweet in it, a green box never. This can be learned by every child (and even by a rat or a monkey). In one experimental group of children the presentation of the red box was further accompanied by the utterance of the word 'red'—this group of children learned the distinction between two boxes very much faster.

An interpretation of this result in Pavlovian terms could be expressed as follows. The children who are offered additionally the word 'red' learn faster because not only the first but also the second-signal system are brought into play to make the distinction. One might equally well express it by saying that the stimulation had become more varied and richer in contrasts. Whereas in every other respect—form, size and weight—the boxes were alike and were presented by the same person and under identical environmental conditions, with color only functioning as a distinguishing stimulus; in the case of the experimental group, the word, i.e., a vocal stimulus, was added as a further discriminator.

This experiment can be related to KAMINSKI's example of 'fruit' and 'vegetable' discussed earlier in this book in connection with mediation theories (pp. 181 f.): the sight of the banana evokes at the same time the mediating response 'fruit' and the appropriate stimulation; it is the additional stimulation which helps us to distinguish 'bananas' from 'cucumbers'.

The fact that the sound pattern of the word, defined by certain critical attributes, functions in turn as an attribute of the referent is supported by an everyday observation. If children are asked whether it is possible to call a cow 'horse' or 'water' instead of calling it 'cow', this suggestion, according to VIGOTSKY and BROWN (BROWN, 1958a, p. 208), will be rejected on the grounds that cows give milk while horses are for riding on. Here, by the way, is also the psychological reason for the view (discussed on p. 149) of the *orthotes onomaton*: it is experienced as a feeling of inevitability that the name, this attribute with the highest degree of discriminatory power, cannot be purely accidental or conventional.

The sound pattern of a sign—itself a class of events defined by critical attributes in relation to speaking and hearing—is at the same time an attribute of the reference category and therefore contributes to the stabilization of the latter.

CASSIRER has put it in quite a similar fashion when he wrote: "Through the sign that is associated with the content, the content itself acquires a new permanence" (1953, p. 89).

We viewed previously the tendency to categorize and to establish constancies (of a sign and a referent) as naturally given. We now add that the tendency to relate verbal and conceptual categories appears to be deeply rooted and to precede anything that might be learned by experience. The argument that the sign is an attribute of the reference category and that thus a link is created between the two constancies must now be taken a step further. Whenever we hear for the first time a new term, and only the term, we put a kind of empty category in readiness, which is expected to be filled with substantive content. The new word does not yet point to anything definite; it merely signals that something is there. If in a zoology lecture we hear for the first time (to use BROWN's illustration) the term 'coelenterate', we don't think that the lecturer suddenly intersperses a series of nonsense sounds; we know that a non-linguistic counterpart, a reference category, corresponds to this sound sequence. The new word now functions—as BROWN (1958a, p. 206) says appropriately—as "a lure to cognition". This creates a kind of magnetic pull directing perception and thought towards the empty space to which the new word draws attention. Cognition being *a priori* oriented towards the discovery of meaning, and the function of language being creative rather than representative (CASSIRER), it follows that perception and thought are challenged to supply material to fill the empty category.

What we have described is a fact of decisive importance: let us consider what it means when a linguistic category exercises, so to speak, its 'magnetic pull' upon perceiving and thinking to create from the raw material of available percepts and memories a reference category corresponding to the new word. It means that the category prepared by linguistic convention is the determinant (or at least a co-determinant) of the way in which the 'objective world' of reference categories is organized. The organization of language does not passively reflect the organization of the world but actively organizes this world—another lead to the ideas to be examined in the final chapter.

At the same time, this inherent human tendency to treat a new word as an attribute of an unknown 'real' reference category accounts for the fact that talking about abstractions can easily lead to reification. Wherever there is a word there must be a *real* object, something tangible described by that word. Psychological thought in general—in particular the field of personality psychology—has been prone to be drawn into many such blind alleys by the lure of words. The word 'trait' is a good example in this respect (HÖRMANN, 1964)[1].

Starting from MOWRER's autism theory of word learning we have discussed first the orectic factor which refers to the undifferentiated mixture of emotion and drive. At a later stage we saw that a further symbolic factor was added to the orectic factor. This symbolic factor, although biological in its deeper origins, is, in its manifestations and in its closeness to cognition, specifically human. This added symbolic factor was viewed up to now, in a somewhat restricted fashion, as a process of categorization. The process of fusion of the orectic and symbolic factors will now be discussed once more in relation to the genesis of predication or of propositions.

Orectic factors seem to us to be the primary motor in the development of speech. Animal communication follows this principle, frequently hemmed in and directed by instinctive mechanisms. It develops into human language at the point where propositions and predication occur. CASSIRER describes it vividly in the following terms: "The difference between *propositional language* and *emotional language* is the real landmark between the human and the animal world" (1944, p. 30). The following sections are concerned with that border area.

The infant—at the level of MOWRER's autism—produces speech sounds as a kind of substitute satisfaction. The mother may not be present, but by imitating the sounds heard in her presence the infant can soothe himself. Underlying this imitative trend is therefore an instinctive-

---

[1] *Translator's note.* The author refers to the German word *Eigenschaft*, the approximate equivalent of 'trait'. (Other examples in English-speaking psychology would be 'instinct', 'need' or 'drive'.)

emotional tendency. Since the child does not live by himself, but in a social environment which is receptive to signals, these sounds act instrumentally: mother comes and does whatever is needed. What she does *may* not be exactly what the child would have liked her to do, because the sound sequence produced by the infant does not as yet contain any information; the mother is simply likely to perform whatever the situation as a whole suggests.

This is to say that up to this point meaning is conveyed almost completely by the situation. The sound sequence produced as a result of orectic pressures is rather like a non-specific signal to do *something*. It does not yet point to an object (and is clearly not yet conventionalized), nor does it say what is happening or ought to happen with regard to this object nor does it express a hope or a fear.

If we refer once more to BLOOMFIELD'S model of the speech act as a link between two practical events (cf. p. 210) and remind ourselves that the speech act does not connect two unconnected events, but, on the contrary, permits the separation of two neighboring links in the chain of events, we can now raise the question whether this separation which is dependent upon the speech act can be related to the genesis of predication.

The next step which characterizes this development is the following situation: the baby sits in his play-pen and cannot reach the ball outside. He reaches towards the ball and whimpers. In one way this is entirely emotional, yet in another we see here the beginnings of predication. The gesture of the hand, as BROWN (1958a, pp. 197-198) says, defines the function of whimpering. The coordination of gesture and sound means 'Please, Mummy, give me the ball'.

Bearing in mind CASSIRER'S thesis of the boundary between animal and human life, we can ask whether there is a further parallel in the animal world for this process. It can be seen in the example of a dog which, wanting to be taken for a walk, runs to the door and whines.

On the next level of development the infant no longer simply whimpers; he says 'ball' or 'want'. For the first time a word is used here to bridge, in a specific way, the gap between two practical events (the infant seeing the ball outside and the mother giving the ball to the infant). We are faced here, for the first time, with a verbal event which can be described as a sentence—admittedly, a sentence in which either only the object (ball) or the predicate (want) is encoded in a socially binding fashion.

Such sentences are called *one-word sentences*. In this situation the single word 'ball' means 'Give me the ball'; in another situation the same word 'ball' may mean 'This is my ball' or 'This is a lovely ball'. The single word 'want' in this situation means 'I want the ball'; in another it might mean 'I want something to eat'.

These one-word sentences or holophrastic words are discussed in detail in psychological writings. What CLARA and WILLIAM STERN wrote on this subject at the beginning of the century constitutes one of the classical texts in the literature of psychology.

The one-word sentence is the first instance of a sound combination or word establishing the link between two practical events. This also explains why the first infantile utterances in genuine language always relate to an immediate situation and not to the past or future[1]: the contribution of the concrete situation is still an essential part of the meaning-carrying process. Likewise the receiver still needs to know the concrete situation to be able to decode the message. This, in effect, means that the one-word sentence is not a true sentence. The so-called one word sentence 'want' is more accurately a two-term sentence; it is already a kind of predication. The child utters the predicate that goes with a non-symbolized, physically present object of the sentence, the ball lying outside the play-pen and pointed to by the child. He does not have to say 'ball' because he can point to it.

And vice versa, he can confine himself to designate the ball by a word, while the predicate can be added by means of a gesture and the situation. Accordingly, MOWRER calls the one-word sentence "quasi-predication".

We have to ask ourselves again whether we are still in the transitional field where man and animal can perform in a comparable way. MOWRER has pointed out that this quasi-predication can also exist in animals. If a bee has found nectar and wants to inform other members of the hive of the location, it performs, as we know, a round-dance or a wagging-dance. But the bee has no word for nectar; instead, it has to carry a small amount of nectar which it shares with some of the spectators of the dance. The object of the 'sentence' is not represented by a sign but is given by the actual substance, while the predicate ('fly 500 meters north') is encoded in the subsequent dance pattern.

At this level the encoding capacity of the sign maker is not adequate to put the whole message into words; part of it must still be carried by the situation; or to put it differently, words still serve only to define more precisely the meaning of the total situation.

This limited capacity of the sign-maker (and correspondingly of a sign-receiver operating at the same level) was already encountered when we discussed LURIA'S twins Liosha and Yura (p. 270). But in certain circumstances, e.g., under conditions of neglect, hurry or laziness, even the adult who has full command of the power of speech may regress to this stage of development. Messages are left incomplete because the receiver can complete them on the basis of previous experience or situational context.

---

[1] This observation was made by LEWIS, for example, as in MCCARTHY, 1954, p.557.

An impressive confirmation of our thesis that the degree of elaboration of speech is inversely related to the degree of communicative support supplied by the situation is given by a relevant finding of MEIER's linguistic statistics. Among the texts examined by MEIER for sentence length the dialogue in a film ("In Those Days" by H. KÄUTNER) displays the highest frequency of extremely short sentences (MEIER, 1964, p. 191). The sequence of visual events acts as communication to such an extent that extreme shortness of sentences is possible.

But as soon as an utterance refers to something which is not here and now, constructions of more than one-word length are needed. The object which is not present cannot be referred to by a gesture; it must be 're-present-ed' by a word.

The preliminary schema of predication discussed so far must be further refined and differentiated. At the level of the primitive two-word sentence two words are simply put together. This combination in itself contains more information than the information contained in the two words separately. The extent of the information transmitted by the two words is, however, further increased if they are not simply placed together but if they take on specific grammatical functions. The possibilities of coordination of words in a sentence rise sharply as soon as the speaker has at his disposal more complex rules of grammar than those of simple linear addition.

In this connection it is possible to look at the sudden rise of interactive possibilities from a different point of view. Grammar is the system of a language. The child cannot learn all word combinations which are possible in a particular language (his life would not last long enough to do that), nor is it indeed necessary to learn them, because by using language he learns rules enabling him to produce even sentences which he himself has never heard in this particular form before, but whose formal properties are implicit in anything he has heard.

The reader will recall CHOMSKY's view discussed on pages 45ff. according to which a grammar is a tool kit, a collection of rules or a program for generating such sentences as are recognized by the native speaker to be grammatical. "Language is the prime example of rule-governed behavior" (MILLER, 1965, p. 17).

How does the knowledge of these rules develop in the child? At the age of approximately eighteen months he begins to utter two-word sentences. After a further eighteen months he can already construct nearly all sentence types which are possible in the particular language[1]. Can the development in these eighteen months be further analyzed? And in connection with such an analysis the following question deserves

---

[1] See on this point, among others, STERN, 1930, pp. 132f.

our attention. What evidence is there to say that the child constructs his utterances in accordance with these rules and does not simply repeat a sentence previously heard ? It is only if this can be proved that one can say that he has learned the rules.

One possibility of determining what language rules a child knows is to analyze the mistakes he makes when he speaks. If a child employs the plural correctly and says 'dogs', it cannot be inferred whether he imitates a particular word (perhaps he has heard his parents say this word) or whether he has already mastered the plural rule and constructs plurals accordingly. But if the child says, 'Two mans', the mistake indicates that he has begun to construct forms according to rules—even though in this instance the use of the rule was inappropriate. He is unlikely to have ever heard 'mans', but constructs this word according to the rules applicable, for example, to 'dogs'.

Modifying this incidental observation into an experimental procedure, collaborators of BROWN, in particular, have carried out systematic studies. One of these investigations, a study by BERKO (1958), will be described.

A total of 50 children (one group of four-and-a-half-year-olds, another group of five-and-a-half-year-olds) were shown line drawings as illustrated in the accompanying figure (Fig. 68).

This is a wug.

Fig. 68. BERKO, 1958, p. 154   *Now there is another one.*
There are two of them.
There are two....

The rule of plural formation is studied in the following way. The investigator points to the first picture and says: "This is a wug. Now there is another one (second picture). There are two of them. There are two ...". If the child has mastered the rule he will complete the sentence and say "two wugs". The mastery of the rule for the comparison of adjectives is tested with another example. The child is shown a picture of a spotted dog, next to it a dog with more spots, and next to him again a dog with many more spots. The experimenter points to the first dog and says: "This dog has quirks on him. This dog has more quirks on him. And this dog has even more quirks on him. This dog is quirky. This dog is ... And this dog is the ...". If the child employs the rule for the comparison of adjectives, he will insert "quirkier" and "quirkiest".

BERKO'S investigation shows how these rules gradually appear during the growth of the child; but there are considerable differences in difficulty of different grammar rules. Unknown words are treated by children according to the rules which are applied most frequently and have the smallest number of exceptions.

Presumably here, too, development starts out from an analysis of undifferentiated structures. It is as if the child took a sentence as a whole and systematically experimented which variations (of place or direction) in this sentence are possible. There is evidence from numerous studies that such experimentation has at least a part to play (although it is not known how large a part) in the acquisition of grammatical rules. According to these studies, children literally practice how to speak grammatically. Of particular interest are the monologues spoken by a two-and-a-half-year-old boy in the evening before going to sleep, which RUTH WEIR has recorded. One of these monologues was as follows: "What color/what color blanket/what color mop/what color glass". The substitutability of nouns is practiced here. Or: "Big Bob/Little Bob/Big and little/Little Bobby/Little Nancy/Big Nancy". The possibility of pronoun substitutions is explored in the following monologue: "Take the monkey/ Take it/Stop it/Stop the ball/Stop it". And: "I go up there/I go/She go up there".

The stages of development in child language between 18 months and three years have been investigated by BROWN and BELLUGI (1964) and by BRAINE (1963a).

BROWN and BELLUGI have studied the verbal utterances of two only children, Adam and Eve. At the time the studies began Adam was 27 months old, and Eve 18 months. Every second week recordings were made of what the child uttered and heard.

As one would expect, imitation plays a considerable part. The mother says something and the infant copies it. But what is this imitation like?

Table 24. *Some imitations produced by Adam and Eve* (based on BROWN and BELLUGI, 1964, p. 136)

Model utterance	Child's imitation
Tank car	Tank car
Wait a minute	Wait a minute
Daddy's brief case	Daddy brief case
Fraser will be unhappy	Fraser unhappy
He's going out	He go out
That's an old time train	Old time train
It's not the same dog as Pepper	Dog Pepper
No, you can't write on Mr. Cromer's shoe	Write Cromer shoe

The order of words remains identical. This is by no means obvious; but in this way the order of words which applies to grammatical sentences, hence their comprehensibility, is guaranteed. Only short sentences are copied completely. If the sentences exceed a length of three or more morphemes the child omits words. The cause for these omissions cannot lie in the limitations of the child's vocabulary (the omitted words are known to him) nor do the limitations of his immediate memory account for them; for the child's spontaneously produced sentences are also only of this length. It is probable that a child can only plan utterances of a restricted length[1].

At this point it is once more appropriate to recall what we described as the separation of practical events. For a child the linguistic bridge to be built between the practical events cannot yet be very long.

The limitations of his planning capacity compel the child, when he copies, to omit some of the words of the model. It becomes evident that these omissions are not accidental. Omissions include inflections, auxiliaries, articles, prepositions, and conjunctions. These words are comprehensively referred to by some linguists as 'functors', because their grammatical function is more important than their semantic content. Among the words copied and not omitted by the child are nouns, verbs and adjectives, i.e., words which are important not for their function in the sentence but for their content.

The child proceeds exactly like an adult composing a message in telegraphic style: words with a high information content are kept; those with a low information content are dropped.

However, we are not forced to assume that the child undertakes an analysis in terms of information theory followed by a sifting process of what he has heard. His procedure is facilitated by a device which is much more obvious to the ear: the child can confine himself to copying the stressed words because they are the content words.

Following our earlier discussion on the role of speech as a link between practical events (p. 210), it is important to note that the child copies those words which could not be guessed from the context.

The recordings show that it is not only the child who copies the sentences spoken by the mother but also the mother who copies sentences first uttered by the child (Table 25). It should, of course, be noted that while the majority of the child's imitations entail a reduction of the heard utterance, the mother expands the child's utterance; and more specifically, she again adds those functors which are absent in the child's speech. Such expansions on the part of the mother were found in approximately a third of the data collected by BROWN and BELLUGI.

---

[1] For the role of planning in speech see pp. 250f.

Table 25. *Expansions of child speech produced by mothers* (based on BROWN and
BELLUGI, 1964, p. 141)

Child	Mother
Baby highchair	Baby is in the highchair
Mommy eggnog	Mommy had her eggnog
Eve lunch	Eve is having lunch
Mommy sandwich	Mommy'll have a sandwich
Sat wall	He sat on the wall
Throw Daddy	Throw it to Daddy
Pick glove	Pick the glove up

The verbal interaction between mother and child consists largely of a
cycle of reductions and expansions. The modifications made by the
infant are perfectly predictible so that a machine could be programmed
to turn a mother's sentences into baby-talk; but the expansions which
the mother adds when she repeats the child's utterances cannot be
specified so well. In the above examples the child always produces a proper
name plus a common noun. The mother turns these into quite a variety
of sentences. Thus the child's 'Eve lunch' is not expanded into 'Eve's
lunch' nor into 'Eve will have lunch', but into 'Eve is having lunch',
because in this particular situation this expansion is more appropriate.
Therefore the expansion encodes aspects which the child, instead of
encoding, had left to the situation to express. The expansion on the part
of the mother translates from the situational into the verbal the functional entity of a message which had relied less on specific verbal elements.
The inserted functors give information about the time at which the
action is set (e.g., in the past), whether it is completed, and what the
relationship is between participants; e.g., 'Throw daddy' will be interpreted more precisely as 'Throw it to daddy'. By expanding the child's
sentences, the authors argue, the mother teaches more than just grammar;
she teaches a world-view.

In this investigation by BROWN and BELLUGI the central question has
been: what rules govern the omissions which occur in infant speech?
Another question is: how does a child learn to construct new sentences
in such a way that the words appear in the order in which they are
regarded as syntactically correct in the language in question. BRAINE
(1963a) has studied this problem.

Our discussion thus returns to a problem considered in detail at an earlier stage.
Learning the grammar of a language means learning a structure which is not tied
to any particular group of words; it enables the learner to construct new sentences
which have never been heard before in such a way that they conform to the same
general structure to which previously-heard sentences also conform. Approaching

this question from the point of view of developmental psycholinguistics, we are led once more to a problem which engaged our attention when we discussed the psychological reality of grammar (pp. 230ff.). In spite of the risk of being repetitious, we will describe the following investigations in detail because they enable us to give an account of the chronological sequence of the acquisition of grammatical rules and structures.

How do we learn the general structure which determines word order in a sentence? To answer this question one must no doubt fall back upon the notion of generalization. BRAINE specifies this concept further by referring to 'contextual generalization' which he defines as follows: "When a subject, who has experienced sentences in which a segment (morpheme, word or phrase) occurs in a certain position and context, later tends to place this segment in the same position in other contexts, the context of the segment will be said to have generalized ..." (1963a, p. 323).

BRAINE made children of different age levels learn miniature artificial languages. This procedure suggested that what is learned is the localization of a linguistic unit within a larger more comprehensive unit. Unit formation, it appears, occurs on different levels so that a hierarchy of units, is formed. Within the sentence it is possible to isolate, as a first unit, the so-called primary phrase ('the book', 'has thrown'); within the primary phrase the units generally consist of a noun or verb and one or several words from such form classes as articles, auxiliaries, etc.; the latter—we recall BROWN and BELLUGI'S functors—indicate the relational order of content words and facilitate the recognition, identification and learning of the primary phrase. They are designated as functors or pivot words.

The organizing and cementing function of these pivot words has already been indicated in the investigation by GLANZER (see pp. 236f.).

The primary phrase consisting of a content word and one or two pivot words is a characteristic feature of speech development. It can be seen from Table 26 below that the grammar of the child in question could be expressed in the following generative rule: first take a pivot word (i.e., a word from class M), then add a word from the large class of content words N.

These two classes M and N, which are here needed to describe the child's grammar, no longer occur in the language of the adult. Between the stage of language development described here and that of the adult, there is not only an increase in differentiation and complexity of the generative rules that come into operation (to be discussed later, pp. 295f.), there is also a change of the functional classification of the vocabulary, to which we are now turning. The child, for example, must learn that 'a' and 'two' do not belong to the same class since 'a' is followed by a singular and 'two' by a plural. He must also learn that the word 'more' is followed by

Table 26. *Noun phrases in isolation and rule for generating noun phrases at Time 1*
(based on BROWN and BELLUGI, 1964, p. 145)

A coat	More coffee
A celery[1]	More nut[1]
A Becky[1]	Two sock[1]
A hands[1]	Two shoes
The top	two tinker-toy[1]
My Mommy	Big boot
That Adam	Poor man
My stool	Little top
That knee	Dirty knee
NP → M + N	

M → a, big, dirty, little, more, my, poor, that, the two.
N → Adam, Becky, boot, coat, coffee, knee, man, Mommy, nut, sock,
stool, tinker-toy, top, and, very many others.

[1] Ungrammatical for an adult.

a plural of some words ('more nuts') and the singular of others ('more coffee').

The organization and re-organization of such classes can be accounted for in terms of JENKINS' mediation processes (cf. p. 181).

Table 27, taken from BROWN and BELLUGI, will show the stage of differentiation attained 16 weeks after the stage described above.

Table 27. *Subdivision of the modifier class at Time 2* (based on BROWN and BELLUGI,
1964, p. 147)

A. Privileges peculiar to articles

Obtained	Not obtained
A blue flower	Blue a flower
A nice nap	Nice a nap
A your car	Your a car
A my pencil	My a pencil

B. Privileges peculiar to demonstrative pronouns

Obtained	Not obtained
That my cup	My that cup
That a horse	A that horse
That a blue flower	A that blue flower
	Blue a that flower

In the earlier two-word utterances, the article had appeared immediately before a noun as in other examples the demonstrative. At this stage in three-word utterances the article normally occupies the first position and other modifiers ('nice', 'blue') are placed between the article and the noun. If a demonstrative appears, it may be placed in front of the article. At Time 1 the generative rule M + N was sufficient; to describe what is happening now requires far more complicated rules:

$$\text{Dem.} + \text{Art.} + \text{M} + \text{N} \text{ or}$$
$$\text{Art.} + \text{M} + \text{N} \quad \text{or}$$
$$\text{Dem.} + \text{M} + \text{N} \quad \text{or}$$
$$\text{Art.} + \text{N}$$

or generalized: $(\text{Dem.}) + (\text{Art.}) + (\text{M}) + \text{N}$[1].

And six months after Time 1 of the investigation, Adam had already subdivided his large class M into five different sub-classes.

BROWN and BELLUGI'S concluding remark that the development of the noun phrase alone is more like the biological development of an embryo than like the acquisition of a conditioned response makes it evident that the learning theories of general psychology do not offer a model which is sufficiently flexible to account for the acquisition of grammar. We have already discussed in a different context how the more recent psychological investigations on the reality of grammar cope with this problem.

While the BROWN and BELLUGI study is more ideographic, i.e., describes an individual case, the procedure employed by PAULA MENYUK (1963, 1964) is more nomothetic. Her aim is to demonstrate by means of cross-sectional studies the age dependency of the complexity of grammatical structures employed by the child. MENYUK, like others, employs CHOMSKY'S generative model to describe the structures the child makes use of.

The data of the investigation consist of the verbal utterances which children at different age levels produced in more or less standardized situations. Each sentence, in accordance with CHOMSKY'S model, was converted into a rule according to which it had been generated. It is obvious that, in this way, rules are made, some of which also occur in the standard language of the adult, while others by adult norms lead to incomplete ungrammatical sentences.

The results of this investigation show that all basic structures of adult grammar are already present in the language of the pre-school child. As the child grows up, syntactic structures are linked with each other so that the sentences formed become longer.

---

[1] ( ) means class within parenthesis is optional.

The use of non-standard rules does not decline in a linear fashion with rising age; the decline forms a wave pattern. The use of non-standard rules rises again somewhat whenever the child advances to more complex structures. MENYUK concludes from her results that language acquisition and development cannot be said to be based simply on imitation. Between the acts of hearing and self-expression certain operations must be carried out which enable the child to sort the heard data according to the categories of grammar. If imitation were decisive for speech production, then the child ought to produce sentences with omissions in the earliest stages (because of the limitations of his memory) and only afterwards complete sentences.

The objection that other types of incorrect sentences resulted from the imitation of other *children* is not defensible because, if that were so, one would expect greater chance variations in the production of incorrect sentences than actually occur. The mistakes a child makes point to his increasing capacity to employ more and more differentiated rules in the formation of sentences. The fact that the basic structures of an adult standard grammar are already present in a three-year-old child indicates how early the analysis in terms of grammatical categories begins. On the other hand, the extent to which transformations are used increases markedly with age. The preschool years in this development are a relatively quiescent period; during this time there is less experimentation with language than practice of already acquired rules.

We can see that little is as yet known about the mechanisms of language acquisition; even the phenomenology of the chronological sequence of this acquisition is not yet refined enough. We can further see—and this is what this chapter should have made clear—that an accurate and adequate conception of the structure and functioning of speech cannot be attained without constant reference to genetic and child psychology.

Chapter 15

The Influence of Language on Man's View of the World

Semantic implications of grammatical wordclasses — The object-forming function of language — Formation of categories through language — Language as a teacher of discrimination and non-discrimination — Kinship terms as an illustration — Status and solidarity of address — WHORF and the thesis of linguistic relativity — LENNEBERG'S methodological argument — Color coding and its problems — GLANZER'S verbal-loop hypothesis — Towards linguistic universals — General Semantics.

In the last chapter we saw how language in the child gradually evolves as an instrument of the human mind. However, language is more than a passive instrument; it influences its user. This influence of language upon the way in which the speaker views and confronts the world is the problem of this final chapter.

Our discussion may begin where we left off in the preceding chapter in which it was shown how the child, in the course of his development, learns the formal structure of the language so that he can operate in accordance with the rules of this structure. For example, on the basis of communalities of forms, he learns to establish classes of words to be treated alike. This takes us back to what we said about the *paradigm* elsewhere in this book (p. 128). There are different sentence frames; at certain places within the frame, word substitutions may be made. Or, to put it in more precise terms, any word that can be substituted without breaking up the frame is considered to belong to the same class; it conforms to a single rule. 'The ... is good': whatever fits into the slot or can be substituted (disregarding exceptions at this point) is a noun in our language. The frame is broken if, say, the word 'beer' or 'child' is replaced by 'up' or 'little'.

In this way the wordclass 'noun' has been purely formally defined. In twentieth century linguistics (e.g., in the work of FRIES) such formal definitions are common because semantic or notional definitions have too many exceptions. A notional definition of a noun or substantive would be, for example: a noun or substantive is the name of a thing. The term 'substantive' in itself shows that earlier epochs of linguistic science used to define notionally. The notional definition is appropriate for 'house', 'ball' or 'tree', but not for 'warmth' or 'justice'.

It could now be imagined—and this is a thesis put forward and empirically tested by BROWN (1957)—that in the early stages of the acquisition of language in the child the formal and notional aspects are not yet differentiated, with the practical consequence that the child ascribes to a word functioning as a noun properties of substance, and to words functioning as verbs the characteristics of action.

BROWN spent a month recording utterances which he heard in pre-school sessions. A comparison of the words he noted with words which appeared in the language of adults produced the following results. While 16 percent of the nouns used by adults refer to objects with a visual contour, in the case of children this applies to 67 percent of the nouns used. This finding could be formulated equally as follows: children use more concrete nouns than adults. As for the verbs used by adults, only one third of the adults' verbs but two thirds of the children's verbs refer to movement.

The semantic implications which a noun has as 'the name of a thing' and a verb as 'referring to action' is more consistent in children's speech than in the speech of adults. At the later stages the notional or semantic uniformity of the form classes declines. The same rules which are applied to 'car', 'block', 'ball' and 'auntie' are applied to the non-concrete words which belong to the form class of nouns.

What function does this initially high correlation between formclass and semantic content fulfill? It has a dual function: in the first phase it facilitates learning; at a later stage it acts as a 'lure to cognition'—and this is what this final chapter is about.

Suppose an adult shows a glass of water to a child and says 'water', the child is not yet able to say what this unknown word refers to: vessel, color, content, drinking or the like. The child does not yet know what feature is to be picked out by the new word as an invariant category. He can gain this knowledge only by observing that in other situations only one feature is constant: water; everything else changes: form of vessel, location, and color. The constant feature among all the variations is then associated with the constant term.

This process is extremely lengthy and its result is uncertain. The child is helped in picking out the relevant aspects from the total situation by the adult guiding his learning. The new word is not isolated; it is presented in a sentence; in this way the child is informed about the part of speech to which the word belongs. We don't say 'dog', but 'Look at the little dog running along the road' and thus mark the word 'dog' as a noun. This characterization limits the possible meanings of 'dog'; it can only be something that can be seen running along the road.

In this sense LEISI (1961) speaks of linguistic hypostatizing. Every word category hypostatizes something specific: the noun represents the referent as an object, the adjective represents it as a property and the verb as an activity. WEISGERBER (II, 1962b, p. 301) calls these three representations of the word "not only copies of reality but guides to reality".

The formclass of a word is, in BROWN'S view, therefore an attention-directing device. BROWN has tested this assumption empirically by presenting to children artificial words which clearly belong to a certain formclass and then questioning the children about their meaning. He made use of three formclasses: verb, mass noun and count noun.

As is known, English treats certain nouns such as 'snow', 'milk', 'rice', or 'dirt' differently from others such as 'house' or 'dog'; we say 'some milk', but 'a dog'. When we use a count noun, e.g., dog', and say 'some dogs', 'dog' is plural, whereas in the case of a mass noun, e.g., 'milk', it always remains in the singular; hence, 'some milk'.

After BROWN had noticed that the children use words such as 'milk', 'orange juice' or 'dirt' correctly, i.e., only in the singular, he undertook the experiment proper: first, they are shown a picture of a pair of hands kneading a mass of confetti-like material in a striped container. The movement would be described by a verb, the confetti-like mass by a mass noun, and the container by a count noun. It was justifiable to assume that the children had no words for any these.

If we now investigate whether a child has an idea of the common notional significance of verbs (action or movement), the child is asked the following question: "Do you know what it means to sib? In this picture you can see sibbing. Now show me another picture of sibbing", and he is immediately presented with three further pictures which show either only the movement (applied to a different kind of material) or only the material (with different movements) or only the container (with another material).

If one wished to study whether the child has an idea of the common notional significance of all count nouns, the question is: "Do you know what a sib is? In this picture you can see a sib. Now show me another picture of a sib."

The results of this investigation are presented in the following table:

Table 28. *Picture selections for words belonging to various parts of speech* (based on BROWN, 1957, p. 4)

Depicted category	Verbs	Count nouns	Mass nouns
actions	10	1	0
objects	4	11	3
substances	1	2	12
no response	1	2	1

The result can be interpreted to mean that classification of an unknown word under a particular formclass offers the learner a hint as to the kind of substantive meaning of this particular word.

It appears that the acquisition of the system of formclasses of a language is generalizable to a high degree and intervenes as a steering device in the acquisition of semantic relationships.

On the other hand, the inherent suggestion to classify a word as belonging to the formclass of nouns ("This is probably a thing or a substance"), which helps the child in the acquisition of language, can also mislead, or misdirect the child's (or the adult's) thoughts or expectations. "When the word *justice* comes into one's vocabulary it comes as a noun and may, as a consequence, be endowed with thing-like attributes borrowed from blocks and trucks. It would then be quite natural to make statues and paintings of justice" (BROWN, 1958a, p. 247).

We have described BROWN's investigation in detail because it forms a bridge between the acquisition of grammatical structures discussed in the last chapter and the problem which is the subject of the present chapter: the problem of the influence of language upon thought.

Naively looked at, language is the means of representing the reality which is perceived independently from it. When, for example, in BÜHLER'S model (see pp. 18ff.), language is characterized by the remark of "one person talking to another about things", then the things about which the one person talks to the other have an existence and form of appearance which is quite independent of whether and in what way they are talked about.

The question of the influence of language upon the way a speaker sees his world and thinks about it originated, as was seen in the last chapter, in the developmental characteristics of categorial behavior. If the question is to be discussed in the present chapter as a problem in its own right, it takes us back to the philosophical thought reported in chapter 12. These reflections form the wider horizon against which to view these questions.

In chapter 12 we discussed in detail the philosophical argument which caused the independence of thing and language (or of *res* and *intellectus*) to be called into question. We noted at that point how the world-creating rather than the world-representing function of language, which appears with particular clarity in WITTGENSTEIN's 'language-game', had been developed—in the work of PEIRCE and MORRIS—as a result of taking into account pragmatic elements in the complex of *meaning*.

The problem of the influence of language upon man's view of the world has a respectable philosophical ancestry. KANT postulated that space and time are modes of perception of the human mind, which, therefore, to put it crudely, the human mind adds to objective reality. Objective reality can only be recognized with the help of the spectacles of these modes of perception (which may actually distort reality).

The chief criticism which HERDER made of KANT'S *Critique of Pure Reason* was that KANT completely neglected the problem of language. Is it not possible that analogously language can influence the process of perception ?

When HUMBOLDT said, "Language is the thought-forming organ" (1949 edition, p. 52), he made the decisive move away from the copying function of language, implied in HERDER'S criticism. Or to quote HUMBOLDT again: "It is the subjective activity of thinking which creates an object. For there is no single kind of idea which can be regarded as a purely receptive contemplation of an object previously given. The activity of the senses must be combined into a synthesis with the inner activity of the mind ... To do this language is essential" (p. 55). HUMBOLDT further wrote in the *Academy Treatise on Comparative Philology*[1]: "The mutual interdependence of thought and word makes it evident that languages are not really means of representing already known truth, they are means of discovering hitherto unknown truth" (1905a, p. 27).

There is no doubt that this thesis has far-reaching implications. If it is right to say that world or truth is not something to be known prior to language or independently of it (merely to be put into words), but that it can only be perceived and thought about with the help of speech, it may lead to the assumption that a particular language is a co-determinant of the world-view of the members of a speech community; the particular language would further determine the world-view differently from the way another language would determine the world-view of another speech community.

HUMBOLDT saw this consequence of his thesis with complete clarity: "The mental characteristics and the development of language of a nation are so intimately bound up with each other that if the one were known the other could be completely deduced from it. For intellect and language permit and develop only forms which are mutually compatible. Language can be said to be the outward manifestation of the mind of nations. Their language is their mind, and their mind their language. One must imagine them as completely identical" (p. 41).

It follows that the image which man receives through cognition (KANT) or language (HUMBOLDT) does not depend alone on the nature of the perceived object but always includes an active contribution of the cognizing individual or speaker. It is, as CASSIRER put it, not imitation *(Abbild)* but creation *(Urbild)*.

---

[1] *Translator's note:* The German title of this treatise is: *Akademie-Abhandlung über das vergleichende Sprachstudium.*

The characteristic way in which every language organizes its content, the world-view of the language, is called by HUMBOLDT the *inner form of the language.*

HUMBOLDT'S idea has been developed further in several directions and by several disciplines. To name a few of such developments: CASSIRER in philosophy, SAPIR and WHORF in ethnology, WEISGERBER in linguistics, KORZYBSKI and HAYAKAWA in General Semantics. As early as 1931 WEISGERBER formulated the fundamental principle of all such developments in the following terms: "It must be recognized to what extent the individual by virtue of his membership of a language community incorporates its characteristic mentality and is shaped by it in such a way that his mental activity is more strongly determined by the world-view of his native tongue than by his individual personality" *(Report of the Twelfth Congress of the German Psychological Association, 1931* [1932, p. 197]).

In a certain way one can refer to this, quite realistically, as word magic; for—in ALDOUS HUXLEY'S terms—the word forms the mind of him who uses it. "Conduct and character are largely determined by the nature of the words we currently use to discuss ourselves and the world around us" (1940, p. 9).

In the same year as WEISGERBER (1931), SAPIR, in an American investigation on the conceptual categories in primitive language, wrote —certainly completely independently of WEISGERBER—: "The relation between language and experience is often misunderstood. Language is not merely a more or less systematic inventory of the various items of experience which seem relevant to the individual ... but is also a self-contained creative symbolic organization, which not only refers to experience largely acquired without its help but actually defines experience for us by reason of its formal completeness and because of our unconscious projection of its implicit expectations into the field of experience" (1931, p. 578).

Thus, language is included among the factors which modern psychology recognizes as co-determinants in the development and quality of the processes of perceiving, learning and thinking. Gestalt psychology (in particular the Berlin School) laid emphasis upon the sensory determination of units in the field of perception and therefore looked for structuring factors in the interaction between stimulus intensity and sense organ. The 'new look' of social perception stressed the contribution of motivational and experiential factors in the organization of perception and learning. Among these autonomous factors of perception or cognition, speech occupies a special position: it is less powerful than the biological and physiological factors which apply virtually to the entire species, but its influence is more powerful than that of all other sociological, situational or personality determinants. It is not so much that an individual's direct experience and his personal motives contribute to his world-view, rather it is that language—comparable to the sense organs of our physical equipment—puts at his disposal the tools necessary for gathering experience; and these are tools which the individual cannot help using. "To find words for what we have before our eyes can be most arduous. But once they have appeared, they work upon reality as if they were little hammers used by a craftsman to hammer an image out of a copperplate" (BENJAMIN, 1963, p. 44).

The linguist SEILER has attempted to analyze this whole group of problems in terms of three questions:

"1. To what extent are categories of thought determined, prepared or influenced by the categories of language within which such thought occurs ?

2. What distinguishes the thought or knowledge of a community A with language A from the thought or knowledge of community B with language B ?

3. Applying purely linguistic criteria, what are the decisive differences between language A and language B ?" (1960, p. 43).

In SEILER'S view, the linguist must first answer the third question so that research workers in other disciplines can investigate the first two questions. This is, however, an erroneous argument. The question of the decisive differences between languages A or B cannot be treated independently of the processes referred to in questions 1 or 2; for 'decisive' must always mean 'decisive for something'. A linguist may well regard the difference in the verb structure in languages A and B as decisive, whereas for the difference of thought habits between nations A and B differences in the speed of speech utterances may be 'decisive'.

The second defect of SEILER'S approach is less an error of thought; he makes an unrealistic presupposition: the comparison of linguistic and thought categories, which he regards as necessary, presupposes that thought categories can be conceived independently of speech. But it is precisely the feasibility of this undertaking which has been questioned (by scholars ranging from WITTGENSTEIN to WHORF).

There is simply no patent recipe to solve 'finally' or 'decisively' the problem of the influence of language upon the world-view of man. What we may reasonably expect and what we are going to attempt to do is, by approaching the problem from various angles, to delineate the presuppositions and variables which are implicit in the study of this problem.

In the preceding paragraphs a great deal of importance was attributed to the process of categorization or formation of classes. It is, therefore, natural to ask whether this process is not the basic mechanism that accounts for the variations in world-views determined by language. Even in the work of WEISGERBER, whose frame of reference is entirely un-psychological, thoughts leading in this direction occur: "I can call the shape I hold in my hand a 'rose', because I recognize and identify it as a rose" (1962a, I, p. 55). The process of identification is without doubt the same as the process of classification; the exemplar in question is classified as a rose because its properties are identified sufficiently in agreement with the criterial attributes of this class. What is happening is more than mere recognition; there is also a component of a subjective judgment: "The attributes I recognize are sufficient to identify the exemplar as a rose".

A first source of possible differences of categorizing behavior in individual languages is the *level* of categorization. An example (BROWN, 1958b, p. 14) will illustrate this point. A brown shadowy movement is seen outside. We say this must be:

> 'an animate being'
> 'a quadruped'
> 'a dog'
> 'a boxer'
> 'the landlord's dog, named Prince'.

If we say 'a dog' we have decided upon a particular level. We might equally have chosen the level of 'quadruped', because for the use of this category or this level a smaller number of criterial attributes is sufficient.

The next question that therefore arises is how large is the area of freedom within which we can move in a given case and what factors determine the decision. We can here immediately recognize the over-whelming influence of language: in practice we can only choose a level for which our language offers us a term. We can only classify according to categories available in the particular language. WHORF's great merit has been to draw attention to the differences between these possibilities in different languages.

Before we consider his contribution in more detail, a question which has already been mentioned here must be discussed: which factors influence the decision to select from two or more categories available in *one* language a particular one and no other?

This is, first of all, a factor determined by age and stage of development, because the attributes which are regarded as critical for a given category change and are revised in the course of individual growth. The study of these changes is closely associated with PIAGET's name. Thus, the child has, for example, a category 'weight' for which the attribute of conserva-tion or constancy is not yet critical. And, vice versa, whereas form is still a critical attribute of mass for the child, this is not so for the adult; thus, a child might say that a plasticine cube becomes 'smaller' when it is flattened. The change in complexity of attributes which are critical for a category, a concept, or the use of a word must not be interpreted only in terms of genetic psychology. A comment which at this point is worth recalling is CARROLL'S (discussed on pp. 279f.) that the adult, too, is satisfied, when using the category 'size', with a smaller number of critical attributes than would be needed to understand the theory of relativity. The adult may do this because in general it does not matter whether or not he takes these additional attributes into account, because they are not critical.

This leads us to the second factor which determines the level of categorization: utility or relevance. Thus, when talking about an automobile one may well refer to it as a 'Volkswagen' or 'Ford' or' Cadillac', but in the case of coins we are hardly likely to speak of a 1960 dime or a 1962 dime. BROWN, who has discussed this question in a valuable investigation, "How Shall a Thing be Called?" (1958b), comments that we make distinctions where it matters. Among coins we have to distinguish nickels, dimes and quarters, but for anyone who is not a coin collector it is of no importance whether a dime carries the 1960 or the 1962 imprint.

At this point we can pursue two lines of thought; one leads us back to a group of problems discussed previously and the other takes us further in the discussion of the theme of the present chapter.

We can think, firstly, of the number of words to be subsumed under one concept (e.g., under the concept 'vehicle': 'Ford', 'convertible', 'Mercedes', 'truck', etc.), and, secondly, of the degree of completeness or appropriateness of comprehension. If a given group of persons are in agreement as to which words to classify under a certain concept (e.g., words suggested by the term 'vehicle'), this leads to safer and better communication (see JOHNSON, 1962). Here we are very close to what we had already discussed under the heading of 'associative meaning' and in connection with the semantic differential.

Let us now briefly sketch the second line of thought (we distinguish among cars but not among dimes). In general we operate at the level of categorization which is common to the majority of language users. At this level the most usual term is applied; and this level also provides a norm of constancy[1]. It serves as a reference level. Dogs are generally called 'dogs' because this term delimits a category which for society is functionally defined. It makes little sense to say that one was disturbed in one's sleep by the barking of a mammal; but it is equally pointless to indicate the color or breed of the barking mammal. As BROWN expressed it

---

[1] The reader is reminded of what was said in our earlier discussion of the concept of meaning about the establishment of constancy (see pp. 278f.).

(1958 b, p. 16): our naming practices for people and coins correspond to our non-linguistic practices; it is immaterial with which coin
we pay, but it is not immaterial with which person we go out for the
evening.

As a child learns the common terms he learns to make those distinctions which his parents make and fails to make distinctions which, following the model of his parents and other language users, are unnecessary
in the particular cultural context.

It can be predicted that such distinctions correlating with language
occur particularly wherever 'reality' does not in an obvious way provide
classifications and gradations. We shall see later how restricted in fact
the area is which is determined by 'reality'. In chapter 12 we had already
seen how altogether difficult it is to operate in a philosophically adequate manner with the notion of 'reality'.

One area in which language can presumably exercise a determining
influence upon perception and thinking is the sphere of religion. Here
words are particularly powerful because religion is concerned with things
which are 'difficult to put into words'. It is a major issue to what extent
thought on Christianity is affected by linguistic relativity. What changes
in the 'deeper substance' of the Christian faith are produced by translations into Greek, Latin, German or Swahili? Is it still the same message
in all the languages? Modern theological work very largely consists in a
search for the undistorted below layers of distortions.

In the social field the classifications implicit in *kinship terms* offer an
excellent illustration for the fact that relationships which appear to be
completely determined by 'reality' can be viewed linguistically in the
most varying ways. The lexical units of kinship terminology, following
LOUNSBURY (1963), can differ in two aspects: the 'personnel-designating'
aspect and the 'role-symbolizing' aspect. The meanings of the 'father'
terms in two languages can in one case be distinguished as to who may
be named 'father', and, secondly, what it means to be a 'father' in that
linguistic community. In the European languages an individual employs
the word 'father' only to refer to the male parent (apart from the exception of 'step-father', 'father-in-law' or the priest addressed as 'Father').
In all those societies having what anthropologists call 'Iroquois-type'
kinship systems, it is not only the father in the European sense who is
called 'father' but also the brothers of the father and male cousins.
In societies having 'Crow-type' kinship systems (the Crows—like the
Iroquois—are North American Indian tribes), the term 'father' applies
to the father, the father's brothers, the father's sister's sons, the sons of
the father's sister's daughters, and at times also to the brothers of the
father's mother.

Let us consider the following tabulation (cf. LOUNSBURY, 1963, p. 571):

1. Brother, sister.
2. Father's brother's son, father's brother's daughter.
3. Mother's sister's son, mother's sister's daughter.
4. Father's sister's son, father's sister's daughter.
5. Mother's brother's son, mother's brother's daughter.

In our kinship usage types of 2 to 5 are classed as cousins. In the Iroquois-type usages, the 1, 2 and 3 types are all brothers and sisters; only 4 and 5 are classed as cousins. In the Crow-type usages 1, 2 and 3 are classed as brothers and sisters, 4 as father and aunt whereas the relationships under 5 are designated as son and daughter by a man while a woman refers to them as nephew and niece.

Corresponding to this linguistic division, our society attributes greatest importance to degree of collaterality whereas it is only of secondary importance to which generation a person belongs. In the Iroquois system generation and bifurcation are the principal dimensions while in the Crow system a peculiar, skewed generation membership is of particular importance (i.e., females rank a social generation higher than their male siblings). The undifferentiated use of the term 'cousin', as it is customary in our society, would be experienced as either ridiculous or immoral in some other communities (cf. SHLIEN, 1962, p. 161).

Here, then, the linguistic term is closely linked with the social structure which is perceived as the norm (an extreme adherent of the WHORF thesis of linguistic relativity might say: the linguistic designation determines the social structure perceived as norm). In the same way, the availability of a term describing a social relationship can legitimize this relationship which, if it were not for this term, might not be sanctioned by the moral system of the society. Thus, the invention in Germany of the term 'Onkelehe' ('uncle marriage') was a factor in the development of postwar German society, the importance of which should not be underrated[1].

From this angle it is possible to approach KORZYBSKI's, HAYAKAWA's and JOHNSON's General Semantics. But we will leave this until later, so that for the present we may complete the discussion of kinship terms.

Kinship terminology not only reflects the sociological structure of a society or linguistic community, but beyond that implicitly suggests psychological relations which are both the basis and result of this sociological structure. KROEBER has emphatically declared that kinship terminology is a subject of social *psychology*. In a similar manner, GIFFORD considers

---

[1] *Translator's note.* The term 'Onkelehe' refers to a man and a woman living together as husband and wife, without being legally married, in order to evade higher income tax or loss of social security benefits.

that kinship terms are primarily *linguistic* phenomena whereas the social phenomena are secondary; they reveal the modes of thought in a given society's language. Kinship terms have a high degree of stability and they can only partially or occasionally be influenced by social structure (SHLIEN, 1962).

Whether or not one is inclined to regard the linguistic aspect so unreservedly as primary, it is incontestable that an established kinship terminology exercises a structuring and structure-preserving influence.

The subject of kinship terminology was on the border between psycholinguistics and sociolinguistics. The next topic, forms of address, takes us plainly back into the field of psycholinguistics. Each time someone is addressed a renewed act of decision occurs between forms which the language puts at the speaker's disposal (e.g., 'Mr. Smith'—'John', or in German the formal 'Sie' versus the familiar 'du'). Here psychological factors of more restricted scope can manifest themselves whereas kinship terms represent a supra-individual deposit preserved in the repertoire of the language available to all speakers alike. In kinship terminology the issue was how we speak *about* a person; here we consider how we speak *to* him. We therefore inquire into differences in behavior which are related to differences in linguistic forms.

"Forms of address are relational forms—the selection is not governed by properties of the speaker alone or of the addressee alone but by the properties of the dyad", i.e., the sociopsychological structure of the dyadic group (BROWN, 1962, p. 664). Titles, first names, family names and pronouns of address are forms which can connect all members of a society with each other.

BROWN—partly in collaboration with GILMAN—has investigated the dual forms of address in thirty different languages (1960). To begin with he distinguishes two types: a reciprocal or symmetrical pattern and a non-reciprocal, asymmetrical pattern. In the case of the reciprocal type, both members of the dyad use the same form. Thus both parties can address each other with a first name or both use 'Mr. + family name' or, in German, both use the familiar 'du' or the formal 'Sie'.

BROWN describes pronouns of the type 'du' (German), 'tu' (Italian and French) comprehensively as belonging to the T class, which he contrasts with the V class pronouns: 'vous', 'vos', 'lei', 'Sie'.

The difference between reciprocal patterns is one of degree of intimacy, friendship or familiarity or, as BROWN puts it, of solidarity, based on shared interests and values.

In the non-reciprocal pattern, one of the parties, for example, uses the Christian name, 'Jim', whereas the other says, 'Mr. Jackson'. One partner in German might use the formal 'Sie' and the other the informal 'du'.

In medieval Europe the knight spoke to the commoner in the T form and the commoner to the knight in the V form. Even today the non-reciprocal form of address expresses a status distinction, an unequal possession of attributes valued by the society. This status distinction is chiefly manifested in different degrees of social power.

It appears to be a linguistic universal (i.e., a phenomenon common to all languages) that forms of address code the two dimensions of solidarity and status. These two dimensions can have common *formal* definitions for all languages; solidarity is based on equality, and status on inequality with regard to valued characteristics. From the point of view of *content* there are marked differences between different languages with regard to what creates equality or solidarity and inequality or differential status: age, vocation, lineage, wealth, religion, education and so forth.

But not only is it common to all languages to code solidarity and status in the form of the address, a second phenomenon is also universal: the form of address (e.g., the T form) used reciprocally between intimates is used equally in the non-reciprocal pattern downward from the higher to the lower status, whereas the form of address normally used reciprocally between distant acquaintances is, in the non-reciprocal pattern, used upwards. The intimate address form is, therefore, always also the condescending form, whereas the more formal address, is at the same time, always also the deferential mode of address.

There is no logical reason why the relationship could not equally well be reversed. But since this does not appear to happen, it is natural to ask whether this finding can be explained on psychological grounds. BROWN puts forward the following hypothesis: although in Europe inequality of status is generally no longer expressed in a non-reciprocal form of address (the European 'boss' addresses his subordinates in the V form), such inequality has an important part to play in the shift from one form of address to the other. Two people nowadays are likely to use a mutual V form of address to begin with. There may well be a move to a reciprocal use of the T form. The transition has, however, a non-reciprocal aspect. The person of higher status must initiate the change. This element of non-reciprocity becomes particularly evident in languages such as German where this transition almost amounts to a rite, *Brüderschaft*[1]. The speed of transition from status difference to solidarity is always determined by the person of higher status, although the person of inferior status is more highly motivated towards such a transition because solidarity enhances his status[2].

---

[1] *Translator's note.* The transition from the V form to the T form *(Brüderschaft)* is marked by the rite of both parties drinking each other's health with arms linked.

[2] The fusion of intimacy and condescension which was common in 19th century Europe is still shown in Yiddish today (SLOBIN, 1963).

Up to this point we have considered the two areas of religion and society to find out how far the forms implicit in the structure of language determine the thinking which takes place in the language. But in other areas, too, in which no abstract concepts are involved, but which deal with concrete objects, the formative force of language can be seen. If, however, language determines how the members of the speech community view the world and think about it, the differences among various languages lead necessarily to the conclusion that members of different language communities see and think of the world in different ways or, in other words, that each language implies a particular world view.

The foregoing sentence summarizes WHORF'S interpretation of the arguments of his 'predecessors' (from HUMBOLDT to SAPIR). The first proposition contained in it ('Language determines thought') is frequently referred to as the *principle of linguistic determinism*, the second ('Every language embodies a definite world view') is known as the *principle of linguistic relativity*. The first is of primary importance because, if it is valid, the second is a necessary consequence.

In the last two decades, the WHORF hypothesis has been received by scholars with much interest and sympathy. What is its position within the whole field of psycholinguistics ? The WHORF hypothesis is concerned with the relationship between linguistic data (e.g., the structural organization of word classes) on the one hand and non-linguistic data (e.g., processes of perception or thinking) on the other. But this relationship has been the major theme of psycholinguistics since its beginnings. To give only one illustration from this book, the investigation by MILLER and SELFRIDGE, discussed on pp. 102f., also had as its subject the relationship between a linguistic set of data (i.e., approximation levels of verbal material to normal text) and a non-linguistic set of data (i.e., speed of learning of such verbal material).

Therefore, in short, the WHORF hypothesis represents a special case of what in general terms is the subject of psycholinguistics as a whole. What accounts for the fact that this particular case has aroused such widespread interest in so many different disciplines leading to an overall intensification of psycholinguistic research ? It is certain that there are several reasons.

Our age no doubt provides the right climate for it. International tensions and misunderstandings are brought close to us through press and radio. We know that such tensions and misunderstandings can threaten our existence directly. Thanks to good communications and a change-oriented structure of society, we are informed of strange ways of life which are most clearly manifested in a foreign language. And, finally, the ideological debates whose din reverberates around us let us feel bitterly the relativity of words ('Christian', 'democratic', 'freedom', and 'socialism'). Thus, WHORF, by considering the linguistic aspect of the relationship, postulates interlinguistic rather than intralinguistic distinctions, and by attempting to match them with differences in ideologies, has found a cause which we experience as our own. It can, in fact, be argued that this special position of the WHORF thesis is not justified. For even within one idiom, as PLESSNER once expressed it, language may think for us or against us, in any case beyond us. In a later discussion, we will see that General Semantics represents a movement which aims at the elucidation of relativity and determinism within a single language.

Another reason for the receptivity to WHORF's hypothesis lies in the fact that WHORF had the great skill of presenting his thesis in an exceedingly vivid and convincing way by comparing heterogeneous languages. He confronts American Indian languages and Eskimo with what he calls 'Standard Average European' (SAE), interpreted by him as the undifferentiated communality of English, French, German, Italian and so on. The structure of Indian languages is so radically different from SAE that culture-bound or language-bound differences between the corresponding speech communities can be particularly clearly and persuasively demonstrated. Such comparisons will now be illustrated, first by a lexical example, and then by some grammatical items.

In SAE there is a uniform category called 'snow'. That is to say that a single word ('snow' in English) is used to refer to falling snow, snow on the ground, packed snow, slushy snow, etc. To an Eskimo, to whom snow matters more than to an average European, this would seem extraordinary. He sees different things—and designates them by different words—in these varying modes of appearance of a substance which is always the same to us. To use the terminology of the previous paragraphs, the Eskimo categorizes on a different level. By contrast Aztecs, for whom snow is probably less important, treat this aspect in an even more undifferentiated manner: 'cold', 'ice' and 'snow' are all represented by the same root with different endings.

In this case, an intercultural comparison lends support to the view discussed above, i.e., that one cannot acquire the language of a community without at the same time adopting the perceptual distinctions which are normally—and perhaps inevitably—made in that society.

In order to be able to employ correctly the English word 'snow' (or its equivalents in other European languages), one must learn to distinguish, on the one hand, snow from grass, earth, rain, etc., but, on the other hand, one must also learn to treat as equivalent slushy snow, powdery snow, dirty snow, icy snow, falling snow and snow on the ground. And since in English there is the uniform category 'snow', it can be argued on the basis of the thesis of linguistic determinism that the user of English learns to regard snow as something unified. At this point we again encounter the process of categorization in the act of recognition which was discussed on pp. 303f.

Here it is appropriate to point out once more that the mediating response functions as a unifier. The reader will recall that on two earlier occasions in this book (pp. 181f. and pp. 283f.) we pointed out the unifying effect of the terms 'fruit' or 'vegetable'; in these cases, too, cognition followed language.

Even more impressive than such differences in the vocabulary of a language are the examples of structural differences gathered by WHORF. In SAE we divide most of our words into nouns and verbs. "Our language thus gives us a bipolar division of nature. But nature herself is not thus polarized. If it be said that 'strike, turn, run', are verbs because they denote temporary or short-lasting events, i.e., actions, why then is 'fist' a noun? It also is a temporary event. Why are 'lightning, spark, wave, eddy, pulsation, flame, storm, phase, cycle, spasm, noise, emotion' nouns? They are temporary events. If 'man' and 'house' are nouns because they are long-lasting and stable events, i.e., things, what then are 'keep, adhere, extend, project, continue, persist, grow, dwell,' and so on doing among the verbs? If it be objected that 'possess, adhere' are verbs because they are stable relationships rather than stable percepts, why then should 'equilibrium, pressure, current, peace, group, nation, society, tribe, sister,' or any kinship term be among the nouns? It will be found that an 'event' to US means 'what our language classes as a verb' or something analogized therefrom. And it will be found that it is not possible to define 'event, thing, object, relationship,' and so on, from nature, but that to define them always involves a circuitous return to the grammatical categories of the definer's language" (WHORF, 1956, p. 215)[1].

In Hopi, one of the North American Indian languages, events are indeed defined according to duration. 'Lightning, wave, flame, meteor, puff of smoke or pulsation' are necessarily verbs here, while 'cloud' and 'storm' are approximately at the lower limit of duration for nouns. In Hopi there is therefore a closer correlation between formal and semantic pecularities of word classes (at least in this example) so that there is less danger in Hopi than in SAE of thought being misled by the formal attributes of words.

In the following example taken from WHORF, a structural distinction between SAE and Hopi has been pursued because of its non-linguistic implications for world-view. "In our language, that is SAE, plurality and cardinal numbers are applied in two ways: to real plurals and imaginary plurals ... We say 'ten men' and also 'ten days'. Ten men either are or

---

[1] The studies and experiments by BROWN, reported on pp. 298ff., started out from this line of argument.

could be objectively perceived as ten, ten in one group perception—ten men on a street corner, for instance. But 'ten days' cannot be objectively experienced. We experience only one day, today; the other nine (or even all ten) are something conjured up from memory or imagination. If 'ten days' be regarded as a group it must be as an 'imaginary', mentally constructed group. Whence comes this mental pattern ?" It originates " . . . from the fact that our language confuses the two different situations, has but one pattern for both. When we speak of 'ten steps forward, ten strokes on a bell', or any similarly described cyclic sequence, 'times' of any sort, we are doing the same thing as with 'days'. Cyclicity brings the response of imaginary plurals. But a likeness of cyclicity to aggregates is not unmistakably given by experience prior to language, or it would be found in all languages . . ." (p. 139); i.e., they would be what CARROLL (cf. p. 282) calls 'conceptual invariants'. "In Hopi there is a different linguistic situation. Plurals and cardinals are used only for entities that form or can form an objective group. There are no imaginary plurals, but instead ordinals used with singulars. Such an expression as 'ten days' is not used. The equivalent statement is an operational one that reaches one day by a suitable count. 'They stayed ten days' becomes 'they stayed until the eleventh day' . . . Our 'length of time' is not regarded as a length but as a relation between two events in lateness. Instead of our linguistically promoted objectification of . . . 'time', the Hopi language has not laid down any pattern that would cloak the subjective 'becoming later' that is the essence of time" (WHORF, p. 140).

WHORF characterizes the thought habits, corresponding to and related to these different linguistic structures, thus: "The Hopi microcosm seems to have analyzed reality largely in terms of events (or better 'eventing') . . ." (p. 147). "A characteristic of Hopi behavior is the emphasis on preparation. This includes announcing and getting ready for events well beforehand . . ." (p. 148). They do not have a number of separate time elements but one continuum. Prayer, song, the preparation of special food, running, racing, dancing, all these are preparatory acts which are frequently repeated. And since time for the Hopi is not a motion but a 'getting later' of all previous events, repetition is not wasted but accumulated.

In contrast to this, SAE, corresponding to our quantified and spatial conception of time, expresses our interest in exact chronological localization, bookkeeping, time wages (equal portions of time have equal value), also our interest in speed and economy of time.

WHORF is not the only one to have demonstrated by means of such intercultural comparisons (i.e., by comparing two speech communities) parallels between linguistic and non-linguistic facts. For example, HOIJER (1951, 1953, 1954) has pointed out the fact that in Navaho, another

North American Indian language, two kinds of verbs perform an important function. Neuter verbs appear to designate 'eventings solidified' into states of being, by virtue of the withdrawal of movement. Active verbs, on the other hand, represent 'eventings in motion'. The nature, direction and status of a movement can be described in this language in a most precise way.

Corresponding to these linguistic facts there are certain parallels in cognition, culture and ideology. The Navahos are nomads. Their gods, too, wander from place to place seeking to maintain by their motion the dynamic flux which, in the Navaho conception, characterizes the universe.

Whereas in SAE sentences frequently present an action and its agent, a person in Navaho is not cause or originator of an action but only associated with it. This is in keeping with what KLUCKHOHN and LEIGHTON (1946) have said about the Navahos and their ideology: they do not strive to master nature but to influence her with songs and rituals.

These examples must suffice. Although they impress, they leave a certain uneasiness. The impression is gained that WHORF, HOIJER and other workers in this area with enormous skill and subtlety have searched out and discovered parallels between intangible sociocultural phenomena and linguistic structures.

It is, however, possible to question the parallelism between them. WHORF'S principle of linguistic relativity and linguistic determinism does not say anything about the manner in which the two are related, nor does it predict where such parallelism is to be expected. However impressive the data are, as scientific evidence they are far too anecdotal and do not lead to precise and testable hypotheses. Nevertheless, these data have enormous value in providing suggestive leads.

Equally suggestive are also the acute observations of poets and writers who have spoken of language as guides to thought. SIMONE DE BEAUVOIR (1958) recounts how her early experiences remained shapeless without words and how the simple vocabulary of her parents, which she adopted, modelled and distorted her experiences without her being able to prevent it, although she was aware of the distortions. The German dramatist KLEIST (1806) spoke of the word as the flywheel on the axle of thought (in MUELLER, 1946).

The critique of WHORF'S views—which, by the way, was less directed against WHORF himself than against some of his over-eager adherents—can be summarized as follows: cases that fit and have a certain plausibility are reported; but no question is raised whether there are not also other cases which do not fit. Since it is impossible to estimate the number of possible kinds of relationships between linguistic and non-linguistic data, it is not possible to say how much importance can be attributed to the individual case in which the relationship has been proved.

The method which has been employed in this area has been made clear by LENNEBERG and ROBERTS (1956) in a fictitious but by no means absurd illustration. Let us assume the claim that there is a relationship between language (C) and national character (K); accordingly, the following matched pairs are produced:

Language conditions (C's)			*National character traits* (K's)	
Japanese:	harsh sounds	purported to correspond to	harsh discipline
German:	complicated sentence structure	purported to correspond to	complicated philosophical thoughts
English:	preponderance of monosyllabic words	purported to correspond to	conciseness; thriftiness

Such matchings are entertaining, perhaps even impressive, but they have no scientific value. The vigor of the Whorfian thought is indicated by the fact that psychologists and anthropologists have felt impelled to take up these ideas and during the past decades have tried to support the WHORF thesis by empirical inquiries.

The basic design of such investigations has been outlined by LENNE-BERG in a fundamental article (1956). Variations of linguistic conditions are matched with variations of non-linguistic behavior in the following manner:

$$C_1 \text{ corresponds to } K_i$$
$$C_2 \text{ corresponds to } K_{ii}$$
$$C_3 \text{ corresponds to } K_{iii}$$
$$\dots\dots\dots\dots\dots\dots\dots$$
$$C_n \text{ corresponds to } K_N$$

The first criterion which must be met in such an investigation consists in defining what varies under C and what varies under K. In the fictitious example quoted above, it is clear that neither in C nor in K are the variations in the same dimensions. LENNEBERG speaks of the *criterion of variation*.

He, secondly, introduces the *criterion of universality*. The feature investigated must be present in all cultures under investigation. For example, the question of whether the Germans have developed their philosophy because of their language or whether the Bororo Indians—equally on account of their language—lack any formal epistemology is in principle unanswerable.

The third of LENNEBERG'S criteria is that of *simplicity*. Commensurability presupposes the construction of descriptive parameters. Thus it is possible to compare measurements of weight because they vary along a single dimension. But if we want to describe the social actions which can be designated by the term 'justice', we need a large number of parameters. The system of co-ordinates required would be so incredibly complex that it would be impossible to describe exactly the difference between the actions to which the term 'justice' applies in the two different cultures.

LENNEBERG now singles out one area which satisfies all three criteria and which is excellently suited to test the WHORF hypothesis: the language of sensory perception, i.e., the words and structures used to designate the sensations of temperature, humidity, light or color. Thus, we reach the major testing ground of the WHORF hypothesis: color coding.

Even in this specialized field there are historically interesting predecessors of modern thought. HOMER'S translators had great difficulties in translating the Greek color terms so that for a time it was thought the Greeks were color-blind. We note here again the tendency to explain a behavioral feature found in many people in terms of a universal physiological characteristic instead of attempting to find an exogenous (sociological or linguistic) determinant of the common feature. In quite a similar way it has long been customary to account for the phenomena of adolescence in terms of biological changes until anthropologists reported the absence of these phenomena in other cultures where the biological changes of puberty are the same as in our own culture.

The earlier examples of the use of the word 'snow' illustrated how a certain sector of nature is coded uniformally in SAE, i.e., is conceived as a single word, while in another language, Eskimo, instead of being coded uniformally, it is subdivided. The two languages dispose of different numbers of words for a certain sector of physical reality. LENNEBERG and BROWN have spoken of the varying degrees of 'codability' of this sector in different languages.

The concept of codability is not confined in its application to lexical items and physical reality; it can equally be applied to grammatical operations (e.g., the differences in arrangement of word-classes discussed on p. 312) and to non-physical realities (e.g., kinship structures).

Prima facie, therefore, this presents only a coding phenomenon or differentiation of linguistic organization. This observation becomes an argument in favor of WHORF only through the claim that non-linguistic distinctions correspond to the linguistic differentiation.

How does this apply now to color perception ? The human organism can distinguish approximately 7,500,000 hues. English has nearly 4,000 color terms, but only eight of these are used frequently. Broadly expressed, it can be said that in order to encode 7,500,000 possibilities, 4,000 terms (and eight common words) are available. In this area too—as always in most natural languages—coding involves a marked reduction of multiplicity.

Different languages use different color categories. In the Iakuti language there is only one term for what is named by two in SAE: blue and green. In SAE, therefore, one region or dimension of experience is differentiated which is undifferentiated in the Iakuti language.

Now all color dimensions are continuous: red is linked to orange through gradual transition; orange merges gradually into yellow and then into green, and so on.

One objection may be expected at this point; what about the 'primary colors'? Where do they come in? Why is there a tendency to regard red, blue and yellow as primary colors, or why is it sometimes claimed that red, blue, yellow and green are primary colors? There are no arguments on physical grounds for the assumption of certain colors as primary. All that the so-called color-mixing rules claim is that one has to operate with three colors if one wants to produce all the shades of the color circle. Even certain findings made by GRANIT, which may establish probable physiological connections with the primary color problem do not affect the conclusion that the question, 'What are the primary colors?' should be treated mainly as a semantic problem (cf. WEISGERBER, 1962b).

Where language draws sharp boundaries there are no corresponding physical boundaries. There is no physical criterion to determine up to what point one has to use the term 'red' and from which point onwards one has to say 'yellow'.

Let us assume a speaker of SAE is asked to name a point × on the spectral continuum (Fig. 69). He will probably hesitate whether to call it green, blue, or blue-green, etc.

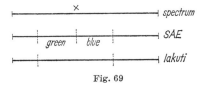

Fig. 69

The Iakuti speaker, on the other hand, will use the term applicable to the whole area without hesitation. The hue × is more difficult to code in SAE than in Iakuti.

From this observation we are led to the fundamental question of psycholinguistic interest: does the difference in codability affect the nonverbal behavior? A positive reply to this question would broadly lend support to the validity of the WHORF thesis at least in its general form.

This question has been studied experimentally by BROWN and LENNEBERG (1954). Their experiment, which is particularly noteworthy because it stands in contrast to the prevailing tendency to speculate about this question, deserves to be examined in detail.

As a first step, the concept of codability had to be defined operationally. This was done by asking five judges to pick out the 'best' red, orange, yellow, green, blue, purple, pink and brown from 240 chips showing all the hues of the color circle. This indicated a very high degree of agreement among the judges. A further 16 hues were added to those eight so that the choices ranged as evenly as possible over the whole color circle.

In the first experiment carried out with the material which had thus been prepared, 24 subjects had the task of naming as rapidly as possible each color chip as it was presented. Among the measures calculated were the following:

(a) the number of syllables which on the average were used to name a particular color.

The authors thus follow a suggestion made by DOOB (1952), i.e., to relate the WHORF thesis to the results of ZIPF'S investigations. According to ZIPF, the more frequently a term is used in a language, the shorter it is likely to be. From this, one can in turn infer that the number of syllables (or phonemes) offers a clue to the currency of a term in a particular language. BROWN defines this conclusion as follows: the existence of a monosyllabic term in preference to a polysyllabic one suggests a high degree of cognitive availability of the particular principle of categorization.

(b) average reaction time from the moment of presentation of the color to the utterance of the color term as another measure of the relationship between codability and availability.

(c) the degree of agreement in the terms used by the subjects for a particular color.

These (and some other) measures were correlated. Table 29 presents the results.

Table 29. *Correlation matrix for five indices of codability* (based on BROWN and LENNEBERG, 1954, p. 459)

Measure	1	2	3	4	5
Number of syllables					
Number of words	.425*				
Reaction-time	.387	.368			
Interpersonal agreement	.630*	.486*	.864*		
Intrapersonal agreement	.355	.537*	.649*	.773*	
k from second factoring	.589	.587	.787	.976	.795
Communality from first factoring	.403	.378	.671	.873	.653

* $p \leq .05$

If one factor is extracted from this matrix, only a few correlations are left. This means that a single factor is sufficient to account mathematically for these coefficients of correlation. BROWN and LENNEBERG have named this factor 'codability'.

In this way, it was, first of all, possible to define operationally the factor of codability as the exact composite value of the above measures; and only after that was done was the attempt made to correlate it with non-linguistic behavior.

The non-linguistic behavior selected by the authors was color recognition. A set of four colors was presented to each subject simultaneously. After an interval the subjects were asked to pick out the same colors from a color chart consisting of 120 different colors.

The question to be studied was whether codability had an influence upon retention and recognition. The answer to this question lies in the correlation coefficient between codability and recognition score: .415. The more easily a color is coded, the better it is remembered. The conclusions of the BROWN-LENNEBERG study can be formulated as follows. Differences in codability are related to differences in availability. And if instead of this restricted formulation one prefers a more generalized one, it may be said that a connection between verbal and non-verbal behavior —as postulated by the WHORF hypothesis—is probably established.

This investigation was made within one culture; that is to say, it investigated distinctions, matched by verbal differences, within one culture or speech community. The fundamental relevance of such studies for the discussion and evaluation of the WHORF hypothesis has already been explained above (p. 310). Nevertheless, complementary cross-cultural comparisons are also of great interest; such a study was carried out by LENNEBERG and ROBERTS (1953, cited in BROWN and LENNEBERG, 1954, p. 461).

In Zuni there is only one term for yellow and orange. If the above experiment is repeated with Zuni Indians, it appears that yellow and orange are confused much more frequently by Zuni Indians than by English-speaking Americans. It is interesting to note that the performance of those Zunis who also speak English falls between that of monolingual Zunis and monolingual English-speaking Americans.

Confirmation of the evidence provided in these investigations for the validity (or, perhaps better, the fruitfulness) of the WHORF hypothesis, can be found in numerous studies quite unconnected with psycholinguistics, which have demonstrated the positive influence of verbal coding on learning and retention. Anything which can be named or can be given a verbal label is learned more easily and less easily forgotten. The concept of 'schema', which has profitably been employed by investigators, ranging from HEAD via BARTLETT to PIAGET, in the study of memory and intelligence, is generally applied to a verbally encoded schema.

Of particular interest in this connection is a new development within the psychology of perception. In contrast to the traditional conceptions of the act of perception, in which between seeing the stimulus and the response an organization-phase is interposed, GLANZER has developed the verbal-loop hypothesis. The notion of the organization-phase had, largely as a result of Gestalt psychology, found recognition in the explanation of the act of perception. Thus, four dots : : are organized into a whole. GLANZER specifies the concept of organization which, in his view, is too vague, as covert verbalization. According to his view, the subject sees the stimulus, translates it into words and according to this translation makes his response. The most impressive evidence for this theory is the following. A stimulus is all the more difficult to identify accurately (accuracy being defined as correctness of reproduction) the more complicated and longer the words in which it can be formulated. If GLANZER'S results are confirmed in investigations under varying conditions, this would constitute one of the weightiest arguments for the heuristic value of the WHORF hypothesis—at least in its more restricted form (see below for what is meant by this restriction).

GLANZER'S views make it possible, however, to relate the WHORF hypothesis of linguistic determinism to a totally different sector of psycholinguistics, i.e., LIBERMAN'S motor theory of speech perception (see pp. 62ff.). According to this theory, the perception of speech involves the covert repetition of the articulation needed for speech production. The speech event to be perceived must in a kind of way be spoken by the listener or repeated in his own voice before he can register it. GLANZER, going beyond that, makes such verbalizing not only a necessary phase of speech perception but of perception in general. If, therefore, in this process verbal and non-verbal stimuli confronting us have to run through a phase of translation into language or verbal encoding on their way to apperception, it is reasonable to assume that such apperceptions—our view of the external world and our thinking about it—are partly determined by the verbal containers and structures which are at the disposal of the receiving individual for this intermediate phase. It is now possible to understand that not only those items which are available in verbal concepts (which belong to what WEISGERBER would call 'the linguistic intermediate sphere') are subject to linguistic relativity; even the things of direct reality are passed through a grid of verbal structures and distorted. Whether certain plants are 'weeds' in a country depends on the language of the inhabitants of this country. Likewise, the snow falling from the sky and melting in spring is a problem of semantics. If ARIS-

TOTLE had spoken a different language, say Chinese or Hopi, instead of Greek, we would operate today with a different kind of logic[1].

The thesis of language as a determiner of thought and perception and especially the thesis of psycholinguistic relativity of the thought in a given language have both been very influential in recent years. Nevertheless, criticisms have been voiced and objections have been raised which have somehow reduced the claim of absolute validity with which the WHORF hypothesis (less by WHORF himself than by his disciples) has been put forward.

The criticism of WHORF'S method of inquiry has already been reported. In the following paragraphs the objections to be outlined are those that have been made from the psycholinguistic and philosophical point of view.

Among these are certain findings in developmental psychology which need mentioning first of all. The absence of parallelism in linguistic and cognitive growth in childhood has been stressed repeatedly—to name only a few— by KÖHLER, VIGOTSKY and PIAGET, who have demonstrated, in different ways, intelligent and cognitive operations in non-verbal behavior.

If, for a moment, we assume the validity of the WHORF thesis, it would mean that it would be impossible for intercultural differences in nonverbal areas (e.g., of concepts) to be greater than the differences in verbal fields. It is certain that WHORF has given a picture of the differences between languages which is too one-sided. Besides the differences to which WHORF has drawn attention, there are also communalities which we are inclined to accept as a matter of course. GREENBERG, OSGOOD, MILLER and others have opposed the concept of language universals to the WHORF notion of linguistic relativity.

Such language universals have already been encountered in BROWN'S investigation in the forms of address (pp. 308f.). Universals occur on different levels. Thus, for example, all languages can be analyzed into sequences of a few phonemes. Approximately a dozen phonological features are sufficient to signal the required distinctions. In all languages can be found a restricted number of syntactic classes. In all languages the admissible word sequences (sentences) are produced with the help of a finite number of grammatical rules. All languages have subject-predicate constructions.

It is around this point that the sharpest controversy rages among the experts (e.g., WHORF on one side and GREENBERG on the other). In this respect it would indeed appear to be a matter of greatest importance for psycholinguists to clarify whether the subject-predicate construction is a universal. In an earlier chapter

---

[1] e.g., it would in all probability not contain the law of excluded middle.

(pp. 285ff.) we discussed in detail the role of predication in the language development of the individual.

All languages know the principal verbal operators ('and', 'not', 'or'); all languages tackle in some way the notions of space and time. 'I', 'you' and 'he' occur in all languages. Everywhere, questions and answers follow an alternating pattern[1].

These language universals are so much a matter of course that they are noticed less than the more striking interlinguistic differences which constitute the basis of the thesis of linguistic relativity.

OSGOOD (1962a), for example, recognizes the evidence reported above for the reality of linguistic relativity. He calls it 'denotative relativity'; but on the basis of his own inquiries he is able to oppose it with the existence of 'connotative universality'. In different languages, ratings on the semantic differential of a particular word and its translation into other languages produce congruent results.

Such observations suggest that it depends on the subject of investigation whether we will find relativity or universality. Investigations on denotative relations produce evidence for the thesis of relativity; inquiries on connotative relations yield results supporting the thesis of universality.

At any rate the existence of such language universals draws attention once more to the biological basis of language, hence to features which apply to the whole species. The arbitrariness of the decision to play a certain language-game, as suggested by WITTGENSTEIN, is kept within bounds by what is biologically given (LENNEBERG, 1960).

The WHORF thesis assumes the unidirectional determination of language giving form to thought. If linguistic universals are taken into account, the view reached will be that of MILLER, who writes: "If it is true, as WHORF and SAPIR believed, that our language shapes our psychology, then it is at least equally true that our psychology shapes our language" (1963, p. 418).

The relationship between codability and availability, which has been adduced as evidence for the validity of the case for relativity, has been critically examined by FRENCH (1963), among others. In the BROWN-LENNEBERG type of investigation, codability has generally been interpreted either as uniformity of designation attributed to an object by different speakers or as brevity of designation. But there are, of course, also unusual 'original' terms which, in spite of their novelty, may be understood by the listener immediately. If a speaker calls a particular color 'Swiss-cheese colored', he employs an unusual term of considerable phonemic

---

[1] This does not mean to say that both partners cannot talk simultaneously. The masking capacity of the human voice is not sufficiently great to exclude this possibility.

length which nevertheless conveys a uniform meaning to speakers of English.

Here an impression is encoded in an unusual form; but a non-linguistic uniformity within the linguistic community, i.e., everybody knows Swiss cheese, guarantees the consistency of the listener's reaction to this unusual creation: a member of the speech community will, for example, easily remember the color so described.

This leads us to one of the principal objections to WHORF's procedures. They are linguistically too atomistic. He takes isolated words from different languages ('snow') and, comparing these, notes that the category which this word designates in one language has not the same coverage as the category designated by the translation 'equivalent' (which is not an equivalent). As the grids in the two languages do not coincide, he is led to the conclusions which are embodied in the theory of linguistic relativity.

In the analysis of structural peculiarities, too, WHORF proceeds in the same atomistic manner: for example, he notes that the verb in one language functions differently from the verb in another language. However, the work and function of a language do not result from the sequential arrangement of separate words, nor from the stringing together of single word classes or other grammatical structures. If the word A in language Alpha is not matched by a similarly defined word A' in language Beta, who can say that in Beta one cannot express with the words A' + F' + N' what in language Alpha has been expressed with A? Even if—in contrast to Navaho—we have no special class of verbs to express 'eventings solidified' by class membership, we may still be capable, by means of corresponding adjectives and adverbs, to express the state which the Indian speaker wants to express and no doubt expresses more succinctly.

The WHORF view is based entirely on the notion of an independent study of semantics. But in an earlier part of this book (chapter 8) we have already explained in detail why the meaning of a word cannot be reduced to an unambiguous and simple word-thing relationship. The inclusion of the language-user and of the situation leads beyond the simple reference function of language which WHORF had in mind. (WHORF, so to speak, 'blames' language for imperfections in the word-thing relationship.) LONGACRE (1956), in a subtle criticism of the WHORF thesis in which he contrasts the views of WHORF and URBAN, emphatically stresses that language is less a grid than a calculus. The context of a word always participates in a decisive manner in the specification of its pragmatic-semantic meaning. WHORF is so concerned with the process of classification—a process which is undoubtedly present in language—that his thesis is basically more a thesis of the relativity of lexical and grammatical features than of the relativity of language in general. In spite of difficulties, translation *is* possible, and the distinction between 'amour' in French and 'love' in English is no greater than the distinction between the meanings of Jack's 'love' and of Jill's 'love'.

WHORF emphasises the differences between languages. He denies the justification of speaking of language in general: "'It may even be in the cards that there is no such thing as "Language" (with a capital L) at all'" (from LONGACRE 1956, p. 300). Opposed to this we find BÜHLER'S view that the whole enterprise of language theory (and we might add of psycholinguistics) is based on the presupposition of the existence of 'human language in the singular' (1934, p. 141).

In a similar way, although supported by different arguments, criticism from a Marxist point of view has been put forward against WHORF and the related notions of General Semantics (still to be discussed below). The case for relativity as an approach to reality had been made in Marxist terms by MARR. Language is dependent upon society and social class, and differences will correspondingly be found. This view, however, offends the Marxian doctrine that reality can be grasped by the human mind: the thesis of linguistic relativity is apt to lead to questioning the validity of linguistically formulated ideologies. It is therefore quite understandable that STALIN himself (1950) upheld against MARR'S 'deviation' the view that language was universally binding for all members of society. According to the theories of linguistic relativity and linguistic determinism, human behavior is so much determined by verbal signals that, in the opinions of Marxian theorists (e.g., BRUTYAN, 1962, and NEUBERT, 1962), this approach implies an underestimation of the importance of economic factors.

The view that different languages reflect reality in different ways and therefore necessarily introduce an element of distortion (because reality can only be reached by means of language) has been attacked from two sides: by ST. AUGUSTINE and WITTGENSTEIN. ST. AUGUSTINE says: "If no one asks me, I know; but if I want to explain to someone who asks me, I do not know." This refers to a form of knowing preceding verbal formulation and at the same time resisting such formulation. If this kind of knowledge is possible, language is a prison which man enters by speaking.

On the other hand, WITTGENSTEIN adopts an extreme Whorfian view by making such statements as: "Grammar tells what kind of object anything is" (1958, § 373). WITTGENSTEIN goes so far as to make the question of the relationship between language and reality meaningless—a question which is central to WHORF because, according to WITTGENSTEIN, reality is only constituted in language and by means of language. There is no fixed reference point by means of which the internally completely consistent language-game could be made relative to something else. Whereas in ST. AUGUSTINE'S view man enters the prison of language only by speaking, in WITTGENSTEIN'S view there is no question of imprisonment because there is nothing outside it.

The attempt to establish a philosophical formulation of WHORF'S metalinguistics leads to no conclusion, except to the sceptical questioning whether language is an instrument in the hands of human thought or whether thought is drawn along avenues prepared by language.

From this sceptical position two trends of thought have developed: one, in a somewhat naive way, aims at language improvement in the expectation of making language more effective, and the other, more profoundly, tries to change our attitude to language and therefore to reduce human conflicts. The first can be found here and there in different places, while the second has been formalized under the name of General Semantics.

The attempt to improve the effectiveness of language — which inevitably leads to the question of the criterion by which to measure such improvement — can be illustrated for example by STEGER'S argument[1]: the standard language must always be a tool which is appropriate to the thought of a given age. The boldest discoveries of our time are expressed in the special languages of chemistry, mathematics and physics; for example, in our everyday standard language, the sun still 'rises' and 'sets' in spite of the fact that it has been known for five hundred years that the sun does not do anything of the sort. Our language can make the poetry of the eighteenth and nineteenth centuries ring in our ears, yet it is quite incapable of expressing the newer discoveries about the universe. "An improved, i.e., more consistent use of language than the common standard language would be able to express thoughts in a more profound and more comprehensive way" (1962, p. 196).

This view — like, incidentally, also that of the General Semanticists — expresses an enviable belief in progress. Yet a thoughtful observer will ask whether the sun does not 'rise' and 'set' after all: in other words, whether the world of the physicist or of the scientist in general must necessarily form the basis of everyday language. Is everyday language most effective when it is determined by the sciences ? In STEGER'S view everyday language should be guided by the current state of knowledge — but is it not equally possible that the current thought of an age is guided by everyday language ? It would be a rewarding task for diachronic psycholinguistics to analyse the *Zeitgeist* ('mind of an age') from this point of view.

A further attempt to improve the effectiveness of language is a partial task of what is commonly known as 'cybernetics'. The application of a

---

[1] *Translator's note.* HUGO STEGER is a distinguished contemporary Germanist.

terminology, originally developed in technology, to such areas as biology, psychology, sociology and even educational science has undoubtedly enormously enriched these disciplines. Formulations have been found for new relationships, and new connections have been made visible, thus confirming in a most eloquent way the interdependence between language and thought. Equally, however, this kind of development reveals the other side of the coin: the terminology developed round the original cybernetic model exercises a directing influence upon the biologist, psychologist, or any other scientist who operates with it. It is quite possible that those who make use of these concepts do not even know to what extent their thinking follows avenues determined by the language they employ.

General Semantics is less concerned with the improvement of the effectiveness of language than with the improvement of human relationships. This discipline is in a way an 'applied' science. It aims at creating an awareness of linguistic relativity and linguistic determinism in order to prevent language from taking over thought.

As a school of thought, General Semantics was established by KORZYB-SKI, a Pole who came to live in the USA. His principal work significantly carries the title of *Science and Sanity*. His views largely coincide with those expressed by WHORF, although both developed their ideas independently of each other. One difference, however, is that KORZYBSKI and, following him, HAYAKAWA, JOHNSON, RAPAPORT and others have drawn pedagogical consequences from the interdependence of language and thought. In WHORF'S work the relationship between language and *thought* is central, while in General Semantics the central relationship is between language and *thinker* (or more precisely the relationship between language and the inadequate thinker). The individual who is the primary concern of General Semantics is the person who identifies the structure of language with the structure of reality. The chief principle of General Semantics is that language and reality are related in the same way as a map is to the terrain to which it refers (i.e., the principle of *non-identity*). Language, therefore, is not an image of *reality*: at best it is an image of the *structure* of reality.

From this follow a number of interesting implications. In WHORF'S view—inasmuch as he comments on this at all—reality is unstructured. It is given structure by the language in which it is conceived. For KORZYB-SKI, however, reality *is* structured: the map, therefore, can be more or less accurate. The structural concordance between map and terrain, which is of interest to General Semantics, is akin to the principle of isomorphism of Gestalt psychology where, equally, similarity of structure, for example, links different levels: stimulus, retina, cortex, etc. in an act of perception (cf. KÖHLER, 1924).

The second principle of General Semantics is *incompleteness*. The representations in language are always less than what is represented. The map inevitably ignores details of the terrain.

Finally, the third principle of General Semantics is that of *self-reflexiveness*. We use language to speak about language; we make judgments about judgments; we evaluate values.

All these principles can be considered to be features of the process of abstraction which is fundamental to all language. This process of abstraction can be removed to varying degrees from the level of the concrete event. If, for example, we speak of 'a statement about a statement', the word 'statement' is used on two different levels of abstraction. Such terms are described in General Semantics as multiordinal; 'yes', 'no', 'true', 'false', 'agreement', 'non-agreement', 'relationship', 'number', 'structure', 'love', 'hate'—all these and many other words are multiordinal. It is characteristic of these multiordinal words that they have different meanings on different levels of abstraction; the first 'statement' in our example is on a higher level of abstraction than the second.

The multiordinality of many words enriches our vocabulary in an extraordinary way, but it is also a source of misunderstandings and conflicts if one is not aware of them.

In this connection the reader will recall the discussion in chapter 8 of BERTRAND RUSSELL'S theory of types. The example of the lying Cretan showed that, if a judgment is made about all judgments of a given class, this judgment does not itself fall into the same class. General Semantics would in this instance point out the multiordinality of the word 'judgment' and recommend as a measure of precaution the distinguishing subscripts judgment$_1$ and judgment$_2$.

There is a certain Socratic note about General Semantics which rests upon the conviction that making oneself aware of the traps of language is sufficient to circumvent them.

Once we know that a verbal statement is not reality, that past is not present, that Communism$_{1950}$ is not Communism$_{1965}$, that intelligent$_{John}$ is not intelligent$_{Jack}$, we will no longer regard the linguistic event as the signal for a ready-made, prejudiced reaction ('He is an American, no wonder ...'). Instead, we will conceive the verbal event as such, i.e., as a symbol; therefore we will not react to the verbal event but to the non-verbal reality symbolized by the verbal event.

General Semantics sees as its aim an education for 'extensional orientation', i.e., an orientation towards the reality of the world. This stands in contrast to 'intensional orientation', orientation towards words or verbal labels. Man's behavior must not be directed by 'semantic' or 'signal' reactions, i.e., reactions evoked by the sound of what is heard or thought, therefore reactions which are prefabricated and hence prejudiced. In order to react it is not sufficient to identify the stimulus in a rough and ready manner (e.g., as the term 'police') and then to make the stereotyped response (e.g., to police-in-general). It is important to control behavior in such a way that pauses may be interposed between the verbal stimulus and the response, so as to identify the symbol as a symbol, to advance from the symbol to the object symbolized and to grasp it with its differentiations (which are always simplified by the symbol). In this way the delayed symbol reaction will not be guided by a word but by reality.

The thesis of linguistic determinism leads to this realization: language is not simply an instrument we control; it controls us. The same language which adds a dimension of freedom to our existence appears to us at the end of this book as a power in its own right and, indeed, as overpowering. To a certain extent language seems to travel past what we proudly feel to be our 'real' capacities. Through language many bygone generations help to shape our thoughts. As we speak we 'educate' future generations as yet unborn.

We can look at language in another way, somewhat less pessimistically. Man is not always and not only the victim of his language. Whoever creates language, which in its purest form will be poetic creation—but in effect such creations can occur anywhere—shares in the creation of our world. Whoever forms new sentences about a sunset enriches the nation whose language he speaks. The psychology of language ends where poetry begins. Somewhere between the gain and loss of freedom which the possession of language implies is the true center of human existence. The self is surrounded by the mirrors of language.

Bibliography

ACH, N.: Zur psychologischen Grundlegung der sprachlichen Verständigung. Ber. 12. Kongr. Dtsch. Ges. Psychol., Hamburg, 1931. Jena: Fischer 1932, 122—133.

ACKER, L. E., EDWARDS, A. E.: Transfer of vasoconstriction over a bipolar meaning dimension. J. Exp. Psychol. **67**, No. 1, 1—6 (1964).

ADELSON, M., MUCKLER, F. A., WILLIAMS, A. C.: Verbal learning and message variables related to amount of information. In: Information Theory in Psychology. Edited by QUASTLER, H. Glencoe, Ill.: Free Press 1955, 291—299.

AEBLI, H.: Über die geistige Entwicklung des Kindes. Stuttgart: Klett 1963.

AJURIAGUERRA, J. DE, BRESSON, F., FRAISSE, P., INHELDER, B., OLÉRON, P., PIAGET, J.: (Eds).: Problèmes de psycholinguistique. Paris: Presses Universitaires de France 1963.

ALBRECHT, E.: Beiträge zur Erkenntnistheorie und das Verhältnis von Sprache und Denken. Halle (Saale): Niemeyer 1959.

ALLESCH, J. von: Zur nichteuklidischen Struktur des phänomenalen Raumes. Jena: Fischer 1931.

—: Über das Verhältnis des Allgemeinen zum realen Einzelnen. Arch. ges. Psychol. **111**, 23—38 (1942).

AMMER, K.: Sprache, Mensch und Gesellschaft. Halle (Saale): Niemeyer 1961.

APEL, K.-O.: Sprache und Wahrheit in der gegenwärtigen Situation der Philosophie. Philos. Rdsch. **7**, 161—184 (1959a).

—: Der philosophische Wahrheitsbegriff einer inhaltlich orientierten Sprachwissenschaft. In: Sprache—Schlüssel zur Welt. Festschrift für L. Weisgerber. Düsseldorf: Päd. Verlag Schwann 1959b, 11—38.

—: Sprache und Ordnung. In: Das Problem der Ordnung. 6. Dtsch. Kongr. Philos. München, 1960. Edited by KUHN, H., WIEDMANN, F. Meisenheim am Glan: A. Hain 1962, 200—225.

—: Die Idee der Sprache in der Tradition des Humanismus von Dante bis Vico. Arch. Begriffsgesch. 8, (1963).

—: Sprachanalyse als Metaphysikkritik. Lecture at the Free University of Berlin, February 22, 1965.

ATTNEAVE, F.: Applications of information theory to psychology: A summary of basic concepts, methods, and results. New York: Holt, Rinehart and Winston 1959.

AUSUBEL, D. P.: A subsumption theory of meaningful verbal learning and retention. J. Gen. Psychol. **66**, No. 2, 213—224 (1962).

BARTLETT, F. C.: Remembering. A study in experimental and social psychology. Cambridge: Cambridge University Press 1950 (1st Ed. 1932).

BASILIUS, H.: Neo-Humboldtian ethnolignuistics. Word, 8, 95—105 (1952).

BAY, E.: Principles of classification and their influence on our concepts of aphasia. In: Disorders of Language. Ed. by DE REUCK, A. V. S., O'CONNOR, M. London: J. and A. Churchill 1964, 122—142.

BEAUVOIR, S. DE: Mémoires d'une jeune fille rangée. Paris: Gallimard 1958.

BECKER, K. F.: Organismus der Sprache. Frankfurt (Main): G. F. Kettenbeil 1841.

BELLUGI, U., BROWN, R. W. (Eds.): The acquisition of language. Monogr. Soc. Res. Child Develpm. **29**, No. 1, serial No. 51 (1964).

BENJAMIN,W.: San Gimignano. In: Städtebilder. Frankfurt (Main): Suhrkamp 1963.

BENTLEY, M., VARON, E. J.: An accessory study of 'phonetic symbolism'. Amer. J. Psychol. **45**, No. 1, 76—86 (1933).

BERGIUS, R. (Ed.): Handbuch der Psychologie. Vol. 1: Allgemeine Psychologie, Part 2: Lernen und Denken. Göttingen: Verlag für Psychologie 1964.

BERGSON, H.: L'Evolution créatrice. Paris: Félix Alcan 1907. English Edition: Creative Evolution. Translated by MITCHELL, A. London: Macmillan 1954.

BERKO, J.: The child's learning of English morphology. Word **14**, Nos. 2—3, 150—177 (1958).

—, BROWN, R. W.: Psycholinguistic research methods. Handbook of research methods in child development. Edited by MUSSEN, P. H. New York: Wiley 1960, 517—557.

BERLYNE, D. E.: Novelty and curiosity as determinants of exploratory behaviour. Brit. J. Psychol. **41**, Nos. 1—2, 68—80 (1950).

—: Knowledge and stimulus-response psychology. Psychol. Rev. **61**, No. 4, 245—254 (1954a).

—: A theory of human curiosity. An experimental study of human curiosity. Brit. J. Psychol. **45**, No. 3, 180—191 (1954b).

BETZ, W.: Zur Überprüfung des Feldbegriffs. Z. vergleich. Sprachforsch., **71**, 189—198 (1954).

BIXLER, R. H., YEAGER, H. C.: It may have begun with 'mama'. Psychol. Rep. **4**, 471—475 (1958).

BLOCH, E.: Tübinger Einleitung in die Philosophie. I. Frankfurt (Main): Suhrkamp. 1963.

BLOCK, J.: Commonality in word association and personality. Psychol. Rep. **7**, 332 (1960).

BLODGETT, H. C.: The effect of the introduction of reward upon the maze performance of rats. University of California Publications in Psychology. **4**, No. 8, 113—134 (1929).

BLÖSCHL, L.: Neue Experimente zum Problem der vermittelten Assoziationen. Z. exper. angew. Psychol. **8**, 297—310 (1961).

BLOOMFIELD, L.: A set of postulates for the science of language. Language **2**, 153—164 (1926). Reprinted in Psycholinguistics. Edited by SAPORTA, S. New York: Holt, Rinehart and Winston 1961, 26—33.

—: Language. New York: Henry Holt 1933.

BOUSFIELD, W. A.: The occurrence of clustering in the recall of randomly arranged associates. J. Gen. Psychol. **49**, No. 2, 229—240 (1953).

—: The problem of meaning in verbal learning. In: Verbal Learning and Verbal Behavior. Edited by COFER, C. N. New York: McGraw-Hill 1961, 81—91.

—, WHITMARSH, G. A., BERKOWITZ, H.: Partial response identities in associative clustering. J. Gen. Psychol. **63**, No. 2, 233—238 (1960).

BRACKBILL, Y., LITTLE, K. B.: Factors determining the guessing of meanings of foreign words. J. abnorm. soc. Psychol. **54**, 312—318 (1957).

BRAINE, M. D. S.: On learning the grammatical order of words. Psychol. Rev., **70**, No. 4, 323—348 (1963a).

—: The ontogeny of English phrase structure: the first phase. Language **39**, No. 1, 1—13 (1963b).

BRIDGMAN, P. W.: The nature of physical theory. New York: Wiley 1964.

—: The operational aspect of meaning. Synthèse **8**, 251—259 (1950—51).

—: The way things are. Cambridge, Mass.: Harvard University Press 1959.

BRINKMANN, H.: Der deutsche Satz als sprachliche Gestalt. Wirkendes Wort. (Supplement) 1952, 12—26.

—: Die Struktur des Satzes im Deutschen. Neuphilol. Mitt. 60, 377—401 (1959).

BROADBENT, D. E.: Perception and communication. London: Pergamon Press 1958.

—: Behaviour. New York: Basic Books 1961.

— : Perceptual and response factors in the organization of speech. In: Disorders of language. Edited by DE REUCK, A. V. S., O'CONNOR, M. London: J. and A. Churchill 1964, 79—92.

BROWN, R. W.: Language and categories. In: A study of thinking by BRUNER, J. S., GOODNOW, J. J., AUSTIN, G. A.. New York: Science Editions 1956, Appendix, 247—312.

—: Linguistic determinism and the part of speech. J. abnorm. soc. Psychol. 55, No. 1, 1—5 (1957).

—: Words and things. Glencoe, Ill.: Free Press 1958a. —

—: How shall a thing be called? Psychol. Rev. 65, No. 1, 14—21 (1958b).

—: The language of social relationship. Proc. 16th Int. Congr. Psychol., Bonn, 1960. Amsterdam: North-Holland 1962, 663—667.

—, BELLUGI, U.: Three processes in the child's acquisition of syntax. Harv. educ. Rev. 34, No. 2, 133—151 (1964).

—, BERKO, J.: Word association and the acquisition of grammar. Child Develpm. 31, No. 1, 1—14 (1960).

—, BLACK, A. H., HOROWITZ, A. E.: Phonetic symbolism in natural languages. J. abnorm soc. Psychol. 50, No. 3, 388—393 (1955).

—, DULANEY, D. E.: A stimulus-response analysis of language and meaning. In: Language, thought and culture. Edited by HENLEY, P. Ann Arbor, Mich.: University of Michigan Press 1965, 49—65.

—, FORD, M.: Address in American English. J. abnorm. soc. Psychol. 62, 375—385 (1961).

—, FRASER, C.: The acquisition of syntax. In: Verbal behavior and learning. Edited by COFER, C. N., MUSGRAVE, B. S. New York: McGraw-Hill 1963, 158—197.

—, GILMAN, A.: The pronouns of power and solidarity. In: Style in language. Edited by SEBEOK, T. A. New York: Wiley 1960, 253—276.

—, LENNEBERG, E. H.: A study in language and cognition. J. abnorm. soc. Psychol. 49, No. 3, 454—462 (1954).

—, NUTTALL, R.: Method in phonetic symbolism experiments. J. abnorm. soc. Psychol. 59, No. 3, 441—445 (1959).

BRUNER, J. S.: Going beyond the information given. In: Contemporaty approaches to cognition. By BRUNER, J. S. et al. Cambridge, Mass.: Harvard University Press, 1957a, 41—69.

—: On perceptual readiness. Psychol. Rev. 64, 123—152 (1957b).

—, GOONDOW, J. J., AUSTIN, G. A.: A study of thinking. New York: Science Editions 1956.

—, BRUNSWICK, E., FESTINGER, L., HEIDER, F., MUENZINGER, K. F., OSGOOD, C. E., RAPAPORT, D.: Contemporary approaches to cognition. Cambridge, Mass.: Harvard University Press 1957.

BRUTYAN, G. A.: A marxist evaluation of the WHORF hypothesis. ETC.: A review of general semantics, 19, No. 2, 199—220 (1962).

BUBER, M.: Urdistanz und Beziehung. Heidelberg: Schneider 1951.

BÜHLER, K.: Das Ganze der Sprachtheorie, ihr Aufbau und ihre Teile. Ber. 12. Kongr. Dtsch. Ges. Psychol., Hamburg, 1931. Jena: Fischer 1932, 95—122.

—: Sprachtheorie. Jena: Fischer, 1934.

CARMICHAEL, L. (Ed.): Manual of child psychology. New York: Wiley 1954.
—: The early growth of language capacity in the individual. In: New directions in the study of language. Edited by LENNEBERG, E. H. Cambridge, Mass.: M.I.T. Press 1964, 1—22.

CARNAP, R.: Philosophy and logical syntax. London: K. Paul, Trench, Trubner 1935.
—: The logical syntax of language. Translated by SMEATON, A. London: Routledge and K. Paul 1937.
—: Introduction to semantics. Cambridge, Mass.: Harvard University Press 1948.
—: Empiricism semantics and ontology. Rev. int. de Philos. 4, No. 11, 20—40 (1950).

CARROLL, J. B.: Diversity of vocabulary and the harmonic series law of word-frequency distribution. Psychol. Rec. 2, 379—386 (1938).
—: The study of language. A survey of linguistics and related disciplines in America. Cambridge, Mass.: Harvard University Press 1955.
—: Review of "The measurement of meaning" by OSGOOD, C. E. et al. Language, 35, No. 1, 58—77 (1959).
—: Language and thought. Englewood Cliffs, N. J.: Prentice-Hall 1964a.
—: Words, meanings, and concepts. Harv. educ. Rev. 34, No. 2, 178—202 (1964b).
—, KJELDERGAARD, P. M., CARTON, A. S.: Number of opposites versus number of primaries as a response measure in free-association tests. J. verb. Learning verb. Behavior 1, No. 1, 22—30 (1962—63).

CARTERETTE, E. C., MØLLER, A.: The perception of real and synthetic vowels after very sharp filtering. Proc. Speech Communication Seminar — 1962. II. Stockholm: Speech Transmission Laboratory, Royal Institute of Technology, 1963.

CASSIRER, E.: Die Sprache und der Aufbau der Gegenstandswelt. Ber. 12. Kongr. Dtsch. Ges. Psychol., Hamburg, 1931. Jena: Fischer 1932, 134—145.
—: An essay on man — An introduction to a philosophy of human culture. New Haven: Yale University Press, 1944.
—: Philosophie der symbolischen Formen. I: Die Sprache. Darmstadt: Wissenschaftliche Buchgesellschaft 1964. English Ed.: The philosophy of symbolic forms. I: Language. Translated by MANHEIM, R. New Haven: Yale University Press 1953.

CATTELL, J. McK.: Über die Zeit der Erkennung und Benennung von Schriftzeichen, Bildern und Farben. Philos. Stud. 2, 635—650 (1885).
—: Psychometrische Untersuchungen. Philos. Stud. 3, 452—492 (1886).

CHERRY, C.: On human communication. A review, a survey, and a criticism. New York: Wiley 1957.

CHOMSKY, N.: Syntactic structures. 's Gravenhage: Mouton 1957.
—: Review of "Verbal behavior" by SKINNER, B. F. Language 35, No. 1, 26—58 (1959). Reprinted in: The structure of language. Edited by FODOR, J. A., KATZ, J. J. Englewood Cliffs, N. J.: Prentice-Hall, 1964, 547—578; and: Readings in the psychology of language. Edited by JAKOBOVITS, L. A., MIRON, M. S. Englewood Cliffs, N. J.: Prentice-Hall 1967, 142—171.
—: Some methodological remarks on generative grammar. Word 17, 219—239 (1961).
—: Aspects of the theory of syntax. Cambridge, Mass.: M.I.T. Press 1965.
—: Cartesian linguistics. New York: Harper and Row 1966.
—: Language and mind. New York: Harcourt, Brace and World 1968.

CHURCH, J.: Language and the discovery of reality. New York: Random House 1961.

COFER, C. N. (Ed.): Verbal learning and verbal behavior. New York: McGraw-Hill 1961.

—, FORD, T. J.: Verbal context and free association-time. Amer. J. Psychol. **70**, No. 4, 606—610 (1957).

—, MUSGRAVE, B. S. (Eds.): Verbal behavior and learning: Problems and processes. New York: McGraw-Hill 1963.

—, YARCZOWER, M.: Further study of implicit verbal chaining in paired-associate learning. Psychol. Rep. **3**, 453—456 (1957).

COHEN, B. H.: Role of awareness in meaning established by classical conditioning. J. exp. Psychol. **67**, No. 4, 373—378 (1964).

COLEMAN, E. B.: Sequential interferences demonstrated by serial reconstructions. J. exp. Psychol. **64**, No. 1, 46—51 (1962).

—: Approximations to English: Some comments on the method. Amer. J. Psychol. **76**, No. 2, 239—247 (1963).

—: Supplementary report: On the combination of associative probabilities in linguistic contexts. J. Psychol. **57**, No. 1, 95—99 (1964a).

—: Generalizing to a language population. Psychol. Rep. **14**, 219—226 (1964b).

CRAMER, P.: Successful mediated priming via associative bonds. Psychol. Rep. **15**, 235—238 (1964).

CURTIUS, G.: Grundzüge der griechischen Etymologie. Leipzig: Teubner 1858. English Ed.: Principles of Greek etymology. Translated by WILKINS, A. S., ENGLAND, E. B. London: Murray 1886.

DAVIS, E. A.: The development of linguistic skill in twins, singletons and only children from age five to ten years. Minneapolis, Min.: University of Minnesota Press 1937.

DAVIS, R.: The fitness of names to drawings. A cross cultural study in Tanganyika. Brit. J. Psychol. **52**, No. 3, 259—268 (1961).

DAY, E. J.: The development of language in twins. Child Develpm. **3**, No. 3, 179—199 (1932).

DE CECCO, J. (Ed.): The psychology of language, thought and instruction. New York: Holt, Rinehart and Winston 1967.

DEESE, J.: Serial organization in the recall of disconnected items. Psychol. Rep. **3**, 577—582 (1957).

—: Influence of inter-item associative strength upon immediate free recall. Psychol. Rep. **5**, 305—312 (1959a).

—: On the prediction of occurrence of particular verbal intrusions in immediate recall. J. exp. Psychol. **58**, No. 1, 17—22 (1959b).

—: From the isolated verbal unit to connected discourse. In: Verbal Learning and Verbal Behavior. Edited by COFER, C. N. New York: McGraw-Hill 1961a, 11—41.

—: Associative structure and the serial reproduction experiment. J. abnorm. soc. Psychol. **63**, No. 1, 95—100 (1961b).

—: On the structure of associative meaning. Psychol. Rev. **69**, No. 3, 161—175 (1962).

—: Form class and the determinants of association. J. verb. Learning verb. Behavior, **1**, No. 2, 79—84 (1962—63).

DOOB, L. W.: Social psychology: An analysis of human behavior, New York: Holt 1952.

DREHER, J. J., O'NEILL, J. J.: Effects of ambient noise on speaker intelligibility for words and phrases. J. acoust. Soc. Amer. **29**, No. 12, 1320—1323 (1957).

DUNCAN, C. P.: Mediation in verbal concept learning. J. verb. Learning verb. Behavior, 4, No. 1, 1—6 (1965).

DURKHEIM, E.: Les règles de la méthode sociologique. Paris: F. Alcan, 1918. English Ed.: The rules of sociological method. Translated by SOLOVAY, S. A., MUELLER, J. H. New York: Free Press of Glencoe 1938.

EHRLICH, S.: The role of temporal perception span in the perception of language. Proc. 16th Int. Congr. Psychol., Bonn, 1960. Amsterdam: North-Holland 1962 684—685.

ENTWISLE, D. R., FORSYTH, D. F., MUUS, R.: The syntactic-paradigmatic shift in children's word associations. J. verb. Learning verb. Behavior, 3, No. 1, 19—29 (1964).

EPSTEIN, W.: The influence of syntactical structure on learning. Amer. J. Psychol. 74, No. 1, 80—85 (1961).

—: A further study of the influence of syntactical structure on learning. Amer. J. Psychol. 75, No. 1, 121—126 (1962).

ERDMAN, N. B., DODGE, R.: Psychologische Untersuchungen über das Lesen auf experimenteller Grundlage. Halle (Saale): Voss 1898.

ERDMANN, K. O.: Die Bedeutung des Wortes. Leipzig: Avenarius 1925.

ERTEL, S.: Die emotionale Natur des 'semantischen' Raumes. Psychol. Forsch. 28, 1—32 (1964).

—: Weitere Untersuchungen zur Standardisierung eines Eindrucksdifferentials. Z. exper. angew. Psychol. 12, 177—208 (1965).

—, DORST, S.: Expressive Lautsymbolik. Z. exper. angew. Psychol. 12, 557—569 (1965).

ERVIN, S. M.: Changes with age in the verbal determinants of word-association. Amer. J. Psychol. 74, No. 3, 361—372 (1961a).

—: Learning and recall in bilinguals. Amer. J. Psychol. 74, No. 3, 446—451 (1961b).

—: The connotations of gender. Word, 18, 249—261 (1962).

—: Correlates of associative frequency. J. verb. Learning verb. Behavior, 1, No. 6, 422—431 (1962—63).

—, FOSTER, G.: The development of meaning in children's descriptive terms. J. abnorm soc. Psychol. 61, No. 2, 271—275 (1960).

—, OSGOOD, C. E.: Second language learning and bilingualism. In: Psycholinguistics. Edited by OSGOOD, C. E., SEBEOK, T. A. J. abnorm. soc. Psychol. 49, Supplement, 139—146 (1954).

ESCH, H.: Über die Schallerzeugung beim Werbetanz der Honigbiene. Z. vergl. Physiol. 45, 1—11 (1961).

FELDMAN, M. J., LANG, P., LEVINE, B.: Word association disturbance, learning, and retention. Psychol. Rep. 5, 607—608 (1959).

FILLENBAUM, S.: Semantic generalization in verbal satiation. Psychol. Rep. 13, 158 (1963).

—: Semantic association and decision latency. J. exper. Psychol. 68, No. 3, 240—244 (1964).

FISCHER, H.: Die Allgemeine Semantik. Eine nicht-aristotelische Wertungslehre A. Korzybskis. Stud. Gen. 6, 361—388 (1953).

FISHMAN, J. A.: A systematization of the Whorfian hypothesis. Behav. Sci. 5, 323—339 (1960).

FLANAGAN, J. L.: Speech analysis. Synthesis and perception. Berlin/Heidelberg/ New York: Springer 1965.

FLAVELL, J. H.: A test of the Whorfian theory. Psychol. Rep. 4, 455—462 (1958).

—, DRAGUNS, J., FEINBERG, L. D., BUDIN, W.: A microgenetic approach to word association. J. abnorm. soc. Psychol. 57, No. 1, 1—7 (1958).

FLESCH, R.: The art of plain talk. New York: Harper 1946.

—: Measuring the level of abstraction. J. appl. Psychol. **34**, No. 6, 384—390 (1950).

FODOR, J. A., KATZ, J. J. (Eds.): The structure of language. Englewood Cliffs, N. J.: Prentice-Hall 1964.

FORCHHAMMER, E.: Über einige Fälle von eigentümlichen Sprachbildungen bei Kindern. Arch. ges. Psychol. **104**, No. 7, 395—438 (1939).

FOSS, B. M.: Mimicry in mynas (Gracula religiosa): A test of MOWRER's theory. Brit. J. Psychol. **55**, No. 1, 85—88 (1964).

FRANK, H.: Über eine informationspyschologische Maßbestimmung der semantischen und pragmatischen Information. Grundlagenstudien aus Kybernetik und Geisteswissenschaften, **1**, 37—40 (1960).

FRENCH, D.: The relationship of anthropology to studies in perception and cognition. In: Psychology. A study of a science. Vol. VI. Edited by KOCH, S. New York: McGraw-Hill 1963, 388—428.

FRENCH, N. R., STEINBERG, J. C.: Factors governing the intelligibility of speech sounds. J. acoust. Soc. Amer. **19**, No. 1, 90—119 (1947).

FREYTAG-LOERINGHOFF, B.: Discussion. Das Problem der Ordnung. 6. Dtsch. Kongr. Philos. München, 1960. Edited by KUHN, H., WIEDMANN, F. Meisenheim am Glan: A. Hain 1962, 240.

FRIES, C. C.: The structure of English. An introduction to the construction of English sentences. New York: Harcourt, Brace 1952.

—: Meaning and linguistic analysis. Language **30**, No. 1, 57—68 (1954).

FRISCH, K. VON: Über die „Sprache" der Bienen. Eine tierpsychologische Untersuchung. Jena: Fischer 1923.

—: Erinnerungen eines Biologen. Berlin/Göttingen/Heidelberg: Springer: 1962a. English Ed.: A biologist remembers. Translated by GOMBRICH, L. Oxford: Pergamon Press 1967.

—: Dialects in the language of the bees. Sci. Amer. **207**, No. 2, (1962b) 79—87.

FRY, D. B.: Communication theory and linguistic theory. Proc. First Symp. Information Theory. London, 1950, 120—124.

—: Aspect informationnel de la phonétique. In: Communications et langages. Edited by MOLES, A. A., VALLANCIEN, B. Paris: Gauthier-Villars 1963, 161—176.

FUCKS, W.: Zur Deutung einfachster mathematischer Sprachcharakteristiken. Forschungsberichte Nordrhein-Westfalen: Köln-Opladen, No. 344, (1956).

GABELENTZ, G. VON DER: Die Sprachwissenschaft, ihre Aufgaben, Methoden und bisherigen Ergebnisse. Leipzig: Tauchnitz 1901.

GADAMER, H.-G.: Die Natur der Sache und die Sprache der Dinge. In: Das Problem der Ordnung. 6. Dtsch. Kongr. Philos. München, 1960. Edited by KUHN, H., WIEDMANN, F. Meisenheim am Glan: A. Hain 1962, 26—36.

GALTON, F.: Psychometric experiments. Brain **2**, No. 2, 149—162 (1897).

GARSKOF, B. E., HOUSTON, J. P.: Measurement of verbal relatedness: an idiographic approach. Psychol. Rev. **70**, No. 3, 277—288 (1963).

—, —: Relation between judged meaning similarity, associative probability, and associative overlap. Psychol. Rep. **16**, 220—222 (1965).

GEHLEN, A.: Der Mensch, seine Natur und seine Stellung in der Welt. Bonn: Athenäum-Verlag 1950.

GESELL, A., ILG, F. L.: Infant and child in the culture of today. New York: Harper 1943.

GIFFORD, E. W.: A problem in kinship terminology. Amer. Anthropol. **42**, No. 2, part 1, 190—194 (1940).

GLANZER, M.: Toward a psychology of language structure. J. Speech Res. 5, No. 4, 303—314 (1962).

—: Grammatical category: a rote learning and word association analysis. J. verb. Learning verb. Behavior 1, No. 1, 31—41 (1962—63).

—, CLARK, W. H.: Accuracy of perceptual recall: an analysis of organization. J. verb. Learning verb. Behavior 1, No. 4, 289—299 (1962—63).

—, —: The verbal loop hypothesis: Binary numbers. J. verb. Learning verb. Behavior 2, No. 4, 301—309 (1963).

—, —: The verbal loop hypothesis. Conventional figures. Amer. J. Psychol. 77, No. 4, 621—626 (1964).

GLAZE, J. A.: The association value of non-sense syllables. J. genet. Psychol. 35, No. 2, 255—267 (1928).

GLINZ, H.: Die Leistung der Sprache für zwei Menschen. In: Sprache—Schlüssel zur Welt. Festschrift für L. Weisgerber. Düsseldorf: Päd. Verlag Schwann 1959, 87—105.

—: Ziele und Arbeitsweisen der modernen Sprachwissenschaft. Arch. f. neue Sprachen 200, 161—181 (1964).

—: Grammatik und Sprache. In: Das Ringen um eine neue deutsche Grammatik. Edited by MOSER, H. Darmstadt: Wissenschaftliche Buchgesellschaft 1965, 42—60.

GOETHE, W. VON: Faust. Translated by SWANWICK, A. London: George Bell 1879.

GOLDMAN-EISLER, F.: Hesitation, information, and levels of speech production. In: Disorders of language. Edited by DE REUCK, A.V. S., O'CONNOR, M. London: J. and A. Churchill 1964, 96—111.

GOLDSTEIN, K.: Die pathologischen Tatsachen in ihrer Bedeutung für das Problem der Sprache. Ber. 12. Kongr. Dtsch. Ges. Psychol., Hamburg, 1931. Jena: Fischer 1932, 145—164.

—: Language and language disturbance. New York: Grune and Stratton 1948.

GOODALL, J.: My life among wild chimpanzees. National Geographical Magazine 124, No. 2, 272—308 (1963).

GOSS, A. E.: Acquisition and use of conceptual schemes. In: Verbal learning and verbal behavior. Edited by COFER, C. N. New York: McGraw-Hill 1961a, 42—49.

—: Verbal mediating responses and concept formation. Psychol. Rev. 68, No. 4, 248—274 (1961b).

—: Early behaviorism and verbal mediating responses. Amer. Psychol. 16, 285—298 (1961c).

—: Verbal mediation. Psychol. Rec. 14, 363—382 (1964).

GRANIT, R.: Sensory mechanisms of the retina. New York: Hafner 1963.

GREENBERG, J. H.: Concerning inferences from linguistic to nonlinguistic data. In: Language in culture. Edited by HOIJER, H. Chicago: University of Chicago Press 1954, 3—9.

—: Essays in linguistics. New York: Wenner-Gren Foundation for Anthropological Research 1957.

—: Review of "A course in modern linguistics" by HOCKETT, C.F. Amer. Anthrop. 63, No. 5, part 1 (1961), 1140—1145.

—: (Ed.): Universals of language. Cambridge, Mass.: M.I.T. Press 1963.

GREENSPOON, J.: The reinforcing effect of two spoken sounds on the frequency of two responses. Amer. J. Psychol. 68, No. 3, 409—416 (1955).

GUIRAUD, P.: Les caractères statistiques du vocabulaire. Paris: Presses universitaires de France 1954.

GUIRAUD, P.: Structure des répertoires et répartition fréquentielle des éléments: La statistique du vocabulaire écrit. Communications et langages. Edited by MOLES, A. A., VALLANCIEN, B. Paris: Gauthier-Villars 1963, 35—48.

HALL, J. F.: Learning as a function of word frequency. Amer. J. Psychol. 67, No. 1, 138—140 (1954).

HALLE, M., STEVENS, K.: Speech recognition: A model and a program for research. IRE Transactions on Information Theory, IT-8, No. 2, 155—159 (1962).

HARE, R. D.: Cognitive factors in transfer of meaning. Psychol. Rep. 15, 199—206 (1964).

HARLOW, H. F.: Mice, monkeys, men, and motives. Psychol. Rev. 60, No. 1, 23—32 (1953).

—: Motivational forces underlying learning. In: Learning theory, personality theory, and clinical research. Kentucky Symposium, New York, 1954, 36—53.

—, WOOLSEY, C. N. (Eds.): Biological and biochemical bases of behavior. Madison, Wis.: University of Wisconsin Press 1958.

HAYAKAWA, S. I.: Language in thought and action. New York: Harcourt, Brace and World 1949.

—: The aims and takss of general semantics: Implications of time-binding theory. ETC.: Rev. gen. Semant. 8, No. 4, 243—253 (1951).

HEBB, D. O.: The organization of behavior: A neuropsychological theory. New York: Wiley 1949.

HEIDEGGER, M.: Was heißt Denken? Tübingen: M. Niemeyer, 1954. English Edition: What is called thinking? Translated by WIECK, F. D., GRAY, J. G. New York: Harper and Row 1968.

HEIDER, F.: Trends in cognitive theory. In: Contemporary approaches to cognition. By BRUNER, J. S. et al. Cambridge, Mass.: Harvard University Press 1957, 201—210.

HENLE, P. (Ed.): Language, thought, and culture. Ann Arbor, Mich.: University of Michigan Press 1965.

HERDAN, G.: Language as choice and chance. Groningen: Noordhoff 1956.

HERDER, J. G.: Abhandlung über den Ursprung der Sprache. Berlin: C. F. Voss 1772.

HERNÁNDEZ-PEÓN, R., SCHERRER, H., JOUVET, M.: Modification of electric activity in cochlear nucleus during 'attention' in unanesthetized cats. Science 123, No. 3191 331—332 (1956).

HERRMANN, T.: Syntaktische Untersuchungen zum unmittelbaren Behalten von Wortketten. Z. exper. angew. Psychol. 9, No. 4, 397—416 (1962).

HOBBES, T.: Leviathan. London: A. Crooke 1651.

HOCKETT, C. F.: Review of "The mathematical theory of communication" by SHANNON, C. L., WEAVER, W.: Psycholinguistics. Edited by SAPORTA, S. New York: Holt, Rinehart and Winston 1961, 44—67.

HÖRMANN, H.: Aussagemöglichkeiten psychologischer Diagnostik. Göttingen: Verlag für Psychologie 1964.

HOFSTÄTTER, P. R.: Farbsymbolik und Ambivalenz. Psychol. Beitr. 2, 526—540 (1955).

—: Über sprachliche Bestimmungsleistungen: Das Problem des grammatischen Geschlechts von Sonne und Mond. Z. exper. angew. Psychol. 10, 91—108 (1963).

HOIJER, H.: Cultural implications of some Navaho linguistic categories. Language 27, No. 2, 111—120 (1951).

—: The relation of language to culture. In: Anthropology today. Edited by KROEBER, A. L. Chicago: University of Chicago Press 1953, 554—573.

—: (Ed.): Language in culture. Chicago: University of Chicago Press 1954.

HOLLAND, M. K., WERTHEIMER, M.: Some physiognomic aspects of naming, or, maluma and takete revisited. Percept. mot. Skills 19, No. 1, 111—117 (1964).

HORVATH, W. J.: A stochastic model for word association tests. Psychol. Rev. 70, No. 4, 361—364 (1963).

HOUSTON, J. P.: Ease of verbal S-R-learning as a function of the number of mediating associations. J. verb. Learning verb. Behavior 3, No. 4, 326—329 (1964).

HOWES, D.: On the interpretation of word frequency as a variable affecting speed of recognition. J. exper. Psychol. 48, No. 2, 106—112 (1954).

—: On the relation between the probability of a word as an association and in general linguistic usage. J. abnorm. soc. Psychol. 54, 75—85 (1957).

—: Application of the word-frequency concept to aphasia. In: Disorders of Language. Edited by DE REUCK, A. V. S., O'CONNOR, M. London: J. and A. Churchill 1964, 47—75.

—, OSGOOD, C. E.: On the combination of associative probabilities in linguistic contexts. Amer. J. Psychol. 67, No. 2, 241—258 (1954).

—, SOLOMON, R. L.: Visual duration threshold as a function of word-probability. J. exper. Psychol. 41, No. 6, 401—410 (1951).

HULL, C. L.: Knowledge and purpose as habit mechanisms. Psychol. Rev. 37, No. 6, 511—525 (1930).

—: The meaningfulness of 320 selected nonsense syllables. Amer. J. Psychol. 45, No. 4, 730—734 (1933).

—: Principles of behavior. New York: Appleton-Century-Crofts, 1943.

HUMBOLDT, W. VON: Über das vergleichende Sprachstudium in Beziehung auf die verschiedenen Epochen der Sprachentwicklung. Gesammelte Schriften, Vol. 4. Berlin: Königlich-Preußische Akademie der Wissenschaften, 1905a (1st published as Abhandlungen hist.-philol. Kl. Königl. Preuß. Akad. Wiss. 1820—1821. 1822, 239—260).

—: Über den Nationalcharakter der Sprachen. Gesammelte Schriften, Vol. 4. Berlin: Königlich-Preußische Akademie der Wissenschaften, 1905b (1st published in Z. Völkerpsychol. u. Sprachwiss. 13, 1882, 211—232).

—: Über die Verschiedenheit des menschlichen Sprachbaues und ihren Einfluß auf die geistige Entwicklung des Menschengeschlechts. Gesammelte Schriften, Vol. VII, Part 1. Berlin: Königlich-Preußische Akademie der Wissenschaften, 1907 (also introduction to Über die Kawi-Sprache auf der Insel Java. Darmstadt 1949. 1st published in Berlin, 1836.)

HUMPHREY, G.: There is no problem of meaning. Brit. J. Psychol. 42, No. 3, 238—245 (1951).

HUSSERL, E.: Formale und transzendentale Logik. Halle (Saale): Niemeyer 1929.

HUXLEY, A.: Words and their meanings. Los Angeles: Ward Ritchie Press 1940.

IPSEN, G.: Der alte Orient und die Indogermanen. In: Stand und Aufgaben der Sprachwissenschaft. Festschrift für W. Streitberg. Heidelberg: C. Winter 1924, 200—237.

—: Der neue Sprachbegriff. Z. Deutschk. 46, 1—18 (1932).

IRWIN, R. J.: Can animals talk? Percept. and mot. Skills, 18, No. 2, 369—374 (1964)

JAKOBOVITS, L. A., LAMBERT, W. E.: Semantic satiation among bilinguals. J. exper. Psychol. 62, No. 6, 576—582 (1961).

—, —: Mediated satiation in verbal transfer. J. exper. Psychol. 64, No. 4, 346—351 (1962a).

—, —: Semantic satiation in an addition task. Canadian J. Psychol. 16, No. 2, 112—119 (1962b).

JAKOBOVITS, L. A., LAMBERT, W. E.: Stimulus-characteristics as determinants of semantic changes with repeated presentation. Amer. J. Psychol. 77, No. 1, 84—92 (1964).

—, MIRON, M. S. (Eds.): Readings in the psychology of language. Englewood Cliffs, N. J.: Prentice-Hall 1967.

JAKOBSON, R.: Kindersprache, Aphasie und allgemeine Lautgesetze. Universitets Arsskrift (Uppsala) 9, 1—83 (1942).

—: Aphasia as a linguistic problem. In: On expressive language. Edited by WERNER, H. Worcester, Mass.: Clark University Press 1955, 69—81.

—: Why 'Mama' and 'Papa'? In: Perspectives in psychological theory — Essays in Honor of Heinz Werner. Edited by KAPLAN, B., WAPNER, S. New York: Internat. Universities Press 1960, 124—134.

—: In: Zeichen und System der Sprache. Vol. II (Veröffentlichung des 1. Internationalen Symposiums „Zeichen und System der Sprache", Erfurt, 1959). Berlin: Schriften zur Phonetic Sprachwissenschaft und Kommunikationsforschung, No. 4, 1962, 50—56.

—: Toward a linguistic typology of aphasic impairments. In: Disorders of language. Edited by DE REUCK, A. V. S., O'CONNOR, M. London: J. and A. Churchill 1964, 21—40.

—, HALLE, M.: Fundamentals of language. 's Gravenhage: Mouton 1956.

—, —: Phonology and phonetics. In: Fundamentals of language. Edited by JAKOBSON, R., HALLE, M. 's Gravenhage: Mouton 1956, 1—51.

JAMES, W.: As William James said: Extracts from the published writings of William James. Edited by ALDRICH, E. P. New York: Vanguard Press 1942.

JASSEM, W.: In: Zeichen und System der Sprache. Vol. I (Veröffentlichung des 1. Internationalen Symposiums „Zeichen und System der Sprache", Erfurt, 1959), Berlin: Schriften zur Phonetik, Sprachwissenschaft und Kommunikationsforschung, No. 3, 1961, 78—79.

JENKINS, J. J. (Ed.): Associative processes in verbal behavior. Minnesota Conference, 1955.

—: Cited in HOWES, D. H. On the relation between the probability of a word as an association and in general linguistic usage. J. abnorm. soc. Psychol. 54, 75—85 (1957).

—: The change in some American word association norms in the twentieth-century. Proc. 15th Int. Congr. Psychol., Brussels, 1957. Amsterdam: North-Holland 1959, 583—584.

—: Commonality of association as an indicator of more general patterns of verbal behavior. Style in Language. Edited by SEBEOK, T. A. New York: Wiley 1960, 307—329.

—: Mediated associations: Paradigms and situations. In: Verbal behavior and learning. Edited by COFER, C. N., MUSGRAVE, B. S. New York: McGraw-Hill 1963, 210—245.

—: Mediation theory and grammatical behavior. In: Directions in Psycholinguistics. Edited by ROSENBERG, S. New York: Macmillan 1965, 66—96.

—, RUSSELL, W. A.: Associative clustering during recall. J. abnorm. soc. Psychol. 47, 818—821 (1952).

—, COFER, C. N.: An exploratory study of discrete free association to compound verbal stimuli. Psychol. Rep. 3, 599—602 (1957).

JESPERSEN, O.: Language, its nature, development, and origin. New York: W. W. Norton 1964.

JOHNSON, N. F.: Linguistic models and functional units of language behavior. In: Directions in Psycholinguistics. Edited by ROSENBERG, S. New York: Macmillan 1965, 29—65.

JOHNSON, R. C.: Linguistic structure as related to concept formation and to concept content. Psychol. Bull. 59, No. 6, 468—476 (1962).

JOHNSON, W.: Studies in language behavior. I. A program of research. Psychol. Monogr. 56, No. 2, 1—15 (1944).

JUNG, C. G.: Diagnostische Assoziationsstudien. Leipzig, Vol. I, 1906; Vol. II, 1910. English Ed.: Studies in word-association. Translated by EDER, M. D. London: W. Heinemann 1918.

KAEDING, F. W.: Häufigkeitswörterbuch der deutschen Sprache. Berlin: Selbstverlag des Herausgebers, Mittler Sohn 1897.

KAINZ, F.: Psychologie der Sprache. Vol. II: Vergleichend-genetische Sprachpsychologie. Stuttgart: Enke 1943.

—: Die Sprache der Tiere, Tatsachen — Problemschau — Theorie. Stuttgart: Enke 1961.

KAMINSKI, F.: Ordnungsstrukturen und Ordnungsprozesse. In: Handbuch der Psychologie. Vol. 1: Allgemeine Psychologie, Part 2: Lernen und Denken. Edited by BERGIUS, R. Göttingen: Verlag für Psychologie 1964.

KANUNGO, R., LAMBERT, W. E.: Semantic satiation and meaningfulness. Amer. J. Psychol. 76, No. 3, 421—428 (1963).

KAPLAN, B., WAPNER, S. (Eds.): Perspectives in psychological theory — Essays in Honor of Heinz Werner. New York: Internat. Universities Press 1960.

KARWOSKI, T. F., SCHACHTER, J.: Psychological studies in semantics: III. Reaction times for similarity and differences. J. soc. Psychol. 28, 103—120 (1948).

KELCHNER, M.: Kummer und Trost jugendlicher Arbeiterinnen. In: Forschungen zur Völkerpsychologie und Soziologie. Vol. VI. Leipzig: C. L. Hirschfeld 1929.

KELLER, H.: The story of my life. New York: Grosset and Dunlop 1905.

KENDALL, M. G., BUCKLAND, W. R.: A dictionary of statistical terms. Edinburgh: Oliver and Boyd for the International Statistical Institute 1960.

KENT, H. G., ROSANOFF, A. J.: A study of association in insanity. Amer. J. Insanity 67, No. 1, 37—96 (1910); Part II, 67, No. 2, 317—390 (1910).

KIRCHHOFF, R.: Über pragmatische und semantische Handlungen. Jb. Psychol. Psychother. 10, (1963) 104—118.

—: (Ed). Handbuch der Psychologie. Vol. 5: Ausdruckspsychologie. Göttingen: Verlag für Psychologie 1965.

KLAPPENBACH, R., MALIGE-KLAPPENBACH, H.: Zur Bedeutungsanalyse des Wortes. Forschungen und Fortschritte, 39, 54—57 (1965).

KLEIST, H. VON: Über die allmähliche Verfertigung der Gedanken beim Reden. (1806). In: Vom Gespräch. Edited by MUELLER, A. H. Hamburg: 1946, 24—32.

KLUCKHOHN, C., LEIGHTON, D.: The Navaho. Cambridge, Mass.: Harvard University Press 1946.

KOCH, S. (Ed.): Psychology. A study of a science. Vols. I-VI. New York: McGraw-Hill 1959—1963.

KÖHLER, W.: Intelligenzprüfungen an Menschenaffen. Berlin: Abhandlungen d. Preuß. Akademie d. Wissenschaften 1917. Later Ed.: Berlin: Springer. English Ed.: The mentality of apes. Translated by WINTER, E. London: Routledge and K. Paul 1956.

—: Die physischen Gestalten in Ruhe und im stationären Zustand. Erlangen: Philosophische Akademie 1924.

—: Gestalt Psychology. New York: Liveright 1947.

KOFFKA, K.: Die Grundlagen der psychischen Entwicklung. Osterwieck (Harz): A. W. Zickfeldt 1921. English Ed.: The growth of the mind. Translated by OGDEN, R. M. New York: Harcourt, Brace 1931.

KORZYBSKI, A.: Time-Binding: The general theory. Lakeville, Conn.: Institute of General Semantics, 1949.

—: Science and sanity. An introduction to Non-Aristotelian systems and general semantics. Lakeville, Conn.: International Non-Aristotelian Library 1958.

KRASNER, L.: Studies of the conditioning of verbal behavior. Psychol. Bull. 55, No. 3, 148—170 (1958).

KROEBER, A. L.: Classificatory systems of relationship. J. Royal Anthropological Institute 39, 77—84 (1909).

KÜNG, G.: Ontologie und logistische Analyse der Sprache. Wien: Springer 1963.

KÜPFMÜLLER, K.: Die Entropie der deutschen Sprache. Fernmeldetechn. Z. 7, No. 6, 265—272 (1954).

LADEFOGED, P.: The perception of speech. Proc. Symp. Mechanization of thought processes, Vol. 1 (Teddington, England. National Physical Laboratory, Symposium No. 10, 1958). London: Her Majesty's Stationery Office 1959, 399—409.

—, BROADBENT, D. E.: Information conveyed by vowels. J. Acoust. Soc. Amer. 29, No. 1, 98—104 (1957).

LAFFAL, J.: Response faults in word association as a function of response entropy. J. abnorm. soc. Pyschol. 50, No. 2, 265—270 (1955).

—: Linguistic field theory and studies of word association. J. gen. Psychol. 71, No. 1, 145—155 (1964a).

—: Psycholinguistics and the psychology of language. Amer. Psychologist, 19, 813—815 (1964b).

—, FELDMAN, S.: The structure of single word and continuous word associations. J. verb. Learning verb. Behavior 1, No. 1, 54—61 (1962—63).

LAGUNA, G. A. DE: Speech: its function and development. Bloomington, Ind.: Indiana University Press 1963.

LAMBERT, W. E., JAKOBOVITS, L. A.: Verbal satiation and changes in the intensity of meaning. J. exper. Psychol. 60, No. 6, 376—383 (1960).

—, HAVELKA, J., CROSBY, C.: The influence of language-acquisition contexts on bilingualism. J. abnorm. soc. Psychol. 56, 239—244 (1958). Reprinted in: Psycholinguistics. Edited by SAPORTA, S. New York: Holt, Rinehart and Winston 1961, 407—414.

LANE, H.: Psychophysical parameters of vowel perception. Psychol. Monogr. 76, No. 44, (1962).

—: The motor theory of speech perception: A critical review. Psychol. Rev. 72, No. 4, 275—309 (1965).

LANGER, S. K.: Philosophy in a new key. Cambridge, Mass.: Harvard University Press 1963.

LASHLEY, K. S.: Studies of cerebral function in learning. IV: Vicarious function after destruction of the visula areas. Amer. J. Physiol. 59, No. 1, 44—71, (1922).

—: Learning. I: Nervous mechanisms in learning. In: The foundations of experimental psychology. Edited by MURCHISON, C. Worcester, Mass.: Clark University Press 1929, 524—563.

—: Basic neural mechanisms in behavior. Psychol. Rev. 37, No. 1, 1—24 (1930).

—: The problem of serial order in behavior. In: Cerebral mechanisms in behavior. The Hixon Symposium. Edited by JEFFRESS, L. A. New York: Hafner, 1951, 112—136. Reprinted in: The neuropsychology of LASHLEY. Edited by BEACH, E. A., et al. New York: McGraw-Hill 1960, 506—528.

LASHLEY K. S. In search of the engram. In: The neuropsychology of LASHLEY — Selected papers of K. S. LASHLEY. Edited by BEACH, F. A., HEBB, D. O., MORGAN, C.T., NISSEN, H. W. New York: McGraw-Hill 1960, 478—505.

LEES, R. B.: Models for a language user's knowledge of grammatical form. Cited in JOHNSON, N. F.: Linguistic models and functional units of language behavior. (p. 31). In: Directions in psycholinguistics. Edited by ROSENBERG, S. New York: Macmillan 1965, 29—65.

LEIBNIZ, G. E.: Unvorgreifliche Gedanken betreffend die Ausübung und Verbesserung der teutschen Sprache. Beiträge zur deutschen Sprachkunde, vorgelesen in der Akademie der Wissenschaften zu Berlin, I, 1794. (Unpresumptuous thoughts concerning the practice and improvement of the German language. Contributions to the knowledge of the German language, read before the Academy of Sciences at Berlin, I, 1794).

LEISI, E.: Der Wortinhalt. Seine Struktur im Deutschen und Englischen. Heidelberg: Quelle Meyer 1961.

LENNEBERG, E. H.: Cognition in ethnolinguistics. Language 29, No. 4, 463—471 (1953).

—: A note on CASSIRER's philosophy of language. Phil. phenomenol. Res. 15, No. 4, 512—522 (1955).

—: Language, evolution, and purposive behavior. In: Culture in history: Essays in Honor of Paul Radin. Edited by DIAMOND, S. New York: Columbia University Press 1960, 869—893.

—: Understanding language without ability to speak: A case report. J. abnorm. soc. Psychol. 65, No. 6, 419—425 (1962).

—: (Ed.): New directions in the study of language. Cambridge, Mass.: M.I.T. Press 1964 a.

—: A biological perspective of language. In: New directions in the study of language. Cambridge, Mass.: M.I.T. Press, 1964 b, 65—88.

—, ROBERTS, J. M.: The denotata of color terms. Paper read at the Linguistic Society of America, Bloomington, Ind., August, 1953. Cited in BROWN, R. W., LENNEBERG, E. H. A study in language and cognition. (p. 461). J. abnorm. soc. Psychol. 49, No. 3, 454—462 (1954).

—, —: The language of experience. In: Psycholinguistics. Edited by SAPORTA, S. New York: Holt, Rinehart and Winston 1961, 493—502.

LEONTIEV, A. N.: Learning as a problem in psychology. In: Recent Soviet Psychology. Edited by O'CONNOR, N. Translated by KISCH, R., CRAWFORD, R., ASHER, H. Oxford: Pergamon Press 1961, 227—246.

LERSCH, P.: Aufbau der Person. Munich: Barth 1962.

LEWIS, M. M.: Infant speech — A study of the beginnings of language. New York: Humanities Press 1951.

—: Language, thought and personality in infancy and childhood. London: George G. Harrap 1963.

LIBERMAN, A. M.: Some results of research on speech perception. J. Acoust. Soc. Amer. 29, No. 1, 117—123 (1957). Reprinted in: Psycholinguistics. Edited by SAPORTA, S. New York: Holt, Rinehart and Winston 1961, 142—153.

—, COOPER, F. S., HARRIS, K. S., MACNEILAGE, P. F.: A motor theory of speech perception. Proc. Speech Communication Seminar — 1962 — II. Stockholm: Speech Transmission Laboratory, Royal Institute of Technology, 1963.

—, DELATTRE, P. C., COOPER, F. S.: The role of selected stimulus-variables in the perception of the unvoiced stop consonants. Amer. J. Psychol. 65, No. 4, 497—516 (1952).

LIBERMAN A. M., DELATTRE, P. C., COOPER, F. S., GERSTMAN, L. J.: The role of consonant-vowel transitions in the perception of the stop and nasal consonants. Psychol. Monogr. 68, No. 8, (1954).

—, —, —, —: Tempo of frequency change as a cue for distinguishing classes of speech sounds. J. exper. Psychol. 52, No. 2, 127—137 (1956).

—, HARRIS, K. S., HOFFMAN, H S., GRIFFITH, B. C.: The discrimination of speech sounds within and across phoneme boundaries. J. exper. Psychol. 54, 358—368 (1957).

LICKLIDER, J. C. R.: Effects of amplitude distortion upon the intelligibility of speech. J. Acoust. Soc. Amer. 18, No. 2, 429—434 (1946).

—, MILLER, G. A.: The perception of speech. In: Handbook of experimental psychology. Edited by STEVENS, S. S. New York: Wiley 1951, 1040—1074.

LINDAUER, M.: Communication among social bees. Cambridge, Mass.: Harvard University Press, 1961.

LOHMANN, J.: Sprache und Zeit. Stud. Gen. 8, 562—567 (1955).

—: Das Ordnungsprinzip der Sprachwissenschaft. In: Das Problem der Ordnung. 6. Dtsch. Kongr. Philos. München, 1960. Edited by KUHN, N., WIEDMAN, F. Meisenheim am Glan: A. Hain 1962, 225—236.

LONGACRE, R. E.: Review of "Language and reality" by URBAN, W. M., and "Four articles on metalinguistics" by WHORF, B. L. Language 32, No. 2, 298—308 (1956).

LORENZ, K.: Die angeborenen Formen möglicher Erfahrung. Z. Tierpsychol. 5, 235—409 (1943).

LOUNSBURY, F. G.: A semantic analysis of the Pawnee kinship usage. Language 32, No. 1, 158—194 (1956).

—: Linguistics and psychology. In: Psychology. A study of a science. Vol. VI. Edited by KOCH, S. New York: McGraw-Hill 1963, 552—582.

LÜDTKE, H.: In: Zeichen und System der Sprache, Vol. I (Veröffentlichung des 1. Internationalen Symposiums „Zeichen und System der Sprache", Erfurt, 1959). Berlin: Schriften zur Phonetik, Sprachwissenschaft und Kommunikationsforschung, No. 3, 1961, 249ff.

LURIA, A. R.: The directive function of speech in development and dissolution. Word 15, (1959), part I: 341—352, part II: 453—464.

—, YUDOVICH, F. I.: Speech and the development of mental processes in the child — An experimental investigation. London: Staples Press 1959.

LYONS, J., WALES, R. J. (Eds.): Psycholinguistic Papers. Edinburgh: Edinburgh University Press 1966.

MACLAY, H.: Linguistics and language behavior. Cited in JOHNSON, N. F.: Linguistic models and functional units of language behavior (p. 31). In: Directions in psycholinguistics. Edited by ROSENBERG, S. New York: Macmillan 1965, 29—65.

—, OSGOOD, C. E.: Hesitation phenomena in spontaneous English speech. Word 15, 19—44 (1959).

MALINOWSKI, B.: The problem of meaning in primitive languages. In: The meaning of meaning by OGDEN, C. K., RICHARDS, I. A. London: Kegan Paul, Trench, Trubner 1936.

MALMBERG, B.: Structural linguistics and human communication. Berlin/Göttingen/Heidelberg: Springer 1963. (2nd Ed. 1967).

MALTZMAN, I., MORRISETT, L., BROOKS, L. O.: An investigation of phonetic symbolism. J. abnorm. soc. Psychol. 53, 249—251 (1956).

MANDELBROT, B.: Structure formelle des textes et communication; deux études. Word 10, 1—27 (1954).

MARKS, L. E., MILLER, G. A.: The role of semantic and syntactic constraints in the memorization of English sentences. J. verb. Learning verb. Behavior 3, No. 1, 1—5 (1964).

MARSHALL, G. R., COFER, C. N.: Associative indices as measures of word relatedness: A summary and comparison of ten methods. J. verb. Learning verb. Behavior 1, No. 6, 408—421 (1962—63).

MARTIN, R. B., DEAN, S. J.: Implicit and explicit mediation in paired-associate learning. J. exper. Psychol. 68, No. 1, 21—27 (1964).

MARTINET, A.: Eléments de linguistique générale. Paris: Colin 1960.

—: A functional view of language. Oxford: Clarendon Press 1962.

McCARTHY, D.: Language development in children. In: Manual of child psychology. Edited by CARMICHAEL, L. New York: Wiley 1954, 492—630.

McGINNIES, E.: Emotionality and perceptual defense. Psychol. Rev. 56, No. 5, 244—251 (1949).

McKEAN, K., SLOBIN, D., MILLER, G. A.: Cited in MILLER, G. A. Some psychological studies of grammar (p. 757). Amer. Psychologist 17, 748—762 (1962).

McNEILL, D.: The origin of associations within the same grammatical class. J. verb. Learning verb. Behavior, 2, No. 3, 250—262 (1963).

MEHLER, J.: Some effects of grammatical transformations on the recall of English sentences. J. verb. Learning verb Behavior 2, No. 4, 346—351 (1963).

MEIER, H.: Deutsche Sprachstatistik. Vols. I and II. Hildesheim: G. Olms 1964.

MENYUK, P.: Syntactic structures in the language of children. Child Develpm. 34, 407—422 (1963).

—: Alternation of rules in children's grammar. J. verb. Learning verb. Behavior 3, No. 6, 480—488 (1964).

MERLEAU-PONTY, M.: Sur la phénoménologie du langage. In: Problèmes actuels de la phénoménologie. Edited by VAN BREDA, H. L. Paris: Desclée de Brouwer 1952, 91—109.

MEUMANN, E.: Die Entstehung der ersten Wortbedeutungen beim Kinde. Leipzig: W. Engelmann 1908.

MEYER-EPPLER, W.: Grundlagen und Anwendungen der Informationstheorie. Berlin/Göttingen/Heidelberg: Springer 1959.

—: Problèmes informationnels de la communication parlée. In: Communications et langages. Edited by MOLES, A. A., VALLANCIEN, B. Paris: Gauthier-Villars 1963, 51—65.

MILLER, G. A.: Language and communication. New York: McGraw-Hill 1951a.

—: Speech and language. In: Handbook of experimental psychology. Edited by STEVENS, S. S. New York: Wiley 1951b, 789—810.

—: The magical number seven, plus or minus two: some limits on our capacity for processing information. Psychol. Rev. 63, No. 2, 81—97 (1956).

—: Decision units in the perception of speech. IRE Transactions on Information Theory, IT-8, 81—83 (1962a).

—: Some psychological studies of grammar. Amer. Psychologist 17, 748—762 (1962b).

—: Review of "Universals of language", edited by GREENBERG, J. H. Contemp. Psychol. 8, No. 11, 417—418 (1963).

—: Language and psychology. In: New directions in the study of language. Edited by LENNEBERG, E. H. Cambridge, Mass.: M.I.T. Press, 1964, 89—107.

—: Some preliminaires to psycholinguistics. Amer. Psychologist 20, 15—20 (1965).

MILLER, G. A., BRUNER, J. S., POSTMAN, L.: Familiarity of letter sequences and tachistoscopic identification. J. gen. Psychol. 50, No. 1, 129—139 (1954).

—, FRIEDMAN, E. A.: The reconstruction of mutilated English texts. Inform. Control. 1, No. 1, 38—55 (1957).

—, GALANTER, E., PRIBRAM, K. H.: Plans and the structure of behavior. New York: Henry Holt 1960.

—, HEISE, G. A., LICHTEN, W.: The intelligibility of speech as a function of the text of the test materials. J. exper. Psychol. 41, No. 5, 329—335 (1951).

—, ISARD, S.: Some perceptual consequenses of linguistic rules. J. verb. Learning verb. Behavior 2, No. 3, 217—228 (1963).

—, LICKLIDER, J. C. R.: The intelligibility of interrupted speech. J. Acoust. Soc. Amer. 22, No. 2, 167—173 (1950).

—, McKEAN, K.: A chronometric study of some relations between sentences. Quart. J. exper. Psychol. 16, No. 4, 297—308 (1964).

—, NICELY, P. E.: An analysis of perceptual confusions among some English consonants. J. Acoust. Soc. Amer., 27, No. 2, 338—352 (1955). Reprinted in: Psycholinguistics. Edited by SAPORTA, S. New York: Holt, Rinehart and Winston 1961, 153—175.

—, SELFRIDGE, J. A.: Verbal context and the recall of meaningful material. Amer. J. Psychol. 63, No. 2, 176—185 (1950).

MOLES, A. A.: Les bases de la théorie de l'information et son application aux langages. In: Communications et langages. Edited by MOLES, A. A., VALLANCIEN, B. Paris: Gauthier-Villars 1963, 15—33.

—, VALLANCIEN, B. (Eds.): Communications et langages. Paris: Gauthier-Villars 1963.

MORRIS, C. W.: Foundations of the theory of signs. International Encyclopedia of Unified Science 1, No. 2. Chicago: University of Chicago Press 1938.

—, Signs, Language and Behavior. New York: G. Braziller 1955.

MOSER, H. (Ed):. Das Ringen um eine neue deutsche Grammatik. Aufsätze aus 3 Jahrzehnten. Darmstadt: Wissenschaftliche Buchgesellschaft 1965.

MOWRER, O. H.: Preparatory set (expectancy) — some methods of measurement. Psychol. Monogr. 52, No. 2, whole No. 233 (1940).

—: The psychologist looks at language. Amer. Psychologist 9, No. 11, 600—694 (1954).

—: Learning theory and the symbolic processes. New York: Wiley 1960.

MÜLLER, A. L.: Experimentelle Untersuchungen zur stimmlichen Darstellung von Gefühlen. Dissertation, Göttingen, 1960.

NEUBERT, A.: Semantischer Positivismus in den U.S.A. Halle (Saale): Niemeyer 1962.

NEWMAN, S. S.: Further experiments in phonetic symbolism. Amer. J. Psychol. 45, No. 1, 53—75 (1933).

NOBLE, C. E.: An analysis of meaning. Psychol. Rev. 59, No. 6, 421—430 (1952a).

—: The role of stimulus meaning (m) in serial verbal learning. J. Exper. Psychol. 43, No. 6, 437—446 (1952b); 44, No. 6, 465.

—: Meaningfulness (m) and transfer phenomena in serial verbal learning. J. Psychol. 52, No. 1, 201—210 (1961).

—, McNEELY, D. A.: The role of meaningfulness (m) in paired-associate verbal learning. J. Exper. Psychol. 53, No. 1, 16—22 (1957).

—, STOCKWELL, F. E., PRYOR, M. W.: Meaningfulness (m') and association value (a) in a paired-associate syllable learning. Psychol. Rep. 3, 441—452 (1957).

ÖHMAN, S.: Wortinhalt und Weltbild. Stockholm: Thesis Stockholms Högskola, 1951.

—: Theories of the 'linguistic field'. Word 9, No. 2, 123—134 (1953).

OGDEN, C. K., RICHARDS, I. A.: The meaning of meaning. London: Kegan Paul, Trench, Trubner 1936.

OLDFIELD, R. C.: Individual vocabulary and semantic currency: A preliminary study. Brit. J. soc. clin. Psychol. 2, No. 2, 122—130 (1963).

—, MARSHALL, J. C. (Eds.): Language: Selected readings. Harmondsworth, England: Penguin Books 1968.

OLÉRON, P.: Reconstitution des textes français ayant subi divers taux de mutilation. Psychol. Franç. 5, 161—174 (1960).

—: Les habitudes verbales. In: Problèmes de psycholinguistique. Edited by DE AJURIAGUERRA, J., et al. Paris: Presses universitaires de France 1963, 73—103.

OSGOOD, C. E.: Method and theory in experimental psychology. New York: Oxford University Press 1953.

—: A behavioristic analysis of perception and language as cognitive phenomena. In: Contemporary approaches to cognition. By BRUNER, J. S., et al. Cambridge, Mass.: Harvard University Press 1957, 75—118.

—: The representational model and relevant research methods. In: Trends in content analysis. Edited by POOL, I. DE S. Urbana, Ill.: University of Illinois Press 1959.

—: Some effects of motivation on style of encoding. In: Style in language. Edited by SEBEOK, T. A. New York: Wiley 1960, 293—306.

—: Comments on "The problem of meaning in verbal learning" by BOUSFIELD, W. A. In: Verbal learning and verbal behavior. Edited by COFER, C. N. New York: McGraw-Hill 1961, 91—106.

—: Psycholinguistic relativity and universality. Proc. 16th Int. Congr. Psychol., Bonn, 1960. Amsterdam: North-Holland 1962a, 673—678.

—: Studies on the generality of affective meaning systems. Amer. Psychologist 17, 10—28 (1962b).

—: Psycholinguistics. In: Psychology. A study of a science. Vol. VI. Edited by KOCH, S. New York: McGraw-Hill 1963, 244—316.

—, SEBEOK, T. A. (Eds.): Psycholinguistics. A survey of theory and research problems. J. abnorm. soc. Psychol. 49, (1954), Supplement. Reprinted as: Psycholinguistics. A survey of theory and research problems. With: A survey of psycholinguistic research 1954—1964. By DIEBOLD, A. R. Bloomington and London: Indiana University Press 1965.

—, SUCI, G. J., TANNENBAUM, P. H.: The measurement of meaning. Urbana, Ill.: University of Illinois Press 1957.

PALERMO, D. S., JENKINS, J. J.: Sex differences in word associations. J. gen. Psychol. 72, No. 1, 77—84 (1965).

PAUL, H.: Prinzipien der Sprachgeschichte. Tübingen: Niemeyer 1960.

PAVLOV, I. P.: Conditioned reflexes: An investigation of the physiological activity of the cerebral cortex. Translated by ANREP, A. V. New York: Dover Publications 1960.

—: Lectures on conditioned reflexes. Translated by GANTT, W. H. New York: Internat. Publishers 1963.

PEIRCE, C. S.: Collected papers, Vol. II. Edited by HARTSHORNE, C., WEISS, P. Cambridge, Mass.: Belknap Press of Harvard University Press 1960.

PENFIELD, W., ROBERTS, L.: Speech and brain-mechanisms. Princeton, N. J.: Princeton University Press 1959.

PETERSON, M. J.: Effects of delay intervals and meaningfulness on verbal mediating responses. J. exper. Psychol. 69, No. 1, 60—66 (1965).

—, COLAVITA, F. B., SHEAHAN, D. B. III, BLATTNER, K. C.: Verbal mediating chains and response availability as a function of the acquisition paradigm. J. verb. Learning verb. Behavior 3, No. 1, 11—18 (1964).

PETERSON, M. S., JENKINS, J. J.: Word association phenomena at the individual level: A pair of case studies. Minneapolis, Min.: Technical Report 16 ONR Contract, N8 onr 66216, 1957.

PIAGET, J.: Le développement des quantités chez l'enfant. Conservation et atomisme. Neuchâtel: Delachoux et Niestlé 1928.

—: La formation du symbole chez l'enfant. Neuchâtel and Paris: Delachoux et Niestlé, 1945. English Ed.: Play, dreams and imitation in childhood. Translated by GATTEGNO, C., HODGSON, F. M., London: W. Heinemann 1951.

PICK, A.: Die agrammatischen Sprachstörungen, Studien zur psychologischen Grundlegung der Aphasielehre. Part 1. Monographien aus dem Gesamtgebiete der Neurologie und Psychiatire, No. 7. Berlin, 1913.

PODELL, H. A.: A quantitative study of convergent association. J. verb. Learning verb. Behavior 2, No. 3, 234—241 (1963).

PÖTZL, O.: The relationship between experimentally induced dream images and indirect vision. Z. Neurol. Psychiatr. 37, 278—349 (1917). Reprinted in: Psychol. Issues, 2, whole No. 7, 41—120 (1960).

POLLACK, I.: The information of elementary auditory displays. J. Acoust. Soc. Amer. 24, No. 6, 745—749 (1952).

—: Assimilation of sequentially encoded information. Amer. J. Psychol. 66, No. 3, 421—435 (1953 a).

—: The information of elementary auditory displays. II. J. Acoust. Soc. Amer. 25, No. 4, 765—769 (1953 b).

—, FICKS, L.: Information of elementary multidimensional auditory displays. J. Acoust. Soc. Amer. 26, No. 2, 155—158 (1954).

—, PICKETT, J. M.: Intelligibility of excerpts from fluent speech: Auditory vs. structural context. J. verb. Learning verb. Behavior 3, No. 1, 79—84 (1964).

POLLIO, H. R.: Composition of associative clusters. J. exper. Psychol. 67, No. 3, 199—208 (1964).

POOL, I. DE S. (Ed.): Trends in content analysis. Urbana, Ill.: University of Illinois Press 1959.

PORZIG, W.: Wesenhafte Bedeutungsbeziehungen. Beiträge zur Geschichte der deutschen Sprache und Literatur, 58, 70—97 (1934).

PREYER, W.: Die Seele des Kindes. Leipzig: Grieben 1900.

PUTNAM, H.: Zu einigen Problemen der theoretischen Gundlegung der Grammatik. Sprache im technischen Zeitalter 14, 1109—1131 (1965).

RAPAPORT, D.: Diagnostic psychological testing, Vols. I and II. Chicago: Year Book Publishers 1945—46.

—: Discussion of "A behavioristic analysis of perception and language as cognitive phenomena". In: Contemporary approaches to cognition. By BRUNER, J. S., et al. Cambridge, Mass.: Harvard University Press 1957, 119—125.

RAZRAN, G.: Semantic and phonetographic generalizations of salivary conditioning to verbal stimuli. J. exper. Psychol. 39, No. 5, 642—652 (1949).

—: Experimental semantics. Trans. N. Y. Acad. Sci. 13, 171—177 (1950—51).

REUCK, A. V. S. DE, O'CONNOR, M. (Eds.): Ciba Foundation Symposium: Disorders of language. London, 1963. London: J. and A. Churchill 1964.

RÉVÉSZ, G.: Ursprung und Vorgeschichte der Sprache. Bern: A. Francke 1946. French Ed.: Origine et préhistoire du langage. Translated by HOMBURGER, L. Paris: Payot 1950.

RIEGEL, K. F., RIEGEL, M.: Changes in associative behavior during later years of life: A cross-sectional analysis. Vita Humana 7, No. 1, 1—32 (1964).

RIESMAN, D., DENNEY, R., GLAZER, N.: The lonely crowd. New Haven: Yale University Press 1950.

ROSEN, E., RUSSELL, W. A.: Frequency-characteristics of successive word-association. Amer. J. Psychol. 70, No. 1, 120—122 (1957).

ROSENBERG, S. (Ed.): Directions in psycholinguistics. New York: Macmillan 1965.

—, BAKER, N.: Grammatical form class as a variable in verbal learning at three levels of linguistic structure. Cited in Rosenberg, S., Koplin, J.: Introduction to psycholinguistics. In: Directions in psycholinguistics. Edited by ROSENBERG, S. New York: Macmillan 1965, 3—12.

—, KOPLIN, J. H. (Eds.): Developments in applied psycholinguistic research. New York: Macmillan 1968.

ROSENBLITH, W. A.: Auditory masking and fatigue. J. Acoust. Soc. Amer. 22, No. 6, 792—800 (1950).

—: La perception catégorielle des phénomènes sonores. In: Communications et langages. Edited by MOLES, A. A., VALLANCIEN, B. Paris: Gauthier-Villars 1963, 67-76.

—, ROSENZWEIG, M. R.: Electrical responses to acoustic clicks: Influence of electrode location in cats. J. Acoust. Soc. Amer. 23, No. 5, 583—588 (1951).

ROSENZWEIG, M. R.: Études sur l'association des mots. Année psychol. 57, No. 1, 23—32 (1957).

—: Comparisons among word-association responses in English, French, German, and Italian. Amer. J. Psychol. 74, No. 3, 347—360 (1961).

—: Comparisons among word association responses in English, French, German, and Italian. Proc. 16th Int. Congr. Psychol., Bonn, 1960. Amsterdam: North-Holland 1962, 704—705.

—: Word associations of French workmen: Comparisons with associations of French students and American workmen and students. J. verb. Learning verb. Behavior 3, No. 1, 57—69 (1964).

—, ROSENBLITH, W. A.: Some electrophysiological correlates of the perception of successive clicks. J. Acoust. Soc. Amer. 22, No. 6, 878—880 (1950).

ROTHKOPF, E. Z., COKE, E. U.: The prediction of free recall from word association measures. J. exper. Psychol. 62, No. 5, 433—438 (1961).

RUBENSTEIN, H., ABORN, M.: Immediate recall as a function of degree of organization and length of study period. J. exper. Psychol. 48, No. 2, 146—152 (1954).

—, —: Psycholinguistics. Ann. Rev. Psychol. 11, 291—322 (1960).

RUNQUIST, W. N., FARLEY, F. H.: The use of mediators in the learning of verbal paired associates. J. verb. Learning verb. Behavior 3, No. 4, 280—285 (1964).

RUSSELL, W. A.: Bi-directional effects in word association. In: Associative processes in verbal behavior. Edited by JENKINS, J. J. Minnesota Conference, 1955, 1—12.

—, MESECK, O. R.: Der Einfluß der Assoziation auf das Erinnern von Worten in der deutschen, französischen und englischen Sprache. Z. exp. angew. Psychol. 6, 191—211 (1959).

—, STORMS, L. H.: Implicit verbal chaining in paired-associate learning. J. exper. Psychol. 49, No. 4, 287—293 (1955).

SALZINGER, K., PORTNOY, S., FELDMAN, R. S.: The effect of order of approximation to the statistical structure of English on the emission of verbal responses. J. exper. Psychol. 64, No. 1, 52—57 (1962).

SAPIR, E.: A study in phonetic symbolism. J. exper. Psychol. 12, No. 3, 225—239 (1929).

—: Conceptual categories in primitive languages. Science 74, No. 1927, 578 (1931).

—: Language. Encyclopaedia of the social sciences, 9, 1933 edition, 155—168.

—: Selected writings in language, culture and personality. Edited by MANDELBAUM, D. G. Berkeley, Cal.: University of California Press, 1949.

SAPORTA, S.: Frequency of consonant clusters. Language 31, No. 1, 25 —30 (1955a)

—: Linguistic structure as a factor and as a measure in word association. Associative processes in verbal behavior. Edited by JENKINS, J. J. Minnesota Conference, 1955b, 210—214.

—; (Ed.): Psycholinguistics. A Book of readings. New York: Holt, Rinehart and Winston 1961.

SAUSSURE, F. DE: Cours de linguistique générale. Paris: Payot 1916. English Ed.: Course in general linguistics. Translated by BASKIN, W. New York: Philosophical Library 1959.

SCHAEFER, M., JENKINS, J. J.: Word association phenomena at the individual level: A pair of case studies. Associative processes in verbal behavior. Edited by JENKINS, J. J. Minnesota Conference, 1955, 26—43.

SCHILDER, P.: Medizinische Psychologie. Berlin: J. Springer 1924. English Ed.: Medical Psychology. Translated by RAPAPORT, D. New York: Wiley 1965.

SCHLOSBERG, H., HEINEMANN, C.: The relationship between two measures of response strength. J. exper. Psychol. 40, No. 2, 235—247 (1950).

SCHMETTERER, L.: Sprache und Informationstheorie. In: Sprache und Wissenschaft. Vorträge der Tagung der Jungius-Gesellschaft in Hamburg, 1959. Göttingen: Vandenhoeck Ruprecht 1960, 155—168.

SCHMITT, A.: Helen Keller und die Sprache. Münster-Köln: Böhlau 1954.

SCHUBENZ, S.: Beitrag zu einer Analyse der selbsttätigen Steuerungsvorgänge im Sprechverhalten, untersucht mit der Technik der künstlichen Verzögerung der auditiven Rückkopplung. Dissertation, Berlin, 1965.

SCHWARTZ, F., ROUSE, R. O.: The activation and recovery of associations. Psychol. Issues 3, whole No. 9, 1—140 (1961).

SEBEOK, T. A. (Ed.): Style in language. New York: Wiley 1960.

—: Review of "Communication among social bees" by LINDAUER, M.; "Porpoises and Sonar" by KELLOGG, W. N.; "Man and dolphin" by LILLY, J. C. Language 39, No. 3, 448—466 (1963).

SEGERSTEDT, T. T.: Die Macht des Wortes. Zürich: Panverlag 1947.

SEILER, H.: Sprachsysteme und systematische Sprachbetrachtung. In: Sprache und Wissenschaft. Vorträge der Tagung der Jungius-Gesellschaft, Hamburg, 1959. Göttingen: Vandenhoeck & Ruprecht 1960, 43—50.

SHANNON, C. E.: A mathematical theory of communication. Bell System Techn. J. 27, No. 3, 379—423; (1948); 27, No. 4, 623—656 (1948).

—: Prediction and entropy of printed English. Bell System Techn. J. 30, No. 1, 50—64 (1951).

—, WEAVER, W.: The mathematical theory of communication. Urbana, Ill.: University of Illinois Press 1949.

SHERMAN, M.: The differentiation of emotional responses in infants — II. The ability of observers to judge the emotional characteristics of the crying of infants, and of the voice of an adult. J. comp. Psychol. 7, No. 5, 335—351 (1927).

SHIPINOVA, Y., SURINA, M.: Cited in: Language, thought and personality in infancy and childhood, by LEWIS, M. M. London: G. G. Harrap 1963, p. 36. Also in: Psychology in the Soviet Union. Edited by SIMON, B. London: Routledge and Paul 1957, 198.

SHIPLEY, W. C.: Indirect conditioning. J. gen. Psychol. 12, No. 2, 337—357 (1935).

SHLIEN, J. M.: Mother-in-law: A problem in kinship terminology. ETC: A review of general semantics, 19, No. 2, 161—171 (1962).

SHPOLA, E., WALKER, W. N., KOLB, D.: Task attitudes in word association, projective and nonprojective. J. Pers. 23, 441—459 (1955).

SKINNER, B. F.: The distribution of associated words. Psychol. Rec. 1, 71—76 (1937).

—: Verbal Behavior. New York: Appleton-Century-Crofts 1957.

SLOBIN, D.: Some aspects of the use of pronouns of address in Yiddish. Word 19, 193—202 (1963).

SMILLIE, D.: Language development and lineality. ETC.: A review of general semantics, 17, No. 2, 203—208 (1960).

SMIRNOV, A. A.: Sprachbewegungen und Retention. Proc. 16th Int. Congr. Psychol., Bonn, 1960. Amsterdam: North-Holland 1962, 678—683.

SOMMERFELT, A.: Diachronic and synchronic aspects of language. Selected articles. 's Gravenhage: Mouton 1962a.

—: La linguistique: science sociologique. In: Diachronic and synchronic aspects of language. 's Gravenhage: Mouton 1962b, 36—51 .

—: Sprache und Wissenschaft. Vorträge der Tagung der Jungius-Gesellschaft, Hamburg, 1959. Göttingen: Vandenhoeck & Ruprecht 1960.

STAATS, A. W.: Verbal habit-families, concepts and the operant conditioning of word classes. Psychol. Rev. 68, No. 3, 190—204 (1961).

—, STAATS, C. K.: Attitudes established by classical conditioning. J. abnorm. soc. Psychol. 57, 37—40 (1958).

—, —, BIGGS, D. A.: Meaning of verbal stimuli changed by conditioning. Amer. J. Psychol. 71, No. 2, 429—431 (1958).

—, —, HEARD, W. G.: Denotative meaning established by classical conditioning. J. exper. Psychol. 61, No. 4, 300—303 (1961).

STAATS, C. K., STAATS, A. W.: Meaning established by classical conditioning. J. exper. Psychol. 54, No. 1, 74—80 (1957).

STEGER, H.: Sprachnorm, Grammatik und technische Welt. Sprache im technischen Zeitalter, 3, 183—198 (1962).

STEINBUCH, K.: Automat und Mensch. Berlin/Heidelberg/New York: Springer 1965.

STENZEL, J.: Philosophie der Sprache. Munich/Berlin: Oldenbourg 1934.

—: Sinn, Bedeutung, Begriff, Definition. Jb. Philologie, 1, 160—201 (1925). Reprinted Darmstadt 1958.

STERN, W.: Psychologie der frühen Kindheit. Leipzig: Quelle & Meyer 1930.

STERN, C., STERN, W.: Die Kindersprache. Eine psychologische und sprachtheoretische Untersuchung. Leipzig: Barth 1907.

STEVENS, S. S. (Ed.): Handbook of experimental psychology. New York: Wiley 1951.

—, DAVIS, H.: Hearing, its psychology and physiology. New York: Wiley 1938.

STEVENSON, C. L.: Ethics and language. New Haven: Yale University Press 1944.

STUMPF, C.: Die Sprachlaute. Berlin: J. Springer 1926.

SUMBY, W. H., POLLACK, I.: Visual contribution to speech intelligibility in noise. J. Acoust. Soc. Amer. 26, No. 2, 212—215 (1954).

SWIFT, J.: Gulliver's travels. New York: Harcourt, Brace 1920.

TAYLOR, I. K.: Phonetic symbolism re-examined. Psychol. Bull. 60, No. 2, 200—209 (1963).

TAYLOR, W. L.: Cloze procedure, a new tool for measuring readability. Journalism Quarter. 30, 415—433 (1953).

TELEGDI, Z.: Discussion in: Zeichen und System der Sprache. Vol. I. (Veröffentlichung des 1. Internationalen Symposiums „Zeichen und System der Sprache", Erfurt, 1959). Berlin: Schriften zur Phonetik, Sprachwissenschaft und Kommunikationsforschung, No. 3, 1961, 209—211.

TEUBER, H. L.: Discusssion in: Disorders of language. Edited by REUCK, A. V. S. DE O'CONNOR, M. London: J. and A. Churchill 1964, 255.

THORNDIKE, E. L.: Educational psychology, New York: Lemcke and Buechner 1903.

—: Educational psychology I: The original nature of man. New York: Teacher's College, Columbia University 1913.

—: Educational psychology II: The psychology of learning. New York: Teacher's College, Columbia University 1914.

—: Man and his works. Cambridge, Mass.: Harvard University Press 1943.

—, LORGE, I.: The teacher's word book of 30 000 words. New York: Bureau of Publications, Teacher's College, Columbia University 1944.

THUMB, A., MARBE, K.: Experimentelle Untersuchungen über die psychologischen Grundlagen der sprachlichen Analogiebildung. Leipzig: Engelmann 1901.

TICHOMIROV, O. K.: Review of "Verbal Behavior" by SKINNER, B. F. Word, 15, 362—367 (1959).

TINBERGEN, N.: The study of instinct. Oxford: Clarendon Press 1951.

TITCHENER, E. B.: A text-book of psychology. Part II. New York: Macmillan 1910.

TOLMAN, E. C.: Cognitive maps in rats and men. Psychol. Rev. 55, No. 4, 189—208 (1948).

—: Principles of purposive behavior. In: Psychology. A study of a science. Vol. II. Edited by KOCH, S. New York: McGraw-Hill 1959, 92—157.

—, GLEITMAN, H.: Studies in learning and motivation: I. Equal reinforcements in both end-boxes, followed by shock in one end-box. J. exper. Psychol. 39, No. 6, 810—819 (1949).

TRAUTSCHOLDT, M.: Experimentelle Untersuchungen über die Association der Vorstellungen. Philos. Stud. (Edited by WUNDT, W.), 1, 213—250 (1883).

TREISMAN, A. M.: Contextual cues in selective listening. Quart. J. exper. Psychol. 12, No. 4, 242—248 (1960).

—: The effect of irrelevant material on the efficiency of selective listening. Amer. J. Psychol. 77, No. 4, 533—546 (1964).

TRIER, J.: Der deutsche Wortschatz in Sinnbezirk des Verstandes. Vol. I. Heidelberg: C. Winter 1931.

—: Das sprachliche Feld. Neue Jahrbücher für Wissenschaft und Jugendbildung. 10, 428—449 (1934).

TRUBETZKOY, N.: Zur allgemeinen Theorie der phonologischen Vokalsysteme. In: Mélanges linguistiques dédiés au premier congrès des philologues slaves. Prague: Travaux du Cercle linguistique de Prague I. 1929, 39—67.

—: Grundzüge der Phonologie. Prague: Travaux du Cercle linguistique de Prague. VII. 1939. French Ed.: Principes de phonologie. Translated by CANTINEAU, J. Paris: Klincksieck 1949.

TSURU, S., FRIES, H. S.: A problem in meaning. J. gen. Psychol. 8, No. 1, 281—284 (1933).

TULVING, E.: Forgetting: Another look at an old problem. Paper presented at the XIX. Int. Congr. Psychol., London, July 30, 1969.

UEXKÜLL, J. VON: Theoretische Biologie. Berlin: J. Springer 1928. English Ed.: Theoretical Biology. Translated by MACKINNON, D. L. London: K. Paul, Trench, Trubner 1926.

ULLMANN, S.: The principles of semantics. New York: Barnes and Noble, 1963 (1st Ed. 1957).

—: Semantics: An introduction to the science of meaning. New York: Barnes and Noble 1962.

UNDERWOOD, B. J., RICHARDSON, J.: Verbal concept learning as a function of instructions and dominance level. J. exp. Psychol. 51, No. 4, 229—238 (1956).

URBAN, W. M.: Language and reality. The philosophy of language and the principles of symbolism. London: Allen and Unwin 1939.

VERPLANCK, W. S.: The control of the content of conversation: Reinforcement of statements of opinion. J. abnorm. soc. Psychol. 51, 668—676 (1955).

VIGOTSKY, L. S.: Thought and language. Edited and translated by HANFMANN, E., VAKAR, G. Cambridge, Mass.: M.I.T. Press 1962 (Orig. Ed. Moscow 1934).

VOLKOVA, V. D.: On certain characteristics of the formation of conditioned reflexes to speech stimuli in children. Fiziol. Zh. SSSR, 39, 540—548 (1953). Cited in: RAZRAN, G.: The observable unconscious and the inferable conscious in current Soviet psychophysiology: Interoceptive conditioning, semantic conditioning, and the orienting reflex. Psychol. Rev. 68, No. 2, 81—147 (1961).

WALLACH, M.: Perceptual recognition of approximations to English in relation to spelling achievement. J. educ. Psychol. 54, No. 1, 57—62 (1963).

WATSON, J. B.: Psychology from the standpoint of a behaviorist. Philadelphia: Lippincott 1924.

WEGENER, P.: Untersuchungen über die Grundfragen des Sprachlebens. Halle (Saale): Niemeyer 1885.

WEINREICH, U.: Travels through semantic space. Word 14, Nos. 2—3, 346—366 (1958).

WEIR, R. H.: Language in the crib. 's Gravenhage: Mouton 1962.

WEISGERBER, L.: Sprachvergleichung und Psychologie. Ber. 12. Kongr. Dtsch. Ges. Psychol., Hamburg, 1931. Jena: Fischer 1932, 193—201.

—: Energetische Terminologie in der Sprachpsychologie. Z. exper. angew. Psychol. 6, 621—632 (1959).

—: Von den Kräften der deutschen Sprache. Vol. I: Grundzüge der inhaltbezogenen Grammatik. Düsseldorf: Päd. Verlag Schwann 1962a.

—: Von den Kräften der deutschen Sprache. Vol. II: Die sprachliche Gestaltung der Welt. Düsseldorf: Päd. Verlag Schwann 1962b.

WEISS, J. H.: Further study of the relation between the sound of a word and its meaning. Amer. J. Psychol. 76, No. 4, 624—630 (1963).

—: Phonetic symbolism re-examined. Psychol. Bull. 61, No. 6, 454—458 (1964a).

—: The role of stimulus meaningfulness in the phonetic symbolism response. J. gen. Psychol 70, No. 2, 255—263 (1964b).

WEIZSÄCKER, C. F. VON: Sprache als Information. In: Die Sprache. Vortragsreihe der Bayrischen Akademie der Schönen Künste. Darmstadt: Wissenschaftliche Buchgesellschaft 1959, 33—53.

—: Die Sprache der Physik. In: Sprache und Wissenschaft. Vorträge der Tagung der Jungius-Gesellschaft, Hamburg, 1959. Göttingen: Vandenhoeck Ruprecht 1960, 137—153.

WELLS, R.: Meaning and use. In: Psycholinguistics. Edited by SAPORTA, S. New York Holt, Rinehart and Winston 1961, 269—283.

WERNER, H.: Grundfragen der Sprachphysiognomik. Leipzig: Barth, 1932.

—: Einführung in die Entwicklungspsychologie. Munich: Barth, 1953. English Ed.: Comparative psychology of mental development. Translated by GARSIDE, E. B. New York: International Universities Press 1957.

—: (Ed.): On expressive language. Worcester, Mass.: Clark University Press 1955.

—, KAPLAN, B.: Symbol formation. New York: Wiley 1963.

—, KAPLAN, E.: The acquisition of word meanings: A developmental study. Monogr. Soc. Res. Child Develpm. 15, No. 1, serial No. 51, 190—200 (1952).

WERTHEIMER, M.: The relation between the sound of a word and its meaning. Amer. J. Psychol. 71, No. 2, 412—415 (1958).

WHITEHEAD, A. N., RUSSELL, B.: Principia Mathematica. Vol. I. Cambridge, Mass.: Cambridge University Press 1935.

WHORF, B. L.: Language, thought, and reality. Edited by CARROLL, J. B. Cambridge, Mass.: M.I.T. Press 1956.

WILDE, K.: Naive und künstlerische Formen des graphischen Ausdrucks. Ber. 21. Kongr. Dtsch. Ges. Psychol., Bonn, 1957. Göttingen: Verlag für Psychologie 1958, 157—159.

WILSON, W. C., VERPLANCK, W. S.: Some observations on the reinforcement of verbal operants. Amer. J. Psychol. 69, No. 3, 448—451 (1956).

WISSEMANN, H.: Untersuchungen zur Onomatopoiie. Part 1: Die sprachpsychologischen Versuche. Heidelberg: Winter 1954.

—: Die Rolle des Grammatischen beim Verstehen des Satzsinnes. Indogermanische Forschungen, 66, 1—9 (1961).

—: Die Rolle des Grammatischen beim Verstehen des Satzsinnes. Proc. 16th Int. Congr. Psychol., Bonn. 1960. Amsterdam: North-Holland 1962, 667—673.

WITTGENSTEIN, L.: Schriften: Tractatus logico-philosophicus. Tagebücher 1914—1916. Philosophische Untersuchungen. Frankfurt (Main): Suhrkamp 1963. English Eds.: Philosophical Investigations. Translated by ANSCOMBE, G. E. M. Oxford: Basil Blackwell 1958; and Tractatus Logico-Philosophicus. Translated by PEARS, D. F., McGUINNESS, B. F. London: Routledge and Kegan Paul 1966.

WOODROW, H., LOWELL, F.: Children's association frequency tables. Psychol. Monogr. 22, No. 5, whole No. 97 (1916).

WOODWORTH, R. S., SCHLOSBERG, H.: Experimental psychology (Revised Ed.) New York: Holt, Rinehart and Winston 1954.

WRESCHNER, A.: Die Reproduktion und Assoziation von Vorstellungen. Z. Psychol. Physiol. Sinnesorgane (1907) Supplement 3, 1—599.

WUNDT, W.: Grundzüge der physiologischen Psychologie. 4th ed. Vols. I and II. Leipzig: W. Engelmann 1983; 6th rev. ed. Vol. I 1908, Vol. II 1910, Vol. III 1911.

YAVUZ, H. S., BOUSFIELD, W. A.: Recall of connotative meaning. Psychol. Rep. 5, 319—320 (1959).

YELEN, D. R., SCHULZ, R. W.: Verbal satiation? J. verb. Learning verb. Behavior, 1, No. 5, 372—377 (1962—63).

ZAWADOWSKI, L.: In: Zeichen und System der Sprache, Vol. I. (Veröffentl. 1. Int. Symp. Zeichen u. System d. Sprache, Erfurt, 1959). Berlin: Schriften zur Phonetik, Sprachwissenschaft u. Kommunikationsforschung, No. 3, 1961.

ZAZZO, R.: Les Jumeaux, le couple et la personne. Paris: Presses universitaires de France 1960.

ZEMANEK, H.: Elementare Informationstheorie. Munich: Oldenbourg 1959.
ZIPF, G. K.: The psycho-biology of language. Boston: Houghton Mifflin 1935.
—: The meaning-frequency relationship of words. J. gen. Psychol. **33**, No. 2, 251—256 (1945).
—: Human behavior and the principle of least effort. Cambridge, Mass.: Addison-Wesley 1949.

Author-Index

The numbers given in italics refer to the Bibliography.

Subject Index

Mercedes-Druck, Berlin 61